CREATING ARCHITECTURAL THEORY

DATE DUE

CREATING ARCHITECTURAL THEORY

The Role of the Behavioral Sciences in Environmental Design

Jon Lang

VNR VAN NOSTRAND REINHOLD
New York

Printed in the United States of America
Designed by Azuretec Graphics

Van Nostrand Reinhold
115 Fifth Avenue
New York, New York 10003

Van Nostrand Reinhold International Company Limited
11 New Fetter Lane
London EC4P 4EE, England

Van Nostrand Reinhold
480 La Trobe Street
Melbourne, Victoria 3000, Australia

Nelson Canada
1120 Birchmount Road
Scarborough, Ontario, M1K 5G4, Canada

16 15 14 13 12 11 10 9 8 7 6 5 4 3

Library of Congress Cataloging-in-Publication Data
Lang, Jon T.
  Creating architectural theory.
  Bibliography: p.
  Includes index.
  1. Architectural design—Psychological aspects.
2. Architecture—Human factors. 3. Environmental psychology. I. Title.
NA2750.L36 1987   720   86-28073
ISBN 0-442-25981-6

CONTENTS

PREFACE

This book is motivated by my concern about the quality of the built environment and the education of interior designers, architects, landscape architects, and urban designers. There are many books so motivated. Most of these present proposals for how rooms, buildings, and open spaces should reflect the religious, sociological, spiritual, or technological tenor of the times. The intention of this book is not, however, to propagate a specific new architecture, urban design, or landscape architecture but rather to raise the consciousness of designers to the new insights on the nature of the built environment and the design process that are being yielded by recent behavioral science research.

This book is intended as an introductory statement for students, but it is hoped that practicing designers will find it useful in structuring their thoughts on the concerns and nature of design and design theory. The goal of the book is to enhance our ability to discuss clearly some of the complex issues that we face—in particular, those involving the built environment and what it affords people in terms of activities and aesthetic experiences.

A number of recent writers on environmental design, particularly on architecture, take the position that the speculative theories of the design fields have been successful and that they do not have to borrow any positivistic approach from other disciplines. The theories of the design fields have, however, never been independent of the influences of other disciplines and the knowledge they provide of aspects of the world and how it functions. If the gap between designers' predictions or claims of how their designs will work and how they *do* work is to be reduced, the quality of the knowledge base for design action needs to be considerably enhanced. This is particularly true in addressing the claims that designers make about the impact of their work on people's lives. The contribution of the speculative design philosophies cannot be denied, and they have had a major influence on this book. They are

not, however, a sufficient basis for the further development of design theory.

At present, we designers find many issues difficult to consider explicitly. The reason is that while the design professions have much in the way of *normative theory*—prescriptions for action—they are weak in *positive theory*, or, as some call it, *explanatory theory*, the explicit description and explanation of the phenomena and processes with which they deal. The result is that we designers often jump to erroneous conclusions about the impact of our work on people's lives. This is especially true when we are designing for people whose patterns of behavior and values differ from our own. In this book, it is argued that the behavioral sciences offer the design professions much to help us develop both positive theory and an understanding of our normative theories. The view taken here is that theory-building is a creative act and not simply an analytical one. Theory is created.

This book represents a line of thinking about design, theory, ideology, and practice that has engaged a number of architects, both educators and practitioners, over the last twenty years. The specific effort represented by this book began with a conference and exhibition on *Architecture for Human Behavior* organized by a number of academic institutions in the Philadelphia area under the leadership of the American Institute of Architects/Philadelphia Chapter and held at the Franklin Institute in 1971. The objective of the conference was to bring the attention of architects and students to the research generally subsumed under the rubric "Environmental Psychology." The success of the conference and its proceedings led to the collection and publication in 1974 of a broader set of papers edited by Jon Lang, Charles Burnette, Walter Moleski, and David Vachon under the title *Designing for Human Behavior: Architecture and the Behavioral Sciences*. The book attempted to sketch the nature and scope of a theoretical base for the design fields akin to the theoretical bases of other applied fields such as medicine. It also attempted to explain why the development of such a theoretical base is not only desirable but necessary. The goal of the present book is to take these previous statements a step further with a more detailed explication of those aspects of environmental design theory to which the behavioral sciences can make or have made a major contribution.

The approach to theory in this book extends that characteristic of the major architectural philosophers of this century by broadening the definition of "function" to include all aspects of the built environment that serve human purposes rather than simply those involving efficiency in the carrying out of activities. This book also represents the effort to shift architectural, landscape, and urban design theory from a sole concern with the manifestoes of the major masters (which may be called *normative theory*) to an equal concern with the understanding of phenomena *(positive theory)*, an understanding that can be used as the basis for developing prescriptions for action in the situation at hand. This shift reflects an abandonment of absolutist positions on what constitutes good design and the adoption of a relativist position. It thus reflects a major value change. It also means that the design professions require a broader and more explicit understanding than they currently have of both the person-environment relationship and the processes of design.

This book is not a comprehensive treatise on design theory. The nature of the construction industry and the political and legal framework of professional activities in the design fields are mentioned only in passing. There is little discussion of building technology and materials. The attention of this book is focused on: (1) how the three-dimensional layout of the environment affords human activities, social behaviors, and aesthetic experiences; and (2) the processes whereby designers shape it.

THE OUTLINE OF THE BOOK

There are four parts to this book. In the first, the book's theoretical background is presented; the second part is concerned with positive theory and the third with normative theory; the final part consists of a brief specification of the limitations of the material presented here and how these might be reduced in the future.

Since this book is concerned with theory, it is important to recognize where designers are now—what we have inherited from the Modern Movement. The movement offers us much that should not be rejected, but there are some major limitations in its concepts of theory and of human behavior that

must be recognized. The basic point is that it is useful to distinguish between *positive* and *normative* theory and between *substantive* and *procedural* theory. Once this point has been made, it is possible to discuss the nature and utility of theory, the role of the behavioral sciences in building design theory, and their past and potential contributions. Part 1 of the book is devoted to these issues.

Part 2 is the central portion of the book. In it an attempt is made to present the core of positive theory in architecture to which the behavioral sciences can contribute. It is divided into two parts. The first is concerned with *procedural theory*—the nature of praxis. It discusses not only the nature of the design process but also the question of why good substantive theory is needed to support the process. The second deals with *substantive theory*—the nature of the environment and the nature of human spatial and emotional behavior within it and responses to it. The goal is to present generalizations on what the built environment affords people and a set of concepts for understanding the relationship between architecture and human behavior. These concepts can replace the naive stimulus-response model of human behavior implicit in most architectural discussions today. The important thing is to recognize that there are competing theories of human behavior that lead to different conclusions about the nature of architecture, landscape architecture, and urban design.

Part 3 of the book brings the discussion back to the consideration of *normative theory*. One of the major contributions of the behavioral sciences is in enhancing our understanding of the value orientations of different architects and schools of architectural thought and how these do or do not reflect those of the broader society of which they are a part. It also raises issues whose resolution depends on the perception an individual designer has of his or her own role in society.

While the goal of this book is to give a comprehensive overview of the contribution of the behavioral sciences to architectural theory, there are gaps and inconsistencies in the presentation of both *positive* and *normative* theory. Indeed some critics will no doubt conclude that this attempt to synthesize the disparate and widely dispersed research findings and hypotheses of the behavioral sciences is premature. Be that as it may, without theory it is difficult to focus research to improve the knowledge base of a discipline. Without focused research it is difficult to build theory. In Part 4, the conclusion of this book, the most glaring inconsistencies and omissions in the concepts presented here are reviewed. It is hoped that this review will encourage further research that will result in the development and possible replacement of the ideas presented here with better ones.

ACKNOWLEDGMENTS

In contemplating the nature of designing and the nature of the built world, urban designers, architects, landscape architects, and interior designers have turned to the research of an eclectic group of people interested in similar issues. It will be clear from the most cursory glance at this book that it relies very heavily on the work of others. I am in the position Sir Henry Wotton found himself in when he wrote *The Elements of Architecture* in 1624: "I shall not need to celebrate the subject which I deliver; In that I am at ease. For Architecture can want no commendation. . . . I will spend this Preface, rather about those from whom I have gathered my knowledge; for I am but the gatherer of other mens stuffe, at my best value."

In thinking about the nature of theory I have been influenced by the writings of Barclay Jones, Abraham Kaplan, and two of my colleagues at the University of Pennsylvania, Britton Harris and Seymour Mandelbaum. The ideas of cognitive psychologists and decision theorists such as Herbert Simon have exerted a profound influence on the thinking of many architects about the nature of the design process and the creative act. The writings of Marvin Manheim, Raymond Studer, Gary Hack, Horst Rittel, Don Schon, and Hayden May have shaped developments in procedural theory. The work of environmental psychologists such as Harold Proshansky and his colleagues at the City University of New York have had a similar influence on substantive theory. The efforts of Amos Rapoport, Constance Perin, William Michelson, C. Douglas Porteous, and Thomas Saarinen in synthesizing this research for designers have been of immense help in this work. Many of the ideas presented here have been borrowed from the writings of recent architectural philosophers such as James Marston Fitch, Christian Norberg-Schulz, Robert Venturi, and Denise Scott Brown; another source has been the seminal work in the design fields of people, such as Kevin Lynch, who have made contributions to psychological theory. Psychologist James J. Gibson provided the concept of *affordance* so basic to the understanding of the relationship between the built environment and human behavior. In spirit this book owes a lot to Appollinari K. Krasovsky, Nikolai Aleksandrovich Ladovsky, and Moisei Ginsburg, the major philosophers of the Rationalist and Constructivist schools of Soviet architecture and among the first modern architects and educators to stress the need for systematic, explicit, and well-tested theory in architecture, and to Walter Gropius and Hannes Meyer, two very different directors of the Bauhaus.

If this book stimulates some designers to apply and test the knowledge and ideas of these and the other people, too numerous to mention, that are presented in this book, and if it stimulates other designers and behavioral scientists to carry out the research needed to develop more rigorous theory, it will have served its purpose. If it provides design students with a framework for building their knowledge of how the built environment serves mankind and the nature of the design process, it will have served its purpose. These were the goals of the Franklin Institute Conference and of *Designing for Human Behavior,* both of which generated considerable discussion. If this book takes this discussion a step further, it will be a success.

The original impetus for the Franklin Institute Conference and for *Designing for Human Behavior* came from Charles Burnette while he was Executive Director of the American Institute of Architects/ Philadelphia Chapter. Without his participation and encouragement, none of these efforts would have come to fruition. Over the years, Walter Moleski, Executive Director of the Environmental Research Group in Philadelphia, has provided steadfast support in developing this book. Many of its insightful contributions are his. Mark Francis, William Sims, Carole Treinan, Seymour Mandelbaum, Richard Dober, Raul Garcia, Ernest Arias, and Mark Heyman, as well as anonymous reviewers, have provided invaluable help in improving the manuscript. Perhaps most of all, however, the challenges, criticism, and support received from both undergraduate and graduate students at the four Philadelphia schools of architecture and environmental design—Drexel, Penn, Spring Garden, and Temple—have to be acknowledged. Not only have they contributed directly to the compilation of this volume, but they have also provided the stimulation without which this volume would not even have been contemplated.

PART I

THE MODERN MOVEMENT, ARCHITECTURAL THEORY, AND THE BEHAVIORAL SCIENCES

Architects, landscape architects, and urban designers have long been borrowing ideas from the behavioral sciences and from speculative philosophies on the nature of human acting and thinking. They have done this, however, without ever developing a coherent body of knowledge about the built environment and what it affords people or about design praxis; there has been little coherent environmental design theory. This is changing.

This century has seen an unprecedented growth in human knowledge, major social changes, and increases in the standard of living in much of the world. Rather than making design praxis easier, these developments have made it more difficult. The reasons are clear. We now have the technological ability (and often the technological itch) to construct buildings, neighborhoods, and cities in a wide variety of ways without fully understanding the ramifications of these designs for human behavior. We do know that in the past simplistic evaluations of changes to be made in our habitat have resulted in unanticipated and undesirable side effects. At the same time, architects are faced with more discriminating clients. Society now takes for granted that certain demands are easy to meet. Rayner Banham (1960) notes:

> The average automobile of today, running on such roads as have been specially contrived for it, provides transport more sumptuous in vehicles more gorgeous than palanquin-borne emperors knew how to desire.

Much recent architecture, landscape architecture, and urban design, however, shows that many of our beliefs about what constitutes a good environment for people is not perceived by them as such. Much of what has been perceived by designers to be good is perceived by others to be cold, inhuman, and boring.

Fields of inquiry and action become very critical and concerned about their theoretical bases when they are under challenge and stress or are undergoing change. This is particularly true of architecture and urban design today. During the last decade some critics have come close to repudiating the entire contribution of the Modern Movement in architecture, with the concomitant danger of obscuring the significant contribution that has been made by it. Chapter 1, "The Legacy of the Modern Movement," is concerned with identifying some of these contributions as well as some of the basic limitations of modern architectural thought. It will be claimed that one of its basic limitations is its underdeveloped theoretical basis. This has been recognized by many people (such as Norberg-Schulz 1965, Brill 1974, Perin 1970). The design professions have a poor history of scholarship; we depend almost entirely on other fields for our knowledge base. We have also been slow at recording and transmitting the knowledge developed through practice. Yet there has been considerably less thought on what it means to have "a stronger theoretical base."

An examination of environmental design theory is made more difficult by the ambiguity of the term *theory*. Almost all schools of design have courses titled "Theories of Architecture," "Theories and Principles of Architecture," and/or "Theory and History of Architecture." The very nature of "theory" is seldom discussed in these courses, however, nor has a clear model of "architectural theory" emerged in them. The objective of Chapter 2, "The Nature and Utility of Theory," is to produce a model of theory that can serve the design professions well.

It must be recognized that many designers, particularly architects, are happy with the way things are at present. They believe that the knowledge required to create good design requires no further organization than what occurs intuitively. They believe that the knowledge available to them as a result of their superior "common sense" is sufficient and that the goal of architecture is to express their "own autonomous personalities" (Norberg-Schulz 1965). Although many fine designs have been generated this way, the increased cost of building and the diversity of users of the professionally designed environment make design based on personal whimsy a foolhardy thing. The underlying thesis of this book is that there is much knowledge in the traditional academic disciplines of anthropology, sociology, and psychology that can be brought to bear on architectural theory and hence on architectural practice. The purpose of chapter 3, "The Behavioral Sciences and Architectural Theory," is to show this.

Chapter 3 outlines the potentials and limitations of the contribution of the behavioral sciences to architectural theory. To understand the requirements of architectural theory, one must first understand the concerns of architecture. This is as much an ideological statement as a scientific one. Some architects believe that architecture is a pure fine art with little social content. Others have a broader view of the field. Chapter 3 thus begins with a preliminary statement on the foci of concern to environmental designers. The boundaries are more difficult and less important to define. There is, in reality, a circular relationship between this chapter and Part 2 of the book. Images of the concerns of the design fields shape the way a designer considers the nature of the environment and the nature of people. Images of the nature of the environment and of people shape one's views on the nature of design. In looking at the behavioral sciences as a source of environmental design knowledge, one needs to avoid getting bogged down in scientific controversies irrelevant to designers' concerns. Some *a priori* model of the concerns of architecture is thus necessary. It will be argued that the one used here provides a sound point of departure. ■

1

THE LEGACY OF THE MODERN MOVEMENT

It is fashionable today to say, "Down with the Modern Movement." The contribution of the Modern Movement in architecture has been vast, however. It parallels the development of sociopolitical thought over the course of the last hundred years. Emerging from the social and philanthropic movements of the nineteenth century, and from the Industrial Revolution and the political and artistic revolutions that accompanied it, the Modern Movement transformed the set of patterns used by architects in analyzing and designing buildings, neighborhoods, and the urban infrastructure. It introduced and developed new construction technologies for building design. Perhaps most important, it made architects and landscape architects more sensitive to the social issues related to the design of housing and the public environment. In education, the Modern Movement broke away from a tired academic approach. Much has been built following the design principles of the masters of the movement. Many of the buildings and urban places so created are very pleasant places. Unfortunately though, much has not worked out as well as was predicted or hoped.

Despite the rise of Post-Modernism in its many forms—a largely unidimensional change in design concerns—much of the current practice in the environmental design professions is based on ideas about architecture and urban design inherited from the major schools of architectural thought associated with the Modern Movement. These schools included the Futurists of Italy, who were particularly concerned with "technology" and "new transportation" modes, the De Stijl group of Holland, the Cubists of France, the Rationalist and Constructivist schools of thought in the Soviet Union, who were concerned with "abstract expressionism," and the Bauhaus in Germany with its concern with "functionalism." In America, the ideas of Louis Sullivan and Frank Lloyd Wright influenced but deviated from the European schools of architectural thought.

Although the ideas of most of these schools of thought go back to the first three decades of the twentieth century, they saw their greatest application in the three decades following World War II. In the 1970s and 1980s, with the growth of Post-Modernism, there has been a shift in the attitudes of many designers toward symbolic aesthetics and at least a partial repudiation of social concern. The result of this, however, has been the development of a new set of aesthetic mannerisms rather than a fundamental shift in thinking (see Blake 1984). During the past decade there has been an increasing concern with the nature of architectural symbolism, but the way of thinking and the proposals of a handful of European and American architects associated with modernism are still so pervasive that it is not unreasonable to continue treating them as primary references for much current architectural and urban design practice.

On the strictly architectural side, the influential ideas include those propounded by people such as

1

2

3

1-1. Beaux-Arts and Modern Concepts of Architecture.
The late-nineteenth- and early-twentieth-century ideologies in architecture were dominated by Beaux-Arts concepts. The concern was with designing buildings and building complexes with elements derived from the classical world and its architectural orders. The building shown in (1) reflects this. Modern architecture was concerned with technical efficiency and aesthetic principles derived from Euclidean geometry (2) and/or Gestalt concepts of expression (3).

Louis Sullivan and Frank Lloyd Wright and by institutions such as Moscow's VKHUTEMAS (State Higher Art and Technical Studios) during the period 1919 to 1932 and, subsequently, the Bauhaus. Their ideas were a response to the academic and elementarist traditions of nineteenth-century educational institutions. The response led to the replacement of a style based on classical orders with a style based on forms derived from simple Euclidian geometry, on the laws, organization, and abstract expression of Gestalt theories of visual perception, and on the rejection of decoration for its own sake. It also led to a series of dicta regarding the goals of design. These include Louis Sullivan's "Form follows function," Frank Lloyd Wright's "Form and function are one," Ludwig Mies van der Rohe's "Less is more," and Le Corbusier's "Machine for living."

In urban design, the influential ideas include the Anglo-American concepts of city and neighborhood layout that emerged from the social and philanthropic movements of the nineteenth century. The best-known are Ebenezer Howard's Garden City (1902), Clarence Perry's Neighborhood Unit (1927), Henry Wright and Clarence Stein's Radburn plan (see Stein 1951), and Frank Lloyd Wright's Broadacre City (1958), as well as a number of less well-formulated plans (see Gallion and Eisner 1963). Other ideas include those of the "continental" or "centralist" group as exemplified by Le

Source: Le Corbusier (1934)

1

Source: Gallion and Eisner (1963)

2

3

1-2. Images of the Modern Movement.
Modern architects have provided many powerful images of what the new city (1), new neighborhoods (2), and new buildings (3) should be. These three examples are not representative of all the images that exist but they have been very influential. They have captured the imagination of many designers who have applied the principles that generated these forms in many parts of the world.

Corbusier's "Radiant City" (1934) and the ideas of the Congrès Internationaux d'Architecture Moderne (CIAM) in the 1930s.

There is a tendency, in much recent criticism, to regard these architectural and urban design ideas and proposals as whimsical ego trips or autocratic exercises in behavioral control. They were, however, carefully worked out responses to what their proponents considered to be the major problems of their times. At the urban scale these included: the uncontrolled growth of the city; polluting industries; long trips to and from work for the poor; the lack of educational and recreational facilities; dismal housing and sanitary conditions; overcrowded dwellings; and the negative impact of automobiles

on the existing infrastructure of cities. In architecture, there was the question of how to house large populations in a short time; there were new activity patterns and social organizations to house and thus new building types to face; there were new technologies to harness and there was the development of an aesthetic philosophy in tune with the machine age and the new political realities. The overall goal was the laudable one of bringing to all people the standard of life that only the wealthy could afford in the nineteenth century.

At the same time, it must be recognized that the results of applying the design principles of the modern masters have not always been what architects predicted. This led to much criticism of the movement and its ideas. In response, some architects have railed at the critics; others have retreated from Modernism to a more romantic image of the architect as a fine artist gratifying his or her own concerns with abstract visual patterns and a view of society as a patron of the arts. The value position taken here is that we must understand the nature of the criticism—its sources and character—so that we can build on the successes of the past and avoid repeating the mistakes. It assumes that the goal of design is to meet human needs. This has been the professed goal of many architects, landscape architects, and urban designers. We must understand the limits of our past success in attaining this goal if we are to do better in the future.

THE CRITICISM OF THE MODERN MOVEMENT

Criticism of the goals, ideas, and work of the Modern Movement has come from social commentators (Wolfe 1981), behavioral scientists (Gutman 1966, Gans 1968, Michelson 1968), architectural critics (Jacobs 1961), architectural educators (Herdeg 1983), and many architects (Norberg-Schulz 1965, Brolin 1976, Rossi 1982). Often it has come from architects who made a substantial contribution to that movement through their works and writings (Fry 1961, Mayer, 1967, Blake 1974).

There have been three major phases to this criticism. The first, in the 1940s and 1950s, was led by a small but important group of architects associated with CIAM who called themselves Team 10. In 1954, Alison and Peter Smithson noted that the very success of modern architects (in getting their ideas accepted by other architects and clients) had led to conditions more subtly inhuman than the degradation and filth of the nineteenth-century industrial cities. Five years later, Aldo van Eyck added:

> Instead of the inconvenience of filth and confusion, we have now the *boredom of hygiene*. The material slum has gone—but what has replaced it? Just mile upon mile of unorganized nowhere, and nobody feeling he is somewhere. (Smithson 1968)

The second phase of criticism resulted from studies of the expectations and outcomes of the large-scale housing and center-city urban renewal projects of the 1950s (Jacobs 1961, Gans 1962, Pawley 1971). The criticism echoed that of the members of Team 10 but went a step further. Whereas the members of Team 10 wanted to replace earlier design prototypes and principles with their own, Jane Jacobs, Herbert Gans, and others were challenging the very heart of architectural thinking, the beliefs

architects have about the impact of their work on human behavior. In her critique of the work of architects and city planners, Jane Jacobs (1961) wrote: "The art of city planning and its companion, the pseudo-science of city planning, have not embarked on the effort to deal with the real world."

The third phase of criticism is more recent and stems from the development of the behavioral sciences themselves. This has resulted in the identification of human needs that frequently are not considered either by clients or designers, and in the identification of problems in the design process used by architects. The former is exemplified by the work of ethologists (such as Hall 1966) and architects (such as Newman 1972) on concepts of territoriality, and the latter by critiques of the architect-client relationship by both behavioral scientists (such as H. Mitchell 1974) and architects (such as Goodman 1971). Paralleling this criticism was the implied criticism in the work of architects as diverse as Frank Lloyd Wright, Morris Lapidus, Bruce Goff, and Herbert Greene, whose designs fall outside the mainstream of the Modern Movement. Their work, largely regarded as eccentric, has had little impact on architectural education or practice, although individually such architects have had their own disciples. In addition, the environmental movement and the social protests of the 1960s and 1970s resulted in many fields questioning their own goals.

This criticism is varied and covers many issues. On closer scrutiny, there seem to be five major observations that have to do with the potential contribution of the behavioral sciences to the practice and education of environmental design professionals.

1. The respective roles of professionals, sponsors, and users of buildings and landscapes in providing information and making decisions need to be rethought (see Goodman 1971, H. Mitchell 1974, Zeisel 1974, 1981).
2. The concept of function in the dictum "form follows function" has been a limited one (see Relph 1976, Fitch 1979, Mukarovsky 1981).
3. Architects have been using a limited model of human nature and behavior as a basis for their work (see Stringer 1980).
4. Architects have an inadequate understanding of the relationship between the built environment and human behavior (see Gans 1968, Lipman 1974, Sommer 1974, Brolin 1976). Thus, their claims about the importance of their work in shaping the experiences of the people who observe and use it is misleading designers themselves and their clients.

All of these can be subsumed into one major overriding problem:

5. The theoretical basis for design is inadequate (see, for instance, Perin 1970).

Let us consider these issues in turn.

The Professional–Client Relationship

Some of the most successful buildings produced during this century have been custom houses. The design of such houses is characterized by a close working relationship between client and professional (Eaton 1969). Moreover, the "sponsor client," the person or group paying for the building, and the "user client," the person inhabiting the building, are one and the same. In some cases the house is a symbol of the client's status in the avant-garde. The architect is selected because his or her taste in art and architecture is similar to that of the client. Thus, to understand the houses one must understand not only the architect but also the client. Le Corbusier's clients seem to have been, for the most part, eccentrics and art collectors (Eaton 1969). This is in strong contrast to Frank Lloyd Wright's clients in Oak Park and River Forest, Illinois, who were self-made men and women, highly creative in manufacturing, who existed outside the social whirl of Chicago. In their life-styles they were

1

Le Corbusier (1960)

2

3

1-3. Architects and Custom House Design.
Some of the most distinctive and individualistic buildings that have come out of the Modern Movement in architecture have been homes specifically designed for their owners. These buildings by Frank Lloyd Wright (1), Le Corbusier (2), and Robert Venturi (3) are very different in character. Each house reflects the shared values and character of its designer and owners. This results from a close working relationship between the two. Architecture has not been so successful when values diverge and a close working relationship between designer and users is nonexistent.

more typical of upper-middle-class people today than of their contemporaries. To understand successful "fits" between users and buildings, one has to understand the relationship between clients and professionals. The same is true of unsuccessful fits.

Many of what we now regard as design failures, be they interiors, buildings as a whole, or landscapes, occurred in situations where there was both a social and an administrative gap between the ultimate user and the designer (Lipman 1974, Zeisel 1974). A "social gap" is a discrepancy between the values of the clients and those of the professional resulting from differences in cultural background, education, and/or income (Michelson 1968). An "administrative gap" exists when the architect deals only with the sponsor of the development and not with the ultimate user. The sponsor is often a poor surrogate for the user. A major social gap often exists between the sponsor and the user client as well.

We designers cannot have all the facts on all populations and life-styles at our fingertips, but we can have better information. We must also have better access to user populations. We need to ask the right questions and be good listeners. To ask good questions we need a sound understanding of the nature of the built environment, the nature of people (including ourselves), and the interactions among all three. Often, however, the users are not present, and we do not have access to them. The decision process must be set up to deal with this. A better understanding of alternative modes of operating the process and of different modes of professional-client interaction is needed. We must understand the nature of design praxis.

The Concept of Function

One of the more enduring slogans of the Modern Movement is, "Form follows function." It is enduring because most designers subscribe to it. Although some critics have said that buildings and urban designs have been made too functional, in reality they have not been made functional enough (Fitch 1979). Often they have been considered too functional if one assumes that the function of the built environment is simply to be efficient in terms of circulation distances and construction techniques (Relph 1976). They have not been functional enough if one considers the other human purposes served by the built environment. These purposes include the need for identity, the provision of security, the need for self-expression, and more broadly, the aesthetic function of architecture (see Mukarovsky 1981).

Gottfried Semper, one of the formulators of the Modern Movement's concept of functionalism, believed that industry and the applied sciences would provide a revitalizing force for the arts. He had the natural rather than the social sciences in mind. He was concerned more with the nature of the building than with what it was to house. Later Le Corbusier and Walter Gropius argued for a machine aesthetic based on the functional purity of engineering products such as airplanes, ships, and grain elevators (Le Corbusier 1923). The result was that, although the Modern Movement was claiming to serve people, its primary concern more often focused on technical efficiency and the internal consistency of building components rather than on meeting a broad range of human needs.

There have been many expressions of concern about this. Gropius himself noted, "Superior phrases like *functionalism* and *fitness for purpose equals beauty* have deflected appreciation of the new architecture into minor and purely external channels" (Gropius 1962). The basic criticism is that much Modern and now Post-Modern design ideology is based on a deficient understanding of what the built environment affords people. The reason for this is that much design ideology is based on a deficient concept of people and behavior.

Models of People, Human Behavior, and Experience

The "model of man" implicit in the arguments of many designers of the Modern Movement is what Joachim Israel (Israel and Tajfel 1972) calls an "organismic" model (Stringer 1980). It assumes that the whole range of human needs can be reduced to a few universal, constant physiological requirements. The organismic model has been contrasted to a "role" model stressing human activities in a social system and to a "relational" or "self-actualizing" model emphasizing social relationships (Maslow 1954). While frequent lip service is paid to social and cultural needs, the organismic model has been the basis for much architectural design. This was particularly true of the Bauhaus—though it was less true of the urban design, landscape architecture, and architecture of people such as Henry Wright and Clarence Stein (see Stein 1951).

Although Hannes Meyer introduced behavioral science courses at the Bauhaus, he was able to think of housing simply as the provision of shelter for a number of activities (Meyer 1928):

- sex life
- sleeping habits

1

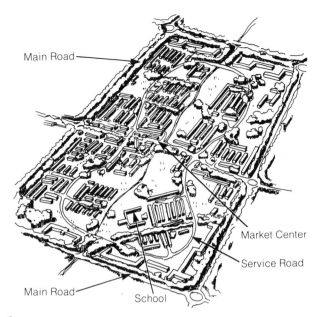

Main Road

Market Center

Service Road

Main Road

School

2

3

1-4. Problems with the Ideology of the Modern Movement.

The high-rise buildings of East Falls Housing in Philadelphia (1) lie vacant now (1985) while planners and architects attempt to find a use for them. The neighborhood unit plan is largely meaningless in Chandigarh, India (2) except as a locational identifier; the low-density garden city layout does not afford the desired lifestyle of its inhabitants. The furniture designed for the Trenton Mall in New Jersey (3) has been removed now. What do these three examples have in common? They are manifestations of design principles that have all worked well in some settings but not in these.

- pets
- gardening
- personal hygiene
- protection against the weather
- hygiene in the home
- car maintenance
- cooking
- heating
- insulation
- service

Issues of territoriality, privacy, security, social interaction, and symbolic aesthetics, for example, simply

are not considered in such a model. Similar questions have been raised about the model of people used as the basis for the design of offices, factories, and city centers (see, for instance: Parr 1967b, Rapoport 1967, Perin 1970, Lang et al. 1974, Blake 1974, Brolin 1976, Fitch 1979). With the rise of Post-Modernism has come an increased concern with the symbolic nature of the built environment, but little evidence exists of any systematic concern with broader human issues or much systematic inquiry into how people experience the symbolic meanings of the world around them or what the importance of these meanings to them may be.

1

3

2

1-5. Symbolism in Architecture.

The TWA terminal building at Kennedy Airport (1) is one of a number of efforts to create new symbolic forms in architecture in the post–World War II era. Currently there is often a much greater emphasis on decoration and the incorporation of historical referents in buildings as part of the Post-Modern Movement in architecture (2). Much recent architecture, however, remains rooted in modernism (3). The emphasis is on the creation of new forms that show a technological dexterity and communicate expressive meaning through line and form.

Both Modern and Post-Modern architectural ideology has tended to neglect cultural differences between people. This was particularly true of the former:

> All men have the same organism, the same functions. All men have the same needs. The social contract which has evolved through the ages fixes standardized classes, functions and needs producing standardized products. . . .
>
> I propose one single building for all nations and all climates. . . . (Le Corbusier 1923)
>
> There is now an approach to architecture that is common to all countries. (Fry 1961)

An underlying tenet of modern architecture is that it is universally applicable. This assumption has been so mauled by critics (for instance, Brolin 1976)

that the systematic analysis of cultural factors in design has become an integral part of the research agenda of the design professionals. Most of this research has focused on the use of space, however, rather than on aesthetic issues. We know very little about how tastes differ among cultures. Victorian artists such as Landseer, Alma-Tadema, and Millais were the last—until, perhaps, very recently—to be held in high esteem by both the art world and the general public. In communicating their ideas, they relied very heavily on associations that were part of the knowledge of broad sections of the population. Cubists and their allies in the design professions who relied on abstract expressionism have had much greater difficulty in communicating their ideas to broad segments of the public. The assumption of the Modern Movement that the aesthetic experience of buildings is based on functionalism and abstract expressionism is thus open to question.

When the architects of the Modern Movement's second generation—the disciples of the masters—realized that buildings do have important symbolic characteristics, they became obsessed with the creation of new symbolic forms. This can be seen in Harrison & Abramovitz's First Presbyterian Church in Stamford, Connecticut, and in Eero Saarinen's TWA Terminal at Kennedy Airport. Post-Modernism, on the other hand, is full of historical allusions to referents such as the classical orders of Greek architecture. We have only a limited knowledge of the success of these ideas as aesthetic philosophies and of the responses of different segments of the population to them. It seems that Post-Modern design is understood by only a small, erudite audience. There has been very little research on tastes in different cultures and the aesthetic appreciation of buildings and landscapes. The result is that the claims we make about the impact of our work on people are extravagant.

The Person-Environment Relationship

The inadequacy of the model of people that has been the basis for much architectural ideology has resulted in a misunderstanding of the nature of the person-environment relationship. Most of the ideological stances in the design fields are based on a naive stimulus-response (S-R) model of the relationship between environment and human behavior. In this model the built and/or natural environment is regarded as the stimulus and human behavior as the response. The result is that architects (and many others) often have assumed that because two variables are correlated, they also are linked causally. This has led to erroneous conclusions about the effect of the built environment on people. A special example of this is the belief in architectural determinism. Let us consider the general case first and then the specific.

It is easy to assume that correlated variables also are linked causally. If variables are linked causally, then changing one should lead to a change in the other. Correlated variables are not always linked causally, however. For instance, in much of the literature on urban design, there is an underlying assumption of both a negative correlation and a causal linkage between population density and the quality of life, but systematic research does not support this conclusion (Leary 1968). Variables such as the paucity of behavior settings, noise pollution, and specific population characteristics intervene (Bechtel 1977). Density itself is not an indicator of much apart from population-per-unit-area. Thus, we must treat with great caution the conclusion that reducing population densities in residential areas will automatically improve the quality of life. Both low- and high-density environments can be desirable. One has only to consider Southampton and Sutton Place in New York, Chestnut Hill and Society Hill in Philadelphia, or Vaucluse and Wharoonga in Sydney to illustrate this point. The reverse is also true. Much has been written about high-density slums, but examples of low-density slums abound.

The writings of interior designers, architects, and landscape architects contain many assumptions regarding the effect of the characteristics of the built environment on human behavior. Community facilities are said to create communities, parks to reduce vandalism, architectural unity to create social unity, architectural magnificence to lift spirits. Often these pairs of variables are indeed correlated, but to assume that they are linked causally without considering intervening variables is a foolhardy belief in architectural determinism.

Content analyses of the writings of architects show that much architectural ideology is based on a belief in the built environment as a major determinant of human social behavior (Broady 1966, Boughey 1968, Lipman 1974, Brolin 1976, N. Dostoglu 1986). Written statements are particularly bold: "Architecture or revolution," wrote Le Corbusier. Oral statements are much softer.

The belief in architectural determinism is particularly apparent in the design of institutions, shopping areas, housing developments, and neighborhoods. In the design of jails, for instance, architecture was perceived as an instrument of reform. In the nineteenth century it was perceived as an active instrument of the correctional officer. This is no longer the case. Rather, the built environment of jails reflects the attitudes of a society toward prisoners and what they are and are not allowed to do (R. Evans 1982). Even in places where the residents find the built environment and landscape very pleasant (such as Columbia, Maryland), the social objective of establishing a cohesive community through the physical layout of neighborhoods has not been achieved (Brooks 1974). Social variables, such as similarity of values of the population, rather than architectural factors are the major determinants of social patterns. Many architects now recognize this.

> We all naively thought that if we could eliminate the very bad physical dwellings and surroundings of slums, the new sanitized dwellings and surroundings would almost "per se" cure social ills. We know better now. (Mayer 1967)

It is some time since Albert Mayer made that statement, but little has changed in the mainstream of architectural ideology. Accepting his observation would mean that the profession has to accept a less grandiose self-image than in the past. In accepting Mayer's observation, some architects have gone to the other extreme, however, and have assumed that the built environment has no impact on social behavior patterns. Such a position is equally erroneous. If we are going to predict the outcomes of our design efforts better than we have in the past, we will need something better than a simple S-R model of the relationship between environment and behavior.

The Nature of Architectural Theory

What is it that characterizes all of the problems described above? It is what scientists call the "low external validity" of concepts. Ideas about the built environment may be very consistent internally—that is, they may support each other well—but their ties to reality often are weak. Whatever one's value position on what constitutes a "good environment," the predictive power of many of the beliefs that designers hold about the interrelationship of the built environment and human behavior and experience is lower than most would like it to be. We need to design from "knowledge not belief" (B. Jones 1962); we need to be guided by "tangible observations rather than abstract speculations" (Neutra 1954). The difficulty has been to turn these instructions into a way of structuring thought about the nature of the environment (natural and artificial), design fields, and designers.

The shortcomings of much design philosophy arise from a general lack of understanding of the intricacies of life and what different patterns of the built environment afford people. Conclusions about how a particular design will work tend to be drawn from casual experience of the world rather than from a body of systemic and systematic knowledge. We do this, often, because we have no knowledge base for more informed conclusions. Often, however, we do this because we lack the systematic organization of knowledge that would facilitate recalling it.

In considering the knowledge base—the theoretical base—that any profession needs for guiding its actions, one first has to devise a useful structure for it. At present, architectural theory is concerned mainly with a set of ideologies held by individual architects or schools of architectural thought. It is focused on the architect as artist and on his or her beliefs about what constitutes good architecture. The reasoning behind these ideologies—these beliefs about the operation of the world—seldom is stated explicitly. We design professionals have an extraordinary amount of accumulated knowledge about the world, but it is internalized in our minds. One designer's knowledge is not accessible to another—it is not available for application or testing.

Many people have been concerned about the knowledge base of the environmental design professions. During the past two decades there has been much soul-searching but also much research on the built environment and its inhabitants and on the processes of designing. This research is having a negligible impact on design, however. Some professionals, particularly behavioral scientists, believe this is because the research is not sufficiently empirical. The fundamental reason, however, seems to be that designers have few organizing models for the bodies of knowledge they use. The design professions have had no model of the nature of the theory they require for education or practice. This is being remedied.

ADDITIONAL READINGS

Allsop, Bruce. *Towards a Humane Architecture*. London: Frederick Muller, 1974.

Blake, Peter. *Form Follows Fiasco*. Boston: Atlantic–Little, Brown, 1974.

Brolin, Brent. *The Failure of Modern Architecture*. New York: Van Nostrand Reinhold, 1976.

Herdeg, Klaus. *The Decorated Diagram, Harvard Architecture and the Failure of the Bauhaus Legacy*. Cambridge, Mass.: MIT Press, 1983.

Jacobs, Jane. *The Death and Life of Great American Cities*. New York: Random House, 1961.

Lang, Jon, Charles Burnette, Walter Moleski, and David Vachon, eds. "Emerging Issues in Architecture." In *Designing for Human Behavior: Architecture and the Behavioral Sciences*. Stroudsburg, Pa.: Dowden, Hutchinson and Ross, 1974, pp. 1–14.

Montgomery, Roger. "Comment on 'Fear and House-as-Haven in the Lower Class.'" *Journal of the American Institute of Planners* 32 (January 1966): 31–37.

Pawley, Martin. *Architecture versus Housing*. New York: Praeger, 1971.

Wolfe, Tom. *From Bauhaus to Our House*. New York: Farrar Straus Giroux, 1981.

2

THE NATURE AND UTILITY OF THEORY

Theory is an ambiguous word. It means different things to different people. To some people a theory is a system of ideas or statements—a mental schema—that is believed to describe and explain a phenomenon or a group of phenomena. This schema may be an untested act of faith or, ideally, one that has been tested using scientific methods. This type of theory will be referred to here as positive theory. This may cause some confusion. The term *positive theory* is used because it consists of positive statements, assertions about reality. This should not imply that it also coincides with the tenets of positivist epistemology, which holds that no truth exists beyond the bounds of possible verification and falsification (Ricouer 1977).

"Theory" is used in at least three other ways. It can refer to a *model*, a way of perceiving reality that imposes a structure on that reality. The model of the concerns of environmental design presented in the next chapter is of this type; it is more correctly a philosophical position. Theory can also refer to a prediction that a certain outcome will be achieved by a certain action; such predictions will be referred to as *hypotheses* in this book. The other way "theory" will be used here is as a prescription for action; this is *normative theory*. In architecture, "design principles," "standards," and "manifestoes" are examples of such theory. They are based on an ideological position on what the world, good architecture, landscapes, and urban designs should be.

POSITIVE THEORY

Consciously or unconsciously we designers, like everybody else, build positive theories about the world and the way it functions as part of our everyday activities. Elements of the world occur in patterns. Some of these patterns are invariant, some occur with a high degree of regularity, and some occur randomly. The ability to predict how these patterns will occur is central to human existence. Actions are based on them.

The regularities of the world may be observed and described casually or systematically. Much of our knowledge of the world comes from the casual observations we make as part of our everyday lives and thus it is highly biased. Scientific or even quasi-scientific research procedures reduce this bias (Conant 1953). Assertions about reality, however, generally do not come from scientific research. A scientific hypothesis is "an imaginative preconception of what the truth may be" (Medawar 1983).

Theory building involves more than describing the world. It involves explanation. It is a creative process in that it involves the construction of conceptual structures both to order and explain observations. The goal is to be able to use these structures to describe what is happening and to predict what is going to happen. The value of positive theory depends on its explanatory and predictive power. Abraham Kaplan (1964) notes:

> A theory is a way of making sense of a disturbing situation so as to allow us most effectively to bring to bear our repertoire of habits, and even more importantly to modify or discard them altogether, replacing them by new ones as the situation demands.

Successful theories consist of simple but powerful generalizations about the world and how it operates that enable us to predict accurately future operations. It is essential for applied fields such as the environmental design professions to have such theories.

It is tempting to think of positive theory as an accumulation of facts about the world. The history of science suggests that we should be more cautious. Positive theory is "intrinsically tentative and subject to revision in the face of the first deviant case that does not conform to its explanation and prediction" (Roberts 1969). A theory cannot be proved. It stands until it is disproved.

Scientists may use empirical techniques to test theories, but fields such as history, and often architecture, have to rely on quasi-scientific methods. Thus positive theory in architecture cannot fulfill the requirements of the philosophy of logical positivism proposed by A.J. Ayer (1936). It is nevertheless possible, using quasi-scientific approaches, to build systematic theories that are open to discussion and challenge. The environmental design professions have been slow in doing this. Designers often have taken the position that sound common sense is all that is needed to practice well. The complexities of the world suggest that this position places high expectations on the mental capacities of the designer. Another position often taken is that theory and practice are mutually exclusive—which, as this book argues, makes theory irrelevant. Theory must address the issues of practice (see Rosmarin 1984).

Recent critics of the environmental design professions suggest that one of the major reasons for this lack of explicit positive theory is a fear among designers that systematic research will lead to the public challenge of some cherished beliefs about the nature of architecture, landscape architecture, and urban design. Certainly there is often major opposition to new data and theories that imply a need to modify or discard a traditional way of operating. Those people with a major investment in traditional practices are understandably loath to give them up. Designers know much about people

and design issues, but if one recognizes the limitations of knowledge in the professions—the limits of the traditional functional theory that architects and urban designers have inherited from the Modern Movement—then one realizes the benefits that will accrue to the design professions from having a stronger positive theoretical basis.

The Functions of Positive Theory

In response to the need for greater knowledge in the practice of environmental design, educators have developed longer educational curricula for design students. Architectural education in the United States may take as long as seven years of full-time study. A number of design theorists, including Horst Rittel (1971), quote Kenneth Boulding (1956) in this regard:

> ... the academic world generally goes on the assumption that the more we know of everything the better.... The student has always known better than this. He has usually operated on the principle of knowing as little as he can get away with. It is time, perhaps, for this principle to be made respectable. ... Any economizing in learning, therefore, is highly desirable.

Boulding also suggests how this might be achieved:

> If a single theoretical principle can be shown to apply over a wide range of the empirical world, this is economy in the learning process.

This function of theory has been called the "economy of thought." The basic goal of positive theory is to enable people to derive a large number of descriptive statements from a single explanatory statement. If one understands, say, the nature of the symbolic territorial markings of the environment by people, then one can generate any number of building patterns that meet territorial requirements. Thus theories can replace knowledge of myriad descriptive statements about the world.

The economization of knowledge is only a byproduct of the central purpose of positive theory, which is to make sense of what otherwise might remain unmeaningful. In the design professions one of the functions of positive theory is to raise to consciousness behaviors in the built environment that are important to people and that therefore should have an impact on design decisions. Recent explorations of territorial behavior and the built environment (for instance, E. Hall 1966, Newman 1972, 1979, Becker 1978, El-Sharkawy 1979) have brought to the designer's attention relationships that often were understood unconsciously. Now issues of territoriality can be discussed with some clarity. Prior to this, some designers seemed to have designed intuitively, or coincidentally, for human territorial needs. These needs, however, were not met and were not even considered in many instances, although territorial behavior is exhibited by almost everyone. There are often such gaps between our ability to carry out behaviors unconsciously and our ability to design intuitively for them.

Much knowledge about human territorial behavior is now openly available to all designers (and laymen too), and so it can be considered explicitly in the designing of rooms, buildings, and public and private open spaces. The best example of this is Oscar Newman's set of principles for the design of defensible open space based on territorial control. His explicit descriptions of these principles make them accessible to all designers. These descriptions and an understanding of his research methods make the designer aware of why they hold and what their possible limitations may be, as shown by more recent research (Brower 1980, Brower et al. 1983).

The world of theory is often contrasted with the real world. This distinction must be perceived within its proper context. Often one hears the comment, "Design may work in theory but not in practice." Many highly practical theories do specify conditions that cannot exist in the everyday world —perfect competition or frictionless movement, for example. These theories, nevertheless, enhance our understanding of phenomena. The impact of other variables must, of course, be understood. If positive theory for the design professions is not helpful in making design decisions leading to predictable outcomes, then it is irrelevant. Abraham Kaplan (1964), who has written on theory with great clarity, notes:

> Theory is of practice, and must stand and fall with its practicality, provided that the mode and contexts of its applications be suitably specified.

This is particularly true of applied fields such as architecture and landscape architecture. If theory does not do this, it is irrelevant.

An explicit positive theoretical base is necessary for any discipline if it is to respond to the issues that face it, conduct the research necessary for its progress, develop logical normative statements for its actions, and understand the limits of its understanding (see Churchman and Ginsberg 1984). It presents the basis for arguments about the direction in which a profession should go. Theory-building, testing through research or practice, and evaluation are linked in a continuous process. This is how a discipline makes progress.

Positive Theory—Value-free?

Positive theory sometimes is presented as being value-free. Many people have challenged this assumption—and quite rightly. A researcher decides to address certain questions because they appear to the researcher to be useful or interesting ones or ones that will attract funding. The choice is based on some concept of people (Lee 1971). The presentation of positive theory in architecture in Part 2 of this book is, for instance, based on a model of the concerns of environmental design that, in turn, is based on a particular ideological position. In addition, research often is funded by organizations with specific goals in mind. Similarly, the explanations a person develops to account for the phenomena observed are likely to be biased by that person's world view. This is certainly true for economics, where Marxist and capitalist explanations for the same phenomena exist side by side. The same is true for the positive theory of the design professions.

The goal of positive theory is, nevertheless, to be value-free, to avoid bias, to look for alternative explanations, and to apply the rules of scientific method to observation and explanation. This involves the operational definition of the variables being analyzed so that there can be no ambiguity in the interpretation of terms, followed by controlled observation and repeated observation. It is frequently impossible to carry out such studies on topics of concern to the design professions. We have to rely on quasi-scientific procedures. Understanding the scientific process and its intellectual basis gives us a yardstick against which we can measure our own research methods—their strengths and weaknesses. Explanations should be consistent and confirm other descriptions. If they do not confirm past studies, there is a problem either with the present explanation or with previous ones. The openness of this type of research makes it accessible for examination and challenge and reduces its biases. The goal of being value-free is itself, of course, a value-laden statement!

NORMATIVE THEORY

Normative theory is an ambiguous term. To some it means, "What has been consensually agreed upon, the norms for a given time"; to others it consists of statements on "what ought to be—what a good world is." The latter has been adopted for this text (see also Lynch 1981). Normative theory consists of the overtly value-laden statements of philosophers, politicians, and architects, among others, on what ought to be. Some people have described their normative statements as scientific. This is a contradiction in terms. The scientific method provides rules for description and explanation, not for creation. A design may be derived from scientifically formulated positive theory, but this does not make it scientific. Normative theory is based on an ideology or world view even if this is not explicitly stated. The normative theory of many action-oriented professions, such as engineering, nursing, and architecture, generally consists of deontic statements. The reason is simple: having guidelines and principles simplifies the process of making decisions. This can also lead to unfortunate results.

Normative theories are built on positive ones. They are based on perceptions of how the world works, but they are based also on perceptions of good and bad, right and wrong, desirable and undesirable, what is working well and what is working badly. Sometimes the relationship between positive and normative theories is explicit, but frequently it is not. In the design professions it seldom is. In addition, the professed normative position of a designer often differs from its behavioral correlate—practice. This can occur for a variety of reasons. An individual may simply be misleading himself or herself, or a compromise may be necessary to get something done, or the person believes that theory and practice are independent. Indeed, according to some critics, this is a characteristic of the Modern Movement (see for instance, Rowe 1972, Gadamer 1975, 1976). They say that the claims to functionality and social responsibility of the Modern Movement were mere aphorisms.

CONCEPTS OF THEORY IN THE DESIGN FIELDS

It has been suggested both in this chapter and in chapter 1 that one of the things holding back the intellectual development of the design professions is their lack of an explicit body of positive theory. They are descriptive and prescriptive disciplines. They are normative in character even though the ideological basis for their normative positions is often unclear. It is important to understand the development of the normative positions of designers during the course of history. This will tell us much about the professions and the society of which they were and are a part.

The emphasis in design theory, particularly architectural theory, as it is taught in schools of design today and as discussed by professionals, is on the designer as creator and on the set of principles that he or she uses to design a building or a building complex or an open place. This emphasis is shown in sequence in figure 2-1a. Robert Gutman (1972) notes that when we are talking about architectural theory we usually mean

> . . . the set of principles that guides the architect in making decisions about the complex problems that arise in translating a brief into the design of a building.

The sets of design principles that traditionally have constituted, say, architectural theory have been concerned primarily with the delineation of a system of logic in which the components of the environment are related to each other rather than to human experience. Where human experience is taken into consideration, it is understood as the experience people are supposed to have, not what they do have. If the experience the people do have is different from what the designer believes they should have, then they are often blamed for being poorly educated or for not knowing how to use the environment (Perin 1970). The position taken here is that, while one of the obligations of the design professions is to educate, a lack of knowledge on the part of users cannot be blamed for the failure of the built environment to meet their needs.

The design principles used throughout the design fields are based on some positive assertions about the nature of the built world and human experience. These assertions are based largely on the insights and personal experiences of the individual professional rather than on a well-formulated and systematic body of shared knowledge based on systematic research and/or the cumulative experience of practitioners. Although this means that it is difficult to learn from that experience, it must not be thought that these individual positive theories are inaccurate simply because they are based on presumptions, anecdotes, personal and cultural prejudices, and self-referential information. Many of them have been based on a process that approximates the scientific method in terms of the repetitiveness of observations. Many environmental designers are extraordinarily observant people; many, however, are not. However observant the designer may be, the conclusions he or she draws about the way the world works are biased by that individual's contacts with the world.

The design professions, it has increasingly been recognized, must tap, make explicit, and disseminate the observations that yield predictable results. Environmental psychologist Harold Proshansky (1974) has noted:

It is my contention that most architects, designers and planners have a wealth of "unrefined" data and ideas about people in relation to physical space and its organization which has yet to be tapped in any systematic fashion.

As long as these unrefined data are implicit in the design principles that are taught as truisms over the drawing board, however, it is impossible to test their accuracy or to specify the context in which they hold. It is even impossible to discuss them sensibly or to disseminate them widely. The result, as Christian Norberg-Schulz (1965) noted, is that "in discussing architectural matters we rarely achieve anything but a quarrel about what you like and what I like." An explicit body of positive knowledge certainly would raise the level of discussion, even though arguments over what is liked and disliked will persist.

THE NATURE OF POSITIVE THEORY FOR ENVIRONMENTAL DESIGN

Any statement on what positive theory should encompass is based on a value judgment. The position taken here is that, given the many problems we have had in designing environments in which people can fulfill their perceptions of the good life, and the number of failures we have had in predicting the performances of buildings and neighborhoods in human terms, we need to know more about the way in which the environment is experienced and used and valued by different people (see Michelson 1968). This is not a unique position. It is hardly coincidental that the growth of interest in the development of positive architectural theory coincides with the development of a new pluralism in normative architectural theory. This ideology recognizes the diversity of people and the need for the built environment to respond to this diversity. The resulting focus of concern of positive theory is shown in figure 2-1b.

Positive theory thus encompasses our understanding of the natural and the built environments and their roles in people's lives. It is concerned also with understanding the processes of design. These bodies of knowledge should consist of logically related, complete, internally consistent, and externally valid definitions and explanations. Knowledge propagates itself when united in theories (Kaplan 1964). It has been noted that positive theory, research, and practice should be linked in a continuous way. This is done through the testing of hypotheses—every urban, landscape, or building design is a hypothesis or set of hypotheses—that are a component part of the theory. This can be done through the systematic evaluation of the built form from the designer's, the sponsor's, and the user's viewpoints after it has been constructed and is being used.

During the past decade there has been a dramatic growth in the amount of research being done by architects and behavioral scientists on both the built environment and design praxis. It is now pos-

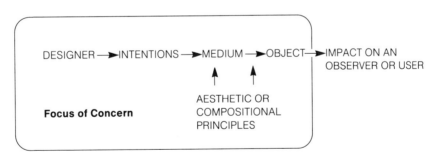

a. A conceptual model of normative theory for the design fields

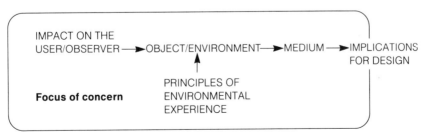

b. A conceptual model of positive theory for the design fields

2-1. Positive and Normative Theory.

Source: Philadelphia Museum of Art

2-2. Positive Theory and Intuition.
If our knowledge of something or some people is weak or lacking we have to rely on our own experiences and intuitions in filling the gap. To the extent our own experiences are valid this is fine. This nineteenth-century Japanese artist's portrayal of a wealthy American woman is based on some image he had of what Americans look like. In completing his work he drew on his own intuitions. Much of the criticism of recent building, urban, and landscape design is that the image of the users, their needs, and their values that is held by designers differs from the realities (Michelson 1968). A strong and explicit *positive theoretical* basis for design would help remedy this.

sible to attempt a synthesis of this research in order to understand our present level of knowledge. A clear conceptual framework is necessary to make this synthesis useful.

A CONCEPTUAL MODEL OF ARCHITECTURAL THEORY

First of all, it is important to differentiate between two fundamentally different types of theory, *positive theory* and *normative theory*.

Positive Theory

Positive theory in the design fields, as for other applied decision-making fields, consists of two components, *substantive theory* and *procedural theory*. *Substantive theory* is concerned with the nature of the phenomena with which architects and other designers have to deal in their work. The concern is with the nature of the environment at both a molecular and a molar level, its qualities and how it functions, and what it affords people for activities, physiological support, and aesthetic experiences. The principal concern is with the environment at a molar level, varying in scale from kilometers to millimeters, from cities to surface textures. This is the level at which the environmental design professions work. In contrast, the physicist and chemist are interested in the environment at a molecular level, while the astronomer's concern is at a scale of light years.

Substantive theory can thus be divided into two principal and interrelated components, *natural environmental theory* and *person-environment theory*. *Natural environmental theory* deals with the physical, chemical, and geological nature of the surroundings of people and other organisms. Its goal is to describe and explain the nature of materials, the nature of geometry, the nature of structures, and the nature of the interplay between natural forces (wind, rain, sun, for example) and the artificial environment. The purpose for the development of this aspect of positive theory is to provide the knowledge base for understanding how the environment can be structured in different ways and how the physical nature of these structures interacts with other aspects of the natural environment. The major contributors to the understanding of these phenomena are the natural sciences—physics, chemistry, and biology.

It is here that the focus of concern of the individual design professions, rightly or wrongly, differentiates them. Landscape architects have a much greater understanding of the processes of some aspects of the natural world than architects have. They must understand much more than architects do, for instance, about plant materials (given the way the design professions are now structured). Architects, for their part, have a much greater understanding of the nature of materials and the physical structuring of the artificial world of buildings. Civil engineers place even more emphasis on the theory of structures.

Person-environment theory might better be called "organism-environment theory," for it should deal with the description and explanation of what the three-dimensional layout of the environment affords different organisms for their habitats. Of concern in this book is the layout at a molar level and, primarily, with the human animal. The concern, therefore, is with the person-environment and person-to-person relationships within the environment. Hence it will be referred to here simply as person-environment theory. This implies an understanding of the human animal as a biological, psychological, social, and cultural being. The purpose in developing this aspect of environmental design theory is to enhance understanding of what architects traditionally have called "architectural form" and its utility for people at both an action level and an emotional level. A greater understanding of these relationships is derived from the insights of designers themselves and, more recently, from the behavioral sciences and behavioral science research within the design professions.

Procedural theory is concerned with the nature of praxis in the environmental design fields. The processes of designing can be subjected to detailed, if not scientific, scrutiny, although they seldom have been. This does not mean that the design process can be scientific—by definition, design cannot be scientific. It means, rather, that the process can be described and explained using the methods of scientific or quasi-scientific research.

The basic issues that researchers will have to address in developing procedural theory include: the nature of the design process as a whole; the nature of human creativity; the natures of analytical, synthesizing, and evaluative processes. Much of our present understanding of these processes is drawn from research in other decision-making fields and from the behavioral sciences in general.

Normative Theory

Normative theory in the design fields is concerned also with *substantive* and *procedural* issues. In contrast to positive theory, normative theory is concerned with the different positions that have been taken or might be taken on what the built environment and/or the design process should be. It is concerned with the views of different designers or schools of design on what the role of the designer is, what a good environment is, and how the design process should be carried out. Normative theory is thus concerned with the advocacies of different designers or schools of thought. One should also, as mentioned earlier, distinguish between the *professed* positions of designers and what is *practiced* by them.

SUMMARY

The major components of architectural theory can be presented in a two-by-two matrix:

Subject Matter of Theory	Orientation of Theory	
	Positive	*Normative*
Procedural		Professed
		Practiced
Substantive		Professed
		Practiced

The objective of this book is to describe and explain the present and potential contribution of the behavioral sciences to the development of this body of theory. Thus, most issues dealing with the natural sciences, other than some aspects of human biology, fall outside its perimeter of concern. This book focuses rather on describing and explaining our present knowledge of the relationship between human activities and aesthetic values and patterns of the built environment on one hand and processes of designing on the other.

While there has been little sustained effort to build a systematic positive theoretical base for the design professions, there have indeed been sporadic efforts, often by major architects. These efforts have been hampered by the lack of a clear distinction between positive and normative positions, but they should not be dismissed. It is much easier to establish a theoretical base now due to the efforts and the systematic questioning and research of the last twenty-five years.

ADDITIONAL READINGS

Banham, Reyner. *Theory and Design in the First Machine Age*. New York: Praeger, 1960.

Deutsch, Morton, and Robert M. Kraus. *Theories in Social Psychology*. New York: Basic Books, 1965.

Kaplan, Abraham. *The Conduct of Inquiry*. Scranton, PA.: Chandler, 1964.

Lynch, Kevin. "Is a General Normative Theory Possible?" In *Good City Form*. Cambridge, Mass.: MIT Press, 1981.

Medawar, P. B. *The Limits of Science*. New York: Harper & Row, 1983.

Perin, Constance. *With Man in Mind*. Cambridge, Mass.: MIT Press, 1970, pp. 260–261.

Rosmarin, Adena. "Theory and Practice from Ideally Separated to Pragmatically Joined." *Journal of Aesthetics and Art Criticism* 43, no. 1 (Fall 1984): 31–40.

3

THE BEHAVIORAL SCIENCES AND ARCHITECTURAL THEORY

Behavioral sciences is a broad term. It is assumed generally to comprise anthropology, sociology, and psychology. Sometimes economics and political science are included under this rubric. These are all fields dedicated to the development of an understanding of human activities, attitudes, and values. The focus of this book is with that subset of these fields concerned with the nature of human habitats and the relationship between the physical structure of the world and human activities and values. This subset goes under various names: *environmental psychology, man-environment relations* (M-ER), *environmental sociology,* or *human ecology.* Here it has been referred to as *person-environment theory.* The name indicates a bias in the focus of attention of those that use it. Person-environment theory subsumes the others.

Environmental psychology has been defined as the "psychological study of behavior as it relates to the everyday physical environment" (Craik 1970, Srivastava 1971). An analysis of the literature in the field, however, shows that the topics subsumed under that label include perception theory, cognition, social and anthropological psychology, the study of social relationships, and the study of culture. The terms *man-environment relations* and *environmental sociology* cover much the same areas, although the latter implies a major concern with correlations between social group membership and the use of and values associated with specific environmental patterns. Although people associated with these areas of study do not seem to recognize

it, they are all concerned with building aspects of positive environmental design theory. This represents a departure from the traditional concerns of behavioral scientists.

The traditional study of psychology has focused on the interpersonal environmental or intra-psychic phenomena. It has tried to explain behavior in terms of relationships between individuals or in terms of states existing within the person (Friedman and Juhasz 1974). Where the physical environment was taken into consideration, as in the research on perception, it tended to focus on the molecular level (such as wavelengths of light) and a molecular level of human behavior (such as galvanic skin responses). This research is very much respected for its experimental design but is of marginal use in building environmental design theory. Where psychological research broke away from these patterns and dealt with the environment in a molar way (as in Gestalt psychology), it has been seized on by architects, for good or for bad (Overy 1966, Senkevitch 1974).

In sociology there has been very little consideration of the physical environment as a component in group processes. The Chicago School of Human Ecology claimed that the nature of the physical environment was of great importance to them (Park et al. 1925, Hawley 1950). A closer examination shows that they "left it behind in the dust"; it was not really part of their research agenda (Michelson 1976). Anthropology, on the other hand, has been concerned with the artifacts of culture and the settings in which they were created, but its focus of attention has been on stable "primitive" societies. This has changed in recent times, as this book will show.

THE CONCERNS OF THE BEHAVIORAL SCIENCES

The fundamental goal of the behavioral sciences is to build *positive theory.* They seek to describe and explain phenomena. If they are able to do this well, then this knowledge can be used to predict future patterns of activities and values. When an anthropologist, psychologist, or sociologist makes a normative statement about the future—that is, when he or she states a preference for one future rather than another—then that person becomes an advocate, or a planner, rather than a behavioral scientist. Behavioral scientists in a democratic society have every right to do this, yet they do this at great risk of criticism by their peers. Planners and designers are always concerned about the future. Every act of an architect, landscape architect, or urban designer is an advocacy for one future rather than another. Designers often want behavioral scientists to tell them what the goals for design should be, as if these were statements of fact rather than of ideology (Gutman 1972). Sensitive behavioral scientists often are reluctant to do this because it means stepping out of their own professional roles.

The research process advocated by behavioral scientists is the scientific method, or as close an approximation of it as possible. The result has been an emphasis on laboratory experimentation in psychology and on as empirical a process as can be achieved in sociology and anthropology. Often the emphasis on rigorous research has resulted in a greater concern with the aesthetics of the research process than with the importance of the questions being asked. In addition, these fields were concerned neither with the built environment nor with testing the belief implicit in this lack of concern—that the natural and built environments are largely unimportant in human behavior. Newly developed research techniques (such as Barker 1968, Michelson 1975, Zeisel 1981) are yielding insights of direct utility to archi-

tects, and behavioral scientists increasingly are concerned with questions about the built environment. One of the problems has been that much of the recent research by both behavioral scientists and designers, presented at conferences such as those of the Environmental Design Research Association (EDRA), is not focused on issues of direct concern to designers. This has led to much discussion of the "utility gap" between research findings and professional practice (see Windley and Weisman 1977, Kantrowitz 1985). Empirical facts in themselves do not guide practice; theory can. Research needs to focus on theory building.

THE CONCERNS OF DESIGN

To be able to discuss the contribution of the behavioral sciences to the development of the theoretical bases for design, one must have an image of the concerns of designers. "To engage in theorizing means not just to learn from experience but to think about what there is to learn" (Kaplan 1964). Any categorization of the concerns of a field is biased by the views of the person making it, because it depends on that person's experience and attitudes.

If one accepts general statements on architecture as exemplars for the design professions, then one finds a general agreement on the concerns of design, although different writers use different vocabularies in stating them (see fig. 3-1). A compelling statement was written by Vitruvius, architect to Caesar Augustus, two thousand years ago. According to Vitruvius a building must fulfill three basic purposes: *utilitas, venustas,* and *firmitas.* This statement has been paraphrased by Sir Henry Wotton (1624) as follows:

> In *Architecture* as in all other *Operative* Arts,
> the *end* must direct the *Operation.*
> The *end* is to build well.
> Well-building hath three Conditions.
> *Commoditie, Firmenes,* and *Delight.*

Wotton expressed some misgivings about subdividing the concerns of architecture in this way, but, like others much later (for instance, Scott 1935), he

Vitruvius	Wotton	Gropius (Modern Functionalism)	Norbert-Schulz	Steele
Utilitas	Commoditie	Function	Building task	Task instrumentality Shelter and security Social contact
Venustas	Delight	Expression	Form	Symbolic identification Pleasure
Firmitas	Firmenes	Technics	Technics	Growth

3-1. The Concerns of the Design Fields as Stated by Different Authors.

found it useful as a point of departure for his analysis of buildings. It is important to remember that these three concerns are interrelated. Geoffrey Scott noted:

> Architecture is the focus of three separate purposes which have converged. They are blended in a single method; they are fulfilled in a single result; yet in their own nature they are distinguishable from each other. . . .

Commodity and firmness are certainly major contributions to delight. The mistake of too many modern architects was to believe that the two were the sole contributors.

Commodity, or what Norberg-Schulz (1965) calls "building task," was regarded as the functional goal of design by modern architects, and *delight,* or "form" in Norberg-Schulz's terms, the aesthetic goal. Architecture also requires *firmness.* Buildings have to endure as long as they are needed. The history of architecture is partially a history of technology. Indeed, technology has been a predominant concern in explaining the evolution of architecture. The major changes in architectural style have resulted, however, from the interrelationships of many factors: the emergence of new types of clients; changes in lifestyle, social stratification, values, and economic cultures; and developments in the technology available or inventable by designers and/or builders.

Separating commodity and delight seems to imply that delight serves no fundamental purpose. This simply is not so. Aesthetic functions must be perceived among other functions served by the physical environment (see Broadbent 1975, Mukarovsky 1981). It is through symbolic aesthetics, in particular, that we create displays that communicate messages to others about ourselves and our aspirations. While there is a certain analytical utility in keeping commodity and delight separate, one must recognize the delight in commodity and the commodity in delight.

A number of attempts have been made to elaborate on the Vitruvian statement. Fred Steele (1973) sees six basic functions of architecture: shelter, security, social contact, and task instrumentality are all aspects of commodity, while symbolic indentification and pleasure are aspects of aesthetics, or, in Wotton's term, delight. Growth is something that pervades all aspects of environmental design, for it involves such things as opportunities for learning for the sake of learning.

It is assumed here that the goal of the designer is to create environments that meet these human needs. Thus, a model of human needs is required for defining the set of concerns of the design fields that have to do with "non-firmness." The model used in this book is that of the humanist psychologist Abraham Maslow (1954). The built environment, if properly configured, can meet aspects of human needs for survival, security, affiliation, esteem, learning, and aesthetics. That is the normative philosophy of this book.

Creating such an environment is no easy task. To understand fully why this is so, we have to recognize the nature of the problems confronting the designer.

THE NATURE OF DESIGN PROBLEMS

To design rooms, buildings, building complexes, and urban areas is a daunting task, because the range of activities and the aesthetic needs of humans are so vast that it is difficult to understand them and to understand what configurations of the environment can best afford them. It requires that we identify exactly what the problem is and find or invent the best solution to it in a particular context. For most environments this is compounded by the requirement that a variety of needs of a variety of users and interested parties be met simultaneously. The needs themselves are difficult to identify. Many are largely unconscious. Clients are not able to articulate them very well, and few designers have been trained to be sensitive to them. One of the objectives of this book is to enhance the sensitivity of designers to the users' needs.

Designers can be described appropriately as problem-solvers. An environmental design problem can be said to exist when there is a discrepancy between the present layout of the environment and a layout that would better meet the needs of an individual or a group of people. This does not mean, however, that the only concern of the designer is the removal of negative barriers to human development. The creation of environments that enhance human experience is also a major concern.

> The creative act is of immense value to people . . . because we only continue to live by adapting ourselves to change. If we stagnate, we perish. But if we create for the future out of the present we have made the necessary adjustment, have changed our environment and have a new viewpoint of life. (Fry 1961)

The problems facing designers in doing this have been called "wicked" (Rittel 1971). Environmental problems are wicked because they are so ill-defined. The nature of the future we want is seldom clear. It is seldom clear exactly what the scope of the problem is, what components of it fall within the designer's control, which components are important for whom, or what the appropriate solutions are. Life is too short to test *all* the possible solutions to any but the very simplest problems. In addition, all environmental design problems are unique and there is no specific formula for dealing with them. It is hardly surprising then that there are some limitations to modern architecture, Post-Modernism, or any other design philosophy. It is unreasonable to expect everybody to be satisfied with any complex building, building complex, or open space design or to expect that any such scheme can meet all needs equally well. We are tempted to protest that it is too demanding to ask us to do better. And, indeed, there are limits to human potential, but we *can* do better. The behavioral sciences offer much in this regard. They will not solve all difficulties, however. Luckily humans are adaptable, so "perfect" solutions are not necessary, but that does not mean that a designer should not strive to "optimize" his or her own work. The behavioral sciences are contributing to the achievement of this end.

THE CONTRIBUTION OF THE BEHAVIORAL SCIENCES TO DESIGN THEORY

The behavioral sciences contribute in several ways to design theory. These ways are diagrammed in figure 3-2 and consist of: (1) *theories* and *models* that enhance understanding of design processes and the relationship between people and the physical—particularly the built—environment; and (2) *research methods*. From time to time the question arises as to which is the more important contribu-

tion, but this seems irrelevant. Both are important.

There are two sets of *theories* and *models* of concern to those who create design theory. The first set has to do with procedural theory and the second with substantive theory. The first has to do with knowledge about the processes of analysis, creation, and evaluation; the second, with knowledge about the world, people's use of it, the way people relate to each other in the world, and their attitudes toward it. If one accepts that one of the problems with the normative stance of the modern masters was that it assumed a universality of application for its design principles, then one is also concerned with models of individual and societal differences.

Designers' normative positions are based on what they know and believe about the world and how the design process should be conducted. Normative positions are shaped by designers' world views, which are shaped, in turn, by the cultures—the broad societal and the narrower professional cultures—to which they belong. Models of world views and the processes by which they are developed are important in understanding the normative stances an architect takes with regard to perceptions of a good world and perceptions of how environmental design praxis should be carried out. Some, like Frank Lloyd Wright, have very clearly articulated world views, but many do not. These views can be studied within a positivist framework (that is, through scientific or quasi-scientific research approaches), but, as has already been pointed out, they are not and cannot themselves be scientific positions. Traditionally these views have been the core of architectural theory. They can be studied much more rigorously than in the past, using present theories of cognition and attitude-formation as well as historical research methods.

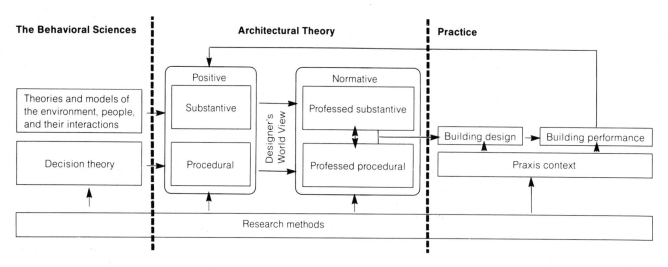

3-2. **The Behavioral Sciences and Environmental Design Theory.**

Research methods are a second important contribution of the behavioral sciences. Designers have always used observation and interview, the basic techniques of behavioral science, for obtaining information about the world, but they have applied these methods very differently. While behavioral scientists have been able to increase the precision and validity of their research findings, designers usually have relied on casual procedures.

The research methods of behavioral scientists are of basic importance to anyone studying the built environment or designing processes. They can be of direct help also to the practicing professional particularly in the programming phase of praxis, as shall be discussed in greater detail later in this book (see also Sanoff 1977, Peña 1977, Palmer 1981). Not all the techniques of behavioral science research are applicable to environmental design research, and there are some areas of concern to designers—symbolic aesthetics, for instance—for which the currently available techniques are not very helpful. It is likely that in the long run, environmental design researchers will design many specific techniques to cope with the specific problems they face. Many methods for environmental research have been ably documented in a number of recent books (such as Michelson 1975, Zeisel 1981), but a brief overview here will give an understanding of their contribution to design research.

While interview and observation are the basic ways of obtaining information for creating design theory and for programming, there are diverse ways of interviewing and observing. The selection of the appropriate technique depends on the problem being addressed. Interview techniques of various types are useful in ascertaining the nature of people's mental involvement with the environment and their hopes for the future (see Goodrich 1974, Marans 1975). They also are used widely to understand how people use the environment. Interview techniques have come under strong criticism in recent times. People find it difficult to talk about their feelings. They also know they are being studied even though the exact purpose of the study may be obscured by the form of the questionnaire or interview schedule. These problems can be overcome by the way in which questions are asked and by the design of modified techniques, which include the charting of daily activities on maps, time-budget recording, and semiprojective games. Although these techniques have limitations, they are the prime means for understanding attitudes and aesthetic values.

Observational techniques vary in scope and rigor. The most systematic is the scientific experiment in which one variable is manipulated to see what impact it has on another while all other variables are held constant. Much of the research on perception and on cognition has involved experimental techniques. This type of research is confined to the laboratory so it has not been very useful in studying human activities. It is possible, however, to set up natural experiments outside the laboratory. In natural experiments elements of the environment are manipulated while the subjects are simply those people who happen to come along. Research on pedestrian and queuing behavior has used this approach. Different layouts are tested to see what impact they have on the way people move through the environment.

The most widely used observational technique is simple observation (see Patterson 1974, Zeisel 1981). In simple observation neither the environment nor the subjects are manipulated. It does, however, involve the systematic recording of observations and great attention to the time periods selected for observation, so that what is observed is a representative sample of reality. Special techniques such as behavioral mapping have been devised to aid the accurate recording of observations. The problem with simple observation is that it is difficult to carry out without the observer becoming intrusive. The use of television cameras, time-lapse photography, and filming all help overcome this problem. This raises ethical questions, however. Participant observation is also an unobtrusive technique that can be used for design research (see Neutra 1954). The researcher in this case becomes a member of the system being observed. The research problem here is that the very presence of the researcher may very well change the behavior of the system.

One of the important contributions that the behavioral sciences can make to environmental design research and theory-building is an attitudinal one. Behavioral scientists are particularly concerned with the objectivity of their methods—that terms and procedures are clearly defined so that other investigators can easily replicate the study or, at least, form their own judgments of the quality of the results obtained. Thus, the research follows a logical, interrelated sequence of steps: formulation of the problem; establishment of the research design; selection of measurement procedures; collection of data; analysis and interpretation of findings; and application of the results to theory-building or testing. The design professions, with little research heritage of their own, have had to turn to the set of techniques developed by others as a starting point for their research efforts. Because we have done so little behavioral research in the past, we also have to rely heavily on research done in other fields to elucidate many of our tasks. An examination of the interaction between the behavioral sciences and the Modern Movement in architecture shows this. It also shows the piecemeal character of much of this borrowing.

THE BEHAVIORAL SCIENCES AND THE MODERN MOVEMENT

The influence of the behavioral sciences, either purposefully or unconsciously, on Modernism has been a major one, but one that is still inadequately understood (see Perez-Gomez 1983). During the past two centuries many designers, architects, landscape architects, and urban designers have turned to the behavioral sciences either to clarify issues of concern to them or to rationalize their normative positions. Many other designers have rejected this approach on the grounds that their common sense is good enough and their creative roles will be diminished if they rely on the sciences. Certainly, the systematic analysis of the potential contribution of the behavioral sciences to design theory is recent. A review of past efforts will illustrate the utility and some of the difficulties in bringing the behavioral sciences to bear on the problems of design.

There are clear linkages between empiricism in philosophy and psychology and the work of romantic classical architects such as Humphry Repton and John Nash at the beginning of the nineteenth century (Hipple 1957); empiricism is linked similarly to the efforts of architects such as Alexander Jackson Downing, during the middle of the century, to justify their normative position that different buildings should be of different styles (Ward 1966).

The contemporaneous development of ideas in psychology and aesthetic theory and in sociology and neighborhood theory began at the beginning of the twentieth century. The explicit concern with procedural theory in the environmental design fields has been considerably more recent, dating from the 1950s. Much of this latter effort was preceded by work in business administration and engineering.

In the first decade of this century, Charles Henry, the French psychologist, was asked to provide corroborating evidence for the beliefs of the masters of the Ecole des Beaux-Arts in Paris (Argüelles 1972). This he failed to do. Instead his studies indicated a possible link between the line and color of drawings and the emotional response of an observer. He assumed this to be true. His writings, which were included in the art journal *L'Esprit Nouveau*, provided the positive justification for the work of cubist architects and artists (Gray 1953).

In America, George Santayana's aesthetic philosophy (1896) was built on the work of psychologist William James (1890). James was also instrumental in initiating a line of research that had a major influence on the aesthetic philosophy of the Modern Movement. He brought psychologist Hugo Munsterberg, the "founder of applied psychology" (Boring 1942), to Harvard. Munsterberg's writings on such topics as "The Aesthetics of Simple Forms" and "Studies in Symmetry" presaged Gestalt theory. Many of his theoretical concepts and research methods were used as the basis for the educational programs and research efforts in the Soviet schools of architecture in the post-revolutionary period. Munsterberg's work had a major influence on Nikolai Ladovsky's attempts to link the study of formal aesthetics with the psychology of perception. Ladovsky established a research laboratory at the VKHUTEMAS (State Higher Art and Technical Studios) in 1920 (Khan-Mahomedov 1971, Khazanova 1971). The objective was to study the aesthetics of shape and form. With the shift to the aesthetic ideology of "social realism," as decreed by Stalin in 1931, the systematic research efforts of the Soviet schools ceased (see Senkevitch 1974). By then many of the people involved had moved to western Europe. Some were teaching at the Bauhaus.

The architecture department at the Bauhaus was founded in 1927. Walter Gropius, who headed the Bauhaus, was critical of the old academies because they did not nurture the study of aesthetics—something few design schools do systematically today. Under Gropius's leadership courses on perception theory were introduced at the Bauhaus. The development of Gestalt concepts of perception in Germany was contemporaneous with the development of the Bauhaus. Gestalt theory justified the aesthetic ideas of artists such as Wassily Kandinsky, Paul Klee, and Josef Albers (Wingler 1969), and these artists were, in turn, influenced by it (Overy 1966). Hannes Meyer, Gropius's successor, broadened the behavioral science component of the educational curriculum at the Bauhaus, although this did not seem to have much of an impact on his own work. He introduced a variety of courses with different theoretical orientations. These included a course on Gestalt theory, a course on what would now be called "ergonomics," and courses on cultural history (Wingler 1969).

The influence of the Bauhaus curriculum on education in western Europe and the United States and ultimately throughout the rest of the world has been a major one (see P. L. Jones 1969, Herdeg 1983). With the coming of Nazism, the teachers of the Bauhaus took positions in schools of design in many countries. Despite all the efforts at the Bau-

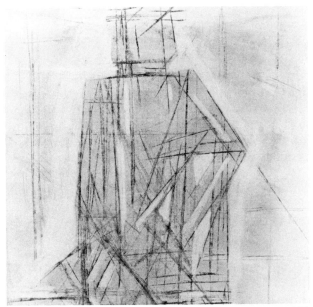

1   Drawing by K. A. Kolnick

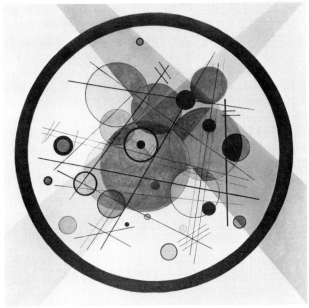

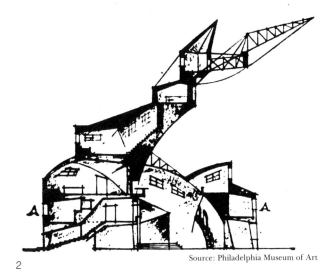

3   Khan-Mahomedov (1970), *Architectural Design* Magazine, London

2

Source: Philadelphia Museum of Art

3-3. Perception Theory and the Aesthetic Ideology of the Modern Movement.

During the course of this century, artists and architects have been very much concerned with the nature of visual perception. Cubist art (for example, Kolnick, 1) relied on the findings of research psychologist Charles Henry to explain the emotional meanings of shapes and patterns. The work of the Rationalist and Constructivist architects of the Soviet Union (2) relied heavily on the work of Hugo Munsterberg at Harvard, while the Bauhaus artists (for example, Kandinsky, 3) had a debt to Gestalt psychology. The problem was that no clear distinction was made between *positive* and *normative* theory or between *perception* and *aesthetic* theories. The result has been considerable intellectual confusion.

haus, however, no clear positive basis for design emerged. The Bauhaus borrowed theoretical ideas from the behavioral sciences but never took the next step, that of initiating the development of an explicit positive theoretical base for design. This was also the situation at other places dealing with design concerns.

In the United States, during the late 1920s and 1930s, there was concern with the physical organization of cities and the development of patterns of layout, which it was believed would enhance feelings of community and reduce the perceived alienation of city dwellers. Sociologist Clarence Perry sought a generic physical unit within which a social unit would develop. He was influenced by the ear-

lier work of Charles Cooley (1909), who stressed the importance of the primary group—the family, the play group of children, and the neighborhood community of their elders—in socializing children and establishing normative patterns of behavior. Cooley thought that face-to-face relationships and a sense of community based on place were particularly important for children. Perry (1927) integrated Cooley's ideas with the practice of providing community centers as the foci of local areas. The resulting "neighborhood unit" has been widely applied throughout the world with varying degrees of success.

Recent research has shown that there is a low degree of congruence between social and physical units in cities (Keller 1968). This finding has had an impact on normative theory in urban design, for instance. The neighborhood-unit concept, widely used in the design of the first generation of British new towns after World War II, was abandoned as the basis for the design of Cumbernauld in Scotland (1966) under the influence of the writings of sociologists such as Peter Wilmott and Michael Young

(Young and Wilmott 1957, Wilmott and Young 1960). Cumbernauld was designed as one large unit to engender more town pride and at higher population densities than the first generation of British new towns. The goal was to provide its inhabitants with a rich set of nonlocal contacts.

The goal of developing "community without propinquity" is even clearer in Milton Keynes, the most recent statement on British new-town design. Future communications technology may further erode the congruence between social and physical space. At the same time, it must be remembered that for many people the locally based community is still important (Hester 1975). It is clear that design concepts of community have been very much influenced by sociological concepts in recent times. It is also clear that the generalizations made by sociologists about social life and physical environment must be enriched. This is being done, as later discussions on social organization and design will reveal.

RECENT EFFORTS

The influence of the behavioral sciences on design theory before World War II was highly fragmentary. This was partially due to the focus of concern of architects on normative ideas, but also partially due to the undeveloped state of the behavioral sciences. It is only when there has been a particular philosophy of architecture, landscape architecture, and/or urban design that a serious attempt to develop the positive theoretical basis for design has been made. The best-known such attempt occurred at the Hochschule for Gestaltung in Ulm, Germany, under the directorship of Max Bill and later Thomas Maldonado. The professed normative position of the school was presented as follows in its bulletin:

> Design as the school sees it . . . requires intense research and methodological work, in order to do justice to all the technical, functional, aesthetic and economical requirements. A good design has to live up to reality. For that reason the work of the school must be done in conjunction with sociology, contemporary history and other disciplines relating to social structure. (Wingler 1969)

Few architects have been enamored with such an approach. Hans Wingler (1969) dismisses it as the "scientific-dogmatic tendencies of Hannes Meyer" or "the last kick of the Bauhaus." The Hochschule, beset with internal dissension, had a short life. One of the basic problems was that those who taught in the design studios, while paying lip service to the findings of the behavioral sciences, were so imbued with the spirit of the Modern Movement that they dismissed evidence contradictory to their own beliefs. Architecture has never had a strong scientific or research base and many practitioners are intimidated by the suggestion that one is possible. Interestingly, it was easier for students at the Hochschule in Ulm to integrate design and ideas of the behavioral sciences than it was for their teachers (Krippendorf 1981).

As late as 1970 there was a profound lack of "human studies" and studies of the design process in the educational curricula of architectural schools in the United States (Perin 1970). This has changed considerably; more and more courses on these topics are being introduced into design schools. Organizations such as the Environmental Design Research Association hold annual conferences (since 1968) at which research papers are presented by designers and behavioral scientists alike. In recent writings (for instance, Rapoport 1977, Holohan 1982, Levy-LeBoyer 1982) an effort has been made to get away from the partisan aesthetic and social ideologies of the modern masters and to present more global treatises on architecture, landscape architecture, and urban design. This does not mean that these books are free of ideology. Rather, it reflects their authors' belief that the design fields can move toward a more rigorous intellectual basis derived from scientific and quasi-scientific research. This movement has by no means been embraced wholeheartedly by architectural educators, and there is a regression to "easier" times in a number of places.

THE FUTURE

There has been considerable concern about the gap between the information generated by environmental design research and the ability of designers to use it (Windley and Weisman 1977). Short-run answers have been suggested by a number of people. These generally have focused on the presentation of research findings in guideline form—that is, in normative statements—because this is the type of information of interest to architects. The best-known such statement is that complied by Christopher Alexander and his colleagues and presented in his book *A Pattern Language* (Alexander et al. 1977). The gap between the behavioral sciences and the design professions seems to run deeper than this, however.

It would be easy to explain the lack of sustained conversation between architects and behavioral scientists by claiming that designers retain the notion that the environments they design are simply an expression of their own beliefs about the world. If one takes this position, then an explicit body of positive theory is largely unnecessary for the design fields. Some architects certainly feel threatened by the challenge to many of their beliefs, social creeds, and design habits presented by the research findings and theory that result from controlled and repeated observation, logical analysis, and the norms of disciplined argument. The main reasons, however, seem to be the continued confusion the profession has about its own activities and purposes and the view that scientists have about the creative act of design.

The fundamental thesis of this book is that it is useful to distinguish clearly between *positive* theory and *normative* theory. This is not always easy to do. The one affects the other. Designers should be clear about the contribution of the behavioral sciences. Whereas the behavioral sciences may clarify the issues that have to be considered in developing a normative position and may clarify the basis for existing normative positions, they cannot, by definition, tell the designer what the goals of design should be. The behavioral sciences can help us to understand the present and what the trends in society are, and they can help us to predict the outcomes of our design proposals for the future better than we do now. The creation of these proposals is not and cannot be a scientific endeavor. As long as designers expect this, they will be disappointed.

Science, as noted above, implies a mode of developing descriptions and explanations. Those aspects of environmental design theory concerned with describing and explaining phenomena and processes will benefit from the theories and research methods of the behavioral sciences. Often, however, there are competing explanations for the same phenomena; there are competing theories. Designers must recognize and be able to work with this ambiguity. It is no longer sufficient for designers simply to take up one theory and develop a normative position on it without recognizing the limitations of that theory.

Interior designers, architects, landscape architects, and urban designers always are dealing with the future. They will always be making decisions with uncertainty. The behavioral sciences may reduce this uncertainty but they will not eliminate it. Providing an organizational model for environmental design theory is a major requirement for clarifying the intellectual basis of the design disciplines. Without such a model the confusion over the role of the behavioral sciences in the development of design theory will persist.

ADDITIONAL READINGS

Alexander, Christopher, et al. *A Pattern Language.* London: Oxford University Press, 1977.

Bailey, Joe. *Social Theory for Planning.* London and Boston: Routledge and Kegan Paul, 1975.

Churchman, Arza, and Yona Ginsberg. "The Uses of Behavioral Science Research in Physical Planning: Some Inherent Limitations." *Journal of Architectural and Planning Research* 1, no. 1 (June 1984): 57–66.

Gombrich, E. H. *Art History and Social Sciences.* Oxford: Oxford University Press, 1975.

Gutman, Robert. "The Questions Architects Ask." In R. Gutman, ed., *People and Buildings.* New York: Basic Books, 1972, pp. 337–369.

Levy-LeBoyer, Claude. *Psychology and Environment.* Beverly Hills, CA.: Sage, 1982.

Lindblom, Charles, and Davis Cohen. *Usable Knowledge: Social Sciences and Social Problem Solving.* New Haven: Yale University Press, 1979.

Michelson, William, ed. *Behavioral Research Methods in Environmental Design.* Stroudsburg, Pa.: Dowden, Hutchinson and Ross, 1975.

Pipkin, John S., Mark E. La Gory, and Judith Blau. *Remaking the City: Social Science Perspectives on Urban Design.* Albany, N.Y.: SUNY Press, 1983.

Proshansky, Harold M. "Environmental Psychology and the Design Professions." In Jon Lang et al., eds., *Designing for Human Behavior: Architecture and the Behavioral Sciences.* Stroudsburg, Pa.: Dowden, Hutchinson and Ross, 1974, pp. 72–80.

Windley, Paul G., and Gerald Weisman. "Social Science and Environmental Design: The Translation Process." *Journal of Architectural Education* 31, no. 1 (September 1977): 16–19.

Zeisel, John. *Sociology and Architectural Design.* New York: Russell Sage, 1975.

———. *Inquiry by Design.* Monterey, Ca.: Brooks/Cole, 1980.

PART II

POSITIVE ARCHITECTURAL THEORY

CONCEPTS OF PRAXIS AND
CONCEPTS OF ENVIRONMENT

The purpose of creating *positive environmental design theory* is to have a body of knowledge that will enable interior designers, architects, landscape architects, and urban designers to better understand the nature of the design process and the present nature of the built environment—how it is experienced and used. This part of the book is divided accordingly into two sections, the first on *procedural theory* and the second on *substantive theory*. The goal is to present explicitly an overview of the body of positive knowledge on the concerns of environmental design to the extent that the behavioral sciences have helped or might help create it. The result will be a more complex picture of the nature of environmental design than that held by many of the design professions at present. At the same time, the knowledge we have at our disposal should help environmental designers deal with this higher level of complexity. This is the advantage of imposing a useful structure on knowledge. The behavioral sciences do more than simply add to our knowledge of the purposes served by the built environment; they change the very structure of this knowledge. The objective of Part 2 of this book is to demonstrate this.

The presentation of positive environmental design theory here will be incomplete in part because many aspects of it—particularly those concerned with the physical sciences and economic theory—fall outside the scope of the book. Another reason is that we have too little knowledge and understanding of how design praxis takes place and how the built environment affects human lives. The scientific study of the concerns, both procedural and substantive, is very uneven. The reasons for this are diverse. Some of the concerns of environmental design—for example, the process of decision-making in an architectural firm—are extremely difficult to study using scientific or quasi-scientific methods. Many topics simply have not attracted the attention of researchers.

Environmental designers have always made decisions with uncertainty and must always do so. We are dealing with the future. The objective of this presentation of procedural theory is to outline our present understanding of the decision process in environmental design—the process whereby designs are created. The discussion also will demonstrate the importance of having an explicit, well-researched, and organized body of substantive theory for the design professions. The objective of the development of substantive theory is to reduce uncertainty about many issues of concern to the designer. The hope for a completely rational understanding of what the environment affords people and the nature of the processes of design is, however, unattainable. There is much, however, that we do know now. ∎

PROCEDURAL
THEORY
Design Methodology

Procedural theory is concerned with descriptions and explanations of the processes whereby the built environment—interiors, buildings, and landscapes—is self-consciously designed. It is concerned with *design methodology,* the study of the processes of designing. In this segment of the book, the concern is thus with that component of environmental design theory shown in the following diagram:

Subject Matter of Theory	Orientation of Theory	
	Positive	*Normative*
Procedural	Part 2 Chapters 4–7	Part 3
Substantive	Part 2 Chapters 8–19	

In other words, the concern here is with the science of *praxis.* The objective of the development of procedural theory is to have a body of knowledge that can enhance both environmental design education and practice. This knowledge, if used thoughtfully, will enable environmental designers to design the process of design in order to deal with the situation at hand instead of relying on habitual processes that are often inappropriate to those circumstances.

Procedural theory in environmental design is weak. Although statements of concern about the lack of an explicit and rigorous body of positive procedural theory in architecture can be traced back at least a hundred years (Senkevitch 1974), a sustained concern with developing it seems to have begun with the work at the Hochschule for Gestaltung at Ulm during the period 1956–1965. The concern there, however, was with making the process "more scientific" through the development of new normative models of the process, rather than with conducting scientific research on how the process is carried out and the results achieved (that is, the environmental quality) as the result of carrying it out in different ways (see Wingler 1969). This being a fairly typical pattern in schools of environmental design, those interested in building procedural theory have had to turn to the literature in other fields and to their own experiences in order to develop some initial hypotheses about the process. During the last twenty years much progress has been made in elucidating the fundamental nature of environmental design praxis, but much remains to be done. There certainly has been an increased willingness for urban designers, architects, and landscape architects to discuss the topic. For a long time this was taboo. It was feared that understanding the process would hamper creative thinking and the creative role of the designer.

One of the difficulties in building procedural theory is simply that environmental design praxis is not easy to study systematically. Longitudinal studies—those looking at particular design efforts from their inception to their conclusion—are extraordinarily time-consuming. If one relies on what designers say they have done, one can be misled. We designers are notoriously bad at describing our own design efforts. An examination of the research literature (such as Eaton 1969, P. Turner 1977) makes one wonder whether we do not often purposely mislead in order to bolster our self-image. The result is that our knowledge is fragmentary and anecdotal. The objective of this part of the book is to put these pieces together in a coherent fashion that will result in the presentation of some basic models of the environmental design process and its subcomponents. This will at least give a preliminary statement on the scope and concerns of procedural theory.

The behavioral sciences can make contributions to the development of procedural theory at two levels. One consists of research findings on the nature of the process as a whole—its overall structure; the other provides an understanding of the subprocesses of *analysis, synthesis, evaluation,* and *decision.* One of the ways in which theory-creation takes place is through the generation and testing of axioms about a phenomenon or, as in the case of concern here, a process. Several such axioms about the general nature of environmental design are presented in chapter 4, "Models of Environmental Design Praxis." These axioms have not been subject to rigorous testing although there have been many reviews of them. In these reviews, designers, particularly architects and urban designers, have examined the axioms in terms of the reviewers' own professional experience. These axioms are not necessarily wrong simply because they have not been tested seriously, but their accuracy as generalizations about the process of environmental design must remain open to question. Many designers, in fact, believe that the processes they go through are too complex to describe and should not be described. This position is rejected here because it largely precludes the asking of serious questions about the field and thus would hamper its advancement.

Chapters 5, 6, and 7 are concerned with the subprocesses of environmental design. Chapter 5 focuses on analytical, or more broadly, intelligence, activities. These are used throughout environmental design praxis whenever there is a need to understand the nature of the problem at hand. Chapter 6 is concerned with the nature of the act of designing itself. This involves both the generation of a variety of ideas and the reduction and synthesis of these into specific solutions. These processes also are used throughout environmental design praxis whenever a decision has to be made. Thus, environmental design programming, sketch designing, and the evaluation of alternative schemes all require creative thought. Evaluation, or more broadly, the choice process, is discussed in chapter 7. Evaluation is used in comparing various design possibilities with each other or against standards or norms of performance. It is an integral part of decision-making—deciding that one possibility is more promising than another. Thus, the whole process of environmental design can be understood to consist of intelligence, design, and choice activities occurring in rapid sequence. Each, however, tends to predominate at one phase of the overall process and gives that phase its basic character. This is recognized in the structuring of the four chapters of this part of the book.

It will be clear from the presentation of procedural theory that however thoughtfully and sensitively the design process is carried out, a whole series of activities cannot be done well without good substantive theory. We cannot ask sensible questions unless we hypothesize about what knowledge is useful; it is chancy to make predictions of the performance of designs that are still on the drawing board unless we have theories on which to base these predictions; it is difficult to identify or design appropriate principles of design for different cultural settings without knowledge of the variables that differentiate one culture from another; systematic evaluation without good substantive theory on which to base predictions of performance is impossible. Good substantive theory—powerful and externally valid theory—is central to the development of the objectives required for solving a design problem and for designing the principles with which to meet those objectives. Many design methodologists —students of the design processes—have failed to recognize explicitly the importance of knowledge about the world in thinking about the process (see B. Jackson 1967). ■

4

MODELS OF ENVIRONMENTAL DESIGN PRAXIS

Making decisions about the future is characteristic of many human endeavors. People have been designing structures and buildings to fulfill present and future needs since prehistoric times. They have used some design process to achieve the results they seek. Christopher Alexander (1964) differentiated between societies in which design is not a self-conscious activity and those in which it is self-conscious. It is largely not self-conscious in societies that have a low division of labor and where design prototypes have evolved over a long period of time in response to stable social and terrestrial conditions. In much of the world today, design is a self-conscious process carried out by professionals. They deal with a series of unique problems for which there are no prototypes, although they usually have had some experience with similar types in the past.

The design of the early cities of the Indus Valley civilization or the temples of Central and South America or the cathedrals of Europe required considerable self-conscious and diligent thought. Early designers must have had some intuitive understanding of the decision process (Bazjanac 1974). There have been comments on the process from Vitruvius's time. According to him, architectural designing is the process of selecting parts to achieve a whole. Alberti (1485) thought about it in much the same way. Descartes (1637) developed a set of ideas for structuring his own creative efforts in his *Discourse on Method*. Following Descartes, architects such as Laugier (1753) described the process of de-

signing as one of decomposing a problem, solving these components, and then synthesizing these partial solutions into whole ones. They referred to this as the *rational method*. This line of thinking has influenced designers up to the present time. Le Corbusier, for instance, describes his own design process in very much these terms in *Vers une architecture* (1923). It is a decomposition/composition process involving a number of steps: the formulation of the problem in terms of the functions to be housed; the formulation of design standards; and the composition of these into built form—"the masterly, correct and magnificent play of masses brought together in light" (Eslami, 1985). Both reason and intuition play a major part in this. Design methodology is the field of study that is leading us to an understanding of these processes and of the overall structure of environmental design praxis and its subcomponents (see also Grant 1975, 1982, Schon 1984).

There are many designers, the majority perhaps, who perceive the design process to be a purely intuitive, indescribable one. Others see it as a rational process, and still others regard it as an argumentative one. Most people who have looked at the process agree, at least, that it is divided into a number of phases. Different people work through these phases different ways (Heath 1984). The objective of this chapter is to review these concepts of design as the basis for synthesizing a model that describes our present understanding of the process.

PRAXIS AS AN INTUITIVE PROCESS

Designing is regarded by many environmental designers, particularly architects, as a sequence of operations that are internalized and undifferentiated. It is recognized that the process consists of analytical, synthetical, and evaluative processes in which the designer is a "black box" turning inputs into outputs by some mysterious process. Different psychological theories of cognition deal with the essence of this process in different ways.

Behaviorist theories of cognition lead to the conclusion that environmental forces in the form of patterns of stimulation that motivate and reinforce behavior act through the individual to determine outputs (Fodor 1981). Psychobiological theories suggest that creative acts depend on the nature of the brain and nervous system—certain abilities, for instance, are associated with certain components of the brain. It is hypothesized that some people have better wired-in processes than others (Garcia 1982). Information-processing theories of cognition, which owe much to recent developments in cybernetics, suggest that the "software" of "mental programs" is superimposed on the "neurological hardware" and that these provide the controlling structure for mental processes. Current research efforts are aimed at developing an understanding of these programs (such as Hunt 1983). Ulrich Neisser (1977) regards them as schemata that are modified

through experience. Gestalt theory postulates the existence of mental processes that are capable of global apprehension and synthesis; these processes occur simultaneously and are affected by the value structure of the social environment. While these views are disparate, they do suggest certain characteristics of the intuitive processes at work in the brain (Garcia 1982).

Many processes in environmental design occur subconsciously based on powerful internal systems of logic that we do not understand. At the same time, we do understand the overall nature of the decision process so that it is not necessary to regard it as a completely unfathomable process. The development of models of the process has been an important step in the development of procedural theory.

MODELS OF ENVIRONMENTAL DESIGN PRAXIS

Most models of the design process are derived from an individual's own experience or are adapted from models of the decision process developed for other fields. A typical model derived from a practicing professional's own experience is that shown in figure 4-1. Developed by Herbert Swinburne (1967), it shows the operation, probably idealized, of his own office in designing a building. Of partic-

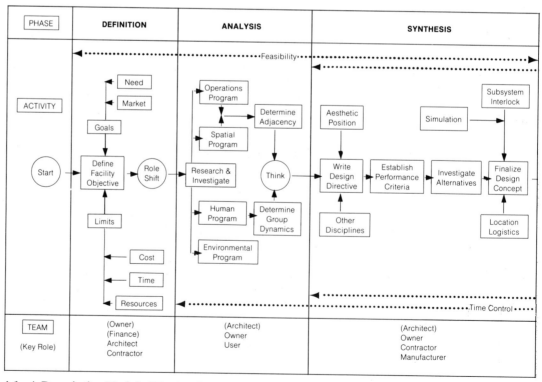

4-1. A Descriptive Model of Design Praxis.

ular interest is the disaggregation of the overall process into a number of phases, each of which has a set of activities and a set of actors associated with it. Even more detailed models are available to designers (Green 1962, Cutler and Cutler 1982), for carrying out portions of a job, such as programming (Sanoff 1977, Preiser 1978, Zeisel 1981). These are important and very useful books. They bring attention to specific functions of designers, but they tell the designer more about what to do than about the fundamental intellectual activities involved in praxis; they are normative in character.

There have been a number of attempts to conduct systematic research to rectify this. One approach has been to get designers to describe aloud what they are doing (Eastman 1970) or to use time-lapse photography to record what they are doing (C. R. Evans et al. 1971). The goal is to record the nature of the process as it occurs. Another approach has been to reconstruct the process after it has been completed (such as Cooper and Hackett 1968, Ruchelman 1977; see also Schon 1984). Based on these studies, on introspective analysis, and on the work of others, some have attempted to describe the broad structure of praxis (for instance, Koberg and Bagnall 1974).

There is a high degree of congruence among the general structures of the various models of the decision process, whether one is dealing with engi-

neering or with one of the fields of environmental design. Swinburne's phases are: definition, analysis, synthesis, development, implementation, operation, and evaluation. Mario Salvadori (1974) has a similar

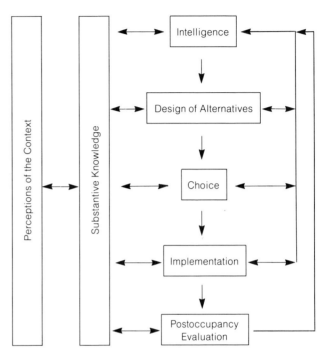

4-2. A General Model of the Phases of Environmental Design Praxis.

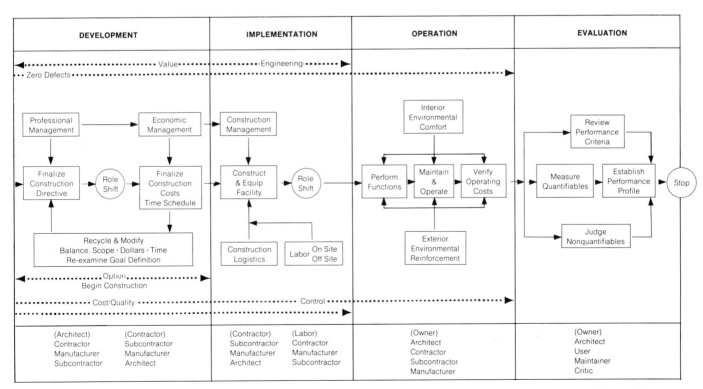

Source: Swinburne (1969)

image of the overall process. He divides architectural praxis into programming, schematic, preliminary design, working document, and construction phases. He describes these as follows:

I) *Programming Phase*—An interactive process aimed at the determination of the "optimal" problem input by resolution of the owner and design team.

II) *Schematic Phase*—A first approximation solution based on the input from Phase I, which ignores "secondary variables" and contains a large amount of undefined data, but is detailed enough to allow a first evaluation of the design "cost." On the basis of the acceptance of Phase II by the owner, certain basic decisions are frozen and will not be challenged in the future, except under extraordinary circumstances.

III) *Preliminary Design Phase*—A second approximation solution in which all the essential variables are considered, many of the undefined data of Phase II are defined, and the conceptual solution to the problem is frozen. At the conclusion of this design phase, i.e. when acceptance is obtained from the owner, the design "cost" is more narrowly established, while some of the program input may have changed, and hopefully frozen.

IV) *Working Document Phase*—A phase in which, through drawings and written specifications, enough detailed information is gathered by the design team to allow the builders to understand what is required of them to execute the design in terms of time, materials, personnel and money.

V) *Construction Phase*—Following acceptance of bids, the contractors produce shop drawings, which represent their interpretations and detailed refinement of the working documents, and the building is erected with minor variations from the design documents of Phase IV under supervision of the design team.

Salvadori notes that in fast-tracked building design the phases of the process are often collapsed. In such a process, parts of the construction phase may be proceeding, while parts of the preliminary design phase may be incomplete. Like Swinburne's model, Salvadori's gives a description of the phases of professional practice but not much feeling for the dynamics of the process or the thought processes or procedural issues involved.

To develop a more generalized understanding of the decision process, environmental designers first turned to the work of cognitive psychologists and operations researchers—people such as John Dewey (1910), Herbert Simon (1960, 1969), and

C. W. Churchman et al. (1967). In these fields the decision process is broken down into a number of phases that go by different names but can be characterized as follows: an *intelligence phase* aimed at understanding what the purpose of the whole activity is; a *design phase* during which possible solutions are generated (or selected from a known set); a *choice phase* during which these solutions are evaluated; an *implementation phase* in which the decision is carried out, and possibly, a *postimplementation evaluation phase* in which results are evaluated leading to an intelligence phase, and so on. This sequence is shown in figure 4-2. This is an idealized model of decision making in the sense that it provides a general framework for considering both positive and normative models of the process.

Environmental design praxis can be considered within this framework. The intelligence phase would involve the development of a program for environmental change; the design phase would involve the development of different sketch plans (for example, potential solutions); the choice phase would involve the prediction of the performance of each possibility and the evaluation that one should be implemented or alternatively that none is good enough. In the latter case, either the statement of the problem would be reconsidered or another design tried. The choice phase is followed by implementation and this is followed, usually implicitly but sometimes explicitly, by further evaluation of the building in use. The whole process is affected by the context in which it occurs and the way in which we look at the world. This, in turn, is very much affected by the substantive theory that we have at our disposal. The substantive theory may be reinforced or changed by the knowledge gained from evaluating the results achieved in practice.

The steps in the model are basically akin to those in the Swinburne model. The important point is, however, that there are some intellectual activities that are carried out repetitively throughout the decision process. Each phase is a decision process itself. Thus the intelligence phase involves the design of a building program. It also, implicitly or explicitly, involves the choice of one potential program over another. It thus involves analytical, synthetic and evaluative efforts. In a similar way the other phases also involve the activities of intelligence, design, and choice. Each phase, nevertheless, has a focus that gives it its basic character.

The nature and interrelationship of the phases of the decision process have been the subject of much debate among design methodologists and professionals. One set of models implies that the process is, or can be, rational and objective, whereas the second group recognizes the argumentative nature of the process. Horst Rittel (1972) calls the first group the "first generation" models and the second the "second generation." Chronologically this distinction is only partially accurate.

MODELS OF ENVIRONMENTAL DESIGN AS A RATIONAL PROCESS

In many early models of environmental design praxis (those developed in the 1960s), the decision process is considered to consist of a discrete set of operations that take place in a unidirectional sequential order. These models owe a considerable intellectual debt to the "rational" models of decision-making in other fields (for instance, Simon 1957, 1960, 1969). They are perceived by some to be based on "the assumption that the ideas and principles of scientific method can be applied to them" (Bazjanac 1974). They are certainly imbued with the idea that more careful analysis of problems, more comprehensive knowledge, and, sometimes, mathematical algorithms lead to better results than are achieved through a purely intuitive approach to

praxis. They also imply a high degree of rationality on the part of the designer. The models tend to be normative ones rather than positive ones, specifying what their designers believe to be better approaches to designing.

One of the most influential models, although now rejected by him, has been that proposed by Christopher Alexander (1964). His model, which is applicable to all the environmental design professions, divides praxis into two major phases: analysis and synthesis. The analytical phase in his approach consists of decomposing a problem into components that are as independent of each other as possible, establishing a hierarchy among them, and then finding patterns of the environment that meet the requirement of each component of the problem. The process of designing is seen as the synthesis of these parts into a whole. Alexander proposed some mathematical routines for the decomposition component of the analysis phase and introduced the concept of "pattern" as a way of linking problem components with solutions. It is the decomposition algorithm based on highly simplistic linkage criteria that Alexander has rejected; the concept of pattern

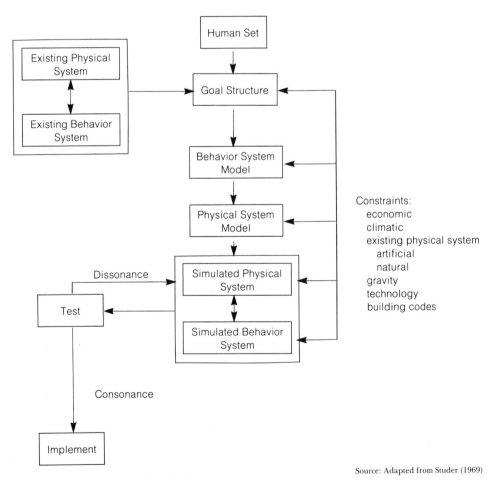

Source: Adapted from Studer (1969)

4-3. A Model of a Behavior-Contingent Design Process.

as a central part of a designer's thought processes has been developed by him and his colleagues in a number of publications (1967, 1969, 1975, 1977, 1979).

Another model, less influential because of its mathematical complexity and concern mainly with product design, is that developed by L. Bruce Archer (1970). He considers the process to consist of three steps: analysis, synthesis, and execution. The first phase is one of observation and inductive reasoning; the second is one of selection and, if absolutely necessary, creative thinking, and the third phase consists of describing, translating, and transmitting the design to those who are going to implement it. Each step in the model consists of a number of serially sequential steps and assumes that each is completed before the next is begun. Feedback processes are not considered explicity.

J. Christopher Jones also suggests a serially sequential model of the decision process in his book *Design Methods* (1970). His model stresses the evaluative activity in the process because he perceives designing as a process in which alternatives are constantly being evaluated and selected. Certainly one of the major activities of the designer is the prediction and evaluation of outcomes of design ideas throughout the design praxis (Wade 1977).

One model that has attracted the attention of many educators and architects because it is perceived as a general "ideal type" model against which any process can be measured is that of Raymond Studer (1970). It also helps clarify the potential contribution of the behaviorial sciences to environmental design theory and practice. The basic steps of the model, shown in simplified form in figure 4-3 are:

1. defining the requisite behavior system;
2. specifying the requisite physical system;
3. realizing the requisite physical system;
4. verifying the resultant environment-behavior system.

In modern architectural terms, the first step is to define the function, the second to design the form, the third to build it, and the fourth to evaluate the function-form relationship.

Studer's model makes explicit many of the things designers claim they are doing intuitively in practice. According to the model, the process of environmental design begins with the recognition that the "existing physical system"—the configuration of the built and natural environments within a geographical setting—is not adequate for the purposes of an individual or group of people. This may occur because a new behavioral system cannot be accom-modated in what exists, or because the existing physical system has deteriorated, or because the standards of acceptability for the function-form relationship have become more stringent. The misfit between the function and form may be on the dimensions of activities, physical comfort, aesthetics, or cost. If the sponsors of the project have the resources to go ahead with it, a new physical system is designed. The whole process, as described by Studer, is implicit in most environmental design practices.

Design usually involves the development first of a simulation of the system to be built. This simulation occurs in the form of drawings and iconic models, that is, models that physically represent the scheme in three dimensions. Perceptions of what this design affords are then checked against the needs of the behavioral system. If the design meets these needs within the resources that are available, the next step is to implement it; if it does not, then either the definition of the behavioral system or the design has to be changed. Many firms go through such a process but not in as systematic a fashion as Studer suggests. For this reason his model is strongly normative in character.

Common Characteristics of Models of Design as a Rational Process

All these early models of environmental design praxis perceive it to consist of analytical, synthetic, and evaluative actions. The models portray the process as a serial sequence of phases. Implicit in this is an assumption that designers have comprehensive knowledge and think rationally. The basic problem with these models is that they avoid dealing with the realities of human capabilities or the realities of the person-environment relationship or such difficult-to-understand variables as the symbolic meaning of the environment. This seems particularly true of those models that suggest mathematical algorithms.

Many of the designers of these "first-generation" models seem to have been more interested in designing internally consistent models rather than in addressing the issue of their external validity. As Herman Neuckermans (1975) has observed, "the attractiveness of the mathematical game tends to obscure the view of the whole," and "a problem is reduced to a caricature whose importance is overestimated under the pretext of rationality and mathematical exactness." In many ways those who assumed a high degree of rationality on the part of designers and clients in the development of their models of the design process fell into the same trap as the masters of the Modern Movement: they had too narrow a definition of function. Too much of their work, though internally consistent, has low external validity; they relied too much on intuitions about what the process could and should be.

The rational models provided a foundation for thinking about the design process. They provided a set of explicit statements about it that are open to challenge. New ideas that add to our understanding of the process have emerged. This is why having explicit positive theory in architecture is important; concepts can be evaluated and improved.

ENVIRONMENTAL DESIGN AS AN ARGUMENTATIVE PROCESS

Most first-generation models of the environmental design process were developed during the late 1960s and early 1970s. Although some of them parallel the development of the rational models of general decision-making in the sixties, the second generation were largely products of the seventies. Like those of the first generation, they are a mixture of positive and normative statements. They owe much to the ferment in city and regional planning and to pleas for greater participation in the decision process of those ultimately affected most by its results (Davidoff 1965). Other spin-offs of this ferment were the "community design" and "participatory design" movements.

Many second-generation models of praxis assumed that the environmental designer is a technician who provides information on which to base decisions. This is a normative statement. Of interest here are, first, the positive assertions about the nature of the process and, second, the criticism of the models that imply a high degree of rationality in conducting the process, made by those who regard design as an argumentative process. The clearest statement on this position is that presented by Horst Rittel (1972) and taken a step further by Vladimir Bazjanac (1974). Bazjanac notes:

> The criticism of the early models of the design process can be summarized in the following way: (a) *design is not a strictly sequential process,* and (b) *design problems are "wicked"* and a linear step-by-step procedure applied to them cannot by itself yield any solutions.

All processes in environmental designing are temporal and sequential but not serially so. In practice, it is often only when one starts to design that the nature of the problems become clear. John Zeisel (1981) notes that there is considerable backtracking in the design process, as the designer comes up against conflicts that cannot be resolved without some redefinition of the problem. He describes designing as a "spiral process" reflecting the following characteristics:

> (1) designers seem to backtrack at certain times—to move away from, rather than toward, the goal of increasing problem resolution; (2) designers repeat a series of activities again and again, resolving new problems with each repetition; and (3) these apparently multidirectional movements together result in one movement directed toward a single action.

Thus, while some basic operations form the core of praxis, the actual sequence and number of times that one goes through it will vary from occasion to occasion (Heath 1984). This is due both to the wickedness of problems and the limits of human rationality.

The concept of "wicked" problems, developed by Horst Rittel, is of fundamental importance for environmental design theory. It has already been introduced in this book but it is important to elaborate on it here. Rittel (1972, Rittel and Webber 1972) contrasts the properties of wicked problems to those of "tame" and "well-mannered" problems. Wicked problems are characterized as follows: they have no definitive formulation (if a problem is definitively stated it is also solved); they have no stopping rule for knowing when to cease asking questions about the nature of problems; they have no definitive set of operations to solve them or to evaluate solutions; experimentation with solutions is impossible except in dealing with repetitive units; each problem is unique. Rittel also adds an ethical statement about the obligations of the designer: "He is fully responsible for his actions"—the designer has no right to be wrong.

Tame problems are those that can be exhaustively formulated, that is, "they can be written down on a piece of paper which can be handed to a knowledgeable man who will eventually solve the problem without needing additional information." Their characteristics are largely opposite to those of wicked problems. This does not mean that tame problems are easy to solve—some mathematical problems and crossword puzzles are extraordinarily difficult—but that there is a recognizable solution. Well-mannered problems fall between the other two. They can be dealt with in a probabilistic, if not a deterministic, manner.

Some problems addressed by interior designers, architects, landscape architects, and urban designers are tame, some are well-mannered, but more of them than we care to admit are wicked. As our substantive and procedural knowledge increases, so the wickedness of problems will be reduced, but not eliminated.

Designers often regard wicked problems as tame ones to achieve a "solution." In thinking about procedural theory, the points to remember are that environmental design problems are poorly structured and that they contain many interacting variables, some of which are difficult to identify and many of which are difficult to measure. Some are overlooked to make the design task manageable.

Recognizing these factors, Rittel suggests that architectural praxis can best be thought of as an argumentative process. He describes the processes of design as follows:

> . . . the designer argues towards a solution with himself and with other parties involved in the project. He builds a case leading to a better understanding of what has been accomplished. In its course, solution principles are developed, evaluated in view of their expected performance and decided upon. The parties commit themselves to specific courses of action and to risks involved in them. In this way better formulations of the problems are being developed simultaneously with a clearer and clearer image of the solution.

There are two major alternating activities in this process: variety generation, the identification or creation of possible problem descriptions or solutions; and variety reduction, the prediction of performance and the evaluation and selection of the most desirable problem description or solution. These activities occur repeatedly. The point is that the process is not a strictly linear one in which a series of steps is executed sequentially. It is a continuous process with much argumentation.

Occasionally environmental designers work through the process by themselves, but usually there is a variety of participants. They all gather information to a greater or lesser extent and prepare arguments, which are the basis of debates that may lead people to change their minds about goals or means. Some arguments are presented more logically, some have a clearer theoretical grounding, some are more forcefully presented than others; some people have more power than others. Expertise and reputation are major bases for the power of environmental designers. A deep understanding of the substantive issues and both substantive and procedural theory gives designers an ability to argue more clearly and logically.

Design as a Learning Process

Another way of looking at environmental design is as a learning process. In this process the designer tentatively formulates a hypothesis about the nature of the problem and then searches for a so-lution. The act of designing raises new problems or a redefinition of the problem. The designer "keeps on learning more about the problem and more about the solution." Bazjanac (1974) describes the process as follows:

> The process is repetitive. The designer keeps redefining and documenting, i.e., putting down on paper new formulations of the problem and the solution until one of the following conditions is met: (a) the incremental gain in knowledge has been insignificant and the understanding of the problem and the solution cannot change enough to warrant further redefinition (i.e., the designer has reached the limits of his understanding); (b) the incremental gain in knowledge has become too costly; and (c) the availability of resources (primarily time) has been exhausted.

One of the important characteristics of environmental designing is that although problems may be wicked, designers do define them. In designing we use all kinds of stopping rules for truncating both analytical and synthetic activities. We run out of time or become bored, or we feel we are getting nowhere. We keep on designing until we have a solution that is good enough in our minds, one that is "satisficing" (Simon 1969).

Design as Hypothesis Formation and Testing

Paralleling the consideration of the design process as a learning process is the perception that environmental designing is a process of hypothesis formation and testing (Colquhoun 1967). The process is perceived to be similar to, if less systematic than, the scientific process in that it also involves conjectures and the evaluation of these (Bartley 1965). It owes much to the philosophical position of Karl Popper (1962) and, according to Colin Rowe (1983), it is similar to the work of detectives in novels. Thus, a building program is regarded as a conjecture about what will solve the problem being addressed; the building design is perceived as a conjecture about what configurations meet the program requirements; the evaluation process is seen as a conjecture about what techniques will predict most accurately how well a building will perform. The tests vary from the subjective evaluation of a drawing on the board to the use of objective measures of the satisfaction that users of the completed building will have with it. The quality of the hypotheses depends on the quality of the substantive knowledge possessed by those making or evaluating the hypotheses and conjectures.

This view of design recognizes that different people have different values and thus different images of the good life and good environments. It also recognizes that different people involved in the process have different types of expertise. This is supported by the research on Frank Lloyd Wright's work in Oak Park (Eaton 1969). His clients provided him with a number of ideas that he incorporated into and made the hallmarks of his work.

Few writers about the process of design have been specific about the role of substantive knowledge in designing. Rittel (1972) argued that there is a symmetry of lack of knowledge between professional and client, although he earlier (1971) argued very strongly for what is essentially a more rigorous positive theoretical basis for design in the terms stressed here.

A MODEL OF THE DESIGN PROCESS

It is clear that the environmental design process can be described in a number of ways and at a number of levels of generalization (see, for instance, Maver 1975). It does consist of a number of basic intellectual activities that are combined in a variety of ways into a number of phases each of which has a distinct character and output. These basic intellectual activities are: analysis, synthesis, prediction, evaluation, and decision. In everyday praxis some of these are carried out very self-consciously, some intuitively, and some by default.

The major phases of the environmental design process can well be considered to be those of any general decision model, since environmental design is one of a family of decision processes. *Intelligence,*

Design, Choice, Implementation, and *Postimplementation Evaluation* are the basic phases of the environmental design process, although people more totally involved in professional praxis may prefer to call them *Programming, Design, Evaluation and Decision, Construction,* and *Postoccupancy evaluation.* There is a general linearity to the process of environmental design, but it must be recognized that each step is not carried out exhaustively and completely before the next is begun and that there is no set of techniques that allows a step to be carried out in a wholly rational and objective way. The process does involve a considerable amount of backtracking when more information is needed or when the designer cannot solve a set of design requirements simultaneously (Zeisel 1981).

The design process *is* an argumentative process involving conjectures and evaluation of these conjectures. Implicit in every design process are conjectures about the functions to be housed, about the requirements of the "physical system" required to meet these needs, about the approaches to design that fulfill these needs, about how these different designs will work, and about the future physical and social environments in which they will have to work. Conjecture involves prediction. Good predictions depend on good theory about the phenomenon that is under concern. Given the purposes of environmental design, this means there must be good theory on the nature of the decision process and good theory on the nature of the person-environment relationship as well as about the nature of technology.

A general model of the main phases of the de-

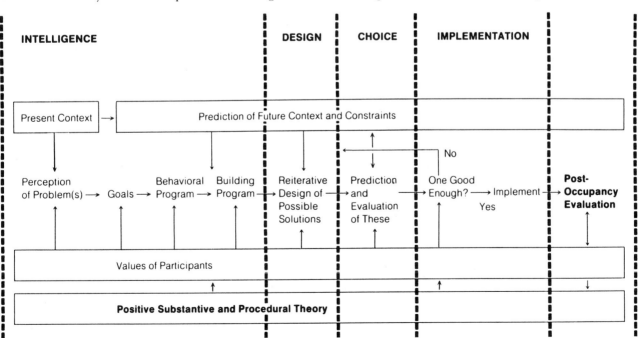

4-4. A General Model of Design Praxis.

sign process is shown in figure 4-4, which builds on that shown in figure 4-2. The diagram shows that perceptions and definitions of a problem occur in a specific physical and social context. Design proposals are created to work in this future environment, and their potential efficacy is predicted and evaluated in terms of images of this future. A decision is then made whether or not to go ahead with the scheme or to return to do more work on defining the problem. If a go-ahead is given, then detailed specifications, in drawings and words, of the potential solution are designed and evaluated. After this the design is implemented. Some sort of postoccupancy evaluation always takes place. Usually this is done in a very casual fashion and problems are rectified. We learn from experience, and our positive theoretical base is enriched by experience. It would be enriched further if systematic postoccupancy evaluations were a routine part of environmental design practice and theory-building.

The three major phases of concern to us here are the intelligence, design, and choice phases. The major intellectual activities that recur throughout the design process are intelligence, design, and choice activities. In other words, each phase consists of the same intellectual activities that characterize all the other phases. Through the provision of basic concepts, the behavioral sciences help us to understand the nature of these activities.

BUT IS ALL THIS THEORY?

It is possible to outline the general activities of environmental design praxis in the form shown in figure 4-4. Such a model provides a basis for asking questions about the nature of environmental design praxis and whether or not it represents what actually occurs. Most decision theorists agree on the basic structure of the model. They agree that it does not consist of a linear sequence of activities because designers do not have comprehensive knowledge about the nature of the built world, nor are they completely rational thinkers. The theorists agree that intuition plays an important part in designing. They agree that the process involves much adjustment of preconceived types to the present situation. Whether this is a desirable process or not is a debated question (see Rowe 1983). Further debate arises when one attempts to model each activity.

Models are abstractions of reality. For a model to be useful, it must correspond closely with the real world, even though it does not fully replicate it. All theories are abstractions of reality; they treat some variables as fundamental to the model, some variables as constants, and other variables as irrelevant,

that is, not important to understanding the system being modeled. The abstractions of the design process that form the basis of current thinking in design methodology pick out the basic structural properties of the process. As such they touch only on what has here been referred to here as procedural theory. Models provide the basis for the development of theory, but theory involves more than model-building. It involves the development of a coordinated set of descriptions and explanations. As such, procedural theory, particularly positive procedural theory, is very limited.

There has been an unwillingness on the part of designers to examine praxis or to have it examined by others. We know that there are major discrepancies between the process as imagined by the people involved in it and as it is viewed by an outside observer. As research progresses, the field of design methodology will be enhanced. Models of the process represent an initial step in the development of procedural theory in environmental design.

ADDITIONAL READINGS

Alexander, Christopher. *Notes on the Synthesis of Form.* Cambridge, Mass.: Harvard University Press, 1964.

Archer, L. Bruce. "An Overview of the Structure of Design." In Gary T. Moore, ed., *Emerging Methods in Environmental Planning and Design.* Cambridge, Mass.: MIT Press, 1970, pp. 285–307.

Bazjanac, Vladimir. "Architectural Design Theory: Models of the Design Process." In William R. Spillers, ed., *Basic Questions in Design Theory.* New York: Elsevier, 1974, pp. 3–17.

Grant, Donald. "Aims and Potentials of Design Methodology." In Basil Honikman, ed., *Responding to Social Change.* Stroudsburg, Pa.: Dowden, Hutchinson and Ross, 1975, pp. 96–108.

Heath, Tom. *Methods in Architecture.* New York: Van Nostrand Reinhold, 1984.

Koberg, Don, and Jim Bagnall. "The Design Process Is a Problem-Solving Journey." In *The Universal Traveler,* Los Altos, Ca.: William Kaufman, 1974, pp. 16–28.

Maver, Thomas W. "Three Design Paradigms; A Tentative Philosophy." *DMG–DRS Journal* 9, no. 2 (April–June 1975): 130–132.

Schon, Don. *The Reflective Practitioner.* New York: Basic Books, 1983.

Simon, Herbert A. *The Sciences of the Artificial.* Cambridge, Mass.: MIT Press.

Studer, Raymond. "The Dynamics of Behavior-Contingent Physical Systems." In Harold Proshansky et al., eds., *Environmental Psychology: Man and his Physical Setting.* New York: Holt, Rinehart and Winston, 1970, pp. 56–75.

Zeisel, John. "Design: Images, Presentations, Tests." In *Inquiry by Design: Tools for Environment–Behavior Research.* Monterey, Ca.: Brooks/Cole, 1981, pp. 3–17.

5

INTELLIGENCE ACTIVITIES AND THE INTELLIGENCE PHASE

The goal of any *intelligence activity* in design praxis is to identify and understand the problems being addressed. The designer engages in basic intelligence actions in response to questions arising throughout the decision process. The intelligence phase however, initiates the overall process. It is concerned with the basic identification of problems, the setting of goals that the design is to achieve, and the constraints under which the future design will have to operate. In professional praxis this phase is often referred to as *facility programming*. The outcome of the intelligence phase, however, is not always a facility program; it may be an educational one, for instance. The procedures for carrying out the programming process have been ably documented (see Peña 1977, Sanoff 1977, Preiser 1978, Palmer 1981, Zeisel 1981). Each documentation has a somewhat different perspective on the process and each, by its very nature, tends to be a normative statement. The objective here is to describe not the specific procedures that environmental designers use but rather the theoretical issues involved.

INTELLIGENCE ACTIVITIES

Intelligence consists of analysis, design, evaluation, and choice. It is, however, fundamentally an analytical activity. Analysis seems to involve the two basic processes of questioning and comparing (Koberg and Bagnall 1974); design involves the processes of divergent and convergent thinking;

evaluation consists of the application of values; and choice, the making of decisions. These processes occur repeatedly throughout design praxis. Behavioral science research also involves all these activities but the goal is different. The purpose of scientific research is to make generalizations about phenomena; the purpose of intelligence activities in designing is to understand more about the specific situation at hand.

Analytical processes, at any phase of design praxis, involve breaking an entity or a problem into components and perceiving order among them. This requires discerning linkages between parts and, possibly, their hierarchical pattern. If the order is difficult to perceive deductively, we often impose an arbitrary order so that we can move on to design. Don Koberg and Jim Bagnall (1974) suggest that the processes of questioning and comparing have a number of purposes:

- to discover interrelationships
- to examine parts in relationships to wholes
- to dissect the problem
- to decompose the problem
- to find out more about the problem
- to get familiar with the problem
- to compare the problem with other situations
- to question or interrogate the problem
- to spread the problem out
- to sequence or order the problem
- to classify the elements of a problem

- to take the problem apart
- to search for insights within the problem
- to attempt to find the recipe of the problem
- to determine what makes the problem what it is.

There are many techniques for analyzing situations. These techniques are used throughout design praxis because each phase involves some analytical activities.

Designing involves generating ideas and putting components of these together to form a whole. It thus involves both divergent and convergent, or synthetic, thinking. Both of these involve much analytical thinking, whether one is designing a building program or a building, because each is itself a decision process. Similarly, *evaluating* ideas, whether subjectively or objectively, involves processes of questioning and comparing. Thus the *choice* phase of praxis also involves intelligence activities. The intelligence phase, in turn, consists of intelligence, design, and choice activities. The focus of concern in the intelligence phase is, however, on establishing what the problem is that the designer *as* designer is required to solve.

THE INTELLIGENCE PHASE

As mentioned above, there are a number of normative statements on programming for environmental design, excellent descriptions of the behavioral sciences methods available to the environmental designer for many aspects of praxis (Michelson 1975, Zeisel 1981), and essays on specific approaches to design research. There is, however, a paucity of research on how designers actually analyze problems in practice—on how the intelligence phase is actually carried out.

We know that it is a well-established procedure to use "building types"—a classification of buildings in accordance with the activities they house and sometimes with their aesthetic characteristics—both to truncate the search procedure for identifying the nature of the problem and to generate a solution to it. Certainly, the definition of the problems to be addressed during the intelligence phase is very much affected by the preconceptions and images in the programmer's mind. Much recent thinking about normative models of the design process suggests that designers should approach the problem without preconceptions, but this appears to be intellectually impossible (Nangara forthcoming).

We also know that the intelligence phase is highly political in an informal way. This is borne out by the findings of systematic research on environmental design praxis as exemplified by the study of the St. Francis Square project in San Francisco by Clare Cooper and Phylis Hackett (1968) and the study of the development of the World Trade Center in New York City by Leonard Ruchelman (1977). These studies give a good description of how decisions are made in practice and, in general, of the highly argumentative and political nature of the intelligence activities that result in building programs and designs. They are political because there are many different participants in the process, each with a set of values that may overlap those of others but may also contain idiosyncratic views. These views are based on the individual's past experience and expertise and on the way he or she appraises the other participants in the process and the consequences that different statements of the problem may have for him or her. The studies reveal that many decisions are made capriciously and that the final product is shaped by many people even though the building or other design that results unmistakably has an appearance that is characteristic of the style of its designer(s).

Any model of the intelligence phase of design praxis is a speculative one. It is, nevertheless, possible to offer a synthesis of present ideas about its constituent elements and how they relate. This model is based on the empirical studies that do exist (such as Cooper and Hackett 1968, Ruchelman 1977, Moleski 1978) and on a variety of existing models that have both a positive and a normative character (Swinburne 1967, Studer 1969, Nadler 1970, Koberg and Bagnall 1974, Hack 1979). These models are based largely on their designer's own introspective analysis.

Implicit, at least, in any intelligence phase are a number of activities. These are aimed at understanding the issues at hand and at developing a partial solution to them. A conceptual model of the phase is presented in figure 5-1. The phase's aims are to: establish goals based on perceptions of what the problem is; specify/design a behaviorial system and identify aesthetic values that will meet the established goals; and identify the characteristics of the physical systems that will enable the social and aesthetic ends to be met. If the present physical system does afford these ends, then the problem is not an architectural, urban, or landscape architectural one but rather an educational one that involves bringing people's attention to how the environment might be used. If it does not, then a decision has to be made as to whether the behavioral and aesthetic system or the physical system has to be changed. If the last-mentioned action is chosen, then a program specifying the changes to be made has to be designed. This again involves setting goals and establishing means. All these activities concern not only the present but also the future. Thus, the intelligence phase involves making many predictions about the future context in which the future design has to work. Every time a design or specification is made it represents a hypothesis about what will work and, presumably, what will work well in the future.

These operations do not take place in a neat sequential order. The results of each step may be changed by new information and/or perceptions of the problem as late as the implementation phase. Problems that arise during the design and evaluation phases frequently necessitate some reprogramming. The whole intelligence process is an argumentative one, but it does implicitly or explicitly follow the general sequence of events described in figure 5-1. As Horst Rittel (1972) has noted, wicked problems have no clear definition, but a preliminary definition of the problem is made to initiate the design phase. To do this a sequence of activities is completed even though these may not be carried out in a linear order or each be totally finished before the next activity is begun. A brief description of the most important of these will clarify the potential contribution of the behavioral sciences to the creation of procedural theory.

Identification of the Problem Situation

The intelligence phase of praxis can be said to begin with somebody perceiving a discrepancy between the present state of the social and/or physical environment and some desired state either known or presumed to exist. The environment is constantly being monitored by individuals or groups of people. Some, such as public agencies, have been given that role in society; others, such as businessmen, are looking for opportunities to invest profitably; still others, such as professional societies, have a quasi-public role in that they monitor the environment, pointing out what they perceive to be problems in terms of their areas of professional expertise. A social-work group may be concerned with the delivery of public services, architects with the nature of the aesthetic environment, historic preservation groups with the preservation of a people's cultural heritage as they perceive it. Thus, many different people can initiate a decision process that results in a building or some other change in the social or physical environment.

Environmental designers are hired to work on many specific types of environmental problems, but they are seldom presented with a general problem-solving task. The people who hire them have been through a decision process already and have already defined the general nature of the problem and the general nature of the solution. They have reached the conclusion that a change in the built environment is necessary to house new activity patterns, or to house existing ones better, or for aesthetic reasons. They have either done this on their own or with the aid of professional consultants. Seymour Sarason (1972) notes that buildings can be "distractions" in thinking about how social services can best be delivered. Many people, he colorfully notes, have

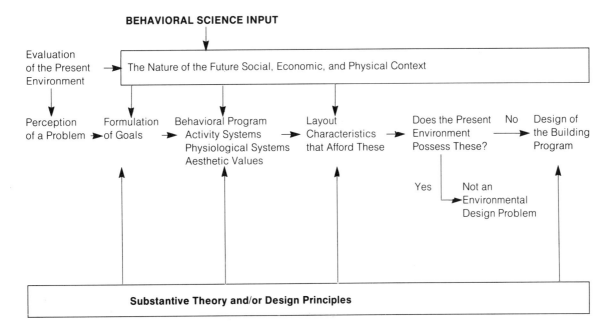

5-1. A Model of the Intelligence Phase of Design Praxis.

an "edifice complex"—they see a building as a solution to all problems (especially if it is to be named after them). By no means is the belief in architectural determinism restricted to architects.

The perception of a problem situation thus involves: a present socio-physical environment operating at a particular level; the recognition and evaluation of its performance in some dimensions important to an individual or a group; and the perception that this performance deviates too much from what is regarded as acceptable and that this discrepancy will persist into the future unless some action is taken. The process is thus a highly value-laden one in which problems are perceived by people with reference to their own values and/or those of others.

Identification of the Groups of People Involved

A number of groups, or stakeholders, are likely to be involved in any process that leads to a decision to change the layout of the environment. As the scale of a proposed project gets larger and the multiplicity of intended activities increases, so the number of people with conflicting objectives and different values is likely to increase. These groups almost always include the following:

- the client and/or sponsor of the project
- design and allied professionals
- regulatory bodies
- contractors.

Each of these groups is subject also to peer-group pressures, so the peer groups of each may themselves be regarded as indirect or hidden participants (see Montgomery 1966 on architects).

During the past two decades the degree to which two other groups should be involved has been the subject of much debate. They are:

- users
- nonusers affected by the proposed scheme.

Often the sponsor acts as a filter for the users' needs and nonusers are seen as competing people. There have been expressions of concern about the lack of consideration of the users of buildings (as in Zeisel 1974), and at least a subset of designers is taking a clear user-needs approach to design. Many other designers regard this as a passing fad, however.

Some of the participants will have more power than others because of their centrality to the problem. There are many normative positions on who should be of central concern in thinking about the

goals and means of design and, in particular, on what the client-professional relationship should be (for example, Goodman 1971, Rittel 1972, H. Mitchell 1974). The participants and the relative importance of each are likely to shift as the process gets under way. Those that originally perceived the problem may give way to others more directly involved; designers are central during the design phase and contractors during implementation. In projects that take a long time to bring to fruition, the sponsor may change between project initiation and the choice phase. This often goes hand in hand with a change in decision criteria and may result in the abandonment of the project or in major revisions to it.

Identification of Constraints

Although no design task operates in a totally constraint-free environment, the level of constraint varies from project to project. The constraints also vary considerably in nature. Laws such as building codes represent the public interest; financial and time constraints usually are imposed by the sponsor; soil conditions are constraints imposed by the environment. Constraints behave like goals: they are needs that have to be met. Goals, however, are ends that one is trying to minimize or maximize.

There is some controversy over exactly where in the intelligence phase constraints should be introduced into the thinking of those involved. The argument for early introduction is that it eliminates effort wasted on trying to attain the impossible. The argument against early introduction is that it prematurely eliminates possibilities that appear to be impossible but are not necessarily so (see Nadler 1970).

The Formulation of Goals

Goals are general statements of intent—they are ends toward which a design tends. Goals are designed. Often they are stated so generally that everybody agrees on them. Translating these into specific *objectives* is likely to involve much argument. Even when the goals of a project remain constant, the objectives are likely to change as the process develops (see Ruchelman 1977).

Implicit in the identification of the problem situation is a basic goal: to change the present situation. Also implicit is some preconception of what the solution is. Certainly there are strong advocates for regarding the whole design process as one of typological adaptations (for example, Eisenman 1982).

The specification of what one is trying to achieve is seldom arrived at in a methodical way.

The different participants in the process are likely to have differing goals or differing values associated with the same goals. Environmental designers, if they are involved at this stage of the decision process, like to believe that they are doing the best job for all concerned but inevitably they become advocates for specific parties or interests.

There is no set algorithm that all designers use for establishing goals. There are, nevertheless, a few steps that usually are used. The first is the establishment of the "perimeters of concern"—in what areas are goals to be established? The second is to answer the question: "What is the range of goals within these areas?" The third involves an examination of the goals to see whether or not they are compatible and mutually supportive. The fourth involves the ranking of goals, and the fifth, the acceptance of them as the basis for moving ahead (see Young 1966, Chadwick 1978). The process is usually an iterative one.

These steps involve a number of processes. Present states of the environment are evaluated, future states are predicted, goals are designed or chosen, goals are evaluated, and a decision is made. The process is an argumentative one, but because of the level of generalization involved, closure on a policy statement is achieved relatively easily. It is in designing to meet the behavioral and physical environmental needs that controversies arise.

Designing the Behavioral Program

The process of environmental adaptation involves changing physical settings in response to changes in activities or aesthetic tastes or changes in demand for congruence between these and the physical setting. Thus, the goals of environmental design depend on the specification of the patterns of behavior needed in order for the people concerned to attain their goals. Who does this design? It is likely to be specialists in the field of concern, such as time and motion researchers and, increasingly, facility programmers—people who understand both the nature of activity systems and the nature of how the built world affects these.

Much of this process is done in a highly subjective manner; much of it is done unconsciously when decisions are made about rooms and spaces. As Constance Perin (1970) has noted, room names become surrogates for a statement of activities that are expected to take place. Increasingly, architects and facilities programmers are using techniques developed in the behavioral sciences to add a level of objectivity to the process.

The explicit consideration of aesthetic and comfort issues traditionally has been deferred to the design phase, since these issues have been considered to fall strictly within the realm of the designer's prerogatives. The explicit consideration of these issues is only likely to occur when they are the central ones. Until an explicit and externally valid positive theory of aesthetics and methods of analyzing aesthetic values for design purposes are created, this situation will prevail. While the positive understanding of aesthetics has been considerably enhanced during recent years, it is still insufficiently developed to act as the theoretical basis for the design of analytical or design methods.

Designing the Physical Layout Requirements

One of the major objectives of the intelligence phase is to specify the patterns of the environment required to meet activity needs as well as physiological and aesthetic needs. This step cannot be carried out deterministically. The programmer draws on his or her substantive knowledge and knowledge of how existing patterns work elsewhere—in other buildings, in urban or landscape designs—in order to make what is essentially a hypothesis about the patterns that will achieve specific ends in the current situation. It involves making a set of predictions about what will work and what will not work. Typological studies are often used as the basis for this.

One of the major reasons for the development of a body of positive knowledge about the built environment and what it affords people is to increase the probability that programmers will make good predictions. It is in this activity, probably more than any other, that architects of the Modern Movement made their major mistakes. They made erroneous predictions about future behavior patterns and the ability of the built environment to cause specific behaviors. They based their decisions, it was noted earlier, on inadequate models of people and human behavior.

Usually this step is carried out only partially before the next step is begun. Then this step is completed with the presentation of a detailed specification for environmental change. Thus, the design of building programs and investigation to see whether the present environment meets requirements are often wrapped up together in what appears to be a single activity consisting of iterative steps.

Evaluating the Present Environment

This is a conceptually important step that is usually implicit in professional practice. Sometimes it is obviously unnecessary to carry it out explicitly, but at other times it is important to do so if resources are not to be wasted. It is unnecessary when a completely new set of activities requires shelter in a place where there is none. In dealing with existing facilities, the sponsors of a project often find that, as a result of carrying out this step, they are able to use their existing facilities or are able to change the way in which activities are carried out so that the existing facilities still meet their needs.

If the built environment consists of the patterns required to house the behavioral program, then an environmental design problem does not exist. There may, however, be an educational problem that involves the designer. It is not always obvious to people how a space might be used. If the present environment does not have the characteristics that will afford the behavioral program and/or aesthetic tastes of those concerned, then a decision has to be made either (1) to change the behavioral program and/or the aesthetic value system so that the present layout affords them, or (2) to specify how the environment should be changed. This specification is the building program.

Designing Building Programs

A building program is a partial solution to the problem. The built environment that results from it is the "solution," for good or bad. The quality of the final outcome is very much dependent on the quality of the building program, but it is not determined by it except in a negative sense: if the program is poor, the building cannot meet the requirements of the situation at hand except by coincidence.

Building programs vary considerably in scope and nature. Traditionally they have consisted of little more than a listing of the rooms a building has to contain and their sizes. Such programs are incomplete statements of intent and require continued analysis to specify intentions on other dimensions of the environment. In professional praxis, building programs have become more and more complex in recent years.

Building programs now often specify performance requirements rather than the square footage of spaces. They often specify the furniture that has to be housed and other requirements, such as those for privacy, territorial control, and aesthetics associated with the activity to occur in that space. They include statements on the flow of goods, information, and people through the system. They may specify the linkages required between indoors and outdoors, the symbolism required of entrances, and the external appearance of buildings.

Such building programs are much more detailed and comprehensive in specifying the ends of design than were those of the past. It is still up to the designer to attempt to resolve conflicts between requirements and to synthesize a design solution. Comprehensive building programs may be a prerequisite for good design. They cannot ensure it.

DEALING WITH UNCERTAINTY IN PROGRAM DESIGN

The intelligence phase is obviously a complex one during which decisions are made under considerable uncertainty about their outcomes. In environmental design praxis, uncertainty is dealt with in a number of ways. The way designers deal with complex problems is to simplify the definition of the problem by eliminating difficult-to-consider variables. The solution is then only a partial answer to a partially identified problem. Provided that the most important aspects of the problem are addressed, this still leads to an adequate solution. People tolerate some discrepancy between the ideal and what they get, based on what they are used to, their personalities, and the costs involved. There are limits to this tolerance, however.

Simplifying the problem by limiting one's scope of concern can be accomplished in a number of ways. Most developers aim for a certain segment of the market when they decide to build, a segment with which they are familiar. Architects may specialize in specific types of buildings or use the same types of materials throughout their work; they may concentrate on meeting the needs of one group of the client population. Each of these approaches reduces the complexity of the definition of the problem being addressed.

Many designers narrow the limits of their professional concern by not getting involved in programming. Their work begins with the program. Praxis, in this case, focuses on generating solutions and on evaluating and implementing phases of professional activity. Other architects are strong advocates of full participation of designers in programming activities (see Griffen 1972). They recognize that this is where the major decisions that truncate the design phase are made.

The enhancement of both substantive and procedural theory in environmental design, particularly during the last decade, has resulted in the development of a set of techniques and a body of knowledge that are becoming part of accepted environmental design practice. In areas where substantive theory is weak, techniques of analysis are weak and designers have to rely (as many prefer to do) on intuition and subjective knowledge. This creates uncertainty. One of the characteristics of creative people is that they are willing to deal with uncertainty, respecting it but not being hamstrung by it.

Uncertainty about the best course of action to take stems not only from a diversity of values but also from the simple fact that buildings have to operate in the future. What are the social and economic forces at some given time in the future? How will these shift? Will people favor simplicity or complexity of forms? Is it worthwhile making systematic predictions about the future? There are techniques for doing this that rely heavily on observation of past trends and on knowledge of the forces that effect change (Bross 1953). The application of these techniques may enhance the probability of accuracy in making predictions, but they will not specify futures with certainty. Having to deal almost constantly with uncertainty may also lead to the arrogance that outsiders often note in architects (T. Wolfe 1981).

OBTAINING INFORMATION FOR ARCHITECTURAL PROGRAMMING

The behavioral sciences, it has already been noted, offer a number of basic techniques for observing present situations, obtaining information, and ascertaining design goals. Many of these are becoming incorporated in environmental design praxis and are shaping designers' views of the nature of the problem. Some of these techniques simply systematize the ways in which designers have always worked; others are new. Some of the techniques are for obtaining information at first hand, others are for obtaining it through some mediational approach—one that involves getting information via another person who is the observer. These approaches can be obtrusive or unobtrusive. They are guided by what one wants to find out and thus by substantive theories of people and environment. These techniques were touched on earlier. The concern here is with how they are and might be used during the intelligence phase of design praxis.

Obtrusive Techniques

Obtrusive techniques are those techniques made known to the person or group being studied. Experimentation is the classic example of an obtrusive observational approach, and interviews and surveys are examples of mediational approaches to information-gathering that are obtrusive. In both approaches, the subjects may not know exactly what is being investigated but they know they are being studied.

Obtrusive observational techniques are more useful in conducting basic theory-building research and testing products than in establishing the issues that have to be addressed in environmental design practice. Interviews and surveys, on the other hand, are widely used in professional work.

In working with either sponsors or users of projects, designers have tended to use the personal interview to obtain information about clients' needs over more structured approaches. Recently environmental designers and facility programmers have used more systematic approaches to sampling and carrying out interviews and surveys of the population of concern to them. When potential users of a potential design are not available (as in the design of a completely new facility or residential development), designers choose a surrogate population (one with characteristics similar to those of the potential users or residents). These techniques are vital in helping designers understand their clients' hopes and aspirations for the future. They are also useful in gathering data about activity systems. It is easier and quicker to obtain information in this way than to carry out systematic observations. Interview and survey techniques, however, also have some basic problems, as environmental designers who rely completely on them have found. These problems place limits on the expected validity of the results obtained and must be recognized by those who use them (Goodrich 1974, Marans 1975).

It is easy to make erroneous assumptions about interview and survey results. Respondents do not always find it possible to verbalize their feelings; often they have limited experience in dealing with the issues at hand and may be unaware of the possibilities available to them or even of the present state of their environments in relation to their activities or tastes. Answers to questions are likely to overemphasize the self and favor the familiar. A number of new techniques have been devised to overcome these limitations. While some of these have been used in professional practice, they have not become part and parcel of many designers' research processes.

Some of these techniques involve sketching to obtain nonverbal responses (as in Van der Ryn and Silverstein 1967); others involve time budgets in which respondents are asked to keep a record of what their activities are and where they engage in them (Michelson and Reed 1975) or to chart them on aerial photographs (Michelson 1970). Another paper-and-pencil technique that has been used to uncover essential information for design purposes is a semiprojective game in which the respondents are asked to make decisions about the options open to them (Sanoff 1968). Despite all these innovations, traditional survey techniques continue to be used widely because they are relatively easy to administer. Designers are recognizing the limitations of these techniques and are supplementing them with other approaches.

The quality of the substantive theory that designers use as the basis for asking questions very much affects the quality of information obtained. This is why even the most sophisticated techniques for obtaining information will not in themselves yield information that will lead to successful design outcomes, whatever measure of success is used. The ability to design good questions depends on having good substantive knowledge.

Unobtrusive Measures

Unobtrusive techniques are those in which the subject is unaware of being studied. They are used to provide the environmental designer with considerable basic information about how the present environment is being used, about the tendencies for people to behave in specific ways, and about the misfits between behavior patterns and the physical environment that exists in a present built environment. The techniques are used when an existing organization is being redesigned and for studying other organizations of a similar type when a new one is being considered (as when designing a new residential area while looking at other residential areas). There is a variety of observational techniques that are unobtrusive in nature and a variety of mediational techniques, such as literature searches and building-type studies, that are used by designers to ascertain the nature of the problems they are addressing without requiring direct, known contact with the sponsors or users of the product to be designed. This raises both methodological and ethical issues. The methodological issues have to do with the ability of a person to be unobtrusive in observational studies and with the validity of data obtained using mediational techniques; the ethical issues have to do with the right of designers to invade the privacy of others. An examination of the procedures themselves clarifies these issues.

Unobtrusive observational techniques include natural experiments, simple observation, participant observation, and the observation of physical traces (Patterson 1974). Natural experiments are those in which the observer may manipulate some elements of the environment (for example, erecting barriers to observe queuing behavior), but the subjects are simply those people who happen by. Simple observation involves the systematic and rigorous recording of behavior without any attempt by the observer to manipulate the environment or select

the subjects. Simple observation is thus not synonymous with easy observation. Participant observation involves the observer becoming part of the system under study (as in Gans 1967). The observation of physical traces involves recording those parts of the environment that have been eroded through use or have been added to in order to better fulfill their users' needs. Some designers find out what is important to people by observing where paths have been worn on floors and lawns or what elements have been added to buildings (Cooper 1975).

A number of specific simple observational techniques that were developed for behavioral science research are being used with increasing frequency in environmental design programming, particularly in the study of the public environments of neighborhoods and urban spaces. These include the behavior-setting survey (Barker 1968, LeCompte 1974, Bechtel 1977, Wicker 1979) and behavioral mapping (Ittelson, Rivlin, and Proshansky 1970). The former involves recording all of the patterns of behavior that exist in a place or organization; the latter involves recording on a map or a grid (if one is dealing with a room) the places where activities actually occur. New technologies have increased the potential of observational techniques. Some researchers have used films (Carr and Schissler 1969), while others have used photography (Davis and Ayers 1975) and television (Helmreich 1974, Scheflen 1976) to record events as diverse as the use of apartment layouts by different ethnic groups, the use of escalators, and life in an undersea habitat.

It is very difficult, in many situations being studied for programming purposes, to be an unobtrusive observer. It is difficult to be unobtrusive in observing how an office or a home is used, although techniques of remote observation through television come close to it; usually people know that an observer is there. In participant observation, the person joining the ongoing behavior of an organization or residential environment may well affect the system. Architect Richard Neutra (1954) claimed that he used this technique in coming to an understanding of the families for whom he was designing new residences, but his presence can hardly have been unobtrusive. One can be unobtrusive in observing physical traces, but here the problem is that it is easy to draw erroneous conclusions about what causes the traces.

Conclusions about Information-gathering Techniques

It is clear that the information-gathering techniques associated with analytical activities all have strengths and weaknesses. There is no single foolproof method for ensuring that the information one is getting is totally reliable and valid. Gaining a good understanding of people's involvement with the environment, their feelings about the present state of the environment, and their desires for the future requires the use of a variety of information-gathering techniques. In practice, the use of the most appropriate technique for a particular task is often bypassed in favor of a technique that is easier, cheaper, and quicker to use. Whatever combination of techniques one uses, if it entails looking at the problem situation itself, it draws on a *malfunctioning* environment to which people have adapted. This is particularly true when looking at an existing organization in its existing physical setting. While designers are usually looking for misfits between behavior and environment as the basis for programming, they are also looking for good fits. These are often less easy to discern.

There also are ethical issues. In designing for a specific organization one is invited in to do studies that will be directly beneficial to the organization. Even so, it might be necessary to disguise what one is doing in order to get information that will be beneficial to the members. This is generally regarded as acceptable. While it has been regarded as acceptable to mount television cameras to observe behavior unobtrusively so long as people know they are being observed, there are still questions about the legitimacy of doing so.

ANALYZING INFORMATION

There has been a tendency among architects, landscape architects, and urban designers toward data collection for its own sake. The analytical process then becomes stylized. The designer believes that certain types of data have to be displayed even if they have no impact on the basic thought processes of design. It has been noted that noncreative work drives out creative efforts (Simon 1960). How designers deal with information and generate ideas is thus an important part of the intelligence effort throughout all the phases of environmental design praxis.

Recording data is often confused with interpreting them. One basic way in which designers analyze information is by comparing one situation with another. The use of statistics is helpful in this regard (see Ferguson 1966, Broadbent 1973), but is seldom used by designers. The data of concern in programming and design are often not amenable to statistical analysis, although something like the use of descriptive and inferential statistics may be going on in the designer's head.

Some designers have found the behavioral science techniques of *sociometric analysis* and *content analysis* useful as analytical tools. Sociometric analysis (Lindzey and Borgetta 1959) is concerned with the spatial distribution of social behavior. This type of analysis is helpful in understanding social organizations, both formal and communal, and how they use the built environment. It is used to identify the physical location of individuals in a group, as well as to test an individual's social position (and the symbolic aesthetic values associated with it) and environmental-use patterns. Content analysis (Fellman and Brandt 1970, Krippendorf 1980) is used in the study of people's attitudes by analyzing what they say about the subject under investigation.

A number of techniques are used by designers to aid the perception of relationships between variables. *Matrix techniques* (see, for example, Sanoff 1968) enable the relationship between components of a problem to be displayed. *Morphological analysis* (Zwicky 1948) is used for essentially the same purpose. It is a technique designers use to force themselves to think about possible relationships between variables by listing the attributes of problems, categorizing them, and determining all the possible combinations that can be derived from linking the attributes. This is only possible for problems having a few key dimensions, however, because the combinations of elements multiply greatly as the variables increase in number. *Synectics*, like morphological analysis, is generally regarded as a method of generating design, but it is also used to analyze the relationships among phenomena. It is one of a class of brainstorming procedures that are widely used by environmental designers, even if in a less systematic way than their advocates recommend. Synectics, like brainstorming procedures as a whole (see Osborne 1957), helps designers probe their subconscious. Synectics makes particular use of analogies, metaphors, and similes to liberate the mind from traditional ways of thinking (Broadbent 1973, Koberg and Bagnall 1974).

The way in which environmental designers have incorporated these and other techniques into their everyday practices has not been systematically examined. There is considerable anecdotal evidence that they used them in a very piecemeal manner, some quite frequently, others less often. What is new is the growing use of more systematic techniques as the problems grow more complex. As this complexity is often accompanied by a major social and administrative gap between architects and clients, designers find systematic approaches helpful not only for their own analytical efforts but also in displaying information to others. While these approaches may aid environmental design praxis, they do not eliminate the difficulties inherent in analytical tasks.

The analytical process is a central one in environmental design. The process of decomposing problems into their components is fundamental to programming and has been described by many architects (such as Le Corbusier 1923). The way this is done very much shapes the product that results. It is not the purpose of the designer simply to accumulate a large body of unrelated facts during the intelligence phase, although the presentation of these can overwhelm a client. Discrete pieces of information are not particularly useful to the designer; they have to be organized into a pattern. The behavioral sciences have provided a number of techniques for enhancing designers' abilities in doing this. Techniques themselves, however good they may be, will not ensure that information is effectively organized in terms of the goals of design. Designers need to be able to ask appropriate questions. A sound body of substantive theory is a precondition for this.

CONCLUSION

Building programs are designed. The whole intelligence phase involves a series of value-laden decisions. It is based on asking questions about the present and the future. The more one understands about the existing situation and about the nature of the environment, about people and about the techniques available for soliciting information and comparing one situation with another, the greater the confidence the designer can have in responding well to the needs of those involved. Good substantive theory is essential to know what to look at and what questions to ask. If, however, the designer takes the normative position that being responsive to the needs of those involved in the overall designing process is irrelevant, then much of the discussion in this chapter is irrelevant.

ADDITIONAL READINGS

Churchman, C. West, Russell L. Ackoff, E. Arnoff, and E. Leonard. "Formulation of the Problem." In *Introduction to Operations Research*. New York: John Wiley, 1967, pp. 105–135.

Koberg, Don, and Jim Bagnall. "Introduction to Analysis." In *The Universal Traveler*. Los Altos, Ca.: William Kaufman, 1974, pp. 46–65.

Palmer, Mickey A. *The Architect's Guide to Facility Planning*. Washington, D.C.: AIA and Architectural Record Books, 1981.

Peña, William. *Problem Seeking*. Chicago: Cahners Books, 1977.

Preiser, Wolfgang, ed. *Facility Programming: Methods and Applications*. Stroudsburg, Pa.: Dowden, Hutchinson and Ross, 1978.

Sanoff, Henry. *Methods of Architectural Programming*. Stroudsburg, Pa.: Dowden, Hutchinson and Ross, 1977.

Zeisel, John. "Research and Design Cooperation." In *Inquiry by Design: Tools for Environment-Behavior Research*. Monterey, Ca.: Brooks/Cole, 1981, pp. 32–50.

6

DESIGNING AND THE DESIGN PHASE

Design has been defined as the effort to generate solutions to problems prior to attempting to implement them (see Simon 1957, Broadbent 1973). It is often regarded purely as a process involving synthesis, but it also requires analysis, evaluation, and the making of choices. The design phase in any architectural, landscape architectural, or urban design praxis is the one in which potential design solutions to the program, designed during the intelligence phase, are created (or selected from a set of potential solutions). The act of designing may reveal new problems and result in a redefinition of the original program, but the focus of concern during the design phase is on the definition of buildings, landscapes, and/or urban designs—the creation of the artifact.

DESIGN

Analysis, it has been noted, involves questioning and comparing. Four basic processes are generally recognized as the basis for creative work in design: *preparation, incubation, illumination,* and *verification* (Dickerson and Robertshaw 1975). Preparation refers to intelligence activities, incubation to the largely unknown intellectual processes that involve the digestion of perceptions of the problems and the development of scenarios for searching for a

solution. Illumination refers to the apparent insights the designer has into the nature of the problem and its potential solutions. Verification is the process by which the designer concludes that a viable potential solution has been found. The whole process is said to involve considerable perspiration. Ultimately, however, the quality of the final product depends on the quality of the substantive knowledge at the designer's disposal and his or her ability to use it creatively. The key to creative thinking is the ability to generate ideas.

There is much about the act of design that we do not understand—much of it remains a mystery —but the behavioral science research of the past fifty years provides many insights to the process. Design seems to involve two basic thought processes: *divergent production* and *convergent production* (Moore and Gay 1967). Divergent production consists of the development of many ideas from a single observation or statement; it is concerned with the generation of a variety of ideas or potential solutions or parts thereof. In contrast, convergent production is the act of synthesis. It involves producing a single idea out of many parts.

Design involves many simultaneous processes that use different schemata embedded in each other (Neisser 1977). It is a process of conceptualization and self-argumentation (Rittel 1972) in which the elements of a problem are related to specific patterns, that are then transformed to get an overall design. This process of synthesis is not merely a matter of combining patterns, because the patterns undergo transformation when thought about convergently.

Not all designing involves creative thinking. The pragmatic, iconic, and canonical approaches to design identified by Broadbent (1973) reduce the process to one that is carried out by habit. In contrast, analogic design and designing using deductive logic involve creative thinking. There are many times when it is quite appropriate to follow habitual processes. Although John Stuart Mill may have been correct in saying that "the despotism of custom is a hinderance to advancement," the abandonment of custom will not automatically lead to advancement. The striving for novelty in architectural design, for instance, often does not appear to have been an objective worth striving for as an end in itself.

A number of cognitive abilities seem basic to successful designing, that is, to devising a solution to the problem at hand. According to Moore and Gay (1967) the abilities, within Western cultures, at least, are:

- to reformulate and properly define the problem in the broadest, least biasing way
- to generate many novel ideas
- to tolerate ambiguity, the lack of sharp boundaries
- to develop overall and strategic attacks on problems
- to look at phenomena in new ways
- to avoid premature criticism
- to avoid premature commitments
- to avoid the fear of making mistakes
- to break free of past ways of doing things
- to judge the appropriateness of ideas

To these may be added the ability to move from generalizations to specifics, from theories to patterns.

It is clear from this list that design involves many evaluative and predictive skills. Every time a designer draws a line on a drawing board, a choice is made from a number of possible lines. Thus the act of designing is a sequential holistic one of creating (or selecting) the problems to be solved, the objectives to be met, the patterns of built form required to meet these objectives, the prediction of how well these selections will work, the evaluation of these predictions, and the decision to take a stand on them. This process is done largely in a subconsciously argumentative way.

THE DESIGN PHASE

Consciously or unconsciously, a designer makes a decision on where to begin the design effort. It might be supposed that the designer starts with the most important problems to be addressed, but this does not seem to be the case. There are various ways of working through the problem. Some designers start with the easiest components of a problem, the ones they feel most certain about; others start with the broadest level, yet others with the details. Often the ones chosen are those that lead to a demonstration of great progress toward a solution. Some architects have been identified as people who work from the inside out (Le Corbusier, for example), while others have been identified as working from the outside in (Mies van der Rohe, for example). Whichever way a designer works, sooner or later he or she has to make a commitment to a design or set of designs. Some designers believe only one potential solution should be produced at a time and defended until it is found to be unacceptable. Others argue that a number of designs should be taken to their logical conclusions and then evaluated. This latter position tends to be supported by research on creative problem-solving (such as Maltzman 1960). Even if this is the case, it may be desirable to present just one design for review in order to maximize the information received from the review.

Many designers seem to have been educated to grasp the first solution they are able to devise and to defend it against all arguments, but a hallmark of creative designers is the capacity to generate many potential solutions. At each step in the process of design they are thinking divergently. A major difficulty in generating potential solutions is to avoid the premature rejection of a pattern that is less desirable in solving part of the problem but that may result in a potentially worthwhile solution to the whole problem if the line of thinking behind it is pursued (B. Jones 1962). To overcome this situation, some designers start the design phase by making only those decisions that impose the most general constraints on what can be done subsequently. The sequence in which decisions are made reflects and is reflected in the style of the designer (Simon 1970, Heath 1984).

A number of strategies designers use at the drawing board can be identified. Hill-climbing—in which a part of a solution is generated, and then the next best step is made, followed by the next, and so on—is one. It may involve facing detours and having to go back, which is something most designers find frustrating. It may involve circling—moving sideways with little apparent success in finding a complete solution (Wickelgren 1974). The biggest danger is that the designer is climbing the wrong hill! Generate-and-test techniques are also used by the designer working intuitively. A pattern is haphazardly chosen and tested; another is chosen, if better, it is retained, otherwise it is rejected. The computer-based algorithms that follow these procedures rely on mathematical procedures for making decisions. The human problem-solver has greater latitude.

As the designer is facing a series of wicked problems in his or her attempt to synthesize a solution, there is no rule for stopping the search for a better answer to the problem at hand. One can go on indefinitely (Rittel 1972). The major factor that keeps prodding the designer to try another approach is a demand for innovation, or the motivation of the architect to do a better job (Dickerson and Robertshaw 1975), or the desire for design awards and other forms of recognition.

People have to have a reason for working hard. The act of designing may be rewarding in itself; a designer may have a strong need for achievement or a fear of losing a job, or the financial rewards may be high. All motivation produces some level of stress. People require a level of stress to work well but a stress level that is too high or too low hinders performance. The major factor that truncates the search for a better solution is the time available. Sometimes, however, the designer may feel exhausted and convinced that no amount of effort will produce a better result. A "trip out of town" may help (Koberg and Bagnall 1974).

A designer cannot generate, predict, and evaluate the performance of all possible solutions to a building program, even a simple one. It is clearly misguided to think of design as an exhaustive process, though it may be an exhausting one. It is pointless to think of the design phase as the search for the optimal solution. This would imply that all possible solutions have been identified and evaluated. Rather, designing involves the search for, or creation of, at least a satisfying solution—one that is good enough (Simon 1960). Some designs are better than others, however, and the attempt to produce better solutions reduces the time available for the task as a whole. It is an inevitable part of environmental design praxis that designers almost always feel that if only they had more time to spend on designing they would come up with better results. The goal is to achieve the best possible design, given time and other resource constraints. Thus, designing—for many architects, landscape architects, and urban designers—is an optimizing process.

Creativity and the Synthesis of Form

Many environmental designers, particularly those who regard themselves as primarily fine artists, have been reluctant to consider the implications of the research on creativity that has been conducted during the course of the twentieth century. This research has focused on two areas: the nature of creative people and the nature of creative thinking. Most attention in the architectural press has been paid to the former, but it may be that the latter will prove more useful in the development of procedural theory. The research on creative people may tell us something about the attitudes required to think creatively; the research on the processes may suggest how we can develop our own thought processes.

Research on creative designers is most closely associated with Donald MacKinnon (1962a, 1962b, 1963, 1967) and Frank Barron (1965). In the environmental design fields it has focused entirely on architects. Creative architects—those whom the members of the profession regarded as the most creative—were found by MacKinnon to be highly productive and highly intelligent people with a great need for achievement. They are also people who value their independence highly, who have a high degree of tolerance for ambiguity, who value intellectual and cognitive matters, and who are very concerned with their adequacy as individuals. It must be noted that high intelligence (as measured on standard I.Q. tests) may be a prerequisite for creativity; but it cannot be equated with high creativity.

Frank Barron's work (1965) was concerned with the personality characteristics of creative architects as measured on the Minnesota Multiphasic Personality Inventory. His studies found that creative people are likely to be somewhat self-centered and moody, particularly steadfast in maintaining their independence of judgment, and somewhat insensitive to the opinions of others. They also show more evidence of psychopathology than less creative people. Thus the personality of creative people stresses individuality and the lack of necessity to "make a good impression." In many ways creative architects and scientists are alike (Manis 1966). This is particularly true in their tolerance for complexity and ambiguity. Barron suggests that this is because they have a "ready acceptance of the unconscious aspect" of themselves. It must be remembered that in all of this research it is the architects themselves who define what is meant by "creative architecture." There is no independent measure of creativity in these studies.

Another line of research on creative people

looks at the age at which they have made their major creative contributions to their fields. There appears to be a high correlation between productivity and the age of creativity. In most fields productivity is greatest when people are in their thirties and forties. In some fields, such as mathematics and chemistry, it has been at a much younger age. In architecture people have been older. The reason for this may be simply that architects do not get their own commissions until they are older. There is another explanation: architecture traditionally has lacked a strong theoretical basis, thus architects have had to learn from experience—and this takes time.

All this suggests certain attitudes that the environmental designer has to bring to bear on his or her own work. The designer has to be self-confident, be *constructively* discontent with the status quo, have a positive outlook, an open mind, and the courage of his or her convictions (Alger and Hayes 1964). These attitudes will not automatically lead to good designs, but they seem to be a common characteristic of creative people, regardless of their personality traits. Above all, creative people tend to have great intellectual curiosity. Organizing the knowledge base of the field within a theoretical framework can only help the professions as a whole. It presents a way of assimilating knowledge more quickly than learning solely by experience as well as a basis for deducing the good questions to raise during designing.

Research on creative processes has used kindergarten children, university sophomores, businessmen, and a wide variety of other people as subjects. Very little of it has focused specifically on the design process as such. One pilot study (Moore and Gay 1967) is highly suggestive about the nature of creativity in architecture but nothing seems to have been done to follow it up. The study by Moore and Gay drew heavily on the major research on creativity by Maltzman (1960), Parnes (1962), and Crutchfield and Covington (1965), and on the model of human intellect posited by Guilford (1959; see Anastasi 1965) to pose a number of hypotheses regarding the creative processes. These were tested with architectural students at the University of California, Berkeley.

The Guilford model is a morphological box portraying a hypothesis about the nature of the human intellect. This is shown in figure 6-1. It consists of three principle dimensions: the *content, operations,* and *products* of intellectual activity. *Content* refers to the manner in which an activity is conceived or expressed. Guilford suggests that it can be thought of in figural, symbolic, semantic, and behavioral terms. For the purposes of the environmental design professions, these can be considered synonymous with graphic, mathematical, verbal, and action contents. *Operations* refers to the processes of usage to which content is put and encompasses the processes of cognition (learning), memory, convergent production (focusing and narrowing), divergent production (expanding and en-

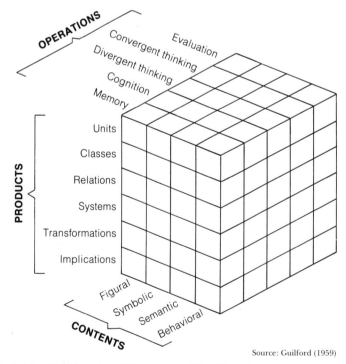

Source: Guilford (1959)

6-1. Guilford's Model for the Complete "Structure-of-Intellect."

larging), and evaluation. *Products* refers to the results of intellectual activity. Guilford identified these as follows: units, classes, relations, systems, transformations, and implications. This model has been used widely by those concerned with the nature of creativity, although the terms often are changed to make them more comprehensible to the members of a particular discipline (for example, engineers in Warfield and Hill 1973).

The other research on which Moore and Gay drew is more directly on creativity itself. The research by Parnes, Maltzman, and Crutchfield and Covington can be synthesized into a number of conclusions: people who are constantly exploring ways of doing things are likely to find new and better ways; the premature closure of a line of thinking should be avoided; all potential solutions should be recorded and evaluated later; and the designer should have a creative attitude in much the terms described above (Koberg and Bagnall 1974).

Pulling these two lines of research together, Moore and Gay suggest that a number of basic skills are necessary wherever design activities take place in architectural praxis. These probably apply to all the design fields. They are:

> *Figural fluency*, or the divergent production of figural units: the ability to generate many visual patterns or images which conform to simple specifications.
>
> *Ideational fluency*, or the divergent production of semantic units: the ability to generate many elementary verbal ideas appropriate to simple requirements.
>
> *Spontaneous flexibility*, or the divergent production of semantic classes: this is the ability to generate categories of ideas spontaneously from a given idea.
>
> *Adaptive flexibility*, or the divergent production of figural transformations: the ability to generate different solutions in response to a particular problem situation.
>
> *Originality*, or the divergent production of semantic transformations: this is the ability to generate remotely associated or uncommon or clever ideas in response to a particular problem situation.

All the above skills involve the divergent production of products of various contents. They all involve variety-generation. Moore and Gay identified two skills involving convergent production, or variety-reducing processes, as being particularly important:

> *Functional redefinition*, or the convergent production of semantic transformations: this is the ability to shift functions of an object, or part of an object, to a new use.
>
> *Figural redefinition*, or the convergent production of figural transformations: this is the ability to shift the shapes of an object so that it can be used in a new way.

They also identify one process of cognition as being important to creative thinking in architecture:

> *Form recognition*, or the cognition [learning] of figural relations: this is the ability to recognize figural relations.

This is an intuitively appealing list of abilities that will enhance creative thinking. Moore and Gay showed that direct training of at least some of these skills can enhance an architectural student's creative abilities. Further research on creative thinking in architecture should not only advance positive procedural theories of design that can be used to enhance practice but also provide the basis for the design of better pedagogical procedures than are currently in use.

METHODS FOR DEVELOPING POSSIBLE DESIGNS

John Alger and Carl Hayes (1964) identify three major activities in developing solutions to problems. These are:

- review of historical information
- individual creative effort
- group creative effort.

They are used throughout environmental design praxis:

Review of Historical Information

Much of an environmental designer's professional activity involves addressing problems similar to those that have been addressed in the past. The review of historical information includes the study of paradigms and typologies, the adaptation of types to meet present needs (Eisenman 1982, Rowe 1983), and the use of design principles and standards. The objective is to understand what others have thought about the problem, and to understand also what variables have been considered to be important and the design patterns used to "solve" the problem.

Paradigms, Typologies, Generic Solutions, and Prototypes in Design

Paradigms refer to patterns—exemplars of certain built form types, such as theaters or plazas. *Ty-*

pology refers to the classification of specimens according to the type of behavior they exhibit; in the field of environmental design, buildings and landscape and urban designs can be classified according to the similarity of their purposes and/or their formal structure. A *prototype* can be either the primary type of anything—in architecture, a building or open space—or a pattern model or standard exemplar. A *generic solution* consists of a combination of design principles that can be applied as a unit to a large group or class of problems.

Paradigms, typologies, generic solutions, and prototypes are used throughout architectural praxis. They are used to help clarify the nature of problems during the intelligence phase, as a basis for generating solutions during the design phase, and as a yardstick of comparison during the choice phase of praxis. Often a designer is faced with a situation in which there is a lack of clarity in the specification of the problem. Design prototypes or generic solutions provide him or her with an understanding of how other people have addressed similar problems in the past. They can suggest the basis for addressing the problem in the new situation. They can also be dangerous.

Designers frequently refer to generic solutions and types in examining present problems. There are numerous books devoted to typological studies (such as Sherwood 1978), and movements in design are recognized by how they categorize and use building types (for instance, the Tendenza movement in Italy, see Rossi 1982). The classification and use of types is based on perceptions of what problems a designer is addressing. This is a value-laden choice. A knowledge of typologies is an important asset to the environmental designer provided it does not hinder him or her from conducting other analyses that will reveal the structure of the situation being addressed. The use of typologies is central to the design process of those who regard design as a process of conjecture, evaluation, and refutation or acceptance of the conjecture.

The Use of Principles and Standards in the Generation of Form

Professionals in all the design fields use design principles very extensively in moving from a series of problem statements to solutions. Design principles are not fundamental truths, laws, or propositions specifying a condition or a relationship. They are rules used for guiding action. They are the basis of canonic design (Broadbent 1973). A standard, according to Walter Gropius (1962), is that simple exemplar of anything in general use which embodies a fusion of the best of its anterior forms—a fusion preceded by the elimination of the personal content of designers and all otherwise ungeneric or non-essential features. Such an impersonal standard is called a "norm"—a word derived from a carpenter's square.

Every designer has a head full of design principles—normative statements—picked up during his or her formal education and developed during practice. Students develop designs in discussion with faculty members who usually are practicing professionals. During this process they develop certain design habits and internalize a set of only partially tested principles. They develop a set of patterns that they tend to use repetitively—a style —and rules of thumb for addressing problems. The reason this occurs is that the design fields have lacked an explicit positive theoretical framework, with the result that those who teach design try to condense the knowledge they have gained through years of experience so they can communicate it to students in as short a time as possible (Alexander 1964, Perin 1970). "Standards" are authoritative or recognized exemplars of correctness for designers to use. Many of these standards are listed in books on various subjects: urban design (De Chiara and Koppleman 1975), the use of trees in cities (Arnold 1980), and others.

Principles and standards are used all the time by designers. They save the designer from having to reinvent the wheel for every problem he or she faces; they enable designers to make decisions on matters about which they know very little; they reduce to design-by-habit situations that really require creative problem-solving. The danger of principles and standards is that they are usually a "combination of rules of thumb, personal experience and professional judgment with limited scientific data" (Perin 1970). This does not negate them, but it does mean they should be used with caution. They will continue to be used because they are easy to use.

Principles are usually deontic statements of the following format: *In Situation X do Y*. Architectural texts are full of such examples:

All ornament should be taken and worked out of solid material and not upon it. (Leighton 1881)

Components which make up the enclosure planes . . . should be compatible with the apparent size of the space they define. (Isaac 1971)

Principles of this type are prescriptive. In this form they implicitly specify not only a solution but also a problem, make no reference to their origin, and tend to inhibit divergent thinking.

These limitations have been noted by a number of people and have provoked the development of both design directives (Kriedberg, Field et al. 1965) and pattern language (Alexander et al. 1967). Design directives have the following format: *(Given Situation X) perform Action Y to solve Problem Z.* The statements of the pattern language developed by Christopher Alexander and his colleagues (1967, 1977) are similar: *If the Situation X occurs, then perform Action Y to solve Problem Z because. . . .* Each statement includes the reason why the relationship of context, action, and problem holds.

Alexander and his colleagues believe that the main strength of their pattern statements is their reusability, which occurs because they are abstract, general, criticizable on specific points, and communicable. The danger is the same as with all design principles: rather than focusing on the existing reality, the designer may tend to read into the situation at hand the context and problem specified in the principle. As long as designers rely so heavily on the use of design principles rather than on theory, these problems will persist. Specifying normative design actions in the form of pattern statements reduces the probability of erroneous analysis of situations, but nothing can eliminate the possibility. Good positive theory will further reduce problems of misunderstanding. Still, this by itself will not lead to good solutions.

Individual Creative Effort

A fundamental requirement for creative problem-solving, as noted above, is a creative attitude. There are also several processes that aid both divergent production and convergent production. Geoffrey Broadbent (1973) identifies three types of techniques that enhance creative thinking. These can be used on an individual or a group basis. They are checklists, interaction methods, and psychoanalytical techniques. Checklists are the simplest. They consists of words and patterns that one scans in the expectation that some will trigger off new ideas. They may deal with either substantive or procedural issues—the built form or the designing process. "Is there sufficient space for the entrance?" is an example of the former. Broadbent (1973) regards Osborne's (1957) concept of vice versa technique as an example of the latter. In this approach the architect uses the opposite of a standard procedure for dealing with a problem and then tests it. This is essentially the process of conjecture and verification (or refutation) of Karl Popper (1962). As an example, Broadbent cites Summerson (1949) on Le Corbusier:

We put it to him that a park is a space for recreation in a town, and he replies, "not at all; in the future the park will not be in the town but the town in the park."

This process does come up with novel solutions, but novelty is not synonymous with success, as the followers of Le Corbusier have found in many situations (Marmot 1982).

An example of an interactional method has already been given. Guilford's model of the human intellect results from this kind of analysis. The method of morphological analysis is an example of a technique that "forces" one to think of possible combinations of elements that would not have occurred to the designer otherwise. The technique was developed by Fred Zwicky (1948) as a means of discovering associations to aid invention, research, and construction. There is little evidence of such a technique being used explicitly and systematically in environmental design, although there are many examples of its use in industrial design. It is quite possible that many of the people engaged in architecture, landscape architecture, and urban design use something like the process subconsciously.

Brainstorming and synectics, whether carried out formally or done haphazardly, are regarded by many methodologists as a fundamental part of the argumentative process that designers go through with themselves or others to generate ideas. Don Koberg and Jim Bagnall (1974) cite Osborne's manipulative verbs—magnify, minify, rearrange, alter, adapt, modify, substitute, reverse, combine—and add a few of their own as a means of encouraging divergent thinking. These actions lead to new potential solutions, which can then be tested and verified.

Synectics involves a number of steps, from stating the problem to summarizing the ideas presented; it relies heavily on the use of analogies (Gordon 1961, 1978). The objective is to encourage divergent thinking in an uncritical atmosphere. Certainly metaphors and analogies have long been used by designers for this purpose.

The Use of Metaphors and Analogies in Design

Metaphors are figures of speech in which a descriptive term is transferred to some object based on some resemblance of a literal to an implied subject. Analogies suggest an equivalence or likeness of relationship between something in one medium and something in another medium. Metaphors have featured in the work of some major architects, but it is analogic thinking that really frees the creative spirit (Black 1962).

The use of typologies is one example of analogic thinking; it is an example of a *direct* analogy. Direct analogies also refer to the process whereby facts in one field are applied to another field faced with similar problems. Broadbent (1973) gives the example of Brunel who, when faced with the problem of building underwater constructions, observed a teredo worm forming a tube for itself as it bored into timber. From this he developed the idea of a caisson. Broadbent also identifies two other types of analogies—personal and symbolic.

Personal analogies involve relating the inanimate world to the animate. "If I were a brick what would I want to be?" Architect Louis Kahn answered: "An arch." The aesthetic philosophies of Bernard Bosanquet were developed along similar lines of thinking (Bosanquet 1931). *Symbolic* analogies are more mystical and involve comparing a situation with an abstract referent. Architects have frequently talked about a "truthful" architecture, for instance. Like all analogies, symbolic ones can free the mind. But they also can misdirect the designer by their colorfulness when this leads to dealing with irrelevant issues.

Group Creative Effort

Much of the professional work in the fields of environmental design is done on a group basis. A design evolves as a number of people make contributions to it. Designs are criticized by other members of the organization and amendments are made. There is often a need to bring the collective knowledge of a number of people to bear on a problem.

Group Designing

Assets	Liabilities
1. Greater sum total of knowledge and information	1. Social pressure for conformity
2. Greater number of approaches to the problem	2. Consensus may come too soon and shut out higher-quality solutions
3. Participation in problem-solving increases the acceptance of the solution	3. A dominant individual may exercise undue sway
4. Better comprehension of the solution	4. The goal of designing a good solution to the problem may be replaced by the secondary goal of winning the argument.

The techniques available are essentially the same as for individual problem-solving, but the need for organizing the interactions between people is higher. There is more pressure for a formal organization of these interactions if expected results are to be yielded. If all goes well, the interaction between the members of a group can lead to outstanding solutions. Interaction can also be chaotic, however. The assets and liabilities of group work are summarized in the accompanying table.

The first and second of the assets have to do with creative design, the third and fourth with the possibility of enhancing the probability of implementation. The liabilities identify some of the psychological factors at work in groups. Awareness of these liabilities as well as strong leadership, both in setting directions and in maintaining the group, are crucial to effective group problem-solving efforts.

RECENT EXPLORATIONS IN COMPUTER-AIDED DESIGN

There is another line of research that is not strictly a contribution of the behavioral sciences to architectural theory, but it does suggest some questions that architects and behavioral scientists, particularly psychologists, might ask about the nature of the act of designing. This is the work being done on design heuristics and computer-aided design. In these fields the search is for algorithms that get better results than those the designer gets working in traditional fashion at a drawing board.

Most of this work has focused on plan-generation based on the adjacency requirements of rooms and on movement patterns. This is a very limited view of the design task of architects. In the long run, however, this research may have a very beneficial impact on the overall design process. It should release the designer to work on those aspects of the synthesis that require major creative efforts. These are certainly beyond those that we can presently perceive as being carried out by computer-based algorithms. There are, however, more important benefits to this research. It may help us further our understanding of the functioning of the human mind.

William J. Mitchell (1977) differentiates between weak and strong synthesis procedures. Strong procedures have major informational demands, weak do not. Linear programming, a resource allocation procedure in which it is possible to maximize (or minimize) some ends given some constraints expressed in linear terms, is an example of a strong technique. It requires that the system under question be modeled prior to the use of the technique. In contrast, the random generating and testing of solutions is a weak procedure because it has low informational demands. These types of procedures have their counterparts in human problem-solving. Weak procedures are those that are not guided by much use of substantive theory in the generation of solutions, only in the evaluation of these solutions. Strong procedures involve the direct application of theory, to the extent it exists, in predicting how patterns of built form that are being designed will work. It shapes the generation of designs as well as the evaluation of them.

There are other procedures that seem to model the human problem-solving processes. A number of computer-based design algorithms are hill-climbing procedures. In the computer algorithms, as with the designer working intuitively at the drawing board, there is often a need to try one's luck on another hill to see whether it is higher. Some designers attempt to carry a number of designs through to their logical conclusions simultaneously. Others, probably most, find it easier to work on one design and then to try to come up with a different one. Design methodologists call the first approach the breadth-first approach and the second the depth-first approach. Here too there are counterparts between computer-based design algorithms and the human problem-solver. The research on creativity does suggest that the breadth-first approach will yield better results, but there seem to be few designers who can work this way. Whether this is due to innate abilities or to the educational process is unknown. In large offices the process may be partially replicated by having different designers, or design teams, working in parallel.

CONCLUSION

There is much that we do not understand about the nature of the act of designing. At the same time, the behavioral sciences have already provided a number of insights into the nature of human creativity and the nature of problem-solving. We now understand something about the nature of creative attitudes and about the creative processes. We understand something about the overall nature of the design phase and about the solution-generation techniques employed by designers.

The ability to develop a strong positive body of knowledge about the act of designing has been hampered by the lack of research. Very little of the existing research on human problem-solving has focused on any of the environmental design disciplines. Most of the conclusions drawn about the nature of design in these fields is extrapolated from generalizations made about the creative processes in other fields. Luckily, there is little to suggest that the procedure of design in the environmental design fields is different from the procedures of other disciplines, although there are major differences in areas of substantive concern.

ADDITIONAL READINGS

Adams, James L. *Conceptual Blockbusting*. San Francisco: Freeman, 1974.

Broadbent, Geoffrey. "The Design Spectrum," and "The Derivation of Architectural Form." In *Design in Architecture, Architecture and the Human Sciences*. New York: John Wiley, 1973, pp. 412–430.

Koestler, Arthur. *The Act of Creation*. New York: Macmillan, 1964.

Koberg, Don, and Jim Bagnall. "Introduction to Ideation." In *The Universal Traveler*. Los Altos, Ca.: William Kaufman, 1974, pp. 66–73.

Le Corbusier. *Creation Is a Patient Search*, James Palmer, translator. New York: Praeger, 1960.

MacKinnon, Donald W. "The Characteristics of Creative Architects and Further Reflections on the Implications for Architectural Education." In Marcus Wiffen, ed., *The Teaching of Architecture*. Washington, D.C.: AIA, 1963, pp. 73–79.

Moore, Gary T., and Lynne Meyer Gay. "Creative Problem-Solving in Architecture—a Pilot Study." Department of Architecture, University of California at Berkeley, 1967.

Osborne, A. F. *Applied Imagination, Principles and Practices of Creative Thinking*. New York: Scribner's, 1970.

Simon, Herbert. *The Sciences of the Artificial*. Cambridge, Mass.: MIT Press, 1969.

7

CHOOSING AND THE CHOICE PHASE

Choosing involves a number of intellectual processes. It requires the prediction of the consequences of actions given a range of possible future contexts; it requires a value to be placed on these outcomes; and it requires decisions to be made based on some criteria. The whole process of design praxis involves a stream of evaluations and decisions. The choice phase of praxis involves either the selection for implementation of one of the possible design solutions generated during the design phase or the decision that none is good enough. In the latter case the whole process is either abandoned or else the problem-solving activity returns to an earlier phase. The choice phase is thus predominantly concerned with evaluation; but it inevitably involves intelligence activities and much design effort.

PROCESSES OF EVALUATION

Decisions are made throughout the design process. Every time a decision is made some sort of evaluation takes place. Since the whole process of designing a building, a landscape, or an urban complex involves a stream of decisions, the application of values is something that goes on continuously. Many decisions are made without conscious thought, but others are made more self-consciously, sometimes subjectively, sometimes objectively, and often through a mixture of the two.

Evaluation is similar to analysis but has another dimension. Analysis is based on description and

comparison. It may also involve prediction. Evaluation involves asking the question: "How good is this . . . ?" There are two major evaluation phases in environmental design praxis. The first is the evaluation of a design on the drawing board before it is implemented, and the second occurs after the design has been built and put into operation. The concern here is with the former.

Values

All decisions involve the application of some sort of value system to the assessment of possible courses of action. If a course of action, place, or event is assigned a positive value, it is regarded as desirable. If a negative value is assigned, it is regarded as undesirable. Usually more than a two-point scale is involved. Clients and designers discriminate between degrees of goodness or badness. Generally a verbal scale is used in which good or bad are qualified by words like "very," "somewhat," and "extremely" (Bross 1953). In environmental design praxis the value system applied is largely an intuitive one.

Many architects, particularly among environmental design professionals, believe that a numerical value system for use in assessing design quality cannot be developed. Designers seeking precision in evaluation may turn to the behavioral sciences for elucidation, but they will find little help. Few behavioral scientists have cared to become involved in research on the modeling of existing value systems, because it is a difficult and highly controversial topic. The consideration of the value of a human life, for instance, raises a host of ethical questions. In much decision-making, however, values are given implicitly to such matters.

Architects talk about seeking truth in design. Implicit in this is a value position. One of the reasons that the design process is argumentative is that there is no single truth nor is there a single objective value system—one in which the dimensions of the evaluation and measuring system are understood by all those involved—with which everyone will agree except in some very limited instances (see also Manheim 1970). These instances concern aspects of the biological and technological nature of the environment.

Close examination shows that environmental designers can and do apply numerical values to the assessment of many items of concern to them. Many things have a market value. A building, its services, and maintenance all have a monetary value as does the work of the designer. Apples and oranges can be compared in monetary terms, but this tells only the measure of demand for them on the market given the costs of production. It does not explain what an individual thinks of the product. Moreover, different people have different reactions to the monetary value of a product.

Psychological research has focused on constructing preference scales to discriminate between the values of different objects. People may be asked simply to rank objects in terms of their preferences or they may be asked to assign a numerical value on, say, a scale from one to ten to show how much they like something. In environmental design there is usually a multiplicity of clients with different values (Manheim 1970). The difficulty is to move from individual values to a group consensus. If one averages the individual values to represent the group's values, one may end up with a value structure representative of no one in the group nor of the group as a whole.

The consequence of all this is that designs are evaluated partially in monetary terms and partially using a verbal scale. The cost of designs is important, but beyond that a verbal, intuitive, and subjective scale is used. This occurs throughout the design process.

THE CHOICE PHASE

Often in environmental design praxis the design and choice phases are merged and only one design is developed. In this case the question is simply: Is this design good enough? More and more often, however, designers are specifically asked to present their clients—usually the sponsors of a project but sometimes the users—with more than one design possibility. In this case, the choice phase is the period in which a discrimination is made between the designs and one is chosen for implementation—at least, if one is acceptable. The major intellectual activities involved in the phase are shown in figure 7-1.

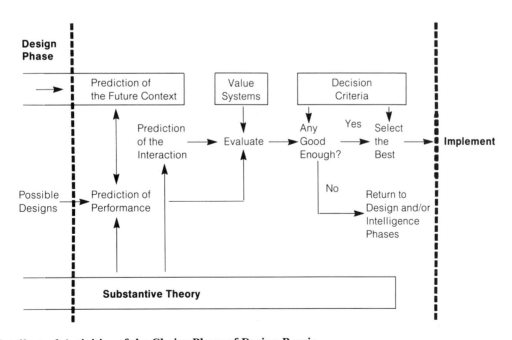

7-1. The Intellectual Activities of the Choice Phase of Design Praxis.

The degree to which the choice is ultimately satisfactory depends on the performance of the design after it has been constructed. If it works out well as a built form, the choice was a good one. Thus, the prediction of the performance of a design once built is an important part of the choice phase. How well the design will work depends not only on its own qualities but also on the nature of the social, cultural, and physical environment in which it will exist. Thus, the nature of the future environment also has to be predicted. Sometimes a designer has control over aspects of the context but more frequently this is not the case. The design-environment relationship is not unidirectional; the design also has an impact on the environment. The prediction and evaluation of the impact of a building, landscape, or larger-scale design on its surroundings is now sometimes legally mandated.

Once a prediction has been made of the performance of a potential solution in the predicted future environment, a value has to be applied to it and a decision criterion applied. Traditionally this whole process has been carried out intuitively, but more and more it is being done in an explicit fashion so that all the people concerned can understand the implications of what is being done.

Prediction

While Section 899 of the Code of Criminal Procedure for New York State still regards the making of predictions as "disorderly" behavior for which "good faith is no defense," implicitly or explicitly architects, landscape architects, urban designers, and their various clients, as noted above, are involved in making a stream of predictions throughout praxis. It was also noted that in the choice phase designers are particularly concerned with predicting the performance of the designs they are proposing in some future context. Several prediction techniques are available to and in use by designers. The most powerful technique is to build a prototype or mock-up of the design and to test it through experimentation. Usually, however, other prediction techniques based on past experiences have to be used. This is where the quality of substantive theory most clearly affects the outcome of a procedural aspect of design praxis. It is difficult to make sound predictions when the knowledge on which they are based is weak.

Experimentation and Simulation in Prediction

Predicting the performance of buildings and other products of environmental design is not easy because prototypes often cannot be built and tested in advance of implementation. The products tend to be unique and the scale and cost of building units that are not unique tend to be prohibitive. With some design products or parts thereof this is, however, possible.

The performance of many industrial products can be evaluated by submitting them to experimental scrutiny. This is possible when the cost of building a prototype is low in comparison with the total number that are going to be built. Items that are going to be mass-produced—like cars, telephones, kettles, and chairs—can be and frequently are subjected to this type of testing. If the prototype does not meet the required standard of performance it can be altered and retested, or, unfortunately, the product can be marketed with its performance inadequacies disguised to be discovered only after purchase. This is also true of buildings.

The elements of the environment at a building or urban-design scale cannot be manipulated in this fashion. Natural experiments can be used to test such things as the impact of the timing of a sequence of traffic lights on traffic flow or changes in the location of a theater ticket office on the flow of people in the foyer. Mock-ups of such settings as dormitory rooms or workstations—that is, repetitive units—can be built but they are not easy to test under everyday operating conditions. We rely on partial tests. Workstations can be tested to see whether they are comfortable and how well they afford the activities that are to take place there. Even their appearance—their aesthetic qualities—can be tested by specific sample populations.

An alternative to experimenting on real systems and mock-ups is to experiment with simulations. In this case, models of the proposed systems are built and tested. There are various types of models. *Iconic models* are those in which the physical features of real systems are represented. Traditional architectural models of buildings are of this type. *Analog models* are another type. Here the model is in a medium different from the real system. Euclidean perspective and orthographic projections are standard models of this type frequently used by environmental designers. Of the various ways they are used, one is to simulate the appearance of what is being designed. A more recent development is the use of computer-generated animated films to simulate the sequence of experiences resulting from a person's movement through cities or buildings. *Symbolic mathematical models* are being used more and more frequently to predict the performance of aspects of buildings.

Many aspects of proposed designs, such as the structure of buildings, circulation patterns, mechanical systems usage, heat loss and gain, maintenance costs, and fiscal performances, can be modeled mathematically. The prediction of performance on these dimensions can be made with a high degree of accuracy. This is only possible because the positive theory in these areas is well developed and the variables involved are described specifically.

It is on other dimensions of concern, particularly those referring to human behavior and aesthetic interpretation of proposed buildings, that such simulations are difficult to design and accurate predictions are difficult to make systematically. Even where mathematical models can be used, limitations of time and money often result in designers relying on their own experiences to make predictions. In so doing they rely on another whole class of prediction techniques, those based on the projection of perceptions of the past into the future.

Prediction Techniques

People, as far as is now known, cannot foresee the future. When designers do not experiment with proposed systems to see how they work, they have to rely on observations of the past in order to predict how the system will work. Recent efforts have focused on doing this less casually.

As the process of designing spirals toward a solution, the predictions need to become more specific. At the outset we may use rules of thumb for predicting how much a building will cost or how deep a floor slab will be. Later in the process the calculations will be made more specifically. It is much easier to predict outcomes well when dealing with these issues than when dealing with variables involving, say, symbolic aesthetic questions.

A number of projection techniques can be identified: persistence prediction, trajectory prediction, and cyclic prediction. These all rely on descriptions of past occurrences. There are also two techniques that involve greater theoretical input: associative prediction and analog prediction. All of these are likely to be used at some time or other during the design of a major project (Bross 1953).

Persistence prediction works well in stable conditions. In using it a designer assumes that the future will be the same as the present—that there will be no change. All he or she needs to know is the present situation. In predicting how a design will perform, the assumption is that present patterns will work as well tomorrow as they do today. When no prediction seems to have been made during the choice phase, especially with reference to the context in which the design must operate in the future, in reality one of three assumptions has been made. The first is that the context is irrelevant; the second

is that it will be the same as today; the third is that the design will function in any possible future context. The second of these involves persistence prediction. This is often an acceptable prediction technique, especially for short-run futures. Activity patterns that exist today will exist tomorrow. Aesthetic values that exist today will exist tomorrow. Building patterns that work today will work tomorrow. These are all persistence predictions. We also know, however, that the world is not as stable as this, that some events are idiosyncratic, and that many things are changing. Thus, using persistence prediction can lead to major errors in anticipating such things as what the context of a building will be like in the future or how the patterns being used in a design will work in the future. We therefore need to consider other techniques.

Trajectory prediction assumes that past rates of change will continue into the future. If there has been no change in the past for the variable being considered—meaning that it is a constant—then tomorrow will be the same as today. If changes have been taking place, it is assumed that they will continue to take place in the same vein. While this is a reasonable method for predicting short-run futures, it is seldom accurate for the long run. Environmental designers, as much as any other people, are concerned with trends—in everything from construction costs to family size to award-winning designs. Few trends continue at the same rate of change into the far future. The context of a building to be designed does not go on changing at the same rate forever.

Cyclic prediction assumes that history repeats itself. This prediction technique requires considerably more historical information than is needed for either persistence or trajectory prediction. It works well for seasonal patterns and many astronomical events that occur in stable patterns of a cyclical nature. Anne Tyng (1975) suggests that popular empathy for complex or simple forms in architecture occurs in cyclical fashion.

Persistence, trajectory, and cyclical prediction techniques can be used throughout all aspects of environmental design praxis. They are descriptive techniques that require no theoretical underpinnings. In research and theory-building the accuracy of the results of using such techniques can provide the bases for asking questions: Why have things changed unexpectedly? Why have they stayed the same when change was predicted? And so forth.

The techniques are widely used in a relatively casual fashion for predicting the performances of buildings and urban and landscape designs. One observes where patterns of other buildings work and assumes that the present patterns being designed will work in a similar fashion. These techniques often work because of the stabilities inherent in the world. Thoughtless reliance on them can be dangerous, however, because the techniques may be inappropriate to the situation at hand. With these techniques conclusions are drawn without any understanding of *why* patterns work the way they do. This is where associative prediction is different.

Associative prediction relies on the use of a positive theoretical basis for making predictions. The predictions can be reliable only if the theoretical basis is reliable. In environmental designing, one goal, presumably, is to predict accurately the performance of the patterns being designed. The better one's knowledge of the range of patterns available, and the greater one's understanding of the affordances of these patterns for different individuals and of why these relationships hold, the more likely one is to predict accurately the performance of specific patterns. The important thing is for the relationships between the variables in the theory to be relevant and externally valid.

Designers in the past made extensive use of associative prediction based on their intuitive understanding of the world around them. When societal changes came slowly and designers and sponsors and users had essentially the same or cooperating values, their predictions were likely to be accurate. It has been argued in this book that such was not and is not the case with the world as it confronted the Modern Movement in design, and that the quality of the positive theory the Modernists have used for making predictions has been deficient and at times simply erroneous. It is hardly surprising that what we hoped would work has so often failed. The current limitations of our positive theory still define our ability to predict accurately.

Analog prediction is another type frequently used by designers. It is based on perceptions of the similarity on a dimension of concern between two different systems. One of these systems is a simple one in which it is possible to see how events will turn out. The observation is then applied to the more complex system. The results achieved by applying the technique depend on the quality of the analog. Architects often use analogs to explain how the building designs they are proposing will work. A powerful and/or colorful analog is a useful way of explaining this. It also can capture the imagination. One of the best-known such analogs is Buckminster Fuller's reference to "spaceship earth." Such analogs can be misleading if the analog is inappropriate, if the performance characteristic of the dimensions of the two systems being compared is not the same. In such cases, if predictions are correct, it is only coincidental.

There are thus a number of prediction techniques used in environmental designing. When it is considered at all, the prediction of the future context of a proposed design is likely to be based on a mixture of persistence, trajectory, and associative techniques. The performance of a building or other environmental design in that context is likely to be based on associative and analog techniques as well as on intuition. In all these cases we now tend to talk about the probabilities of outcomes. We have learned to be modest about our predictive abilities. These will be enhanced, however, as our positive knowledge of the workings of built form is enhanced.

Measures of Effectiveness

Most of the aspects of built form of concern to designers are created to fulfill a multiplicity of objectives. There is a multiplicity of possible ways to meet many of these objectives. Any design that is devised has a multitude of characteristics—too many for all of them to be evaluated. Often the range of characteristics evaluated is very small and restricted to aesthetic ones and traditional functional ones. This is particularly true when designs are evaluated by a panel of experts—the traditional architectural jury system. Juries are used formally to judge design competitions, to review the aesthetics of designs (for instance, by municipal fine-arts review boards), and very extensively as a means of evaluating the quality of students' designs in schools of environmental design.

A study of studio juries in a school of architecture showed that relatively few variables—or what are often called evaluation factors—are considered by jury members (Hassid 1961). The factors selected vary from situation to situation, but they tend to be those involved with circulation and aesthetics. A recent study shows a broader range of issues being raised in juries, with procedural and substantive issues coming under consideration, but the range is still limited (*Architecture Education Study*, Vol. II, 1981). Sometimes the issues are systematically related to the objectives a design is supposed to fulfill, but at other times the objectives are those the jurors believe to be important. There is often confusion in understanding the evaluations, because the evaluation of objectives is seldom distinguished from the evaluation of the means—the design—used to achieve them.

The existence of multiple objectives means that the evaluation process for each potential solution involves the use of a number of possibly incompatible measures of effectiveness. Some variables will have a numerical—usually monetary—value assigned to them, others will have verbal ones. Adding them all up cannot be done objectively. The overall evaluation is argued out.

Several ways have been proposed to enhance this process, and they are slowly coming into use as the pressure for openness in evaluation has mounted. These techniques are used for recording and displaying the evaluations of the performance of buildings and other projects, particularly large-scale environmental design projects such as dams, canals, and subway systems. The methods are essentially "evaluation accounts" involving cost-benefit analysis or cost-effectiveness analysis. The simplest evaluation account is the balance sheet, in which the strengths and weaknesses of each scheme, in terms of the objectives set and the people concerned, are displayed. This is a fairly standard procedure in environmental design. More complex processes include cost-benefit analysis (Litchfield 1960) and the goals-achievement matrix (Hill 1972). The former involves displaying the costs and benefits of each scheme in balance-sheet fashion, whereas the latter extends this by emphasizing the relative importance of the different groups involved and their values. These are considered in assessing how well the objectives of the design have been met. This process recognizes the diversity of values that can be used to evaluate both the objectives of a design and the way in which those objectives have been met. It also recognizes that many of the concerns of design are intangible and that these need to be included in any assessment if it is to have external validity. The problem with all such approaches is that they are time-consuming, because every factor becomes open to argument. For this reason they are seldom employed except on large-scale projects where public accounting is demanded—and often legally required.

Several possible approaches to evaluation have been suggested in the architectural literature (see, for example, J.C. Jones 1970). In all the environmental professions, however, there is a continuing reliance on the jury system using subjective assessment—the black box approach. Construction costs, and increasingly maintenance costs, play an important role in the evaluation of and discrimination between design proposals. However, given two schemes of approximately equal cost, or two schemes with very different costs but also very different performance characteristics, it is largely subjective judgment that is used for evaluation. The quality of the decision depends on the attitudes of the jury—their beliefs about how the project will operate on whatever dimensions they choose to consider and their evaluation of this performance.

Evaluating the Proposed Design-Environment Relationship

Different designers have different attitudes in considering the impact of the projects they design on their surroundings and the impact of the surroundings on their designs. One of the difficulties is in predicting exactly what the environment of the proposed design will be in the future. One of the responses to this is to design buildings, and even urban designs and open spaces, as if they were independent of their surroundings. Designers have gotten away with this in the past, but the general public and people with an investment in surrounding areas have become increasingly aware that neighboring projects have considerable impact on their lives and they are becoming increasingly vocal about this. Architects, in particular, have become more aware of the potential legal consequences if a design impacts negatively on its surroundings (in terms of wind loads and heat gains and losses, for example). Other potential negative side effects are being recognized. Research has shown, for instance, that oversize generators of activities (in terms of the vehicular traffic they create) can have serious deleterious effects on a residential neighborhood by changing traffic patterns, resulting in widened streets and the destruction of traditional territorial markers (Newman 1979).

Discussion of the need to consider the side effects of designs has focused largely on avoiding negative impacts rather than on promoting positive impacts. This is due to the effect of legislation requiring designers, particularly those of large-scale publicly funded projects, to make sure that negative side effects do not occur. On January 1, 1970, the President of the United States signed the National Environmental Policy Act into law (see Jain et al. 1977). This has had an effect on the design of many large-scale facilities, in particular, because it mandated that the impact of the proposed design on its physical and social environment be predicted and assessed. The assessment is biased by legal requirements that emphasize the quantitative measurement of impacts on the natural environment and thus on people. If nothing else, the law has enhanced planners' and designers' awareness that what they do has an impact on the environment. These impacts, it must be remembered, can be both positive and negative.

Decision Criteria

However thoroughly the predictions of the state of the future environment and the performance of the possible designs being proposed within it are carried out, the actual decision to implement one design rather than another is often difficult to make. Designs may perform similarly even though they are very different in character, or each design may have a variety of strengths and weaknesses. Even if one design appears to be the best, given the criteria used by the design team or established during the intelligence phase, the final arbiter's global attitudes may make any systematic evaluation completely irrelevant. This can occur if there is a change of sponsor between the time the intelligence phase of a project is completed and the time the choice phase begins. Many architects have experienced this in the public arena when the government of a country that is sponsoring a scheme changes and with it the perception of what constitutes the problem. Fundamentally, however, people have different attitudes toward the world and this is reflected in the decision criteria they use.

Some people are optimists; they choose the designs they predict will lead to the most favorable result whatever the future holds. Other people are pessimists; they choose the scheme based on their perceptions of the worst possible outcome of each possibility. They select the scheme with the least worst outcome—the one that works best in the worst possible circumstances! Some people are interested in short-run benefits and others in the long run. Many in the design professions see it as their mandate to be advocates of long-term benefits as the major decision criteria. Other decision-makers want a compromise between profit and security. Their dictum would be "Minimize the maximum risk!" A "rational" approach might be to select the design that works best given the most probable future. Which of these approaches is selected depends very much on the personality of the decision-maker.

Carl Jung distinguished between four psychological types depending on the type of data to which they pay attention and how they make decisions. There are two types on each dimension: "sensing" and "intuitive" types on the data dimension, and "thinking" and "feeling" types on the decision dimension. Sensing types focus on hard, empirical data; intuitive types look at situations as a whole using hypothetical scenarios as yardsticks. Thinking types base decisions on impersonal logical reasoning, while feeling types emphasize personal considerations and values. Clashes arise between these types during the design process because each thinks the other is muddleheaded. In reality, each type can make important contributions to decision-making at various points in the overall process (see Mitroff 1983).

Decision criteria are used throughout the design process. The intelligence phase is likely to involve a broad set of these because so many people are likely to be participating. Here it is often the intuitive-feeling types who are good at goal-formulation, while the intuitive-thinking types are good at problem-formulation. In the design phase the attitudes of the designers themselves are paramount. Here the sensing-thinking types may be best at problem-solving. Possibly the best people for carrying out the choice phase would be the sensing-feeling types, but what rules the situation are the design criteria of the person who has, or the group of people who have, the power to make the decision.

CONCLUSION

The choice phase does not always exist as a separate entity in any of the environmental design praxis fields. It is more likely to exist when large-scale landscape and urban-design projects are tackled. It is often merged into the design phase, and sometimes—when small-scale architectural designs are being addressed—with the design phase into the intelligence phase. Choice activities themselves are, however, part of every action throughout the designing process. They involve making predictions, applying values, assessing outcomes, and using decision criteria. There are no rules for ensuring that favorable decisions will always be made.

Prediction systems and value systems being imperfect, designers have to take risks. Will this activity system achieve its specified goals? Will this design house these activities well? How will people respond to the symbolic aesthetics of this proposal? Does it matter? Who will use this building in the future? All these decisions require predictions; some require that values be associated with them; all require some choice to be made. The ability to make good predictions depends on the quality of the positive theory at the designer's disposal. The nature of values depends on the normative theory of those involved in the design process. The degree to which designers promote their own attitudes is part of their normative position.

ADDITIONAL READINGS

Bross, Irwin D. J. *Design for Decision.* New York: Macmillan, 1953.
Chadwick, George. "Evaluation." In *A Systems View of Planning.* New York: Pergamon, 1978, pp. 250–271.
Manheim, Marvin L. "A Design Process Model: Theory and Application to Transportation Planning." In Gary Moore, ed., *Emerging Methods in Environmental Planning and Design.* Cambridge, Mass.: MIT Press, 1970, pp. 331–348.

SUBSTANTIVE THEORY

The Environment and Human Behavior

Substantive theory in architecture is concerned with *descriptions* and *explanations* of the physical nature of the built environment—its materials and structure—and with what it affords organisms. It comprises that segment of environmental design theory shown in the following diagram:

Subject Matter of Theory	Orientation of Theory	
	Positive	*Normative*
Procedural	Part 2 Chapters 4–7	Part 3
Substantive	Part 2 Chapters 8–19	

The concern in this book is with the contribution of the behavioral sciences, thus our interest here is in the human purposes served by the built environment rather than in the way its materials and the facts of geometry allow it to be configured.

The traditional model of the concerns of architecture is that of Vitruvius, which will be the basic organizing model here. There are two concerns basic to all designs: the commodity component and the aesthetic component—the first, providing shelter for activities and the second, a layout that affords delight. It has already been pointed out that delight and commodity cannot be considered as mutually exclusive aspects of design. There is commodity in delight and delight in commodity. To understand more fully the role of the built environment in people's lives, however, we need a basic understanding of the nature of the environment and the nature of human behavior. We now have a much richer and more systematic understanding than was available to the architects of the Modern Movement. The normative position taken here is that we need to *use* it. This discussion of positive architectural theory is divided into three components: Fundamental Concepts of Environment and Human Behavior; Activity Patterns and the Built Environment; and Aesthetic Values and the Built Environment. ■

FUNDAMENTAL CONCEPTS OF ENVIRONMENT AND HUMAN BEHAVIOR

Fundamental to an understanding of the role of the built environment in people's lives is an understanding of what is meant by "environment." The key attribute of any definition is that environments "surround" (Gibson 1966, Ittelson 1973). So any definition, description, or explanation of the nature and functioning of the environment must be with reference to something surrounded. Of particular interest to us is what surrounds people at an ecological level—the level of everyday human behavior. Such a description is presented in chapter 8, "The Nature of the Environment." The basic point made is that the surroundings of humans consist of terrestrial, animate, social, and cultural components. Each of these affects the lives of people and the nature of their attitudes toward the built environment as well as their expectations of the work of designers. What architects create is a *potential environment* for human behavior; what a person uses and appreciates is his or her *effective environment*. The role of positive theory for the design professions is to enhance the ability of designers to predict what the effective environment of people will be when the built environment is configured in a particular pattern.

Any ecologically valid description of the human environment makes some reference to human behavior, thus some assumptions regarding human behavior are made in chapter 8. These observations are taken a step further in chapter 9, "Fundamental Processes of Human Behavior." The goal of the chapter is not to summarize all that is known about human behavior, but rather to concentrate on developing an understanding of spatial behavior and the processes of motivation, perception, cognition, and affect so that designers will be better able to structure environments to satisfy human activities and aesthetic values. One of the problems in attempting to present a conceptually clear statement on the nature of the environment and the nature of human behavior is that there are different and sometimes mutually exclusive theories about the same phenomenon.

Architects have a reputation for grabbing one theory, accepting it as factual, and developing a normative position based on it, or alternatively using it to rationalize a particular prejudice they may have. The acceptance of Gestalt theory and the sociological theories of Mueller Lyer at the Bauhaus were examples of this. Architects have to make decisions, but they need to be aware that much is unknown and that, although it is often necessary to take a stance supporting one theory over another, they are really operating under uncertainty. The conclusions drawn in these circumstances must be held open for future refinement and possibly for refutation.

With a basic understanding of the nature of the environment and the nature of human behavior, it is possible to develop a framework and a set of concepts that will provide a more complete picture of the relationship between environment and behavior than is found in the current ideology of architectural determinism. This is done in chapter 10, "The Built Environment and Human Behavior."

The three chapters of this part of the book provide the basis for developing a model of substantive theory for environmental design. Implicit in the chapters is a preliminary demonstration that existing theories of human behavior can illuminate the concerns of interior design, architecture, landscape architecture, and urban design. ■

8

THE NATURE OF THE ENVIRONMENT

The word *environment* is widely used today, so widely that there is often confusion over what is being discussed. A geographer may be referring to landforms and climate, a psychologist to people and their personalities, a sociologist to social organizations and processes, and an architect to buildings and landscapes. The categorization depends on the purpose it serves (Porteous 1977).

Some analysts distinguish between the *physical*, the *social*, the *psychological*, and the *behavioral* environment. The physical consists of the terrestrial or geographical setting, the social of the interpersonal and intergroup organizations that exist, the psychological of the images that people have in their heads, and the behavioral of those elements to which a person responds. The basic point of such a classification system and others like it is the differentiation between the actual, real, or objective world that surrounds an individual and the phenomenological world that is perceived and that consciously or unconsciously affects people's behavioral patterns and emotional responses.

The distinction harks back, at least, to Gestalt psychology. Kurt Koffka (1935) differentiated between the *geographical environment* and the *behavioral environment*. The geographical environment refers to the objective environment—what is really around an individual; the behavioral environment consists of the cognitive image of the objective environment that forms the basis for behavior. Others (Lewin

1951, Kirk 1963, Gans 1968) make a similar distinction though they may use different terms. Kirk differentiates between the *phenomenal* (Lewin's term) and the *personal* environment, for instance. The personal environment in this case consists of individual images of the world (the behavioral components) and the set of beliefs and attitudes about it (the experiential component). C. Douglas Porteous (1977), influenced by Lewin and by Kirk, adds the "contextual environment" to the concepts of phenomenal and personal environments. He writes:

> Beliefs, attitudes, preferences, and other personality attributes derive from the individual alone, but are largely colored by his experiences as a member of a family, ethnic, social class, cultural, national, and life style groups.

The goal of these categorization schemes is to provide a framework for those things that have an impact on our lives. All the schemes recognize the existence of a *potential* environment for behavior and an *effective* environment that consists of what a person pays attention to and/or uses (Gibson 1966, Gans 1968).

This chapter is concerned with the nature of the potential environment. It focuses on the world around us. It is important to remember that we all create a "mental image" of the world around us and that this image varies from person to person because it does not correspond to "reality." The model of the environment presented here is also an abstraction, an image itself.

THE ENVIRONMENT

Natural scientists have made a number of observations of interest to those interested in developing design theory. One is that organisms are linked in a complex network of relationships. A second is that all organisms, whether animate or inanimate, are affected by internal and external forces, and a third is that they all can adapt to a range of forces. In response to buffeting by their surroundings, some organisms have the ability to adapt to them. To understand the external forces and the adaptation processes one has to understand the nature of the phenomenal world.

There are some generalizations that one can safely make about the phenomenal world. Life, to the best of our knowledge, has developed only in the *terrestrial* environment, which possesses qualities that sustain life as we know it. Different organisms have found different niches in it. The environment of an organism also consists of other organisms. Some of these are of the same species, so that the environment of an individual human can be said to consist of an *animate* or social component. For humans, at least, life is part of and exists within a *cultural* environment.

It is possible to differentiate between components of the environment in other ways, but this model of the environment developed by James J. Gibson (1966) enables a clear statement to be made on the nature of the built, or artificial, environment. This model provides us with a structure for understanding the environment in which we grow up and spend our lives and the environment that affords us some things and not others.

The Terrestrial, or Geographical, Environment

Architects, landscape architects, and urban designers use the term *physical environment* to refer to the nonsocial and noncultural aspects of our surroundings. Buildings along with such things as climate are included in this definition, thus the definition lacks precision. The terrestrial environment, in contrast, refers only to the nature of the earth and its processes at any point on it. It is important to understand these processes because, with the exception of some preliminary explorations in outer space and on the surface of the moon, the environment of people is the planet earth. The built environment consists of adaptations to the terrestrial environment.

All forms of life exist within specific geographic contexts. Some things are constant everywhere on earth but other things vary. Gravity exists everywhere, but the distribution of hills, valleys, trees and other forms of vegetation, as well as seas and lakes, varies. Some areas are more fertile than others. The arrangement of these characteristics at any locale affords different things for different people and thus they have very much influenced behavior. Some aspects of the environment place severe control on human behavior. The earth rotates on its axis and moves around the sun, resulting in diurnal and seasonal cycles. Life is shaped by these cycles. Some areas are uncomfortably hot; others are uncomfortably cold. Some can sustain the life of some organisms and not others. Although humans have developed techniques of reducing the effects of these processes, they remain central to the organization of day-to-day life and in the development of cultural systems (Vayda 1969).

The terrestrial environment consists of solid, liquid, and gaseous components. The rigidity and relative permanence of the solid environment allows animals, including humans, to move from one place to another and to orient themselves accurately (and also to get lost). The materials of the earth can be and have been recomposed into artificial substances by humans and some other animals (von Frisch 1974). People have built new surface configurations that better afford their needs than the natural ones. They have used both organic and inorganic materials to do this.

The sun's radiation has major consequences for life. It regulates the processes of photosynthesis and the carbon dioxide cycle, which are the basic requirements for human existence and for the nutritional cycle for animals. There is one aspect of the sun's radiation that is of central importance in life and in environmental design: light. This is not well understood.

Light

There are many descriptions of the wavelengths of that band of radiant energy we call light. Of interest to the physicist, these descriptions are largely irrelevant to the designer. The analysis of light from an ecological viewpoint is, however, of direct interest to the design professions because it is one of the variables of design.

There are two fundamental types of light, *radiant* and *ambient*. Incandescent substances—such as the sun or light bulbs—emit radiant light, which passes through different media with varying degrees of interference. It passes through a vacuum with no interference, through gases with a little, through translucent substances with more, and not at all through opaque substances. Opaque substances absorb some light and reflect the rest depending on the nature of the surface. The nature of the reflection gives a pigmentation, or color, to the surface. Ambient light consists of the light reflected from the surfaces of the world to any point. Its quality varies by time of day and season and the way artificial sources of radiant light and the surfaces of the world are organized. Only those surfaces directly exposed to radiant light receive it; all other surfaces receive diffused light from the sky or reflected light from other surfaces.

Perception is the physiological and psychological process of obtaining information from the environment. A person who is not blind obtains visual information about the world almost entirely from ambient light. There are other types of ambient information in the environment such as sonic and olfactory information, as any blind person will know (Brodey 1969). Designers are not as sensitive to them as they should be probably because the medium of design communication is the drawing (see Rasmussen 1959). (That is, of course, a normative statement!)

Nonvisual Ambient Information

In addition to the flow of light, the earth's atmosphere allows the transmission of vibrations and the diffusion of volatile substances. Light permits seeing, vibrations permit hearing, and the diffusion of volatile substances permits smelling, provided an organism has the appropriate receptors. The movement of air does not affect the transmission of light, but it does affect the transmission of sound and odors.

Light and sound both move in wave form. Light travels in straight lines, but sounds and smells drift in the wind and go around solid edges, which exclude light. Light is reflected off the surfaces of the earth and is diffused by dust particles in the atmosphere. Sounds may echo to some extent in an enclosed or partially enclosed space, but they do not reverberate like light, nor can they pass through a vacuum. Sounds are caused by a variety of mechanical events such as shearing, collisions, frictional movements, and rolling movements. The wave train that results is specific to the event. People are capable of recognizing a much greater array of sounds and their causes than physicists can describe.

Chemical events give off volatile substances, thus the composition of the air varies from place to place. Different organisms have different abilities and what they can perceive tends to be those types of information that are relevant to them. Some odors are innately pleasant to humans; others are unpleasant. Some have pleasant associations; others have negative ones. We learn to perceive these because much in life depends on this ability. Like sounds, odors are affected by the movement of air, but the strength and nature of an odor is specific to its source. Humans are not very good at describing odors, but our ability to do so in everyday terms is better than in the terms of physics.

Another source of environmental stimulation for animals consists of mechanical contacts with the environment. Humans learn to differentiate between all kinds of mechanical contacts (rolling, rubbing, compression, torsion, stretching) as well as the attributes of the environment that cause the accompanying deformation of the skin. Similarly, people have the ability to detect heat and cold, but not the ability to differentiate between sources of heat and cold except by using their visual, auditory, or olfactory senses.

The terrestrial environment is thus the source of many human experiences: radiant and ambient light, heat, sounds, odors, and mechanical contacts. The way designers structure the environment affects all these. It also affects a very different type of stimulation—social stimulation from other animals.

The Animate Environment

The environment of humans contains other humans and other animals. Some of these have considerable control over their own lives and the degree of stimulation they offer others. The degree of control varies from species to species. Humans have considerable control.

Humans are the source of many simultaneous stimulations. We can provide visual, sonic, chemical, thermal, and mechanical stimulation to other humans, other animals, and the world around us. A very few animals are even sources of radiant light and electrical current. The nature and combination of potential stimulations are unique to each species as are the meanings afforded by them. The relationship of humans to each other is of particular importance in understanding the structure of the world and in changing it.

Social Stimulation and Social Interaction

Favorable natural adaptations have enabled some species to survive better than others. Survival has also been abetted by the sensitivity and support one animal of a species offers another. A social relationship exists between them. This is particularly well developed in higher-order animals, most of all in humans.

Social relationships depend on social stimulation and a response that in turn becomes the stimulation for another response. At least two animals are involved; sometimes it is many more. Social behavior is a basic ingredient of life for all species but it is very elaborate in humans. The *behavioral loop* of social interaction serves both instrumental and symbolic purposes.

These purposes, in turn, serve to meet a variety of needs. The loops are very complex and only recently, with the development of the behavioral sciences, have they been subjected to systematic scrutiny, although novelists and artists have long been interested in them. The extent to which the layout of the environment and the materials of which it is composed affect the channels of communication between the members of a behavioral loop is the extent to which the built environment affects human social processes.

People communicate with each other through touch and sound, visually through facial expressions and body positions, and through odors. Statements about the world, about other people, and about emotions are communicated in these ways. Of particular importance in humans is the use of speech. Speech enables one human to bring the attention of another to characteristics of the environment and events in it that are not immediately present. Writing takes this a step further. People also communicate indirectly with each other through the artifacts, including the buildings, with which they surround themselves (Rapoport 1982).

The Social System

Many animals, but particularly humans, operate within a social system. A social system consists of a set of individuals who directly or indirectly interact on a regular basis for specific purposes. The environment of any individual consists of a number of social systems. Within each of these there is some common expectation about the roles and behaviors of its members. The roles of the individuals reflect the norms of the social system.

Implicit in the concept of "systems" is the notion that a change in one part will affect another part. Thus changes in individual behavior may result in changes in the social system and vice versa. Changes at one level of a system may also lead to changes at another. To survive, each system has to carry out certain functions: it must recruit new members, teaching them the norms of the system; it must deal with internal and external threats and conflicts.

Social systems depend on communications processes for survival. As norms, roles and processes of communication are learned; they vary from culture to culture. Human behavior cannot be understood without reference to a social system and a culture any more than it can be understood without reference to its terrestrial environment. This is true of people generally; it is true of architects, landscape architects, urban designers, and other designers who are members of a smaller environmental design professional subculture as well as a broader societal one. The members of this subculture share some values but also hold different values on some matters.

The Cultural Environment

There are no clear distinctions among the terrestrial, animate, and cultural environments in everyday life, for culture develops out of natural opportunities, human interests, and competencies. One of the characteristics of history is that people have migrated from one part of the world to another taking many aspects of their own culture with them, so that there are many parts of the world where the culture is a symbolic legacy of previous situations.

Our beliefs and attitudes toward other people, the terrestrial environment, our roles in society, and the way we carry out daily activities are all parts of our culture. Writing, painting, and architecture are all means of communicating ideas about society and are culture-bound. They are artificial sources of stimulation and information about the world. The history of peoples can be traced through the artifacts they have created.

> Man is known by his artifacts, he is an artisan, an artificer, an employer of the arts, an artist, a creator of art. . . . The origin of pictures and sculpture can be dated with some confidence. It was achieved . . . some twenty to thirty thousand years ago. . . . Writing can be dated even more exactly since history began with written records. It began around four or five thousand years ago. (Gibson 1966)

Cultural norms are transmitted from one generation to the next through the process of socialization. Loyalty to these customs depends on the perception of the rewards and costs involved. There is considerable debate about the nature of these processes as shall be pointed out in the next chapter. While language, actions, and symbolic media are means for cultural education, many behaviors are learned through experience alone without overt rewards, according to some psychologists.

It must be remembered too that individuals

within a culture do not all behave in the same fashion. There is always some acceptable deviance from the norm. Thus, not all members of the same culture attend to the same things in the environment. Not all opportunities for action are perceived by an individual, nor are all the opportunities that are perceived acted on. The environment is rich in *affordances* for behavior; the set used by any society can be regarded as characteristic of that culture and of individual values and needs. The concept of affordances of the terrestrial, social, and cultural environment is a crucial one and central to the argument in this book. It requires some elaboration here.

THE AFFORDANCES OF THE ENVIRONMENT*

The word *afford* has been used frequently in this book already. It is a common English word. "Affordance," however, does not appear in any dictionary. It was coined by psychologist James J. Gibson (1979). The affordances of anything, be it material or nonmaterial, are those of its properties that enable it to be used in a particular way by a particular species or an individual member of that species. The properties of concern to Gibson are the physical properties of the configuration of an object or setting that allow it to be used for some overt activity. They also afford meanings and aesthetic appreciation. Some things are afforded by an object or environment—terrestrial, animate, or cultural—more readily than others; some activities and/or interpretations are afforded some people and not others by a particular configuration of the built environment. The basic point is that the affordances of a physical setting are what it offers for good or ill because of the characteristics of its configuration and the material of which it is fabricated. Architect Louis Kahn used the term *availabilities* and landscape architect Lancelot Brown the word *capabilities* in much the same way.

The concept of affordance is a simple yet powerful one. It is fundamental to environmental design theory. Different patterns of the built environment afford different behaviors and aesthetic experiences. The affordances of the environment thus limit or extend the behavioral and aesthetic choices of an individual depending on how the environment is configured. People have changed and continue to change the natural and the

artificial environments to alter the set of affordances they possess. Buildings comprise one subset of these changes.

The concept of affordance is related to some earlier concepts (Gibson 1979). Koffka (1935) suggested that objects have a *demand* or *invitational* quality. A mailbox thus invites mailing a letter, or, in Louis Kahn's terms, "a brick wants to be an arch." Gibson traces the concept back to Kurt Lewin's *Aufforderungscharakter* of objects. This has been translated into English as "invitational quality" by one author and as "valence" by another. Lewin, however, used his term differently from the way Gibson uses *affordance*.

Lewin believed that the valence of an object was bestowed on it by the needs and values of the perceiver. Thus the valence of an object changes with the needs of the perceiver. While an object does not change and its affordances do not change, its utility to a person changes with that person's needs. The object, according to Gibson, offers what it does because of what it is. Whether or not an observer recognizes its affordances depends on the nature of the observer, his experience, his competencies, and his needs. People learn the affordances of objects and environments and the culturally appropriate times to use them. The important thing, as Lewin recognized, is that the environment is full of opportunities and constraints because of its characteristics.

THE BUILT ENVIRONMENT

The built environment is a part of the terrestrial and cultural environments. Of concern here is the built environment as part of the habitat of humans, although many of the concepts covered in this book can be extended to include the artificial environments created by other animals, birds, reptiles, insects, and fish (von Frisch 1974). The architectural environment consists of the artificial arrangement of different surfaces of different materials with different pigmentations and/or different textures, illumination, and degrees of transparency or translucency, and of the spaces between them. These are the essential variables of design.

The built environment will be regarded here as the set of adaptations people have made to their terrestrial and cultural environments. The way people structure the surfaces of the world around them affects all the interactions between them and the terrestrial environment. It changes the patterns of heat and light, sound and odors, and the mechanical contacts a person experiences. To some extent it changes or results from changes in the social and cultural environments of people. Any change in the

---

* Parts of this discussion have been published previously. See Jon Lang, "The Built Environment and Social Behavior: Architectural Determinism Re-Examined," *VIA IV*, Cambridge, Mass.: MIT Press, 1980, pp. 146–153.

1

2   Photograph by Lee Copeland

3

8-1. The Concept of Affordance.

Any built environment possesses a set of affordances for human activities and aesthetic experiences. The entry steps in (1) have been complemented with a ramp. This affords people in wheelchairs access to the building. It also helps bicyclists. It was designed originally for elephants and rickshaws. The building in (2) affords various aesthetic interpretations, depending on the viewer's knowledge of the architect's intentions and his or her own associations. The residential area in (3) possesses many affordances that are important in people's lives: shelter, identity, privacy, territorial control—the list is long. It does not afford individual identity or territorial control as easily as does a single-family detached house.

built environment is likely to change the affordances of the world.

The properties of the environment have been changed to afford new activities and new aesthetic experiences or to afford old ones better. Gibson (1966) notes:

> People have paved and straightened the solid surfaces, altered the vegetation, regulated the paths, subdivided the places, eliminated dangers, provided islands of light during the night, and of comfort during the cold. . . . Most strikingly, they have flooded the environment with shapes, sounds and visible patterns which have meaning only to themselves.

These changes have been made so that the terrestrial, animate, and cultural environments should better serve an individual's or group's purposes. The changes reflect the beliefs and attitudes and resources of a time and help provide a pattern for the future. Sometimes everybody gains through the changes that are made; sometimes some people gain at the expense of others; sometimes short-term gains result in long-run losses; sometimes everybody has lost. The ideology of the Modern Movement has resulted in many gains but, if one accepts the analyses of critics, many losses as well (Jacobs 1961, Blake 1974, Brolin 1976).

Self-conscious and Unself-conscious Change

Some changes in the built environment result from natural processes—from wind and rain and sometimes from more violent occurrences such as volcanic explosions. Changes in the built environment initiated by humans result from one of two processes or a mixture of them. They can result from so-called adaptive change, which is incremental and unselfconscious, or they can result from self-consciously planned change (see also Alexander 1964, Broadbent 1973). Planned change involves the decision to make changes and the design of the nature of the changes to be made prior to embarking on them. Whatever process is used, the purpose is to change the affordance of the environment. Interior designers, architects, urban designers, and landscape architects have each taken on specific roles in society to deal with planned self-conscious change.

The Affordances of the Built Environment

The composition of the built environment affords a variety of things to the potential user. It affords visual stimulation and haptic stimulation; it might also provide sonic stimulation and olfactory stimulation. If a person eats it, it will provide another kind of stimulation! In addition to stimulation as such, the built environment affords many other things that support some behaviors and restrict others. The list is almost endless.

A preliminary list of the categories of affordance provided by buildings and other artificial layouts suggests the range of affordances that exist. At the simplest level, the horizontal surface underfoot affords locomotion if it is not liquid. Some surfaces are more slippery than others and afford sliding. In combination with vertical, sloping, and other horizontal surfaces, the built environment might pro-vide shelter from the weather, concealment, and security, as well as places for getting together with other people. These form the most basic affordances. In addition, if properly configured to form specific objects, surface compositions can afford use as toys, tools, and machines. They can also afford associational meanings in displays such as signs and symbols. Some of these affordances may be perceived only by members of a particular culture; some are universally perceived.

The affordances of a particular pattern of the built environment are a property of its layout, of the materials of which it is fabricated, and of the way it is illuminated—with reference, always, to a particular set of people. In terms of the most concrete meanings (such as the perception of depth), the recognition of the affordances of the environment seems to be a function of the biological nature of people; at the symbolic level the affordances are a function of social convention and experience. At that level they are dependent on the socialization that a person goes through as part of a culture. As the perception of affordance is so much a function of individual and group characteristics and human motivations, the fundamental processes of human behavior need to be described in greater detail than in this chapter. A richer description will provide a richer understanding of the built environment and the purposes it serves for people.

ADDITIONAL READINGS

Fitch, James Marston. *American Building 2: The Environmental Forces that Shape It.* New York: Schocken, 1972.

Gibson, James J. "The Environment as a Source of Stimulation." In *The Senses Considered as Perceptual Systems.* Boston: Houghton Mifflin, 1966, pp. 7–30.

Porteous, J. Douglas. "Environments." In *Environment and Behavior.* Reading, Mass.: Addison-Wesley, 1977, pp. 133–147.

9

FUNDAMENTAL PROCESSES OF HUMAN BEHAVIOR

The work of environmental designers is very much influenced by their concepts of human nature. These have varied during history. At one time people are perceived as being free-willed, at another as controlled by their environments. The latter view was central to the thinking of the Modernists in architecture and remains so in much architectural theory today. During one period people are believed to be rational, at another irrational (Neisser 1977). This difference is reflected in the differences between first- and second-generation models of the design process. Anthropological, sociological, and psychological research has reduced some of the mysteriousness of human behavior but much remains unknown. Our present understanding does, however, clarify much about the person-environment interface and thus about environmental design.

The environment is potentially rich in affordances for human experiences and behavior. The basic processes involved in the interaction between people and their environment are shown in figure 9-1. Information about the environment is obtained through perceptual processes that are guided by *schemata* motivated by *needs*. These schemata are partially innate and partially learned. They form the linkage between *perception* and *cognition*. They guide not only the perceptual processes but also emotional responses *(affect)* and actions *(spatial behavior)*, which in turn affect the schemata as the outcomes of behavior are discerned. Human feel-

ings and actions are limited by the affordances of the natural and built environments, the cultural environment, and the intrapsychic states of the people concerned.

The explanation of these processes of behavior is inevitably guided by an overall concept or schema. That given here has been called the "environmental perception and behavior approach" (Patricios 1975). It is a model that focuses on individuals and groups of individuals. This can be contrasted with models that deal with aggregates of people as individuals. The approach used here deals with the fac-

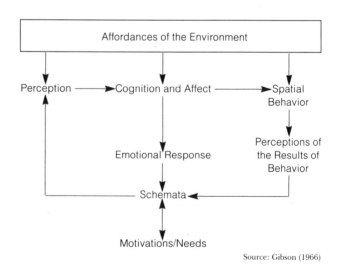

Source: Gibson (1966)

9-1. The Fundamental Processes of Human Behavior.

84

tors underlying behavior at the scale of buildings, urban complexes, and open spaces rather than at a regional scale.

Within the "environmental perception and cognition approach," there are different theories of perception, cognition, and spatial behavior. These theories, although based on research, are often highly speculative and untested. It is important for the designer to understand them so that their implications for the concerns of environmental design can be comprehended. In presenting these theoretical issues, stress will be placed on what designers need to know, and on what we do and do not know in order to clarify positive environmental design theory. The discussion will proceed from *motivation* to *perception* to *cognition and affect* to *spatial behavior* to the subject of *individual differences* in behavior.

MOTIVATION

Motivation is the guiding force behind behavior. Behavior is directed toward the satisfaction of needs. Therefore it is important for environmental design theory to be based on some concept of human needs. A number of such models exist (such as H. Murray 1938, Maslow 1943, 1954, Erikson 1950, Fromm 1950, Whiting and Child 1953, A. Leighton 1959). They all attempt to explain "internal forces"—physiological and psychological, conscious and unconscious—and types of needs from the most basic to the loftiest. Two of the models especially have been used by environmental designers in thinking about what the built environment should afford people: Alexander Leighton's scale of *essential striving sentiments* (1959), and Abraham Maslow's *hierarchy of human needs* (1943, 1954).

Leighton's model has been found by certain writers to be a "convenient handle" for understanding the nature of the built environment with respect to humans (Alexander 1969, Perin 1970). Leighton identifies the following needs: (1) physical security, (2) sexual satisfaction, (3) the expression of hostility, (4) the expression of love, (5) the securing of love, (6) the receiving of recognition, (7) the expression of spontaneity, (8) orientation in terms of one's place in society and the places of others, (9) the securing and maintenance of membership in a definite group, and (10) belonging to a moral order. Some of these needs have to do with what the environment affords at an instrumental level (for example, security, the expression of spontaneity), and others at a symbolic level (for example, recognition, membership). The list is, however, cumbersome and is not ordered in an explicit fashion. Maslow's model, though similar to Leighton's, is easier to re-

late to the concerns of environmental design.

Maslow suggests that there is a hierarchy of needs from the strongest to the weakest, with the stronger taking precedence over the weaker. His hierarchy from strongest to weakest is as follows: *physiological needs*, such as hunger and thirst; *safety needs*, such as security and protection from physical harm; *belonging and love needs*, such as membership in a group and the receiving of affection; *esteem needs*, those desires of an individual to be held in high value by himself or herself and others; *actualization needs*, representing the desire to fulfill one's capacities; and *cognitive and aesthetic needs*, such as the thirst for knowledge and the desire for beauty for its own sake.

This classification provides a framework for thinking about the concerns of environmental design and for the concerns of the designer. The built environment provides for human physiological needs, such as shelter; for safety needs, physical and psychological security; for belonging and esteem needs, through environmental symbolism as well as through specific sets of activities; for actualization needs, through the freedom of choice; for cognitive needs, through access to opportunities for development; and for aesthetic needs, through formal beauty. Much that contributes to the meeting of these needs, however, has very little to do with the built environment.

Some needs are physiologically based, some are sociologically or psychologically based, and some are a mixture. The more basic needs are physiologically based; the need to belong may have a physiological component but is socially and culturally biased, whereas the need for self-actualization and cognitive and aesthetic needs are largely psychological (Moleski 1978). The degree to which each need has to be fulfilled varies from person to person, depending on the individual's philosophy of life, personality, culture, and habituation level—what they are used to. Not everybody seeks a large measure of bodily comfort; some people stress aesthetic needs over physiological ones. Some are prepared to give their lives for what they believe. People do, however, look at the environment partly in terms of their needs; what they discern is largely based on their needs and on what they have learned to perceive.

PERCEPTION

Perception is the process of obtaining information from and about one's surroundings. It is active and purposeful. It is where cognition and reality meet (Neisser 1977). There have been several major attempts to describe and explain why we perceive what we do. They have influenced environmental design theory very much, particularly by their efforts to develop aesthetic philosophies. Designers have not always realized how conjectural these theories of perception are. The result has been that they have drawn very strong conclusions about the purposes of design based on very inadequate evidence.

There are two basic sets of theories of perception. One focuses on the reception of sensory experience and the other on the senses as active and interrelated systems. The first set attempts to explain how sense data, the supposed units of perception, get put together in the brain. *Empiricism* (Titchner 1910, Helmholtz 1925, Carr 1935) suggests by association. *Transactionalism* (Ames 1960, Ittelson and Cantrel 1954), which influenced the writings on environmental design of people such as Walter Gropius (1947), Lewis Mumford (1952), and Clifford Moller (1968), stresses the role of experience. *Nativist and Rationalist* theories (see Cassirer 1954, Piaget 1955, Chomsky 1957) stress the role of innate ideas and the making of rational inferences from sensations. Christian Norberg-Schulz's discourse on design (1964) is very much influenced by this theoretical approach to perception. *Gestalt* theory argues that the basis for the integration is the spontaneous organization of sensory inputs to the brain (Köhler 1929, Koffka 1935, Wertheimer 1938, Ellis 1939), whereas *information-processing* theories suggest that there are computerlike processes in the brain. Gestalt theory has influenced design theory (see Kepes 1944, Ushenko 1953, de Sausmarez 1964, Isaac 1971, Arnheim 1977) more than any other perception theory, whereas information-processing theories are the basis for the writings on aesthetics of people such as Abraham Moles (1966).

In contrast to these theories is the *ecological approach* of James Gibson (1966, 1979) and Eleanor Gibson (1969), who suggest that perception is information based. This should not be confused with the information-processing cybernetic models of perception. The Gibsons acknowledge the reality of sensory experience but regard it as a by-product rather than the "building blocks of perception." Ulrich Neisser (1977) added the concept of *schema* as a "connecting link between perception and the higher mental processes" to the basic theory.

While Gestalt theory has most influenced the ideas of environmental designers during the course of this century, it has been seriously challenged as an explanation of how the world is perceived by transactionalist and ecological theories in recent times. It is important to understand these three interpretations of the processes of perception, because they have influenced and will continue to influence our thinking about the nature of environmental design at all scales.

The Gestalt Theory of Perception

The Bauhaus formulation of basic design was considered to be factual because it drew so heavily on, and/or was so heavily corroborated by, Gestalt theory. Artists such as Kandinsky (Overy 1969) and Kepes (1944) must have been attracted by Gestalt theory's emphasis on pattern perception. The speculative nature of much of Gestalt theory was, however, not clearly recognized. To understand Gestalt theory, its attraction for artists and architects, and what it still affords us in creating positive environmental design theory, one must understand its concepts of *form, isomorphism,* and *field forces.*

Form is fundamental. It is that which stands apart as a closed and structured element in the visual world (Katz 1950). "The *solid figure* appears as something apart, behind which the *ground* seems to extend without interruption like a homogeneous plane" (Köhler 1929). Gestalt psychologists compiled a list of factors that influence the perception of form. Seven of these are of importance to environmental design theory because they tell us much about how units in the environment are perceived. They are the "laws" of *proximity, similarity, closure, good continuance, closedness, area,* and *symmetry.*

Proximity is the simplest condition of organization (Hochberg 1964). According to Gestalt theory, objects that are close together tend to be grouped together visually, the relative closeness offering the least resistance to the interconnection of sensory units. This law is illustrated in figure 9-2a. The rows and columns are seen with equal ease in (i), but in (ii) the pattern is perceived as a set of rows.

Proximity can yield to other factors of organization. Figure 9-2b illustrates the law of similarity. If elements have similar qualities—size, texture, color, and so forth—they tend to be perceived as single units, as in (i) rather than in (ii). In figure 9-2c a conflicting situation is shown. Here it is possible to impose an organization based on similarity or proximity. Artists describe this state as one of tension.

The law of closure states that optical units tend to be shaped into closed wholes (Köhler 1929). In figure 9-2d two such cases are illustrated. The pattern in diagram (i) tends to be seen as a completed circle and (ii) as a triangle. The openings in the figures seem insignificant or extremely important, depending on one's focus.

The law of good continuance states that people

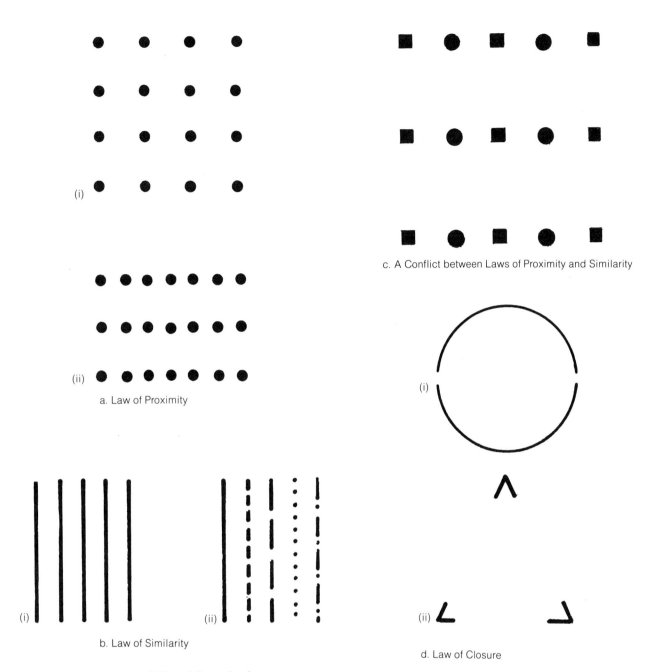

a. Law of Proximity

b. Law of Similarity

c. A Conflict between Laws of Proximity and Similarity

d. Law of Closure

9-2. The Gestalt Laws of Visual Organization.

tend to perceive continuous elements as single units. In figure 9-2e we perceive (i) as two lines crossing and not as two L's. We perceive (ii) as a sine wave on a castellated background, although the law of closedness suggests that we should see it as a set of closed forms. We see (iii) as a two-dimensional representation of a surface extending behind two others.

The other laws of organization are not so fundamental. The law of area states that the smaller a closed area the more it tends to be seen as a figure. The law of symmetry states that the more symmetrical a closed area the more it tends to be seen as a figure. The law of closedness suggests that areas with closed contours tend to be seen as units more generally than those without them. Thus in 9-2f (i) the shape with a closed contour tends to be seen as a unit; we tend to see the frame in (ii) and the window in (iii), while in 9-2g the shaded area appears to be seen as a column on a white background.

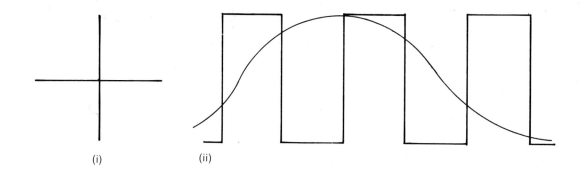

(i)   (ii)

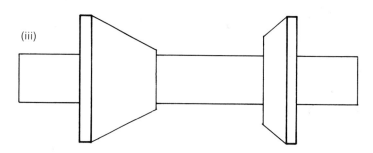

(iii)

e. Law of Good Continuance

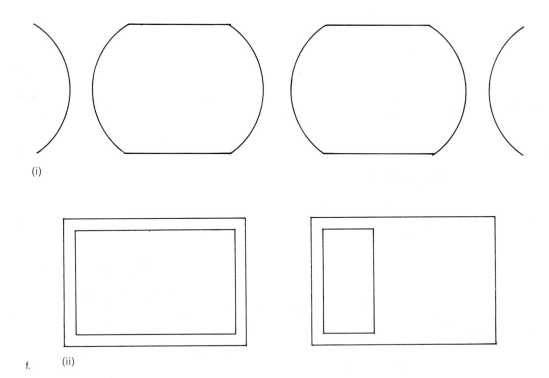

(i)

f.   (ii)

9-2, *continued.*

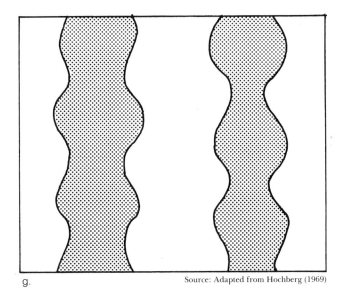

g. Source: Adapted from Hochberg (1969)

9-2, *continued.*

All of these laws are explained in terms of *isomorphism,* an hypothesized parallelism between the form of underlying neurological processes and the form of the perceptual experience (Köhler 1929). Rudolf Arnheim (1965) notes:

> The forces which are experienced when looking at visual objects can be considered the psychological equivalent of physiological forces active in the brain center of vision. Although these processes occur physiologically in the brain, they are properties of the perceived objects themselves.

All these forces are said to occur in some field or environment. *Field forces,* as in mathematics, are said to have an area of application, a direction, and a magnitude. The state of the field is the result of all the forces acting there (Koffka 1935). All these forces are governed by the principle of *Pragnanz.* According to this principle, perceptions take the most stable form under the circumstances.

In summary, Gestalt theory suggests that all our perceptions are organized into figures—this book is a figure with the surroundings as ground. In addition, patterns of lines, planes, and objects appear to have certain "dynamic" qualities—they appear to move, or to be heavy or light, happy or sad. This is explained by the isomorphism between perceptual experience and human neurological processes. This is the basis for the Gestalt theory of expression in art and architecture (Arnheim 1949, 1968, 1977, Levi 1974). According to Gestalt theory these are not subjective associations with visual patterns. They precede the perception of pattern. Arnheim (1968) writes:

The theory would seem to explain why in actual experience the dynamic or expressive aspects are the most powerful and immediate qualities of the percept.

This is a controversial observation, but it is implicit and often explicit in much Cubist art and in modern architectural ideology—normative theory.

The concept of isomorphism has been severely challenged in recent times. R. L. Gregory (1966) notes:

> There is no independent evidence for such brain processes and no independent way of discovering their properties. If there is no way of discovering their properties then they are highly suspect.

There is much experimental evidence that supports this contention (such as Lashley, Chow, and Semmes 1951). The introspective analyses of design theorists have led also to a doubt that it exists (Colquhoun 1967). Recent theories of perception suggest it is unnecessary (Gibson 1966, 1979). Findings can be explained in terms of learned associations of patterns with feelings.

The legacy of Gestalt theory is a major one both in psychology (Gibson 1971) and in environmental design. Its empirical observations of the ways in which we order the environment still offer much for environmental design where formal aesthetic issues of unity often arise. It forms the basis from which the ecological approach to perception is derived (Gibson 1950). At the same time many questions about the processes of perception have been more thoroughly addressed by more recent theories.

The Transactional Theory of Perception

Transactional theory emphasizes the role of experience in perception and focuses on the dynamic relationship between person and environment. Perception is considered to be a *transaction* in which the environment, the observer, and the perception are mutually dependent on each other. William Ittelson (1960) defines the process as follows:

> Perception is that part of the living process by which each of us, from his own particular point of view, *creates* for himself the world in which . . . he tries to gain his satisfaction.

The intellectual underpinnings for this position are in transactional philosophy (Dewey and Bentley 1949), the psychology of Adelbert Ames (1960), and the sociology of George Mead (1903). Transactional theory makes a number of assumptions about the processes of perception, some of which are unique to it and some widely held:

- Perception is multimodal
- Perception is an active not a passive process
- Perception cannot be explained by separating behavior into the perceiver and the perceived
- Perception cannot be explained in terms of conditioned responses to stimuli
- The person–environment relationship is a dynamic one
- The image of the environment that an observer has depends on past experiences as well as on present motives and attitudes
- Past experiences are projected onto the present situation in relationship to one's needs
- Perception is governed by expectancies and predispositions.

The result is that the information a person obtains from the environment has a probabilistic nature which is validated through action (Ittelson 1960).

The information obtained from the environment has symbolic properties that give it meaning, ambient qualities that evoke emotional responses, and motivational messages that stimulate needs. An individual also assigns value and aesthetic properties to it. Because humans need to experience the environment as a pattern of meaningful relationships, past experiences form the basis for understanding the new.

People describe their perceptions either experientially or structurally, according to studies within the transactional approach (Ittelson et al. 1976). Experiential descriptions consist of moods, feelings, and self-reports. Structural descriptions involve reports of what is actually perceived in terms of the physical or social structure of the world. Environmental designers think of the world in structural terms to a greater degree than other people do.

Donald Appleyard, an architect/planner, takes what is essentially a transactionalist view of perception—although his ideas are more directly related to those of Jerome Bruner (1966) than to those of Ittelson (Appleyard, 1973). He organizes perceptual information into three categories: *operational*—that needed by people to attain their goals; *responsive*—the distinctive characteristics that intrude into actions; and *inferential*—that which forms the basis for coding systems for recognizing elements of the world.

The important contribution of transactional theory to environmental design theory is the recognition that experience shapes what people pay attention to in the environment and what is important to them. Any positive theory of aesthetics has to

recognize this. It reminds us that looking at the world as an environment is different than looking at it as an object although we can attend it in that way. There are, however, areas of perceptual research that can enrich environmental design theory that have not been addressed by either Gestalt theory or transactionalism. A coexisting and at least partially contradictory theory of perception—the ecological approach—deals with some of them.

The Ecological Theory of Perception

The ecological approach to perception is a radical one (see Cutting 1982). It contradicts the Gestalt concept of isomorphism and the transactional interpretation of the role of experience in perception. Instead of considering the senses as channels of sensation, it regards the senses as perceptual systems (Gibson 1966). These are listed in the accompanying table.

While the recognition that perception is multimodal is universal (though often neglected by environmental designers), the hypothesis that the structure of light, sound waves, and other sources of perception can convey information about the world directly without the mind having to reconstruct "meaningless sense data" is controversial. In terms of visual perception, the Gibsons note that as long as the environment is illuminated, the sheaf of light rays that converge at a station point is structured by the faces and facets of the world. When a person moves, this structure is transformed. The Gibsons argue that there is information in this structure and in its transformation which is directly perceivable. It does not matter what the level of illumination is except that at low levels the finer details of the structure are lost.

People explore the environment to perceive the finer details by moving their eyes, heads, and bodies. With experience, a person is able to identify the finer and finer details of the world and broader and broader relationships (Gibson and Gibson 1955). With experience, a person learns to pay attention to details of the world that were not attended to before. Any normative movement in environmental design brings people's attention to some variables rather than others.

According to this model, the world consists of surfaces varying from longitudinal to horizontal (see figure 9-3). The texture of the horizontal intensifies with distance from the observer. The ability to recognize this fundamental cue for depth perception seems to be innate (E. Gibson and Walk 1960) and not learned through transactions with the environment. Architects have, from time to time, pur-

The Senses Considered as Perceptual Systems

Name	Mode of Attention	Receptive Units	Anatomy of the Organ	Activity of the Organ	Stimuli Available	External Information Obtained
Basic orienting system	General orientation	Mechano-receptors	Vestibular organs	Body equilibrium	Forces of gravity and acceleration	Direction of gravity, being pushed
Auditory system	Listening	Mechano-receptors	Cochlear organs with middle ear and auricle	Orienting to sounds	Vibration in the air	Nature and location of vibratory events
Haptic system	Touching	Mechano-receptors and possibly thermoreceptors	Skin (including attachments and openings), joints (including ligaments), muscles (including tendons)	Exploration of many kinds	Deformations of tissues, configuration of joints, stretching of muscle fibers	Contact with the earth, mechanical encounters, object shapes, material states—solidity or viscosity
Taste-smell system	Smelling	Chemo-receptors	Nasal cavity (nose)	Sniffing	Composition of the medium	Nature of volatile sources
	Tasting	Chemo- and mechano-receptors	Oral cavity (mouth)	Savoring	Composition of ingested objects	Nutritive and bio-chemical values
Visual system	Looking	Photo-receptors	Ocular mechanism (eyes, with intrinsic and extrinsic eye muscles, as related to the vestibular organs, the head, and the whole body)	Accommodation, pupillary adjustment, fixation, convergence, exploration	Variables of structure in ambient light	Everything that can be specified by the variables of optical structure (information about objects, animals, motions, events, and places)

posefully manipulated these texture gradients to create illusions of depth. This was particularly prevalent during the Renaissance. The permanent backstage of Palladio's Teatro Olimpico in Vicenza is an example of this. He attained an illusion of great depth in a limited space.

Of particular importance in perceiving the structure of the environment, both artificial and natural, is the recognition that some surfaces of the world hide others (see figure 9-4). Even when one is standing on a flat plain, the horizon "cuts off" the world. The actual part that is hidden changes as the point of observation changes (except when one is in a totally enclosed windowless room when everything beyond is hidden). When a person moves through the environment, one vista after another is seen. This occurs in moving from room to room in a building, when reaching the brow of a hill or the corner of a street. Rex Martienssen (1956) analyzes Greek architecture in these terms, and Philip Thiel (1961), Gordon Cullen (1962) and Edmund Bacon (1974) provide many examples of this phenomenon at the urban scale and stress its importance in the aesthetic experience. Much of the work of the land-

scape architect Lawrence Halprin reflects a careful consideration of this concept in design (Halprin 1965). The psychological analysis of the role of movement is one of the Gibsons' major contributions to perception theory (see J. Gibson 1950, 1966, 1979).

Another major contribution to both psychological and environmental design theory has already been introduced. This is the concept of *affordance*. The ability to perceive some of the affordances of the environment seems to be innate or a function of the physiological maturation of people. Others are learned through experience or by having one's attention brought to them. Gibson (1979) notes:

> The human observer learns to detect the value or meaning of things, perceiving their distinctive features, putting them into categories and subcategories, noticing their similarities and differences and even studying them for their own sake apart from learning what to do with them.

To detect meaning, an observer does not have to attend to every variable contained in the optic array. Attention is thus selective. People attend to what

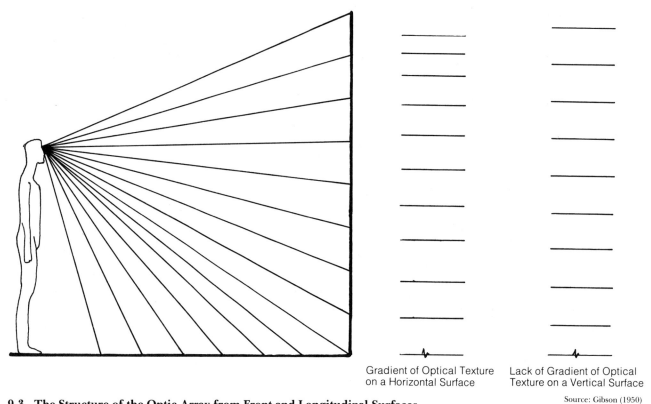

Gradient of Optical Texture
on a Horizontal Surface

Lack of Gradient of Optical
Texture on a Vertical Surface

Source: Gibson (1950)

9-3. The Structure of the Optic Array from Front and Longitudinal Surfaces.

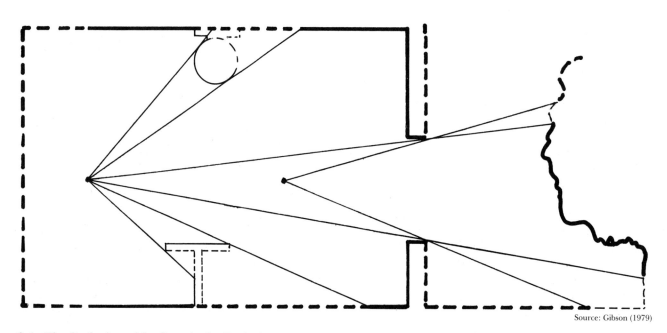

Source: Gibson (1979)

9-4. The Occlusion of Surfaces in the Optic Array.

they know about and what they are motivated to recognize. This depends on their prior experiences.

The linkages of the processes of perception to cognition are unclear in this formulation of perception theory. What goes on in the observer's head? What guides perception? How do we see what we do? Ulrich Neisser (1977) believes that the cognitive structures crucial for perception are anticipatory *schemata*. People can only perceive what they know how to find. The search process is guided by schemata, some of which are innate and some learned. A newborn baby turns toward a sound; it takes much learning to discern the differences among wines, perhaps even more to understand the different aesthetic philosophies in architecture. A schema directs exploration; experience modifies the schema. This involves learning, a basic cognitive process.

Conclusions on Perception

The coexistence of contradictory theories of perception shows the conjectural nature of our understanding of the perceptual processes. There are, however, a number of matters on which there is agreement. Perception is multimodal; movement plays a major part in environmental perception; we learn to differentiate finer details and broader classes of environmental phenomena with experience; the Gestalt "laws" of visual organization may not be the basis of perception, but they may well be ways in which we order the environment; the Gestalt concepts of "field forces" and "isomorphism" and thus the architectural concepts of the universality of "expressiveness" of lines and planes are open to serious question, and the way in which we look at the environment depends on our purposes and experience. Above all, the assumption that perception is largely or completely determined by the characteristics of external stimuli is a dubious one. These factors all need to be recognized in the development of positive theories of the person–environment interface and positive theories of aesthetics.

COGNITION AND AFFECT

Cognitive psychology deals with the acquisition, organization, and storage of knowledge. It focuses on issues of thinking, learning, remembering, feeling, and mental development. *Affect* deals with emotion and is concerned with likes and dislikes. It involves an understanding of values and attitude-formation. An understanding of the processes of cognition and affect can make a major contribution to the understanding of environmental aesthetics and the choices people make in the use of the environment.

Since World War I, the study of cognition has been dominated by the psychoanalytical and behaviorist schools of psychology. The former focuses on the subconscious mind, while the latter focuses on the impact of reinforcement patterns on learning. More recently information-processing models of cognition have become prominent. None of them fully accounts for how people act and interact in the world. The answers to the questions that an environmental designer would ask are thus speculative. How do people look at the environment? How are environmental meanings and their importances learned? How are likes and dislikes developed? Why are some places better remembered than others? These are all questions involving the basic cognitive processes of learning and remembering.

Learning and Memory

Human behavior is highly plastic. So much so that sometimes urban designers and architects, among others, seem to have forgotten that there are limits to human adaptability. People do have, and show, a large capacity to adapt their activities to the affordances of new built environments, to adapt the built environment to their needs, and to learn new aesthetic values. The processes central to this adaptive ability are learning, remembering, and generalizing.

According to behaviorists (for example, Skinner 1938, 1953), learning takes place when an individual associates a new response to a given stimulus, resulting in a permanent change in behavior. This occurs when the event following the response is a positive one such as the reception of parental approval. Punishment, on the other hand, would help to extinguish the response. Other psychologists believe that people learn for subjective satisfaction as well.

What has been learned may not be reflected in overt behavior (Manis 1964). Thus, the behaviorist principle of reinforcement seems to be primarily concerned with performance, not with learning. What we learn, however, does seem to involve some knowledge of the outcomes of behavior and some sort of reinforcement, either internal or external. This applies to environmental attitudes as well as to activity patterns. These attitudes also affect future behavior. Some things are forgotten, however, while others endure in memory.

Remembering and forgetting are serious practical concerns in almost every sphere of human endeavor. The way we use buildings and cities depends partially on how well their structures are remembered from past visits (Lynch 1960, Appleyard 1969, Passini 1984). People tend to forget things over time, but time, itself, does not cause forgetting. Some things are easier to remember than others. The rate at which we forget things depends on their importance to us, how well categorized or organized they are (the Gestalt laws of organization apply here for the built environment), and how deviant they are from the norm. Landmarks tend to be visual phenomena that are deviant from their surroundings (Lynch 1960).

Categorization and Generalization

Studies (such as Carmichael, Hogan, and Walter 1932) have clearly shown that the way in which we categorize and label things can either aid or distort memory. This is particularly true if there is some ambiguity in the original item. For instance, we develop categories of environmental designers (architects, landscape architects, urban designers) and subcategories (Modernists, Post-Modernists) based on certain commonalities in their work. A designer may be classified on one dimension of his or her work but this may be a misrepresentation of the whole body of that designer's work. Future perceptions of that work are then biased by the classification.

The ability to learn how things are related in categories and how to use categories is central to human existence. It depends on the cognitive processes of generalization. Without the ability to generalize from past experience, people would not be able to function as they do. Sometimes premature and erroneous generalizations lead to errors in behavior.

There are two basic types of generalization: *stimulus generalization* in which the same responses are given to a variety of objects or environments or behaviors, and *response generalization* in which different responses are given to the same situation. People respond warmly to many different environments—natural scenes or buildings or room layouts. This is an example of stimulus generalization. At the same time, people learn to respond in different ways to the same affordances of the environment. The response may be due to contextual variables, the mood of the person or the person having different motivations at different times. Environmental design theory must recognize that human behavior—overt or emotional—cannot be explained simply in terms of the phenomenal environment, although many design assumptions, including the naive belief in architectural determinism, are based on this view. How people respond to patterns of the environment depends on how they have categorized the environment and its elements, on the associations they have built up over time, and on the reinforcements they have received.

Much of our behavior is culture-bound. It depends on how we have been socialized to like and dislike patterns of the environment and the successes that we have had in the past in dealing with them. Environmental design education socializes

designers to hold certain values. Often these values deviate from those the person held prior to the education. This change involves the development of new schemata for exploring and dealing with the world.

Schemata

Schemata provide us with algorithms for perceiving, learning, and behaving. We do not know what a schema is like in biological terms. We assume its existence to explain much about learning and behavior. The conjectural nature of a schema is clear from Ulrich Neisser's definition:

> A schema . . . is internal to the perceiver, modifiable by experience, and somehow specific to what is perceived. The schema accepts information . . . and is changed by this information, it directs movement and exploratory activities that make information available, by which it is further modified. (Neisser 1977)

Schemata can be considered to act like templates for action. Extensive schemata have lesser ones buried in them. This explains how we can act, make plans about where we are going and what we are doing, and appreciate the world around us all at the same time. If the schemata are compatible they reinforce each other; if not, one rules. The schemata we have at any given moment offer possibilities for developing along certain lines, but the precise nature of the development is determined by interactions with the environment. People's whole experience influences what they have learned and what they have forgotten and the meanings that elements in the environment have for them. Thus, any theory of aesthetics has to recognize the relativity of environmental quality.

The images that people have of the environment around them are a type of schema. These images can be iconic images (cognitive maps), as discussed by Kevin Lynch in *The Image of the City* (1960), or associational images (more properly, symbolic meanings), as discussed by Anselm Strauss in *Images of The American City* (1961).

Meaning

The subject of meaning is a fundamental one in aesthetic theory. The confused state of the design literature on the subject reflects the confused state of the psychological literature. There are many levels of meaning and many theoretical approaches to the topic. *Empiricist* theories state that meaning has to be supplied to events after the perceiver has registered their structure. *Transactionalists* believe that meaning is given as a perception takes place and past experience interrupts perception to give a new meaning. *Introspective analysis* suggests that meanings are given first. *Gestalt* theorists believe that expressive meanings, at one level, are a function of the geometric character of the environment. *Psychoanalysts* postulate an unconscious component of the mind in which memories are deposited to be awakened by the psyche. Freud postulated an individual unconscious to which Jung added a collective unconscious in which timeless "nodes of energy," called archetypes, evoke images, ideas, and behaviors. Symbols, including the symbolic meanings of the designed environment, provide the medium whereby archetypes are manifested. The most basic of archetypes is the "self," the inner heart of our being, our soul, our uniqueness. One's home is a symbol of the self, for instance (Cooper 1974). The *ecological approach* to perception assumes that all the potential uses and, presumably, meanings of an object are directly visually perceivable in the optic array and/or the structure of nonvisual information obtainable by the other perceptual systems. One just has to know—to have learned, in most cases—what to look for. Certainly, the perception of meaning depends on some schema or other.

A number of classifications of types of meaning exist. Gibson (1950) differentiated polemically among six levels of meaning: first, the primitive concrete; second, use meanings; third, the meanings of instruments and machines; fourth, the value and emotional meaning of things; fifth, the level of signs; sixth, the level of symbols. Architect Robert Hershberger (1974) has a different listing based on a *mediational* theory of cognition akin to that of Ulrich Neisser. This is shown diagramatically in figure 9-5. The development of meaning in this view is a two-step process.

Hershberger identifies five levels of meaning, some of which correspond to Gibson's levels. The first is the presentational meaning, which involves the perception of shape and form (roughly akin to Gibson's first level); the second is referential meaning (akin to Gibson's sixth level); the third is the affective meaning; the fourth is the evaluative meaning—whether something is good or bad (somewhat akin to Gibson's fourth level); the fifth level is prescriptive meaning. The difference between the concept of affordance and the concept of prescriptive meaning is that the latter implies a degree of coercion to behave in a particular way because of the structure of the environment; the affordance of the environment refers to the behavioral possibilities of the structure of that environment.

The built environment, thus, can be perceived to communicate a variety of meanings, from its utility to its symbolism. The symbolism of the built environment is a major concern of environmental designers for it is a major factor in people's liking or disliking their surroundings. The study of symbolism has been approached in a number of ways by different fields. It is a major concern of linguists, for example, de Saussure (1915), whose work has recently very much influenced the thinking of architects, in particular many of the Post-Modernists (Broadbent 1975, Jencks 1977). Within psychology there are a number of approaches, including the Gestalt, psychoanalytical, and behaviorist, each of which has its adherents in the design professions.

There is much conjecturing on why and how these symbolic meanings are developed. The role of learning and thus of cultural differences is particularly important in dealing with symbolic meanings and the development of likes or dislikes of artifacts and patterns of the world. Any artifact or environment carries a number of meanings simultaneously. They are not independent. One level of meaning—the value of things or the affective meaning of things—is central to aesthetic theory.

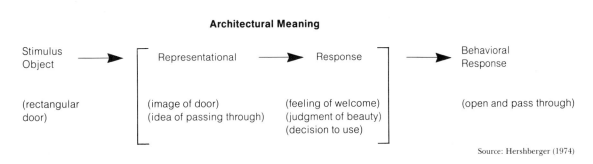

Architectural Meaning

Source: Hershberger (1974)

9-5. Hershberger's Mediational Theory of Environmental Meaning.

Emotional and Affective Meanings

Empirical and experimental research suggests that there are three primary emotional responses: pleasure, arousal, and dominance (Mehrabian and Russell 1974). Pleasure has to do with feelings of liking and disliking; arousal has to do with the interest-evoking qualities of the environment; dominance has to do with the individual's feelings of freedom of action. The concern here is with the interestingness and pleasurableness of environments—their affective meanings.

Different theories of perception and cognition have different postulations about how likes and dislikes develop. According to Gestalt theory, a liking for patterns of the environment would occur because of a resonance between the neurological processes and environmental forms. Psychoanalytical theories would explain preference in terms of the values of the associations between forms and memories in the individual unconscious and/or collective unconscious. Behaviorist theories would explain them in terms of the socialization process and the patterns of the environment that people have been positively reinforced to like. Basic to an understanding of what people find "delightful" in the environment is, however, an understanding of the attitudes they possess and how these develop.

An *attitude* results from combining a *belief* about something with a *value* premise about it. There are several definitions of belief. Most social psychologists consider a belief to be an assertion about an associative characteristic rather than a defining characteristic of a thing. Thus, pointed arches may be a defining characteristic of Gothic buildings; "such windows go well in ecclesiastical architecture" is an associative characteristic. Many such beliefs are verbalized in writings on architecture and interior design, but others can only be inferred from what a designer designs.

Values are related to motivations for they define the attractive and repulsive elements of the world. Patterns of the built environment that people find pleasing have a positive value for them; anything that is disdained has a negative value. Values represent a linkage between a person's motivations, emotional feelings, and behavior. Attitudes toward specific environments and environmental patterns arise from the attribution of a value to a belief.

People strive for cognitive consistency in the attitudes they hold about themselves and their social and physical environments (Festinger 1957, Brehm and Cohen 1962). A number of models of cognitive consistency help environmental designers understand the vagaries of aesthetic analysis. They enhance understanding of how likes and dislikes develop and are maintained.

The simplest model is that of balance theory (Heider 1946). If one person has a positive attitude (likes, promotes, seeks) toward another person or set of ideas (the referent), then the first person's attitude would be positive also toward an inanimate thing that is related positively to the referent. Otherwise the system would not be in balance. This indicates the importance of attitudes toward the referent in understanding people's attitudes toward the symbolic meanings of the built environment. Figure 9-6 portrays the relationship between a person and his or her attitudes toward a referent and an environmental pattern. Figure 9-6a, b, and c show consistent relationships, while 9-6d shows an inconsistent relationship. The basic thesis is that we attempt to eliminate incongruent relationships. The strength with which we hold attitudes indicates which attitude is likely to change to eliminate the incongruity (Osgood and Tannebaum 1955), although sometimes we isolate attitudes that are inconsistent with each other and refuse to recognize the discrepancy (Rosenberg and Abelson 1960). For instance, a person may admire a particular set of design principles but not admire a design according to those principles. This is an inconsistent relationship. The person may deny the inconsistency or strive for consistency by changing his or her attitude toward the principles or the design.

Conclusions on the Processes of Cognition and Affect

It is difficult to separate the processes of perception and cognition; both are guided by schemata. We know much about the processes and how they are linked, but our understanding is by no means fully developed; there are alternative, largely untested, theories that explain them. As a result, designers' theories about human responses to the built environment have to be recognized as conjectural. There are some very important insights about the person–environment relationship that have been yielded by the theories and models of the behavioral sciences. Learning is of fundamental importance because humans are highly adaptive creatures who develop new knowledge, new values, new symbols, and new activity patterns. Social pressures and cultural norms exert a stabilizing force on the patterns of behavior and attitudes that form the basis for an environmental designer's work. This is not a static framework, however. It evolves over time. The work of environmental designers reflects these changes and contributes to them.

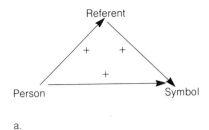

a.

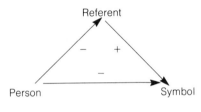

b.

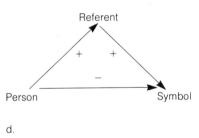

c.

d.

9-6. Balance Theory.

SPATIAL BEHAVIOR

How and why people use the layout of the environment in the way they do as they go about their activities is of central concern to environmental design theory because of the linkages between this spatial behavior and normative theories of functionalism in architecture and the other design fields. The overt spatial behavior of people is something that is directly observable, thus at a descriptive level it is not subject to the controversies that accompany attempts to describe and explain the processes of perception and cognition. Economists, sociologists, anthropologists, and ethologists do, however, focus

on different aspects of behavior and offer different explanations for it. There have been two scales of research in these endeavors (Patricios 1975). The first deals with aggregates of people and the location of activities at a metropolitan and regional scale. An understanding of the distribution of activities and the reasons for this distribution is of concern to city and regional planners. Architects, landscape architects, and urban designers are more concerned with understanding behavior at a microscale—from rooms to neighborhoods and other districts of cities.

Micromodels of Spatial Behavior

The environmental perception and behavioral approach to the study of human behavior suggests that an individual's behavior is a function of his or her motivations, the affordances of the environment, and the images of the world outside direct perception and the meanings those images have for the individual. Within this approach to the study of human behavior and the built environment there are a number of different theoretical orientations.

An *ethological* approach suggests that some of the behaviors we regard as characteristically human are the same as those of other animals. These behaviors are said to be innate although they may be molded by culture. This is the explanation for territorial behavior (see Hall 1966). A number of people (for instance, Newman 1972, 1973, Greenbie 1976) have developed these into design principles. The *behaviorist* tradition stands in strong contrast to this, with its emphasis on the learning of patterns of behavior as the result of reinforcement patterns.

In recent years there have been a great many studies on the built environment, its furnishings, and spatial behavior which do not seem to have a clear theoretical orientation. They seem to be influenced by ethological and behaviorist as well as by psychoanalytic theories. These include much of the work of Edward T. Hall (1966) and Robert Sommer (1969, 1974a), which has strong ethological overtones but is much more eclectic theoretically. Often subsumed under the rubric of *proxemic theory*, their studies of how people relate to each other spatially in each other's presence and how people control space through territorial behavior have influenced the thinking of designers about the layout of rooms, buildings, building complexes, and neighborhoods.

Most environmental design theorists have taken a pragmatic view of the description of spatial behavior. Two concepts have become embedded in environmental design theory. One, the concept of *activity systems* (Chapin 1965), is concerned primarily with the organization of the sequences of activities taking place in buildings, neighborhoods, and cities; the other, the concept of *behavior settings* (Barker 1968, Bechtel 1977, Wicker 1979), is concerned with the relationship between the built environment —the milieu—and the standing, or recurrent, pattern of behavior that takes place within it.

The concept of behavior setting was developed by a group of behavioral scientists who call themselves "ecological psychologists" because they are concerned with human behavior in the everyday environment. Their approach to the study of behavior is similar to that of those who are developing the ecological theory of perception, with one important exception. Ecological psychologists believe that the physical environment exerts a degree of coercion over the behavior of individuals. In this they were influenced, as noted earlier, by the assertion of Kurt Lewin (1936) that the physical environment possesses an "invitational quality." Gibson (1979) does not believe that the physical environment, itself, is coercive in this way. It affords some behaviors and not others. It depends on a person's predispositions whether or not an affordance or set of affordances is or is not used.

INDIVIDUAL DIFFERENCES IN BEHAVIOR

People are socialized differently, growing up as they do in different geographical and social environments. They differ also in their motivations. They look at the environment and use it differently. There is some regularity in these differences. How best can they be classified?

Functional theory in sociology—not to be confused with functional theory in environmental design—provides an approach that has attracted a number of analysts of the built environment and human behavior (such as Michelson 1970, Cranz 1974, Moleski 1978, Sobal 1978). The theory is most comprehensively exemplified by the work of Talcott Parsons (1937, 1959, 1966). It focuses on systems—cultural, social, personality, organismic (or physiological), and environmental—as the basis for examining social behavior. It has attracted the attention of designers because it has a more general application to the development of environmental design theory.

Each of four subsystems—*cultural, social, personality,* and *organismic*—has a primary function in terms of maintaining the internal-external relationships and the mean-ends purposes of a social system. The purpose of the cultural subsystem is to maintain specific action patterns and to manage internal and external tensions for the whole system of action. Integration is the primary purpose of the

social subsystem; goal attainment is that of the personality subsystem; and adaptation is that of the organismic subsystem.

At different times in history the functional relationship of an individual to society varies. There are specific patterns which, nevertheless, seem to be invariant. Parsons identifies a number of these. He draws on *cybernetic theory* to suggest that those subsystems that are high in information and low in energy are the ones that control those that are high in energy and low in information. Culture is at the top of the control hierarchy followed by social group, personality, and organismic subsystems. The subsystems that are low in the hierarchy of control are those that place greater limitations on behavior. Thus, our physiological character is more controlling than the others and so on.

According to this model, culture—the shared system of beliefs, values, symbols, and styles that characterizes a group of people—controls much human behavior. Each culture is unique because it has its own peculiar history. A culture evolves over time as a people develop approaches to dealing with the problems of survival and growth in a particular terrestrial setting. The built environment always exists within a culture and is part of it. Every generation deals with a social and built environment shaped by earlier generations.

People are largely unaware of the constraints imposed on them by their own cultures in their everyday behavior. The impact of a culture on an individual is mediated by norms—"the patterns of commonly held expectations" (Bates 1956). An important consequence of the socialization process for individuals is that they develop the ability to intuit the attitudes and behaviors of others and the meanings of the environment within their own culture. The design professions, as a whole, however, are constantly dealing with different cultures and subcultures, and the intuition of an individual designer alone cannot provide the basic knowledge required for designing habitats congruent with people's lives and values.

Environmental designers, like other professionals, are members of two cultures embedded in each other. Each has its own socialization process. One is the broader society and the other is the professional culture which has its own norms of behavior, values, and expectations. These professional norms and peer-group pressures to conform are extremely coercive in environmental design and in architecture in particular (Montgomery 1966). The result is that the professions have been extremely slow in changing, even when faced with major repudiations of their beliefs. This behavior is true of most professions (Larson 1979).

All the subsystems of human action identified by Parsons occur within a geographic and a built environment that has little influence on what people actually do but has the major influence on what they can do. The limitations of the terrestrial environmental system must be met before people can function at all. As Maslow would also suggest, most basic is the role of the built environment as shelter.

All individuals have organismic and personality traits that make them unique, but they also operate within social and cultural as well as terrestrial contexts. The nature of the built environment to an individual or a group is very much governed by the impact of these subsystems on the processes of perception, cognition and affect, and spatial behavior. Thus they provide us with a useful classification system for considering individual and group differences in the use and appreciation of the built environment. This system helps us ask serious questions about how people might use the environment and the aesthetic experiences they might have. It helps us, too, to take a stand on what activities should be afforded and what aesthetic experiences should be the goals of design.

Individual and Group Competence

The behavior of a person or a group is dependent on its competence in dealing with the world. *Environmental competence* is a term coined by Powell Lawton (1977) to aid in understanding the environmental needs of various segments of the elderly population, but it has general applicability. Everybody has some level of competence in dealing with the social and the built environment. *Competence* is a term that covers a broad set of attributes "such as physical or mental health, intellectual capacity and ego strength" (Lawton 1977). Many of the qualities that contribute to a person's ability to deal with the world are difficult to measure. While it is relatively easy to understand the concept when dealing with physical capabilities such as motor abilities, it is much more difficult to comprehend what it actually means when dealing with cultures and cultural behavior. It is also more controversial. The key point is that the greater the competence of an individual, the greater the behavioral freedom that person has and the less his or her behavior is constrained by the social and physical environments. In environmental design, the question of what competence level should be taken into consideration is a key issue, as shall be explained fully later in this book.

Should people be challenged by their environments or should the environment be made as comfortable as possible physically and psychologically? The answer depends on one's world view.

UNDERSTANDING HUMAN BEHAVIOR FOR ENVIRONMENTAL DESIGN

To understand the role of the built environment in people's lives one has to understand the nature of human behavior. This is the research concern of behavioral scientists. They have developed only a partial understanding of human behavior, however. While there may be general agreement on the basic processes, there is considerable disagreement on how the processes work. Some of these theoretical disagreements have little to do with environmental design theory, but others are central. Different ideas about the nature of interior design, architecture, landscape architecture, and urban design are based on different concepts of human nature and purposes. If designers do not recognize the conjectural nature of their own theories they are fooling themselves. Knowledge of the basic principles and controversies in descriptions and explanations of human behavior helps us clarify our understanding of the relationship between environment and behavior. This, in turn, helps the architect consider how the environment affords people of different backgrounds different aesthetic experiences and activity patterns. As shall be argued throughout, it also enables us to understand what we can predict with confidence and when we are really going out on a limb.

ADDITIONAL READINGS

Gibson, James J. *An Ecological Approach to Visual Perception.* Boston: Houghton Mifflin, 1979.

Hochberg, Julian. *Perception.* Englewood Cliffs, N.J.: Prentice-Hall, 1964.

Ittelson, William, Karen Franck, and Timothy O'Hanlon. "The Nature of Environmental Experience." In Seymour Watner et al., eds., *Experiencing the Environment.* New York: Plenum, 1979, pp. 187–206.

Ittelson, William, Harold Proshansky, Leanne Rivlin, and Gary Winkel. "The Search for Environmental Theory." In *An Introduction to Environmental Psychology.* New York: Holt, Rinehart and Winston, 1974, pp. 61–79.

Neisser, Ulrich. *Cognition and Reality.* San Francisco: Freeman, 1977.

Parsons, Talcott. *Societies.* Englewood Cliffs, N.J.: Prentice-Hall, 1966.

10

THE BUILT ENVIRONMENT AND HUMAN BEHAVIOR

Four basic theoretical positions regarding the relationship between environment and behavior can be identified: a *free-will approach,* a *possibilistic approach,* a *probabilistic approach,* and a *deterministic approach* (see Porteous 1977). The free-will approach suggests that the environment has no impact on behavior. Clearly, since people have severe limitations as biological beings, this is an untenable position. Possibilists perceive the environment to be the afforder of human behavior and little more. It has been argued here that the environment consists of a set of opportunities for behavior upon which action may or may not be taken. The analysis of human behavior suggests that the people are not as completely free to act on their own choices as possibilists assume. Every individual has a set of motivations and competencies that are at least partially conditioned by the terrestrial, social, and cultural environments.

Determinism is the belief that when people are acting out of apparent free will, they are really controlled by their heredity and environment. Environmental determinism, an offshoot of the theory of evolution, holds that it is the environment that is the major determinant of behavior. Environment in this context is generally taken to mean the geographical or terrestrial context (see, for example, Semple

Much of this chapter was presented first in a paper, "The Built Environment and Human Behavior: Architectural Determinism Re-examined," *VIA IV,* Cambridge, Mass.: MIT Press, 1980, pp. 146–153.

1911). It has been easy to assume that the built environment works in the same way.

The deterministic approach to the consideration of the environment–behavior relationship implies a simple cause-effect relationship between the two. It has been noted in this book (see also Lipman 1974, Brolin 1976, Vidler 1973) that much of the ideology of the Modern Movement is based on this assumption.

While recognizing that the environment is full of affordances for human behavior, and that the perception and use of them is very much a function of individual needs and competencies, probabilists take the following position:

> Given an individual A with attributes a, b, c, set in an Environment E with characteristics d, e, f, and with the Motivation for action M, it is probable that A will perform Behavior B. (Prince 1971, reported in Porteous 1977)

This position recognizes the uncertainty of the systems within which human behavior takes place and within which environmental designers act, but it assumes that human behavior is not entirely capricious. The probabilistic position underlies most of the recent research on the relationship between behavior and environmental design.

The goal of this chapter is to clarify our understanding of the relationship between people and the built environment by reviewing existing ideas within the framework of our current understanding of the nature of the environment and the nature of human behavior. The objective is to provide a set of concepts that describe this relationship with some specificity. It will then be possible to draw clearer conclusions on the hypotheses of the person–environment relationship.

"ENVIRONMENTAL DETERMINISM," "PHYSICAL DETERMINISM," AND "ARCHITECTURAL DETERMINISM"

The terms *environmental determinism, physical determinism,* and *architectural determinism* often are used synonomously in the environmental design literature. When this is done, the terms all refer to the belief that changes in the layout of the environment will lead to a change in the social behavior and (when they are considered at all) in the aesthetic values of the persons involved. In behavioral science literature the terms are used much more broadly. In order to clarify the issues facing the design professions, it is important to define these terms more precisely and to define also the different levels of determinism (see also Franck 1984).

Environmental determinism should be used broadly to reflect the belief that it is *nurture* within the setting of our geographical, social, and cultural environments, rather than *nature,* our heredity, that shapes our values and behavior. The nature-nurture controversy has been largely dormant in psychology, although recently, with the rise of the field of sociobiology (Wilson 1978), it has come again to the fore. The question being asked by psychologists today is not whether behavior is genetically or environmentally based, but which aspects of behavior are the one and which aspects are the other.

Physical determinism can best be regarded as the belief that human behavior is determined by the nature of the geographic environment as adapted by people at a particular place. Culture and climate are without doubt interrelated, but the physical determinist would take an even stronger position on the effect of the natural and artificial environment on human behavior. Not everybody uses the term *physical* in this way. Herbert Gans (1961, 1968), for instance, uses "physical environment" in a much narrower way as a synonym for the "planned" or "built environment." This is not the way the term will be used here. Architectural determinism will be used to denote the belief that changes in the landscaped and architectural elements of the environment will result in changes in behavior, particularly in social behavior.

If one acccepts the definitions given here, then we have a hierarchy of beliefs about the impact of the environment on people. Environmental determinism is the belief that changes in the geographic, social, cultural, and built environments shape behavior. Physical determinism is the belief that changes in the geographic environment and "built-form" will result in changes in behavior. Architectural determinism is the belief that built form, composed of artificial and/or natural elements, will lead to changes in social behavior. Given the natural endowment of the individual, the first position seems tenable although it does not account for all interpersonal differences. The others require closer scrutiny.

Aspects of the physical environment are a major factor in human life, but the physical environment cannot be regarded as the determinant of human behavior despite the strong correlations between climate, landform, and culture (Vayda 1969). There are many cultural differences among people living in very similar terrestrial environments (Rapoport 1969). Thus, while it is a source of cultural and behavioral differences, the physical environment is not the only source of influence on social behavior. Architectural determinism requires some elaboration in order to clarify the relationship between built environment and human behavior.

ARCHITECTURAL DETERMINISM

It is not difficult to understand why architects, other environmental designers, and often social reformers believed in the central role of the built environment in determining human social behavioral patterns and values. During the nineteenth century, with the coming of the Industrial Revolution and the large-scale migration of rural workers to the city, many social critics became aware of the strong correlation between the unpleasant conditions in which people lived and their social and psychological conditions. It was easy to conclude that changing the built environment would change not only the living conditions but also the lifestyle and aesthetic values of the people concerned. The whole social and philanthropic movement of the latter part of the nineteenth century, which culminated in the garden cities movement led by Ebenezer Howard (1902) and the settlement-house schemes, was imbued with the spirit of architectural deterministic beliefs.

In the 1930s and 1940s, the principles of housing design generated by successive meetings of CIAM (Congrès Internationaux d'Architecture Moderne) and the public housing movements in many countries were based on a series of assumptions regarding the impact of architecture and urban designs on human behavior (see Le Corbusier 1973). The earlier conferences were concerned with the most fundamental human needs in Maslow's hierarchy—shelter and basic services—while the later ones, such as Bridgewater in 1947 and Oterloo in 1959, were concerned with the social, cognitive, and aesthetic needs, the higher-order needs in Maslow's hierarchy (see Frampton 1980). All of these conferences exhibited a belief that through architectural and urban design all kinds of social pathologies could be eliminated. This belief has been reinforced by the work of sociologists and psychologists. This is particularly so because of the lack of clarity in the specification of the relationship between the independent variables (the environment) and the dependent variables (social behavior) in much of the recent research.

The concept of neighborhood unit emerged from the work of sociologists associated with the University of Chicago between the world wars. It was based on the belief that the localization of facilities would lead to greater face-to-face contact between people, greater participation in community affairs, and hence less anomie and a more democratic society than that found in the heart of major cities. The belief is still very prevalent (see, for example, Sternberg and Sternberg 1971, Alexander 1972, Corbett 1981). Recent research (Bagley 1965, Brooks 1974) has not borne out this assumption, but it has shown that the layout of the environment and the affordances it provides make a difference in people's perception of environmental quality.

The belief in architectural determinism has been further reinforced by a simplistic reading by designers of the work of Leon Festinger (Festinger et al. 1950), William Whyte (1954), Leo Kuper (1953), Herbert Gans (1961), Bert Adams (1968), and Holohan and Saegert (1973). All of these studies showed a powerful relationship between aspects of the physical layout of the environment and human interaction patterns. It must be admitted, however, that neither the relationship between architectural variables and behavioral variables, nor the specific circumstances under which the relationships hold, nor the effect of possible intervening variables is always clearly specified in these studies. The result has been that designers often assume a simple S-R model of the built environment–behavior relationship.

Most recent studies on the built environment and human behavior have stressed the importance of social factors in understanding and predicting the usage of parks and buildings and the interaction patterns of people. As early as 1965 a study in Britain by Christopher Bagley showed that rehousing people from a decaying central city area to new housing had little effect on high delinquency rates: the cultural pattern was not broken. Gans's study of Levittown (1967), while showing a strong relationship between physical proximity and friendship patterns, also showed that friendship is more likely to be based on the perceived homogeneity of values of people or their need for mutual assistance than on anything else. The dimensions along which homogeneity are important are: socioeconomic status and stage in life cycle as well as factors such as similarity in attitudes toward child-raising, leisure-time activities, and general cultural interests. The Westgate study, which showed a strong relationship between the propinquity of residential units and friendship patterns, involved a highly homogeneous population. Gans (1967) points out that where a change in lifestyle accompanies a change in residential environment, there is a predisposition to change and the chosen environment better affords the new lifestyle.

It is highly questionable to claim that a design will have particular behavioral outcomes without first taking into consideration the predispositions and the motivations of the population concerned. If there is no overt or latent desire for interaction between people, for example, then the behavior is unlikely to take place, whatever the layout of the environment might afford, unless there is an accompanying change in the social and administrative environment. Many designers have made very strong assumptions that the spaces that they create will, in themselves, lead to change.

Assumptions have also been made about the ability of "good" design to change people's aesthetic attitudes. Aesthetic attitudes do change over time. This occurs when there is a predisposition on the part of clients for new images to be created and/or a predisposition on the part of a society for change in the formal, or structural, content of buildings and landscapes. Anne Tyng (1975) relates these predispositions to changes in the underlying psychological or personality structure of a society.

Environmental designers have been confused by the seemingly paradoxical criticism leveled at their logic and work by behavioral scientists. Herbert Gans, in the introduction to Clare Cooper's *Easter Hill Village* (1975), reminds the reader of the fallacy of a belief in architectural determinism, but then goes on to describe how the facilities and layout of that housing complex affect behavior negatively. We are now in a position to resolve this apparent paradox.

During the past two decades, with the growth of environmental psychology as a discipline, there has been a major growth in our understanding of the relationship of the built environment and human behavior. The concepts of the environment and of human behavior set forth in the previous two chapters enable a presentation to be made here of a preliminary statement on the relationship of the two from a designer's viewpoint.

FUNDAMENTAL CONCEPTS OF THE PERSON–BUILT ENVIRONMENT RELATIONSHIP

The environment can be considered to consist of interrelated geographic, built, social, and cultural components that afford certain behaviors in consistent ways. The set of *affordances* of the environment at a particular location constitutes the *potential environment* for human behavior at that place. Not all of these affordances are perceived by people, nor are all the perceived affordances used. What is used depends on the nature of the people involved, their *motivations, experiences, values,* and the perceived *costs and rewards* of their engaging in a particular set of activities or aesthetic interpretations of the world around them. The processes of perception, cognition, and spatial behavior are affected by the competencies of the individual and the group of which he or she is a member, as well as by the structure of the built environment. Humans are highly adaptable creatures, but their perceptions of the environment are affected by the things to which they have become accustomed. At the same time, it must be recognized that people do adapt to conditions which threaten to destroy "values which are characteristically human" (Dubos 1965).

The environment consists of a set of *behavior settings*, nested within each other and overlapping. These consist of two major components, a *standing pattern of behavior* and a *milieu* (Barker 1968). The milieu is the physical structure which is composed of surfaces related to each other in specific patterns that constitute landscapes, buildings, rooms, and furnishings. The surfaces are composed of different substances, textures, and pigmentations. They are also illuminated in different ways. A composition affords some things and not others to a potential user. The affordances can be divided into two categories, *direct* and *indirect*. The direct consist of such things as affordances for activities, while the indirect include such things as symbolic meanings which depend on the association of the patterns with a referent and on the utility of a pattern for financial gain. The affordances are the property of the built environment itself within a geographical, animate, and cultural environment. The *effective* environment consists of those elements that are meaningful to the user or observer of a potential

environment. This book is concerned with bringing attention to the affordances of specific patterns of the environment for humans (see fig. 10-2). Others are concerned with other animals, wild or domestic (Leedy, Maestro, and Franklin 1978, Spirn 1984).

Each individual has a variety of competencies in dealing with different aspects of the built environment. Some of these are physiological and some are social and cultural. These differences affect the way the environment is perceived—the images people have of it and the way it can be and is used. The environment in which people are socialized shapes competencies, because what we know and what we learn to look at are shaped by what the environment affords us.

It is quite possible for people to be able to perceive the affordances of the environment for others while being unable to use those affordances themselves because they do not have the competence to do so, or because cultural pressures prevent them, or because they lack the resources in money or time. The lower a person's competencies, the more restrictive—the more pressing—an environment becomes in terms of behavioral opportunities (see fig. 10-3). This restrictiveness can lead to higher rates of mental illness (Klee et al. 1967). In contrast, it has been hypothesized (Lawton 1977) that if the built environment demands less competence of an individual than that individual possesses, then it is too comfortable and not challenging enough. This can lead to the atrophy of a person's abilities. The result, particularly in institutions, is a lack of sharing, deindividuation, and loss of competency (Goffman 1961). Some environments are more challenging than those to which we are habituated. This occurs, for instance, when we move to a new city. We are forced to learn new things. Sometimes we seek especially challenging environments: we learn how to climb cliffs and jump out of airplanes (Klausner 1968). Sometimes people have to live with and adjust to stressful situations (Burton et al. 1982). Provided the people have the competence to adjust, such environments fall into the "zone of maximum performance potential" in the diagram. Some environments are simply beyond our competence to handle.

Even though an environment affords a particular set of behaviors, this does not mean that the behaviors will take place, even though the people perceive the affordances and are competent enough to use them. On the other hand, if the affordances are not there, the behavior cannot take place. The environment can be adapted to afford the desired behavior, or else the people concerned may adapt their behavior to cope with the environment as it is. These adaptations may be accompanied by physio-

1

Photograph by Sei-Kwan Sohn

2

3

10-1. The Perception of Environmental Affordances.
People scan the environment for opportunities to fulfill their predispositions. Certain environments may fulfill latent predispositions—that is, subconscious ones—which become manifested when the affordances of a particular pattern of the environment become clear. Thus, in (1) the steps afford sitting, and the fountain in (2) affords cooling-off behaviors which may have not been considered until the opportunity presented itself. In (3) it is clear that someone has perceived the affordances for adapting the environment to his own needs.

logical or psychological stress. This is particularly likely to occur, as dissonance theory explains, when people are in situations that are not self-chosen (Festinger 1957). The role of the architectural environment is thus accommodative and not deterministic except in the negative sense: if the built environment does not afford a behavior, the behavior cannot take place. What, then, causes behavior and changes in standing patterns of behavior? This is a more difficult question to answer.

Human behavior, both mental and spatial, depends on our intentions and habits as well as on the affordances of the physical and social world we in-

habit. Intentions are some complex function of the schemata we possess, the desirability of a behavior and its perceived consequences, and the social pressure one is under. It thus becomes clear that it is both naive and misleading to try to explain behavior solely in terms of the built environment and to expect much of the built environment in changing social behavior patterns. One has to understand the nature of human motivations because they tell us something about the focus of a person's attention at a particular time. Maslow's model of a hierarchy of human motivations (1943) is a useful one, for we have self-consciously or unselfconsciously shaped

1

3

2

10-2. Bringing Attention to the Affordances of the Environment.

One of the things that entrepreneurs do is identify people's predispositions—or shape them—and create settings which afford the behaviors that are manifestations of those predispositions. In Las Vegas a host of signs, placed so that they afford being seen at different distances, bring attention to available entertainments (1). The sign in (2) does something similar. It brings attention to aspects of the environment that are not discernible. Perceiving the behavior of others also brings attention to the affordances of an object (3), in this case, its clamber-on-ability. It is through the manipulation of the affordances of the built environment that the designer affects human experiences.

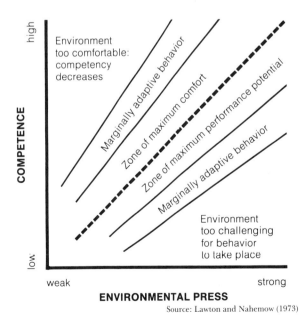

Source: Lawton and Nahemow (1973)

10-3. The Concept of Competence.

the world to better meet our physiological needs, our needs for safety, belonging, esteem, and actualization, and finally our cognitive and aesthetic needs.

Our attitudes are related to our motivations. What we like and dislike, what we believe to be good or bad, important or unimportant—these attitudes are related to the various socialization processes and experiences we have had and thus to the influence of others. We, in turn, try to influence others. Our personalities and our social and cultural backgrounds are all indicators, not perfect predictors, of attitudes toward people and toward characteristics of the built environment. Similarly, what we perceive to be the *rewards* and *costs* of participating in a particular setting affect our attitudes to the setting—to the people in it, to their behavior, and to the milieu, as shown in figure 10-4 (Helmreich 1974). Some settings are highly stressful, but the financial and psychological rewards for being there are high and so we accept the stress. Other settings are highly unpleasant and the rewards for being there are low and the costs high. If there is an alternative, people are likely to attempt to get out of the situation. Sometimes, for those trapped by poverty or authoritarian political powers, there is no alternative. There are also situations where the rewards are high and the costs very low for being there. We cannot expect to always be in such situations.

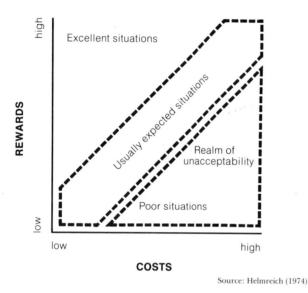

Source: Helmreich (1974)

10-4. The Perception of Environmental Quality in Terms of Costs and Rewards.

CONCLUSION

There are many written expressions of the meaningfulness of the inanimate environment to one's existence. Anyone who has hung a colorful poster on a barren apartment or office wall, or who walks down one street rather than another simply because it is cheerier, or who has selected a house in one neighborhood rather than another because it is more attractive, knows that the quality of the built environment affects one's perceptions of the quality of life. It is tempting to perceive these statements on environment and behavior as pertaining only to the built environment rather than the whole sociophysical environment. It is tempting to adopt a simple stimulus-response model of human behavior. Given the diversity of activities that can take place within the same architectural setting, falling for these temptations would seriously mislead the design professions about their tasks. It has done so in the past.

The architectural environment is more determining, and thus more important, in providing for the basic needs of people—those of shelter and security—than it is in meeting the needs that are a product of interpersonal and social relationships. Yet even here the built environment is important because it does, at least partially, meet needs for self-esteem, affiliation, and aesthetics through the symbolic messages it provides about status, identity, and values. Yet design is limited also in what it can do in meeting social needs.

A building design impinges on people's lives through the affordances it possesses. It cannot be assumed, however, simply because the environment contains a set of affordances for the activities that policymakers or designers believe are good for people or has the aesthetic qualities that designers believe are uplifting, that people in the environment will respond in the desired manner. Not all people perceive the affordances of the environment in the same way.

The effective environment is different for different people. If the differences occurred haphazardly, then the conclusion one would reach is that all that can be achieved through design is to allow for some behaviors and to exclude others—a purely possibilistic stance. Behavior does not, however, occur haphazardly. It has a certain predictability. It is possible to make predictions about who will use what facility, who will bother to look at a particular architectural composition, and who will respond to it warmly and who will not. We can make few of these predictions with certainty. Environmental design theory is not a deterministic science.

It is possible to take a number of normative stances toward positive theory-building based on these observations. Sociologist F. J. Langdon (1966) perceives the role of theory-building and design to be as follows:

> We need to study the social environment so that we can create surroundings which make it easier for people to do what they want to do, to live the way they want; and to make it unnecessary for them to do things they don't want or would otherwise not do.

This is a strong ideological statement. It would, of course, be possible to take the same understanding and create environments that do the opposite.

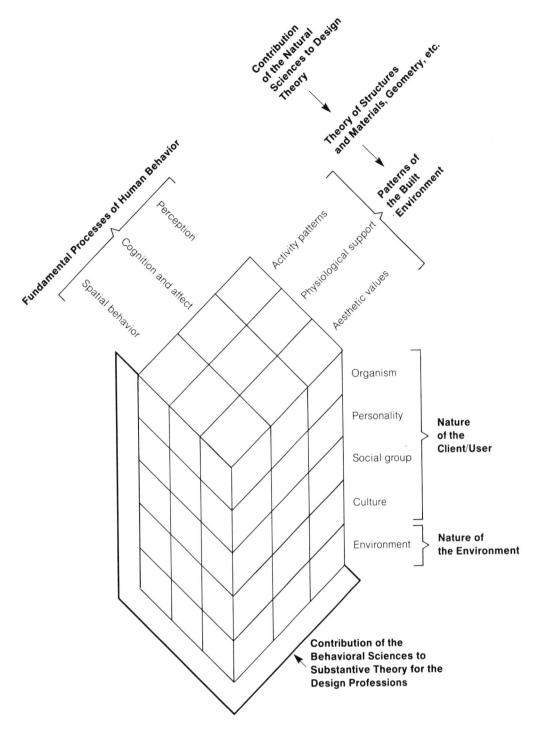

Contribution of the Natural Sciences to Design Theory

Theory of Structures and Materials, Geometry, etc.

Patterns of the Built Environment

Fundamental Processes of Human Behavior

Perception

Cognition and affect

Spatial behavior

Activity patterns

Physiological support

Aesthetic values

Organism

Personality

Social group

Culture

Nature of the Client/User

Environment

Nature of the Environment

Contribution of the Behavioral Sciences to Substantive Theory for the Design Professions

10-5. A Model for Organizing the Contribution of the Behavioral Sciences to Positive Substantive Theory for the Design Professions.

A Model of Substantive Theory for Environmental Design

Figure 10-5 represents an effort to categorize not only what we do know but also what we need to know—a normative judgment! We are concerned with patterns of the built environment and their affordances (A). We need to understand how they afford different human activities and—given that activity—physiological comfort as well. We are also concerned with understanding what patterns afford aesthetic pleasure. Although it is outside the scope of this book because it is an issue of the physical sciences, we are concerned with what patterns are possible from a geometrical and structural viewpoint (B). We are concerned with how people perceive, think about, and react to these affordances (C), and we are concerned with understanding the individual and environmental differences (D) that are good predictors of how people behave and the environmental affordances that are consequently of interest and importance to them. We end up with a three-dimensional matrix of concerns for theory and research. We understand much more about some of the intersections in the matrix than we do about others. We know more about the intersection of culture, territorial spatial behavior, and the patterns of the environment that afford them, for instance, than we know about the interaction between culture, the behavioral processes of cognition and affect, and symbolic aesthetics. One of the objectives of this book is to bring attention to what we do know and to the area where knowledge is skimpy.

The Usefulness of This Matrix of Knowledge

The knowledge provided by such theory will be much more important in the design of some types of buildings than others, depending on their purposes. Kiyo Izumi (Saarinen 1976), suggests that some buildings are designed more for the successful functioning of machines and equipment than for the people who run them. In other buildings the needs of people are paramount (see fig. 10-6). He labels the former type "anthropozemic buildings" and the latter type "anthropophilic." In anthropozemic buildings people have to adapt to the conditions; in anthropophilic buildings the equipment has to be adapted to the conditions of people (Izumi 1968).

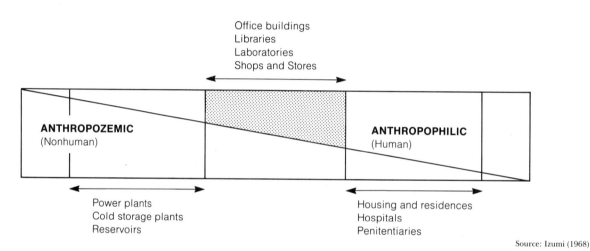

10-6. Anthropozemic and Anthropophilic Buildings.

ADDITIONAL READINGS

Franck, Karen. "Exorcising the Ghost of Physical Determinism." *Environment and Behavior* 10, no. 4 (July 1984): 411–430.

Gans, Herbert. *People and Plans: Essays on Urban Problems and Solutions.* New York: Basic Books, 1968.

Kaplan, Stephen. "A Model of Person–Environment Compatibility." *Environment and Behavior* 15, no. 3 (May 1983): 311–332.

Lipman, Alan. "The Architectural Belief System and Social Behavior." In Jon Lang et al., eds., *Designing for Human Behavior: Architecture and the Behavioral Sciences.* Stroudsburg, Pa.: Dowden, Hutchinson and Ross, 1974, pp. 23–38.

Langdon, F. J. "The Social and the Physical Environment:

A Social Scientist's View." *Journal of the Royal Institute of British Architects* 73 (1966): 460–464.

Proshansky, Harold M., William Ittelson, and Leanne G. Rivlin. "The Influence of the Built Environment on Human Behavior: Some Basic Assumptions." In Proshansky, Ittelson, and Rivlin, eds., *Environmental Psychology: Man and His Physical Setting.* New York: Holt, Rinehart and Winston, 1970, pp. 27–36.

Porteous, C. Douglas. "Environments." In *Environment and Behavior: Planning and Everyday Urban Life.* Reading, Mass.: Addison-Wesley, 1977.

Rosow, Irving. "The Social Effects of the Physical Environment." *Journal of the American Institute of Planners* 27 (1961): 127–133.

Rush, Charles W. "On the Relation of Form to Behavior." *Design Methods Group Newsletter*, October 1969: 8–11.

ACTIVITY PATTERNS AND THE BUILT ENVIRONMENT

"Commodity," Sir Henry Wotton's term for the Vitruvian expression "utilitas," is one of the basic concerns of environmental designers. The purpose of the chapters that follow is to bring attention to the contribution of the behavioral sciences to the enhancement of our understanding of the variables that constitute "commodity." The objective is to enrich the concept of "functionalism" inherited from the Modern Movement. We are concerned with the purposes of the built environment that Fred Steele (1973) called the "shelter and security," the "social contact," and the "task instrumentality" purposes, and the mechanisms that help to attain them. It has to do with the way the built environment houses activities, interactional patterns, and individual movements to attain, at least partially, the specific goals of the individual or the organization. All these may contribute to the fulfillment of any of the needs identified by Abraham Maslow (1943)—the attainment of security, belongingness, esteem, self-actualization, and cognitive and aesthetic satisfaction. The goals are very much interwoven.

The concepts of "behavior setting" and "activity system" embrace the attainment of aspects of all these goals of design and provide a foundation for environmental analysis and design in responding to human needs. The accompanying table shows the correspondence between the human needs identi-

Human Needs and The Sociophysical Mechanisms Required to Afford Them

Need	Steele's Concerns	Sociophysical Mechanisms/Design Issues
Physiological	Shelter and security Task instrumentality	Shelter, access to services
Safety	Social contact	Access to services, privacy, territoriality, defensible space, orientation
Belonging	Social contact Symbolic identification	Access to services, communal settings, symbolic aesthetics
Esteem	Growth, pleasure	Personalization, symbolic aesthetics, control
Actualization	Growth, pleasure	Choice, access to developmental opportunities, control
Cognitive/aesthetic	Growth, pleasure	Access to developmental opportunities, formal aesthetics

fied by Maslow, Steele's list of the functions of the built environment, and the behavior–built environment mechanisms, or patterns, to be described in this book. It can be seen that the same mechanisms contribute to the attainment of more than one function of the built environment, and that the same type of interaction of behavior with built environment, such as orientation, meets a number of goals. Just about everything covered in this section of the book has some relationship to the Vitruvian concerns of "commodity" and "delight."

Chapter 11, "The Behavior Setting: A Unit for Environmental Analysis and Design," is focused on coming to an understanding of the built environment as part of a nested set of behavior settings. This is the part over which the designer has direct control. The way in which the built environment provides support for activity systems, and the degree of ease and comfort involved, are major contributors to subjective feelings of environmental quality.

The meaning of shelter can be understood only by considering the activities to be housed. Shelter needs and their relationship to the physiological characteristics of people have been explored by the fields of *anthropometrics* and *ergonomics*. The former deals primarily with the human body and its dimensions, the latter with the broader issues of human comfort and the ability to carry out tasks, but today the terms often are used interchangeably. The way in which these fields inform environmental design theory is described in chapter 12. The chapter introduces the knowledge base required to address some basic design issues. If the layout of the environment does not afford the behavior patterns required by people to attain their goals, or if it does not provide shelter for these activities, it acts deterministically. Whether or not the built environment

supports the activity patterns of people is closely tied to their competence levels. Of particular concern in recent times has been the effect that traditional patterns of building the environment have had on the mobility of handicapped people.

The layout of the environment also affects behavior in other ways. Behavior in buildings and cities is not only a function of the setting inhabited, but also of the settings that we believe to be available outside our immediate perception. It is a function of the cognitive images we have of buildings and cities. It has to do also with the ease or difficulty we have in finding our way around. Our activities, in turn, affect our images. The physical structure of the environment has a major impact on these images. Chapter 13, "Cognitive Maps and Spatial Behavior," draws on the theoretical work on city layouts, urban design, and architecture of Kevin Lynch (1960) and Romedi Passini (1984), and on the work of Ulrich Neisser (1977) and Gary Moore (1973, 1976) on the psychological development of way-finding abilities. The objective is to show how the layout of the environment affects our images of it, and how these in turn affect and are affected by spatial behavior patterns. These issues of orientation—knowing where one is and how to move toward one's destination correctly—have much to do with meeting the needs for security and belongingness identified by Maslow and with the "psychic security" function of the built environment identified by Steele.

Buildings, landscapes, and urban designs which simply afford human movement patterns are not necessarily perceived as good ones by the people who inhabit them. There are more subtle human behaviors which are largely subconscious but which are affected by the layout of the environment. The research on privacy, personal space, territoriality, and design conducted since Edward T. Hall wrote his seminal book, *The Hidden Dimension* (1966), has considerably enhanced our understanding of the patterns of rooms, buildings, and building complexes in which people feel psychologically comfortable and the reasons for this. These ideas are presented in chapter 14, "Privacy, Territoriality, and Personal Space—Proxemic Theory."

Implicit, and often explicit, in the work of Hall, Sommer, and Altman is that the layout of the environment affects patterns of interaction between people. Many social planners and designers have promoted the role of the built environment in enhancing or hindering interaction patterns between people. The objective of chapter 15, "Social Interaction and the Built Environment," is to present our current understanding of this role.

The following chapter, "Social Organization and the Built Environment," takes this a step farther by relating these findings to the development of social organizations. It deals with the possibility that one layout of the environment may afford the development of a social organization better than another. The chapter thus deals with an issue—the ability to influence social organizational development through design—that has caused designers much trouble in the past. The objective of this chapter is to clarify the role of the built environment in the development of both formal and informal, or communal, social organizations. The topic thus cuts across the discussion of the earlier chapters of this book. The affordances of the built environment for activities, interaction patterns, privacy, and proxemic behavior all contribute to our understanding of social interaction patterns and design.

It would be erroneous to suggest that none of these chapters is concerned with issues of "delight" in and of the built environment. They all are, as indicated in the previous table. At the same time, the visual character of the built environment—both its formal and associative aspects—as perceived by different people, is different from that of the environment's affordances for activities. For this reason it is discussed separately. ∎

11

THE BEHAVIOR SETTING: A UNIT FOR ENVIRONMENTAL ANALYSIS AND DESIGN

One of the basic reasons for creating or redeveloping cities, erecting buildings, making plazas, gardens, and new infrastructure systems is to provide for some existing or potential set of human activities. Sometimes these are the everyday activities of walking, watching, working, sleeping, recreating, and eating, and sometimes they are unique activities. The attainment of almost all human needs involves some sort of gross motor activity—movement. This applies to the actions to meet survival needs, to actions involving access to other people and organizations to meet needs for affiliation and esteem, and to actions involving access to developmental opportunities to meet cognitive needs.

One of the most important developments in the behavioral sciences for design professionals has been the creation of *ecological psychology* by Roger Barker and his colleagues (Barker 1968, Gump 1979). Ecological psychology breaks from traditional approaches to psychological research. It focuses on extraindividual behavior in the field rather than on individual behavior in the laboratory. Moreover, Barker's work is directed at describing patterns of behavior in relationship to their physical setting. This is of fundamental concern to environmental designers as well. David Haviland (1967), for instance, coined the term "activity-space" to describe discrete units of the behavior–environment relationship for architectural design. Ecological psychology provides the concept of "behavior setting," which is essentially the same as "activity-space."

BEHAVIOR SETTINGS

The built environment, it has been noted here, consists of a structured set of surfaces of various qualities. A set may vary from a single surface that affords support to a surface that completely encloses a person. While sometimes these layouts are designed purely for aesthetic appreciation, usually they are designed to afford certain activities. One way for environmental designers to refer to these is in terms of *activity systems* composed of *behavior circuits* (Perin 1970). Behavior circuits have a specific purpose and are differentiated from each other by specific actions, such as a "game of catch" or "microwave component assembly." Constance Perin proposes that the behavior circuit be the unit for architectural analysis and design. She writes:

> . . . what behavior circuit implies is an anthropological ergonomics, tracking people's behavior through the fulfillment of their everyday purposes at the scale of the room, the house, the block, the neighborhood, the city, in order to learn what resources—physical and human—are needed to support, enable or fulfill them.

Roger Barker's work provides the conceptual framework for this.

A *behavior setting* is considered to be a stable combination of activity and place. It consists of:

- a recurrent activity—a *standing pattern of behavior*

113

- a particular layout of the environment—the *milieu*
- a congruent relationship between the two—a *synomorphy*
- a specific time period.

This means that the same physical setting may be part of more than one behavior setting if different standing patterns of behavior occur within it at different times.

A standing pattern of behavior may consist of a number of different behaviors occurring simultaneously:

- overt emotional behavior
- problem-solving behavior
- gross motor activity
- interpersonal interaction
- the manipulation of objects.

The combination of these behaviors, which constitutes a particular standing pattern of behavior, occurs within a particular physical setting—its milieu.

Behavior settings have an internal structure. This may well be accompanied by an internal organization of the milieu. Different individuals or groups occupy different parts of the behavior setting because their roles are different. In a classroom, the teacher occupies a specific area which may be designated by a raised platform that enables him or her to exert greater control over the standing pattern of behavior. Many behavior setting structures are differentiated on the basis of who controls the activity. Barker (1968) calls the area inhabited by the controlling person the *performance zone*. Not all settings have performance zones. Not all performance zones are architecturally differentiated.

Psychologist Paul Gump (1971) gives a good example of a behavior setting in his analysis of a market (see fig. 11-1):

> The person is in a non-human context which has physical boundaries (walls), internal spatial differentiation (aisles) and objects (foodstuffs).
>
> The person is in a behavioral system to which he contributes and which, reciprocally, supports his activity in the store. The market has a sequence of events, a program, which includes buying and selling behaviors. These behaviors constitute the standing pattern of behavior.
>
> The synomorphy is complex. The customer's share of the marketing standing pattern of behavior includes scanning and selecting; the display case presents an array of meats for this process. On one side, the butcher who arranges and replenishes the meats must have ready access to them. But the milieu must

not only fit the separate behaviors of the users but their interactions as well. Thus the display case permits some interaction between customer and butcher (viewing, speaking, passing objects); the customer must scan and select but not touch the meat; he may talk to the butcher but must not enter his supply or work space.

Such analyses begin to show the richness of human behavior and the complexity of behaviors that the built environment has to afford and afford well.

A "behavior setting" enables a person to achieve a "multiplicity of satisfactions" (Barker 1960). These may be of different types for different people. The same behavior setting may, for instance, enable one person to meet his or her needs for affiliation, while for another it meets more basic ends such as earning a living, while for others it may meet both. Similarly, it may meet different needs for an individual at different times.

The Boundaries of Behavior Settings

A clear statement on the nature of behavior setting boundaries has been presented by Robert Bechtel (1977):

> A behavior setting boundary is where the behavior stops. An ideal boundary is a wall, which stops behavior from getting in and out. Such obvious qualities as opacity to sight and sound are important in setting boundaries. Yet it is when behavior setting boundaries are not so obvious that the problems of boundary definition occur.

Boundary problems arise when there is an insufficient segregation of activities that need to be segregated or when there is too much segregation between activities. Special difficulties arise when some but not all aspects of one standing pattern of behavior need to be segregated from another. This occurs, for instance, in open-classroom schools where visual segregation between activities is not necessary but auditory segregation is. Difficulties may arise also when the boundary markers are symbolic—such as a change in floor texture—and not recognizable to some individuals. This is particularly likely to happen in cross-cultural situations where the markers are recognized by one group and not another.

Boundary problems can be resolved in a number of ways. If the problem is one of overlapping behavior settings, then either a physical boundary can be erected or administrative changes can be made. Sometimes only a clear symbolic marker is required. In deciding what boundary conditions are necessary, one must first decide what degree of seg-

1

2

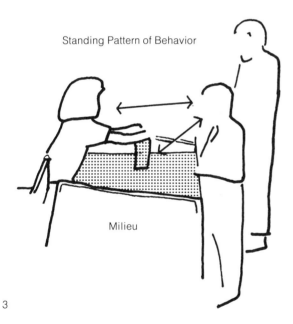

Standing Pattern of Behavior

Milieu

3

11-1. Behavior Settings.
The internal layouts of shops (1) consistently follow certain principles because of the standing patterns of behavior that they have to accommodate. Some of these behaviors are complex and involve the interaction between people and a wide range of behaviors on the part of each. This can be seen in even a relatively simple setting such as at a counter (2). The basic interactions in such a subsetting are shown in (3) (see Gump 1971).

regation is necessary between behavior settings. In interior design the clash may be between the aesthetic values of the architect and the requirements for a layout that affords the activity well. There is often a discrepancy between an ideological belief about how things should occur and the actuality of human behavior. The ideological desire for openness in landscape-type office layouts and school designs, for instance, has been in strong contrast to what people are habituated to and how they actually desire to interact. The building designs have been

more flexible than human behavior.

Roger Barker developed the "behavior setting survey" as a means for differentiating between behavior settings. This has been fully described by Robert Bechtel (1977). The goal is to understand the internal interaction and external links of a set of behaviors. It relies heavily on the judgments of "experts." Certainly, in any organization—formal or communal, large-scale such as a major factory or small-scale such as a single-family house—it is important to recognize the activity systems that are its life, the behavior settings that constitute the activity system, and the degree to which the behavior settings are or should be nested, overlapping, or segregated.

ACTIVITY SYSTEMS

The environment consists of a hierarchy of behavior settings linked together to form activity systems. People's activity systems reflect their motivations, attitudes, and knowledge about (or images of) the world within the constraints of their incomes, competencies, and cultural norms (Chapin and Brail 1969, Porteous 1977). The identification and consideration of existing activity systems and the *design* of potential new ones constitute an essential basis for urban design and architectural and landscape architectural thinking.

Activity systems can be analyzed in a number of ways, including the use of time budgets, censusing, and origination and destination studies—macro approaches to the study of spatial behavior. These techniques are, however, applicable at both a building scale and an urban scale. *Time budgets* enable people's daily, weekly, or seasonal activities to be decomposed into a set of behavior settings that constitute their working day or, more broadly, their lifestyles (Michelson and Reed 1975). Such studies can be used to analyze the nature of organizations as well. *Censusing* is a term coined by ecological psychologists to describe the process of studying all the activities of an individual during a particular time period, using simple observation. Barker and Wright (1951), for example, have studied the behavior of a single child for a whole day. This technique can be used to attain such objectives as the understanding of how a set of workers uses a building, but it is extremely cumbersome to carry out. We resort to shorthand techniques for attempting to ascertain the same information. *Origin and destination studies*, for instance, identify the beginning and end of movement patterns.

Such studies show the actual rather than the imagined standing patterns of behavior that constitute the lives of individuals and organizations. They show the tremendous diversity of human activities and the way patterns of the environment are used. The idealized and implemented designs of many architects, landscape architects, and urban designers are often not nearly as rich in affordances for a variety of standing patterns of behavior in comparison to those afforded by vernacular environments. Much of the criticism of both the Modern Movement and Post-Modernism has focused on this (see also Framptom 1980). If one compares the urban renewal efforts of the fifties, sixties, and seventies to what was replaced, one certainly finds the new environments to be neater and more hygienic than what was there before but also less rich in behavior settings. Many people have recognized this and have been fascinated by unselfconsciously designed environments (Jacobs 1961, Rudofsky 1964). Others (Brolin and Zeisel 1970, Zeisel 1981) have shown conceptually how through observation the richness of the behaviors of a group of people can be discerned and how it can be accommodated in a new building or building complex (see fig. 11-2).

The dullness of environments is often due to the paucity of standing patterns of behavior (hence of behavior settings) as much as to the appearance of the built environment. This cannot be rectified simply by changing the built environment to afford more activities unless there are overt or latent predispositions for those activities. Behavior settings analysis can help designers understand what the former are; one can speculate on the latter based on the perceptions of people's tendencies to behave in specific ways (Alexander and Poyner 1970).

Link Analysis

Behavior settings are linked to form part of an activity system and larger, more encompassing behavior settings. The flow of people, goods, and information between settings can be measured quantitatively. The layout of buildings—houses, offices, stores, building complexes, neighborhoods, and cities—very much affects the efficiency with which these organizations operate (Kantowitz and Sorkin 1983). The normative position of many architects of the Modern Movement was that the affordances for the interference of paths of movement and also the total circulation distance within buildings had to be reduced. This was part of the concept of functionalism.

Efficiency in circulation, it is now recognized, is neither the sole end of a design nor the sole measurement of its quality. The crossing of paths may well serve positive ends such as the need for people to see other people as the basis for potential interactions and furthering a sense of security or belonging. There are many instances, however, when inefficiency in circulation and the moving of goods has had serious deleterious effects on the operation of an organization. Thus, one of the normative questions a designer has to address during the intelligence phase of the designing process is what ought to be the efficiency of operation of an organization in terms of the circulation of people and goods, in comparison to that required for the achievement of other goals.

2. Perspective through Interior Street

OBSERVATIONS AND REQUIREMENTS

12 OBS: After they are ten years old, boys
are generally unsupervised while
outside, and enjoy the freedom to roam
the neighborhood.
REQ: Many places for pedestrian movement.

13 OBS: Groups of teen-agers of different
sexes spend a lot of time "hanging
around" or looking for something to
do. Often they do this with adults
or teen-agers of the opposite sex.
REQ: (A) Connection between boys' group
and peer groups of other statuses.
(B) Connection between boys' and
girls' outside areas and apartments.

14 OBS: Teen-agers gather on corners near
small stores.
REQ: Areas for informal congregating
outside and around commercial areas.

15 OBS: Although boys meet with boys, and
girls with girls, the girls meet near the
corners where the boys hang out.
REQ: Adolescent girls' areas visible to
boys' areas.

16 OBS: Young teen-age girls take care of
younger children on the streets.
REQ: Adolescent girls' areas near
children's play areas.

17 OBS: Both men and women use dress as a
means of self-expression, spending
much money on clothes.
REQ: General visibility among pedestrian,
apartment, commercial, and
recreational areas.

18 OBS: Men wash their cars on the streets
as often as once a week. For men, the
car is important as a means of
expressing their identity.
REQ: Visibility for areas related to
automobiles.

19 OBS: Bars and luncheonettes are places to
exchange news and gossip, as well as
message centers for regular customers.
REQ: (A) Commercial area connected to
living areas.
(B) Commercial area visible from
street and other commercial areas.

20 OBS: Women socialize while shopping.
REQ: Commercial areas visible to and
from streets.

Source: Brolin and Zeisel (1968)

11-2. Field Observations and the Design of Behavior Settings.

THE INFLUENCE OF BEHAVIOR SETTINGS ON THE BEHAVIOR OF INDIVIDUALS

In this book it has been pointed out that different structures, or patterns, of the milieu afford different behaviors and that the set of affordances that is effective for a particular person or group depends on a number of complex factors, including predispositions, competencies, and the perceived rewards and costs of engaging in specific behaviors. Behavior settings as a whole tend to be more coercive than either the standing patterns of behavior or the milieu independently.

Barker's assertions about the impact of the physical environment on behavior are somewhat contradictory. On one hand he asserts that "the non-social, ecological environment does not demand behavior"; on the other, he accepts the Gestalt psychology concept of physiognomic perception. This results in the statement that the milieu has a *demand quality*. Open spaces, he states, invite a child to run. The influence of Kurt Lewin's concept of *invitational quality* (1936, 1951) on Barker's thinking is clear.

Social and socialization forces are strongly coercive. Teachers, legal and administrative systems,

1

2

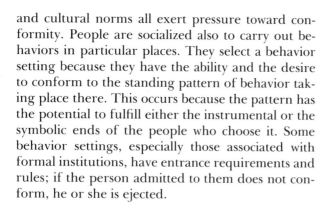

3

11-3. Behavior Settings and Behavior.

A behavior setting such as a city square can be subdivided into a number of subsettings. The liveliness of such places depends on what each subsetting affords and the predispositions of the population. Popular gathering places are those that afford comfortable sitting, good light, and people-watching (1) and something that generates activities, such as a foodseller (2). In contrast, those plazas (3) without such affordances are dead places (Whyte 1975, Lennard and Lennard 1983). There is a reciprocal relationship between the individual and the behavioral system of which he or she is a part. The individual contributes to and is supported by the behavior setting.

and cultural norms all exert pressure toward conformity. People are socialized also to carry out behaviors in particular places. They select a behavior setting because they have the ability and the desire to conform to the standing pattern of behavior taking place there. This occurs because the pattern has the potential to fulfill either the instrumental or the symbolic ends of the people who choose it. Some behavior settings, especially those associated with formal institutions, have entrance requirements and rules; if the person admitted to them does not conform, he or she is ejected.

People also adapt the milieu to better *fit* existing or desired patterns of behavior. Sometimes the erosion of the milieu as the result of constant use reduces its adequacy in affording a pattern of behavior. At some point, if it no longer meets a minimum level of adequacy, it may be abandoned. It may also be adapted or rebuilt.

THE CONCEPT OF FIT

The words *fit, afford, synomorphy,* and *congruence* have all been used to describe the relationship between a pattern of behavior and a pattern of the physical environment. They can all be used in a qualitative sense: some milieus afford (Gibson 1979), or fit (Alexander 1964), a specific pattern of behavior better than others; there is a greater degree of synomorphy (Barker 1968) or congruence (Michelson 1976) between environment and behavior in one instance than in another. Some basketball-court surfaces fit the activities "running, jumping, and bouncing a ball" better than others; some arenas fit the activity "watching a game" better than others; the ambient quality of some milieus simply makes them better places in which to play basketball. The use of the term *fit* in this sense is associated with the work of Christopher Alexander (1960), who points out that we generally are better able to pick out misfits between environments and human activities than good fits.

Evaluating the quality of the behavior–environment fit, or synomorphy, is difficult because one is dealing simultaneously with a multiplicity of variables. One way is to do it entirely subjectively: if people say it is good, it is good. Sometimes apparent misfits in either objective or subjective terms may not matter or may even yield beneficial results.

In many seemingly negative and stressful physical settings the productivity and harmony of the participants is extremely high (Helmreich 1974). Tolerances for the negative aspects of the setting exist because the perceived rewards for being there are high. Thus, perceptions of costs and rewards, individual values and motivations, and individual habituation levels all help to explain different tolerances for how well a milieu fits a pattern of behavior and the difficulty in developing a quantitative method for evaluating the fitness of environments.

It is difficult to build a clear theory of the quality of fit between environments and activities based on the subjective evaluations of people. Some people simply complain more than others; people in good moods give more positive evaluations than people in bad moods; people evaluate buildings and rooms on different dimensions; above all, people's expectations differ (Gutman and Westergaard 1974).

Many discussions of environmental fit tend to assume that a good milieu is one that meets the structure of behavior very tightly. This is not necessarily the case, however. A number of questions arise: How enduring will a pattern of behavior be? How costly will it be to achieve a marginally better fit? Whose values does one consider? The basic goal is to have a milieu that fits the problem at hand. We rely and will have to rely on subjective analyses to a great extent. This is one of the reasons why architectural design is an argumentative process. This is also why an argument is often made for adaptable or flexible or open-ended designs (Rapoport 1967).

Adaptability and Flexibility

With some exceptions, it is possible for many different standing patterns of behavior to occur in the same milieu. A well-illuminated room can serve many purposes, although once it is furnished (internally structured, in Barker's terms) it affords some things considerably better than others. Some layouts, a WC, for instance, are designed for very specific purposes and do not afford very much else. Even a WC, however, affords water play for children if the social environment allows it.

Edward T. Hall (1966) identifies three fundamental types of layout patterns: *fixed-feature space, semifixed-feature space,* and *informal space.* Fixed-feature space is enclosed by elements that are not easily movable: solid walls, floors, windows, and fittings. Semifixed-feature space is that in which furnishings can be moved around. In some instances it is more than this; in the traditional Japanese house, the walls can be moved to create different settings for different activities at different times of the day. Informal space, on the other hand, lasts only for as long as an exchange between two or more people lasts. It is not a stated space and occurs outside awareness.

Some environments afford many activities without restructuring. Some environments are easy to change to afford different activities. Environmental designers use different terms for these two situations. The first will be referred to here as *adaptable* and the second as *flexible,* although often the terms are used as synonyms or in the opposite way.

An adaptable layout is one that affords different standing patterns of behavior at different times without requiring physical changes. It is multipurpose fixed-feature space. A high school gymnasium may house a physical-training class at one time and a dance at another. Architect Robert Venturi (1966) notes: "There are justifications for the multi-functioning building. . . . A room can have many functions at the same time or at different times." In the first of these cases, the behavior settings are adjacent; in the second there is a difference in temporal locus. The placement of doors, windows, and built furniture very much affects the adaptability of spaces such as dormitory rooms. Many designs severely reduce the affordances for different room geographies and the activities that accompany them (Van der Ryn and Silverstein 1967, Sommer 1974b).

Flexible layouts are those in which the structure is easy to change to accommodate different needs. This is more than is generally implied by semifixed-feature space. Usually it implies a change in the enclosing boundary and/or its internal structure. In a "flexible office space" the walls between offices are easily movable. A flexible sports arena may be one that affords easy rearrangement of its seating.

Whatever terms one uses, it is important, in the design of behavior settings, to recognize that the built environment is not simply fixed-feature space. Specific designed environments are seldom tailor-made to cater to only one standing pattern of behavior. As a result, a particular layout often affords one activity better than another and this is accepted because of the perceived psychic or financial rewards in terms of cost savings. Cities and buildings that are adaptable and reasonably flexible are the ones that survive even though they may not be regarded as "well designed"—meaning that there is not a tight fit between behavior and the built environment. Venturi (1966) notes that the important buildings of the past that have survived are the adaptable ones. Jane Jacobs (1969) notes the same thing about the physical layout (and mind-set) of cities that adjust well to changes in their basic activity patterns. Some buildings are also easier to change because of their physical structure (Cowan 1962–63).

BEHAVIOR SETTINGS AND DESIGN

There is a well-developed vocabulary for classifying buildings and rooms. When it is said that a building is a "school" or a "church" or an "office building," people have an image of its physical nature and the standing patterns of behavior that it houses. These images are based on people's own experiences. We designers also rely on our own images. There is often a difference between our images of the patterns we expect to be housed and the actual patterns. Constance Perin (1970) notes:

> Those categories [building type and room type names] should only be a shorthand for expressing the diversity of human behavior, but as they are used, they are made to substitute for knowledge of what it is people do.

This is an inherent danger in the study of architectural typologies as the basis for programming and design. The concepts of activity systems and behavior settings provide the basis for a much richer way of considering the environment than thinking of it merely in terms of land uses and building and room types. They provide a conceptually clear basis for analyzing the existing patterns of behavior and milieus and for thinking about what might exist. The difficulty is that behavior setting analysis takes time

and effort and thus is not without its costs. It is, however, liberating—it helps us to get away from old clichés, from imposing inappropriate images of behavior on people, and from using prototypical designs without thinking. Above all, it makes one consider behavior patterns and milieus as interlocking entities.

INDIVIDUAL DIFFERENCES IN ACTIVITY SYSTEMS

Much effort has been made during the past twenty years to develop generalizations about people's activity systems as the basis for planning and design decisions. These studies are leading to an understanding of the variables that are important and the questions to consider in programming and design. The activities of social classes of individuals (see Michelson 1976), of people in specific places such as public open space (for example, Hester 1975, Whyte 1980), of people at specific stages in their life cycle—the young (Pollowy 1977, Lynch 1977) and the elderly (Howell 1980)—have been studied. Similar efforts (Chapin 1965, Michelson 1975, Hester 1975, Bechtel 1977, Zeisel 1981) have been made to develop procedures for ascertaining the nature of activity patterns that occur in specific problem contexts. Of particular importance has been the effort to do both of these within a cross-cultural perspective (such as Rapoport 1969, 1977). We thus now have the basis for making some preliminary generalizations about human activity systems which illustrate the diversity of human needs. A comprehensive overview is impossible, but a brief review of some of the research on residential environments gives some idea of what behavioral sciences research offers the designer.

The fit between environment and behavior, at a fundamental level, depends on the competence level of the people—their *organismic* characteristics. Since so many human activities involve carrying out operations, the need for the milieu to be congruent with human capabilities is essential. The research areas of human engineering—anthropometrics and ergonomics—have arisen in response to these needs. This research and its theoretical implications are described in the next chapter, which focuses on making the environment and its equipment more usable by people rather than on describing how different organismic characteristics of individuals result in different activity systems.

As people grow up their competencies increase, their use of the environment becomes more broad-ranging. As their competencies decrease as they enter old age or suffer accidents or illnesses, so the

1

2

3

11-4. Environment and Lifestyle.
While almost any residential area affords almost all life-styles, the congruence between some lifestyles and some environmental patterns is higher in some areas than in others. Traditional row-house face blocks (1) afford easy accessibility of people to each other and the housing affords the maintenance of horizontally extended family ties. This lifestyle is not afforded easily by high-rise apartment buildings (2). They afford anonymity very well. The typical suburban environment (3) fits the home-centered life of many nuclear families very well but not the "hanging out" behavior of teenagers or older people.

built environment becomes more restrictive. There is thus a close correlation between a person's stage in life cycle and his or her physiological competencies and activity systems. Stage in life cycle, however, also implies a common focus of concern: growing up, being independent, raising children, and so forth (Michelson 1976). Different patterns of built environments—urban and suburban, play areas, central cities, suburban shopping malls—afford very different experiences for people at different stages in their life cycles and of different physiological competencies.

Neighborhood spaces are heavily used by the

young and the old (Hester 1975). Kevin Lynch (1977) has described what different patterns of residential areas afford children in a number of different countries. Some environments are rich in affordances for children's behavior within their range of competencies; others are not. Children are developing physiologically and mentally and can turn almost any aspect of the built environment into an opportunity for play. Advocates for children, however, note that the growth in the scale of economic activity combined with segregationist land-use policies have decreased the opportunities for learning by self-testing and by observing the activities of adults (Parr 1967b, 1969). One of the responses has been to create adventure playgrounds (Allen 1968) and opportunities for sports activities. Another has been the more traditional concern with neighborhood schools (see Alexander 1977). In multi-cultural areas, however, parents tend to choose schools based on their own values, not on proximity (Keller 1968, Brolin 1976).

The needs of teenagers have been very much neglected by policymakers and design philosophers in the United States (Popenoe 1977, Ladd 1978). The speculation is that in the absence of legitimate sources of self-testing and adventure teenagers often turn to antisocial behavior. Teen centers have been proposed and built in a number of places but these often are used more by subteens (Brooks 1974). Adolescents in many parts of the world describe the environments in which they are growing up, particularly planned environments on the outskirts of cities, as boring (Lynch 1977), offering them nothing that they can control and manage. Often environments are overmanicured with few opportunities for exploration and doing things on one's own.

At the other end of the age spectrum, subsets of the elderly have special needs (Lawton 1975, Howell 1980). Often their range of activity is reduced as they find it increasingly difficult to use transportation to get to existing opportunities for recreation and development or simply to acquire the needs of daily life. There are strong advocates for barrier-free environments (Bednar 1977) that will give access to places for people with low physiological capabilities. This does not, however, deal with the broader issues of what activity systems should be used as the basis for design.

Not only do people's organismic characteristics affect their activities but so do their personality attributes. We do not understand this well. Some intuitively appealing hypotheses about the use of the environment by people of different personality types can be made. For instance, one hypothesis is that extroverts use a broader range of behavior settings and seek closer contact with the external environment than do introverts. It is tempting to take this observation and base, say, the design of the fenestration of houses and other buildings on it. This is a dangerous thing to do. Many intuitively appealing hypotheses about the architectural correlates of personality types are not supported by empirical evidence (Mikellides 1980). There is much more research and evidence available on the correlations between the activity systems of people and their social-group membership and culture.

People of different cultures inhabit different behavior settings because their activity systems dif-

fer. Amos Rapoport (1969) identifies five major aspects of culture that are reflected in the interior organization of houses:

- the way basic activities are carried out
- the structure of the family
- gender roles
- attitudes toward privacy
- the process of social intercourse.

The way such activities as sleeping, cooking, and eating are carried out varies culturally. In some cultures, men eat first; in others, the family eats together. In some cultures people sit on the floor; in others they sit on chairs at tables. This affects such design concerns as window-sill height, space requirements, and location of doors. Similarly, sleeping habits differ. The behavior setting "bedroom" is not a universal type. In warm climates men, in particular, may sleep outdoors. In much of the recent air-conditioned housing in Iran, the pattern of outdoor sleeping continues even though the housing ill affords it.

In the United States, subcultures are reflected in the interior organization of houses. For instance, the activity patterns of lower-income Puerto Rican families result in the kitchen tending to be the place where families entertain guests even if it does not comfortably afford entertaining. Only very special guests are invited to the living room. For Anglo-Saxon families, the living room tends to be the place for entertaining others. The ideal linkage of the front door, kitchen, living room, and dining area thus differs for the two groups (Zeisel 1974).

Historically there has been a clear distinction in most cultures between men's and women's activities in houses. This is more obvious in societies where women are cloistered, such as the traditional Saudi Arabian house (Baleela 1975). As patterns of gender roles shift in society so does the interior organization of houses, the nature of fenestration, the relationship between house and street, and the layout of open spaces. Although the courtyard house makes sense climatically in many parts of the world, it is giving way to the "villa" or "bungalow" because its social function as a segregator of activities by gender is no longer as important as it once was. Many design ideologies involving the centralization of kitchens were based on assumptions regarding the freeing of women to pursue activities other than household ones (Hayden 1976).

Lifestyle can be understood in terms of the roles that people play and the behavior settings they inhabit. One important distinction that has urban and landscape design implications is that between local and cosmopolitan lifestyles. In terms of housing de-

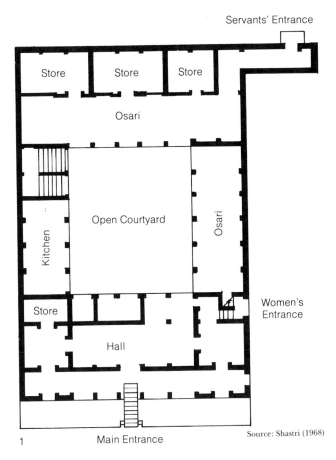

Servants' Entrance

1

Main Entrance

Source: Shastri (1968)

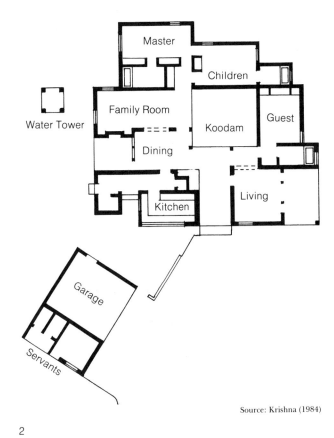

2

Source: Krishna (1984)

3

Source: Aggarawal (1984)

11-5. House Form and Culture.

The subsettings that form the behavior setting "house" may have the same purpose in different cultures, but their nature and the relationships among them may differ. All three examples above are from India. The plans represent differences in attitudes toward activities based on gender roles and segregations, toward the role of servants and children, and toward cooking and ablutions. The courtyard house (1) represents the traditional form while the patterns in (2) and (3) are those of a present house and flat (see also Rapoport 1969).

sign, the place in the house where most activities occur, the nature of interactions between people, the degree of home-centeredness of activities, and the nature of family organization are aspects that seem particularly important in developing design objectives.

Locals are people who use settings close to their place of residence. Cosmopolitans are regional people using city centers and facilities spread across the metropolitan areas and in other cities. Melvin Webber (1963) and Peter Wilmott and Michael Young (1973) believe that the trend is almost inexorably toward cosmopolitan lifestyles (a conclusion that is not based on strong empirical information, however). The British new town of Milton Keynes, with its lack of neighborhood foci, is an example of a design based on this assumption. Cosmopolitan people seek segregation from their neighbors either through distance or by ignoring them. For locals, in contrast, accessibility to facilities and people on a neighborhood basis is important (Michelson 1976). The difficulty is to predict how future developments in communications technology will affect the interaction patterns among people. At present most predictions suggest a greater segregation between people, less reliance on face-to-face communication, and more people working out of their residences—in other words, less need to get together at common venues for work or entertainment. Whether or not this actually will occur is open to conjecture, which is one reason for advocating flexibility and adaptability in the built environment.

An environment with houses close together, with their windows offering easy natural surveillance of the street, and with mixed land-use patterns, affords easy interactions and necessitates movement of its residents through the area. This type of environment is congruent with lifestyles, particularly lower-income lifestyles, that stress family interaction and group integration rather than individual achievement. An area of spread single-family detached homes does not afford this lifestyle very effectively (Gans 1962, Michelson 1976).

Family organization is an important variable in both interior and neighborhood design. A distinction often is made between nuclear and extended families. The latter can be of three types: horizontally extended, vertically extended, or both. In horizontally extended families, those with many same-generation relatives, the demand is for highly adaptable milieus capable of seating large numbers of people on many occasions. With vertically extended families, those consisting of three generations living together, sleeping space becomes more important. When a family is both horizontally and vertically extended (as in Chandigarh, India, as reported by Brolin 1976), space needs become even more extensive.

In nuclear families the intensive interaction is between spouses and children. Outside the family the interaction tends to be with friends and not with relatives. When this pattern is accompanied by a home-centered lifestyle, then the residential area of single-family detached homes, segregated land use, private swimming pools, and backyards works well (Michelson 1976). In such areas the need for an automobile is high. Without a car, and often a second one, access to jobs and recreation opportunities tends to be low. Housewives and teenagers are particularly affected by this (Popenoe 1977).

Cultural difference in working, shopping habits, and recreation also need to be understood (Brolin 1976, Gastal 1982). In some cities, the behavior setting "street" is for handling fast-moving traffic.

In countries like India, however, there are many modes of transportation using the street simultaneously: bicycles, pedestrians, rickshaws (bicycle-, motor-, and person-drawn), bullock carts, camels, and so on. Shops, vendors, and people sleeping also encroach on many streets. In some places the street is also a promenade; in others the railroad station is the place for promenading (Sasuki 1976). Cruising in automobiles is a special type of teenage promenading (Goldberg 1969).

The nature of the *geographic environment,* particularly the climate and topography, very much affects the distribution and nature of behavior settings in a place. Culture and climate are linked. The pace of life, the use of houses, buildings, and open spaces, the nature of activities (particularly recreational activities), reflect the natural features and climate of an area. The correspondence is not total. There are many instances where the climate and natural character of an area afford activities that have not been absorbed into a culture. Nevertheless, there is a strong relationship between the activity patterns of people and the natural features of their environment.

Denver, Colorado and Miami Beach, Florida contain many similar settings, but they also contain many settings that are unique because the affordances of the natural environment have been exploited to fulfill desired activities. Mountains, the warm sea, and frozen lakes afford different activities. A warm, dry climate affords outdoor cafés very well. This does not mean that all cities with such climates have them. And many cities without such a climate, such as Paris, do have them!

Much of the research on behavior settings and activity patterns has focused on the residential environment and public open space. Similar studies can be carried out for other parts of the environment, such as factories and recreation areas. Design, however, involves more than simply catering to existing systems of activities. It also involves asking the question: What behavior settings should exist?

CONCLUSION

Designers think of the environment in terms of spaces or rooms. These are physical configurations—the geometry of the world. It is important for designers to understand what geometrical possibilities exist as the basis for designing. At the same time, much of the debate over the quality of the environment is more concerned with what the geometries afford. Considering the environment as a nested set of behavior settings brings attention to the interdependence of standing patterns of behavior and the built and natural worlds.

Behavioral science research provides the basis for environmental designers and clients asking questions about what patterns of behavior presently exist and what ones should exist in particular situations. Behavioral setting analysis yields a much richer view of human behavior than does intuition alone. It also yields important insights into the nature of individual and group differences in patterns of behavior that enable designers to get away from stereotypical images of people and their activities.

ADDITIONAL READINGS

Ås, Dagfin. "Observing Environmental Behavior: The Behavior Setting." In William Michelson, ed., *Behavioral Research Methods in Environmental Design.* Stroudsburg, Pa.: Dowden, Hutchinson and Ross, 1974, pp. 280–300.

Barker, Roger. "Behavioral Settings: Defining Attributes and Varying Properties." In *Ecological Psychology: Concepts and Methods for Studying the Environment of Human Behavior.* Stanford, Ca.: Stanford University Press, 1968, pp. 183–193.

Bechtel, Robert E. *Enclosing Behavior.* Stroudsburg, Pa.: Dowden, Hutchinson and Ross, 1977.

Hester, Randolph. *Neighborhood Space.* Stroudsburg, Pa.: Dowden, Hutchinson and Ross, 1975.

LeCompte, William. "Behavior Settings as Data-Generating Units for the Environmental Planner and Architect." In Jon Lang et al., eds., *Designing for Human Behavior: Architecture and the Behavioral Sciences.* Stroudsburg, Pa.: Dowden, Hutchinson and Ross, 1974, pp. 183–193.

Michelson, William. *Man and his Urban Environment: A Sociological Approach.* Reading, Mass.: Addison-Wesley, 1976 (revised edition).

Perin, Constance. "Human Studies in the Inception Process." In *With Man in Mind.* Cambridge, Mass.: MIT Press, 1970, pp. 70–107.

Wicker, Alan. *An Introduction to Ecological Psychology.* Monterey, Ca.: Brooks/Cole, 1979.

12

ANTHROPOMETRICS AND ERGONOMICS

In any behavior setting, the milieu has to afford the standing pattern of behavior in order for the behavior to take place. This is basic to the attainment of any of the human needs described by Maslow. In addition, the built environment is expected to provide certain levels of bodily comfort. One reason the built environment is created is to fulfill the basic need for shelter. Buildings have been designed to respond to climatic conditions to a greater or lesser extent in order to meet the basic metabolic needs of people. Feelings of psychological well-being are related to physiological well-being, just as dissatisfaction is related to discomfort (Fitch 1965). At the same time, people are prepared to give up some degree of physiological comfort in order to attain other ends. There are also differences in perception of how comfortable the environment should be. Some people demand high levels of comfort, others believe that this is decadent (Kira 1966, Glassie 1975, Brebner 1982). This depends on expectations and habituation levels. Usually we are unaware of being comfortable. We are more aware when we feel uncomfortable—when the environment is subjectively too hot or too cold, or smelly, or noisy, or badly lit.

Anthropometrics and *ergonomics* are two fields of study that deal with the relationship between human physiological capabilities and metabolic pro-cesses and the built environment. Anthropometrics is the study of human physical dimensions, capabilities, and limitations (Thieberg 1965–70, Croney 1971). Ergonomics focuses more specifically on people and machines (Murrell 1965, de Montmollin 1967, Propst 1970). Often these fields are subsumed under the rubric *engineering psychology* or *human-factors engineering*. There have been three phases to the research in these fields. The first focused on the nature of machines and making people adapt to them; the second was concerned with modifying machines to make them easier and safer to use; and the third, which is emphasized currently, focuses on the whole behavior setting (de Montmollin 1967, Saarinen 1976, Kantowitz and Sorkin 1983).

For a long time we environmental designers thought that our intuitive understanding of human physiology was good enough for design. Le Corbusier developed what he believed to be a universal tool, based on anthropometrical dimensions, for scaling the environment for both use and aesthetic purposes. He called the scale the "modulor" (Le Corbusier 1951). Although Le Corbusier claimed his scale was "anthropocentric" and historically valid, this is hardly so. The basic height taken for a man in the scale—1.75 meters—was chosen for symbolic rather than statistically valid reasons.

We have become increasingly more self-con-

1

Photograph by D. Gorton

2

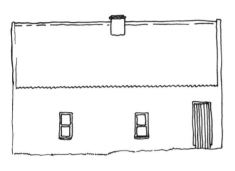

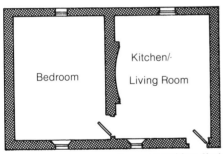

Bedroom

Kitchen/·
Living Room

Source: Adapted from Glassie(1982)

3

12-1. Symbolic Aesthetics and Physiological Concerns in Design.

Although designing for human comfort seems a fundamental goal of designers, people are prepared to forgo bodily comfort to attain other design goals. This is reflected in both vernacular and highly self-conscious design. The chairs by Mies van der Rohe (1) are a symbol of elegance and good taste but they are exceedingly difficult to get into and out of and are not particularly comfortable for a seated person. In much of Chandigarh, India (2), the buildings are set in large open spaces for symbolic reasons. Getting from one to another is arduous for even the heartiest soul especially on a summer day. Even though the technology and resources were available to build houses that afford greater bodily comfort, these Irish cottages (3) were dictated, unselfconsciously, largely by life-style and religious beliefs.

scious about the relationship between the environment and human behavior at a physiological level. There are a number of reasons for this:

1. Some of the best-known pieces of architect-designed furniture have been ridiculed for their lack of comfort and sometimes impossibility of use.

2. The energy crisis has led to questions regarding the heavy reliance on mechanical systems to attain and maintain comfort levels in much recent urban and architectural design. This is a particu-

larly acute issue in building design in resource-poor developing countries (Brolin 1976).

3. There is an increasing awareness of the number of accidents that occur in the workplace and at home due to the lack of congruence between an activity and the milieu affording it (Grandjean 1973).

4. Physiologically impaired people are demanding that they not be handicapped by the layout of the environment (Goldsmith 1976).

5. Designers are increasingly required to ad-

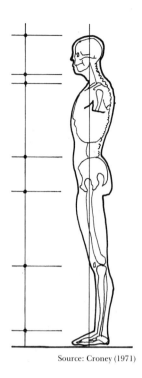

1

Source: Croney (1971)

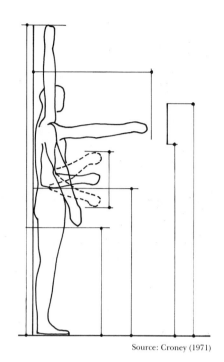

2

Source: Croney (1971)

3

12-2. Anthropometrics and Ergonomics.
Static anthropometrics is concerned with the basic dimensions of the human body (1). Dynamic anthropometrics is concerned with the capabilities of the human body in doing such things as reaching (2). Ergonomics is more especially concerned with the person-machine interface (3) where safety factors are of major importance.

dress these issues to meet the requirements of legislation.

The objective of this chapter is to bring attention to the basic theoretical issues of concern to environmental designers. It is concerned with the fields of anthropometrics and ergonomics and what they afford the designer, and with the issues involved in making the environment usable and comfortable for all. It is thus concerned with individual differences in abilities to use the environment.

ANTHROPOMETRICS

There are several basic points that must be remembered in considering the environment–behavior fit. The physiological capabilities of people differ. They go through rapid change from infancy to adulthood and they vary by gender. A person usually has full strength and mobility in early adulthood, then a gradual degeneration of the morphological systems takes place. There are also ethnic differences in human physiology. Some of these differences are well documented, others are not (see Dreyfuss 1967, Diffrient et al. 1974, Brebner 1982, Kantowitz and Sorkin 1983).

There are many variables of concern in designing the environment to afford specific behaviors. One set is concerned with the specific actions, body postures, and movement patterns of the individual or people involved, and one is concerned with psychological needs such as privacy, personal space, and territorial control. The former are of concern here.

Among the many data sources available to designers, some are specific to specific building types and some are specific to rooms or work settings. K.K.H. Murrell (1965) is particularly concerned with work stations, Franklin Becker (1981) and Etienne Grandjean (1984) with offices; Grandjean (1973) also presents a close analysis of requirements for domestic architecture. Alexander Kira's *The Bathroom* (1966) is a classical analysis of both anthropometric and psychological factors in equipment and room design. These books point out that it is easy to underestimate the amount and type of space that are required to carry out activities comfortably. They also show the interrelationship of physiological, psychological, and cultural variables in designing ostensibly in response to purely human physiological needs.

It should also be remembered that many of the data presented in books on anthropometrics are in guideline form. Many also are gender-biased and dated. They contain strong normative statements based on assumptions of good and bad for an "average" person. What is "good," however, is not a simple scientific fact even when dealing with quantifiable data.

Human Metabolic Processes and the Built Environment

The human body has various thermoregulators that keep the internal temperature constant by adjustments of blood circulation, perspiration, and heat production. The body exchanges heat with its surroundings through conduction, convection, radiation, and evaporation of sweat. The exchange is affected by a number of things: (1) the nature of the ambient and radiant surroundings—the heat-conducting properties of the air and surfaces in contact with the body and the surface temperatures and pigmentations of walls; (2) the pattern of behavior; (3) air movement; and (4) the relative humidity of the air. Thus, perceptions of comfort depend not only on the air temperature but on

whether or not windows and/or walls act as radiant heaters or coolers and on the dampness or dryness of the air. Relative humidities of 40 to 50 percent feel comfortable when heating is needed, while 40 to 60 percent is comfortable in hot weather (Grandjean 1973).

What constitutes a comfortable temperature for an individual depends on that person's activity and clothing and on the characteristics of the person involved. There is considerable variability in what people say is uncomfortable to them (see fig. 12-3, for instance). Suffice it to say here that the nature of the standing pattern of behavior affects perceptions of the temperature required for comfort. Individual expectations and personality differences are also important, however.

As technology has advanced, heating and cooling systems have improved. With this has come a rise in expectation of the quality of comfort afforded by the ambient environment and by the equipment and furnishings of buildings, plazas, and even such places as the queuing areas at amusement parks. There has been a reaction to this, particularly when highly technical equipment has been used in lieu of the thoughtful design use of projecting surfaces, screens, vegetation, and other low-technology means of maintaining comfort levels.

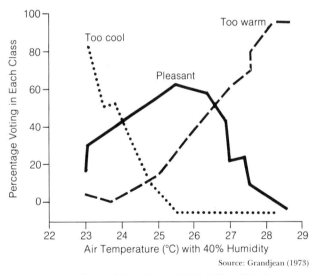

Source: Grandjean (1973)

12-3. Perceptions of Comfort of 845 Office Workers in New York.

Illumination Levels and Design

The level of illumination from natural and/or artificial sources in a setting has both operational and symbolic significance (Hayward 1974). Natural lighting varies over the course of the day, adding to human experience, but artificial light sources are more controllable. Operational factors depend on the nature of the eye and the processes of accommodation and adaptation. Symbolic factors depend on the associational meanings of the illumination level in the specific setting. They are not, however, independent of operational factors.

Accommodation is the ability of the eye to focus sharply on objects at varying distances. Adaptation deals with the ability to deal with differing levels of steady illumination. Sharp constrasts in levels of illumination cause dazzle, which is uncomfortable. People do, however, seem to get aesthetic pleasure from contrasting levels of illumination provided there is no dazzle involved and the eyes can focus sharply enough (Heschong 1979). This occurs, for example, when one is walking through alternating patches of light and shade along a pathway on a pleasant day.

For a behavior setting to be physiologically comfortably lit, light contrasts need to be low. If a room is laid out so that a person carrying out some activity looks into a bright window, a light wall near a dark floor, a dark object on a light background, or highly polished machine parts, that person will be subjected to some level of dazzle (Grandjean 1973). On the other hand, one way of differentiating between behavior settings—giving them a clear contour in Gestalt psychology terms—is by differences in illumination levels rather than by solid barriers. This is done, for instance, in shops where differences in illumination level differentiate between display areas and channels of movement (Hayward 1974).

The Physiology of Color Perception and Design

Color helps to differentiate between elements in a setting and/or between settings themselves. To make the seeing of objects such as knobs and handles easier they can be of a contrasting color to their backgrounds. Large brightly colored areas, on the other hand, fatigue the eye and can produce afterimages, especially when there is variation in the brightness of the surfaces of the environment. Strongly contrasting colors do, however, attract the eye but too many eyecatchers are confusing. Largely by intuition, color theorists have established rules of thumb for dealing with such matters (see, for example, Birren 1965, 1969, Porter and Mikellides 1976).

There is considerable speculation on the psychological effects of the physiology of color perception. It is believed by some (such as Grandjean 1973) that "all dark colors have a depressing effect . . . and all light colors seem to make life easier, brighter, more friendly." This is as much a personal

observation as one based on systematic study. Some colors do seem to make rooms larger by not emphasizing the presence of walls, and some seem to give an impression of warmth. Many of these widely held beliefs seem to be corroborated by everyday experience. Whether or not they are physiologically or culturally determined is not clear. The theoretical backing for many of these observations is unclear, and the various statements on the subject, while providing some mutual support, are also highly contradictory (see Gerard 1958, Bayes 1967, Porter and Mikellides 1976). Grandjean (1973) makes the following observations about the effects of color on perceptions of room size, subjective feelings of warmth, and psychological responses:

Color	Impression of Distance	Impression of Warmth	Mental Stimulation
Blue	farther away	cold	restful
Green	farther away	cold to neutral	very restful
Red	near	warm	very stimulating
Orange	very near	very warm	stimulating
Yellow	near	very warm	stimulating
Brown	very near	neutral	stimulating
Violet	very near	cold	aggressive, depressing

Sound and Noise

The quality of sound associated with a behavior setting affects perceptions of the quality of the setting. Any disturbing sound is called noise. The evaluation of the sound level in a behavior setting depends on a number of things: the sound itself—its intensity, predictability, and pitch, the degree to which it interferes with the activity, and attitudes toward the sound source—as well as the object that is the source of the sound and perceptions of the degree of control that somebody has over it. If sounds are loud and sustained enough they can damage the hearing apparatus of a human (Gibson 1966). More typically they are simply annoying. They interfere with conversations, thinking, and sleeping and can lead to physiological and psychological stress. People in such situations complain of being tired and nervous and display lower levels of vitality as a result (Grandjean 1984).

There are other aspects of sound that are of direct concern to architectural theory. Of particular importance in understanding the performance of the milieu of a behavior setting is its general acoustic properties. There are a number of books that provide guidelines on designing for acoustical quality (such as Lord and Templeton 1983). This information is crucial in understanding the quality of theaters and concert halls, but the acoustical quality of the environment has an impact, often subconsciously, on subjective perceptions of the quality of any behavior setting (Rasmussen 1959, Southworth 1969).

It is well known that different concert halls have different qualities and that different types of music are said to be particularly well suited to the halls' different reverberation times.

Among musicians and music critics there is indeed a preference for performing and hearing the concertos of Bach in small halls with relatively low reverberation times and the richly orchestrated symphonic compositions of the later nineteenth century in larger, relatively reverberant halls (Beranek 1962).

The sound qualities sought after by musicians are complex. It is really the task of the physical rather than the behavioral sciences to elucidate these issues, but the point is that the physical quality affects the subjective impressions of the quality of the whole behavior setting and the pleasure derived from the activities that constitute it. This applies to the design of such places as work stations, corridors, and parks as well as to auditoriums.

BARRIER-FREE ENVIRONMENTS

There are large segments of the population for whom the affordances for mobility in the built environment are severely reduced because these people are physiologically less competent. The most frequent disability is difficulty in walking. This may result from difficulty in balancing, difficulties in moving rapidly, and/or reduced agility (Bednar 1977).

There are several ways in which the affordances of the environment are reduced for such people. If walking surfaces are uneven, with raised joints and other irregularities, they afford tripping. Steps are a problem to a surprisingly large component of the population. The layout of treads, risers, and handrails becomes very important, particularly when they are located outdoors and are thus liable to become wet or icy. Other problems arise with things such as doors that are too heavy or too fast-closing (Bayes and Franklin 1971, Goldsmith 1976, Foott 1977).

Wheelchair-users, as a class, have a wide range of capabilities and disabilities. Some of them have limbs missing or paralyzed, others have difficulty in balancing the upper body; most have problems in reaching. Wheelchairs themselves come in a variety of sizes and weights with different turning radii. Standard ways of dealing with the environment for highly physiologically competent people create special problems for the hard-of-hearing and the blind as well as for people in wheelchairs.

For the hard-of-hearing, clear visual signage and clarity of layouts is a major help in orientation. The problems of the vision-impaired and blind are severe. Shadows create difficulties for the vision-impaired, contours are difficult to see, reflections cause discomfort, colors are not easy to differentiate. Some people are simply color-blind.

Blind people have special problems. The imageability of the environment is especially important to them. They are taught to pay attention to the texture and sounds of the environment in order to form accurate cognitive maps. In most places there are all kinds of things in the environment that present hazards and impede the mobility of the blind. Projections, for instance, especially those that are not detected in the sweep of a cane, are dangerous. The blind can be helped by avoiding such elements and by paying special attention to the sonic environment and the cues it provides for orientation.

As federal, state, and local legislation has been passed during the past few years, so have environmental designers been forced to pay attention to the qualities of the built environment that impede the mobility of handicapped people. There is still much debate on the normative question about the degree to which the environment has to be made accessible to all (Jones and Catlin 1978).

BEHAVIORAL SYSTEM CORRELATES OF ANTHROPOMETRIC DIMENSIONS

The perception of the quality of anthropometrical fit between people and their built environments depends on more than just people's anthropometrical characteristics; it depends also on their personalities and their social and cultural environments. The anthropometrical characteristics of individuals also seem to affect their personality characteristics. To make matters more complex, the way in which people use their bodies to carry out activities depends not only on their anthropometrical abilities but also on social and cultural norms.

There has long been an interest in correlating body types and *personality*. Studies going back sixty years provide support for many popular stereotypes, although the correlations are not as strong as originally expected (Sheldon 1954, Anastasi 1958, Hood 1963). There is a variety of hypotheses about the reasons for the correlations: diet, personality,

1

2

3

12-4. Barrier-Free Environments.
One of the major reasons that people less physiologically competent than the general population are handicapped is because of environmental constraints—the lack of affordances for their modes of mobility. Certainly, steps such as those shown in (1) reduce the mobility of many people. There are, however, an increasing number of examples of innovative designs that meet the mobility requirements of the handicapped without accompanying negative symbolic messages (2). One of the difficulties in design is that people with different handicaps have different needs. Curbs provide cues for the blind but are a hindrance to those in wheelchairs (3).

and physical development go hand in hand; heredity may determine both physique and personality; cultural expectations may lead to specific behaviors; the physical attributes of a person lead to skill development along certain lines. It is highly conjectural whether or not this means that changes in the layout of the environment indirectly affect personality development by increasing or decreasing the success people have in dealing with their environments, as is implicit in the competence-environment press model (Lawton 1977). It is also appealing to believe that there is a correlation between person-

ality and tolerances for fits and misfits between the environment and what it affords for human movement and usage, but the linkages are not clear. A similar situation exists in considering the role of social-group membership in affecting the perceptions of the anthropometric requirements for a good fit between activities and built environment.

There is a positive correlation between *socioeconomic status* and the physical size of individuals (Tanner 1964). Among certain ethnic groups there has been a considerable increase in average physical size since they have had access to better nutrition

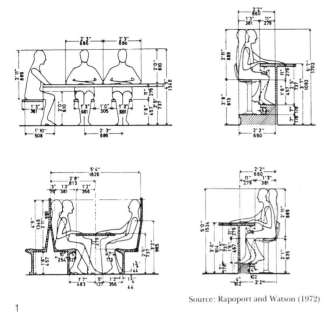

Source: Rapoport and Watson (1972)

1

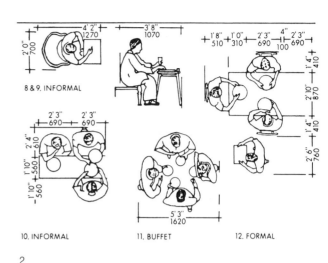

8 & 9. INFORMAL

10. INFORMAL   11. BUFFET   12. FORMAL

2

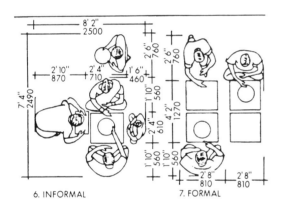

6. INFORMAL   7. FORMAL

3

12-5. The Cultural Relativity of Anthropometric Dimensions.

Even though anthropometric data are "hard," they are not universally applicable. Differences in attitudes toward the way activities should be carried out are deeply ingrained within a culture. The charts in (1) and (2) illustrate the differences between Indian and North American middle-class families in the use of tables for eating. The standards shown in (3) for eating while squatting are largely irrelevant to the American situation (Rapoport and Watson 1972). Traditional ways of doing things do give way as lifestyles and comfort demand change (Drew 1961).

and health care. Thus, furnishings from one era may be too small for subsequent generations. This is also true for door openings and other fixed features of the built environment. Unless great inconveniences occur, these situations generally are regarded with affection and/or amusement because of their associational meanings.

There is sketchy evidence that people of higher socioeconomic status are less willing to accept poor fits between environments and activities from an anthropometric point of view than those who are less well off (Kantowitz and Sorkin 1983). Perhaps the

most important variable is people's aspirations. In many instances, it seems, people are prepared to put up with physiological discomfort in an environment or its furnishings when its symbolic aesthetic value is high or when it is important for them in carrying out some activity.

As Amos Rapoport (1969, 1977, Rapoport and Watson 1972) points out, many differences in the way people carry out basic activities can be attributed to differences in *culture*. Thus, the standing patterns of behavior required to achieve the same ends in different cultures will lead to different structural requirements of the environment. Similarly, although basic patterns may be the same, what is regarded as a good size for a piece of equipment or furniture—the height of a table, for instance—may vary from culture to culture. One must recognize that traditional ways of doing things do give way to more physiologically comfortable or easier ways when the opportunity arises unless they are severely inhibited by the social environment. In the design of housing for Chandigarh, India, "all modern innovations such as high level stoves . . . and so on were welcomed" (Drew 1961).

Cultures occur within *geographic* settings. Some parts of the world are endowed with what are generally regarded as pleasant climates; other parts are not so fortunate. People have moved into all the climatic zones of the world, from the Arctic to the tropics. People learn to adapt and cope with conditions. The built environments they have created modify the terrestrial one. Even so, there are different expectations of the environment–behavior fit based on cultural norms and on perceptions of the costs and rewards of inhabiting a particular behavior setting.

CONCLUSION

One of the goals of design is to create built environments that afford specific patterns of behavior for specific people or ranges of people. One level of affordance that the environment must provide is for motor activity. Another basic one is for physiological comfort. These two are interrelated. What is physiologically comfortable depends on the activity being carried out. The activity being carried out depends, to some extent, on what falls within comfort ranges.

There are fundamental difficulties in designing for human behavior at this level. The designed environment is seldom tailor-made for an individual. There are some instances where this is done: the cockpit of a racing car may be designed for a specific driver, or a wheelchair for a person with special problems, or a house for a specific blind person. These instances are few and far between, however. Generally, the layout of the environment has to cater to a diverse set of users. This is particularly true of the public environment. People of diverse sizes and capabilities—adult and child, athlete and cripple—all have different requirements if the environment is to be comfortable enough or challenging enough for them.

There are many guidebooks which specify what

"good" design is from an anthropometric point of view. Some of these books have a high theoretical content (Olgay 1963, Murrell 1965, Brebner 1982, Kantowitz and Sorkin 1983). This enables the user of the books to understand more fully the implications of the patterns he or she chooses to use in the development of a design. Few of these books deal with culturally defined ways of doing things. Guidebooks such *Time-Saver Standards for Architectural Design Data* (Callender 1974) are highly ethnocentric. People also become habituated to certain layouts and ways of doing things. One of the purposes of anthropometric research is to show people more efficient ways of carrying out activities.

The quality of the environment from an anthropometric viewpoint is fundamental. If the environment does not afford an activity, the activity cannot take place. Some environments afford activities more easily and comfortably than others. There are considerable data and theoretical models on the environment–person interface at this level which can form the basis for environmental design decisions. How one uses them is up to the designer and the other participants in the situation.

ADDITIONAL READINGS

Bednar, James. *Barrier-Free Environments.* Stroudsburg, Pa.: Dowden, Hutchinson and Ross, 1977.

Brebner, John. *Environmental Psychology and Building Design.* London: Applied Science Publishers, 1982.

Grandjean, Etienne. *Ergonomics of the Home.* New York: John Wiley, 1973.

———, ed. *Ergonomics and Health in Modern Offices.* Philadelphia: Taylor and Francis, 1984.

Kantowitz, Barry H., and Robert D. Sorkin, eds. *Human Factors: Understanding People–System Relationships.* New York: John Wiley, 1983.

Kira, Alexander. *The Bathroom.* Ithaca, New York: Center for Housing and Environmental Studies, Cornell University, 1966.

Murrell, K.F.H. *Ergonomics: Man and His Working Environment.* London: Chapman and Hall, 1965.

NASA. "Anthropometric Sources Book, Vol. 1: Anthropometry for Designers; Vol. II: Handbook of Anthropometric Data; Vol. III: Annotated Bibliography of Anthropometry." Webb Associates for NASA, 1978.

Rapoport, Amos and Newton Watson. "Cultural Variability in Physical Standards." In Robert Gutman, ed., *People and Buildings.* New York: Basic Books, 1972, pp. 33–53.

Robinette, Gary O., ed. *Barrier Free Exterior Design: Anyone Can Go Anywhere.* New York: Van Nostrand Reinhold, 1985.

13

COGNITIVE MAPS AND SPATIAL BEHAVIOR

People's spatial behavior depends partially on the images they have of the structure of the environment. The way the built environment is structured very much affects the ease with which people find their way through buildings, neighborhoods, and cities. It is easy to find one's way around some buildings and cities. In other places it is more difficult. The ability to orient oneself, both socially and physically, is a major contributor to an individual's feeling of security.

Labyrinths are designed to make way-finding difficult, but this is seldom a purposeful goal of architectural design except historically for defensive reasons. Despite this, there are some places—residential areas, museums, hospitals, parking garages, and shopping complexes—in which way-finding is notoriously difficult, even for long-time residents (see Passini 1984). The Newmarket shopping complex in Philadelphia, for example, was renovated in 1979 to make destination-finding easier—to make the complex more legible. This had been a particular problem for first-time visitors. The usual response is to resort to the extensive use of signs to point the way. Signs, when properly designed and accurate, are helpful and may be the only way to deal with existing buildings, but there is now much evidence on the organizing elements of the structure of built form.

We have a poor understanding of the impact on people of built environments in which orientation is difficult. Certainly, a person's stress level rises when he or she gets confused about directions. This is particularly true when an individual is in a life-and-death situation, such as being on the upper floors of a high-rise building during a fire. It also holds for more mundane daily experiences. Sometimes we seek this type of experience. Children and adults enjoy tackling labyrinths such as that at Hampton Court (Passini 1984). As tourists, finding our way around cities that we do not know is fun as long as we have a sense of being in control of the situation. Learning the layout of the city is rewarding. The process of learning involves the formation of cognitive maps of one's world.

COGNITIVE MAPS

Cognitive mapping is the process whereby people acquire, code, store, recall, and decode information about the relative location and attributes of the physical environment (Tolman 1932, Moore and Golledge 1976). The images so formed include elements obtained from direct experience, from what one has heard about a place, and from imagined information. They include impressions about the structure or appearance of a place, its relative location, its use, and its values. These images can best be thought of as guiding schemata (Neisser 1977).

Cognitive maps are a central aspect of people's everyday behavior. Roger Downs and David Stea (1973) note:

> We view cognitive mapping as a basic component in human adaptation, and the cognitive map as a requisite for human survival and everyday behavior. It is a coping mechanism through which the individual answers two basic questions quickly and efficiently: (1) Where valued things are; (2) How to get there from where he is.

Spatial orientation has been defined by Romedi Passini (1984) as "a person's ability to determine his position within a representation of the environment made possible by cognitive maps." People who have grown up in cities and buildings orient themselves to the major features of their structures. Of particular importance are continuous elements—rivers, paths, street façades—and specific prominent landmarks. Within buildings, the continuous elements of corridors and the nodal points where they intersect are important image-giving features. People who have grown up in more natural environments use different orienting systems because the features that are important to them are different. Kevin Lynch (1960) describes a number of these personal systems. Some people perceive themselves as the center of the universe; it turns as the individual turns. Some people give directions with reference to the cardinal points of the compass; others rely on the heavenly bodies or on sun or wind directions. Still others may orient themselves with reference to their home territories. Whatever system is used, it tends to be used unconsciously. Its user may well assume it to be a universal system. In this chapter the focus is on the built environments of the world.

THE NATURE AND FUNCTION OF COGNITIVE MAPS

Cognitive maps of the structures of cities, neighborhoods, and buildings are not exact replicas of reality; they are models of reality. The graphic representations of cognitive maps—that is, the drawings people make of areas of cities or buildings —are partial, schematized, and distorted in a manner that reflects both group similarities and individual differences. One assumes that this is a characteristic of mental images: distances and directions are distorted in our memories. Intraurban cognitive distance, for instance, is generally greater than in reality, while there is an underestimation of long distances (Pocock and Hudson 1978). The more we use a place the more accurate the image, but even with heavily used places the process of schematization biases what we remember (Downs and Stea 1973).

Stephen Carr (1967) suggests that we are "victims of conventionality" in this respect. We use "those spatial symbols to which we all subscribe and which we use both as denotative and connotative shorthand ways of coping with the spatial environment." At the city scale we give names to areas that have special meanings for us as individuals or members of a group. We refer to areas as "slums" or "gold coasts." In buildings we refer to rooms by name—for example, the "den." Each such name conjures up an image of the behavior setting associated with it (Perin 1970). We assume that it has specific standing patterns of behavior and patterns of milieu. Such images affect not only our behavior but also our designs.

Stephen Kaplan (1973) suggests that people possess four types of knowledge. Cognitive maps might be thought to provide these as well: the *recognition* of where one is, the *prediction* of what may happen next, the *evaluation* of whether this is good or bad, and knowing what *actions* might be taken. Recognition fulfills the human need for making sense of the environment; prediction, the need to have an intelligent basis for subsequent decisions; evaluation, the need to reduce the discomfort resulting from ambivalence; and action, the need for perception of the consequences of the next action. Understanding the layout of the environment and the behavioral opportunities that exist is thus fundamental to the selection of the activities in which we engage.

The cognitive maps that people have of the layout of cities and buildings differ from person to person. There are, however, certain public images —images that hold for groups of people—that are similar (Lynch 1960, de Jong 1962). They are similar for a number of reasons: the fundamental psychological processes that people possess are the same; the environment may contain recurrent and regular features; and the set of activities that the users of a building or the inhabitants of a city carry out is similar. Individual differences arise from differences in activity patterns and the way people look at the environment.

Image Content

What is it about a building that makes it easy for users to orient themselves there? Most of the research on questions of orientation has focused on the city level, but the findings have been generalized to buildings. There seems to be legitimacy in doing this because the Gestalt laws of visual organization explain most of the findings. Many practicing architects have accepted this and have applied the concepts to the internal organization of buildings and particularly those buildings whose users have a relatively low competence in dealing with the environment. Some psychiatric patients fall into this category (ARC 1975). The recent research of Passini (1984) supports this position.

In the studies on which *The Image of the City* was based, Kevin Lynch found environmental images to be analyzable into three components: *identity, structure,* and *meaning.* Identity refers to objects in the environment having the quality of figure in a figure-ground relationship; structure refers to objects having a spatial relationship to each other; and meaning has to with the emotional or practical utility of the elements. Lynch's work focused on the first two, thus separating the structural, or formal, attributes of the environment from questions of meaning. In reality these go together, but for analytical purposes it is useful to separate them.

In Lynch's study, the structure of the environment was the independent variable and images of cities the dependent variable. His goal was to ascertain what makes cities *imageable* and *legible.* He notes:

> [Imageability is] . . . that quality of a physical object which gives it a high probability of evoking a strong image in any given observer. It is that shape, color or arrangement which facilitates the making of a vividly identified, powerfully structured, highly useful mental image of the environment. It might also be called legibility . . .

A highly imageable city, neighborhood, building complex, or building interior is one that is perceived as a well-structured system of components that are related to each other. This applies to both plan and three-dimensional form for, as Ulrich Neisser (1977) points out, the schemata for exploring and forming images are the same.

The image of a place is enriched and corrected through continual use (Steinitz 1968). If the structure of a place is changed, a person's image of it will change if he or she continues to use it. It may also change if the person is told about alterations to the environment, but this will have less impact. Often there is a considerable time lag between the environmental change and the image change, with the result that in discussions references may be made to the past rather than to the present situation.

The heart of Lynch's work is concerned with identifying the elements of the physical structure of cities that make the cities imageable. He concluded that there are five categories of elements that people use to structure cognitive images of areas. These are: paths, edges, districts, nodes, and landmarks.

Paths are channels of movement. All other elements of the environment are seen from paths—or from corridors in buildings. Corridors, streets, pavements, rivers, or, as in Venice, canals are continuous elements along which people move. For many people they are the predominant elements in their cognitive images of places (Appleyard 1970). *Edges* are boundaries that break or contain or run parallel to the form; they are not used by the observer as paths but they may well be so used by others. In contrast to an edge is a *seam*, which binds areas together rather than subdividing them. Lynch regards seams as a subcategory of edges rather than as separate elements. What is an edge visually may be a seam behaviorally. *Districts* are areas that have a recognizable identity. They possess a homogeneous texture, often accompanied by a homogeneous land use and a clearly defined edge or contour. *Nodes* are places where intensive activity occurs. They are distinctive behavior settings located at places such the intersections of paths. Often they are accompanied by a landmark. Nodes that are the foci of districts may be called *cores* (Porteous 1977). *Landmarks* are points of reference that are external to the observer and are singled out because they are easily distinguishable visually. Like figures in Gestalt figure-ground studies, they are visually distinctive elements in their surroundings.

These elements do not exist in isolation. Mental images consist of clusters of elements. Porteous (1977) notes:

> A marketplace, for instance, is not merely noted as an area formally and functionally distinct from the urban matrix, but it is seen as a node, the meeting place of paths, defined by edges and identified by characteristic landmarks.

Cognitive maps are likely to consist of many such features linked by paths. Not all of these elements are of equal importance in a particular place. Douglas Pocock and Ray Hudson (1978) have assembled the accompanying table, which shows the relative importance of categories of elements in the public image of a number of cities. These studies corroborate Lynch's findings and give an indication of the individual character of each city. Some cities are rich in certain elements and poor in others; other cities are very generously endowed. One thing that most of the cities have in common is weak edges, although Saarinen (1968) found edges to be of some importance in his study of Chicago.

Further studies are necessary to explain why paths, districts, nodes, landmarks, and edges are the important features in the images people have of

Paths

Districts

Landmarks

13-1. The Form-Giving Elements of the Built Environment.

CITY FORM

BUILDING FORM

Edges

Nodes

Source: Pocock and Hudson (1978)

13-1, *continued.*

The Components of the Images of Selected Cities in Europe and North America

City	Paths	Landmarks	Districts	Nodes	Edges
Boston	†	*	*	†	†
Jersey City	†				
Los Angeles	*	†		†	
Chicago	*	*	*		
Englewood	*	*	*		
Amsterdam	*			*	
Rotterdam	*	†		†	
The Hague	*	†	†		
Rome	*	*	†	*	
Milan	*	*	*	*	
Birmingham	*	*		*	
Hull	*	*		*	

* stands for very important
† stands for important

cities. The Gestalt "laws" of visual organization, however, do explain Lynch's observations about cognitive maps. Paths and edges are elements of continuity. Districts can be explained in terms of the proximity and similarity of elements within a good contour; while landmarks consist of elements that are dissimilar to their surroundings. Nodes are difficult to explain in Gestalt psychology terms.

A number of attempts have been made to refine Lynch's work. Christian Norberg-Schulz (1971) identifies three basic elements in cognitive maps: places, paths, and domains. *Places* are specific loci, similar to Lynch's nodes plus landmarks, where events important to the individual take place. *Paths* are continuous elements that provide an overall structure, while *domains* are areas, akin to Lynch's districts, that contain similar elements which are de-

COGNITIVE MAPS AND SPATIAL BEHAVIOR **139**

fined by "closure." Domains act as "ground" for paths and places. The links between Norberg-Schulz's interpretations and Gestalt theory are quite explicit. David Stea (1969) identifies four basic features in cognitive maps: *points, boundaries, paths,* and *barriers.* Points here are similar to Lynch's nodes, and boundaries to his edges, while Stea's barriers are edges that cut across paths.

It is clear from all the research on cognitive maps and human orientation in the built environment that the Gestalt laws of visual organization are important predictors of the features of a city or building that are important to people. Lynch, Norberg-Schulz, Stea, and others (such as Appleyard 1970, Clay 1973) may use different terms for the elements they identify as important in the mental structuring of cities and buildings, but their conclusions are very similar. Order is achieved through the application of the Gestalt principles.

WHY BUILDINGS ARE KNOWN

Donald Appleyard (1969) identified three reasons why some buildings are better known than others. They have to do with *form attributes, visibility attributes,* and *use and significance attributes.* The form attribute that is particularly important is the contour. When buildings have clear contours—sharp boundaries differentiating them from their surroundings—they tend to have a "figure" quality and to stand out from their surroundings. Buildings with contours significantly different from their surroundings also are noticed more easily. Thus the new AT&T building in midtown Manhattan is distinguishable on the skyline because its cornice line deviates from the norm. When each building has a unique cornice, however, there will be uniformity in diversity. Other factors (the complexity of façades, coloring, and illumination of surfaces) that are deviant from those of surrounding buildings were found to be less important, as was the use of signs.

The ability of buildings to be seen—their visibility attributes—is another important explainer of why some buildings are known better than others. Buildings at well-traveled intersections, adjacent to open spaces, or located at bends in highways are likely to be seen and remembered. The *immediacy* of a building to a station point is another good predictor of how well a building is known.

Appleyard's study enriches Lynch's concept of "landmark." Appleyard also found that areas with high *use intensity* (similar to Lynch's "nodes") were important features in the maps people drew of cities. *Use singularity*—the clear identification of a building with a major use, such as a hospital—was also a major factor, but *historical significance* was not.

The image-giving factors identified by Appleyard can also be explained by the Gestalt laws of visual organization. If one adds the concept of "significant usage" to the Gestalt laws, one has a generalized basis for understanding and designing desired levels of legibility and distinguishability of buildings. This understanding can readily be turned into normative design principles.

INDIVIDUAL DIFFERENCES IN COGNITIVE MAP FORM

The maps that people draw of cities in studies differ in size, content, and accuracy. Whether these differences represent differences in the mental images they hold is open to debate. It does seem that there is a correlation between the elements people include in their maps, the order in which they introduce them, and the importance of the features.

Kevin Lynch (1960) found that people approached the mapping task in five ways: (1) some emphasized paths and the elements along them; (2) some drew boundaries first and then filled in the maps; (3) some drew a repetitive system—such as the grid layout of streets—and then filled it in; (4) some drew districts first and then connected them; and (5) some started out drawing the nodal points and then filled in their surroundings. Further analysis suggested that some people have a path-oriented way of conceptualizing the environment while others do it by spatial distribution.

The distinction between path-oriented and spatial styles of cognitive mapping stems from the work of Donald Appleyard in Guyana City, Venezuela (1970). Appleyard concluded that the maps drawn by his subjects were either predominantly sequential or predominantly spatial, as shown in figure 13-2; 33 percent of Appleyard's sample population drew the chain-type maps, 21 percent drew the branch and loop, and 15 percent drew network-type maps. Thus, almost 70 percent of the people drew sequential-image maps. This reinforces the opinion that for most people paths are the major organizing elements of the city.

Gary Moore (1976) believes that the differences in the styles of maps that people draw is associated with stages of individual development (see also Stea and Blaut 1973). Perceptual learning, as noted earlier in this book, is a process of increasingly fine differentiation and categorization of elements of the environment. Moore asks the question: "Is there a discrete set of steps that we go through in learning and remembering our surroundings?"

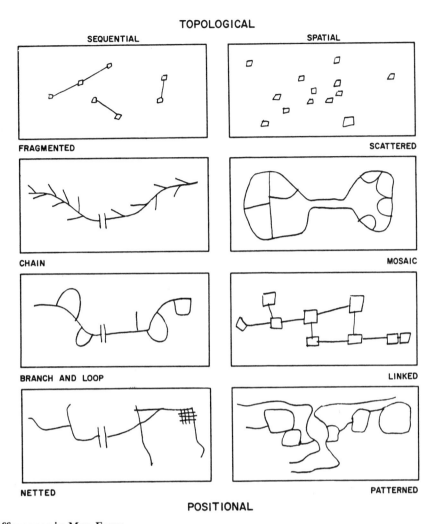

TOPOLOGICAL

SEQUENTIAL — SPATIAL

FRAGMENTED — SCATTERED

CHAIN — MOSAIC

BRANCH AND LOOP — LINKED

NETTED — PATTERNED

POSITIONAL

Source: Appleyard (1970)

13-2. Individual Differences in Map Form.

Moore identifies three major phases in the development of knowledge of, and thus cognitive representations of, the physical environment. These parallel the three major phases of intellectual development identified by Piaget and his colleagues (Hart and Moore 1973). These phases, Moore suggests, are characterized by specific reference systems as follows:

1. an egocentric reference system, that is, one organized around the child's own position and actions in space;
2. several different possibilities of fixed reference systems organized around various fixed, concrete elements, or places in the environment; and
3. an abstract or coordinated reference system organized in terms of abstract geometric patterns including a special case, the cardinal directions.

Moore believes that these steps are developmentally ordered, each being a special case of the next higher order. He suggests that they are not simply different styles of representation. Two studies by Moore (1973, 1976) lend credence to this view.

Much of the research that has followed Lynch's seminal study has sought correlations between individual differences and the nature of the maps drawn. While there is evidence that individual physiological differences affect the way in which people form images of their surroundings, most studies show essentially one thing: cognitive maps are a function of an individual's experience. Experience has been correlated with factors that include gender, socioeconomic status, place of residence and work, length of residence in a location, and types of transportation used.

Organismic differences explain why some brain-damaged people have considerable difficulty in orienting themselves and finding their way from room to room in buildings and around their neighborhoods and cities. Some people whose psychiatric disorders have a physiological base have very reduced and sometimes highly distorted images of their surroundings (Izumi 1967). Psychiatric hospitals resort to painting corridors that link origins and destinations in specific colors, to making behavior settings clearly visible from corridors, and to making objects clearly distinguishable from their surroundings. The goal is to reduce any ambiguity in a person's perception of the structure of his or her surroundings.

Blind people are known to pay attention to very different characteristics of the environment than those noted by sighted people (Brodey 1969). The textures of the surfaces along which they walk, the sounds of the environment, and even such details as the layering of air temperatures are important in differentiating one path from another and one location from another. One would assume that, while the cognitive structures of their representations of the environment may be similar to those of sighted people, continuities in texture and geometries give aid to blind people in structuring their images of the world they inhabit. The Gestalt principles of visual organization seem to hold for the other perceptual modes.

There has been little exploration of *personality differences* in the development of cognitive images, but a considerable amount has been done on *social group differences.*These studies have focused on differences in sex, age, and socioeconomic status.

Several studies (such as Appleyard 1970, Everitt and Cadwallader 1972, Orleans and Schmidt 1972) show that women's images of the environment are different from men's. This seems to be due to role differences rather than biological differences. Women tend to be less mobile than men, with the result that married women, for instance, tend to have maps that are smaller in scale but richer in detail than their husbands' maps (Everitt and Cadwallader 1972); their maps also are domicentric rather than related to standard map coordinates (Orleans and Schmidt 1972).

The mobility of people is very much affected by their stage in life cycle (Hester 1975). Life cycle is closely correlated with age. Even the youngest children, unless they are brain-damaged, can find their way around their own homes. Older people have to contend with images of the past. In a British study, J. Douglas Porteous (1977) found that elderly people often included images of demolished buildings in their images of the city whereas the images of younger people tended to be dominated by "new, highly visible construction projects."

Children pay attention to the seemingly minute and incidental features of the environment. Pocock and Hudson (1978) summarize the research on cognitive maps that children draw as follows:

In Harwich, for instance, the notable landmark of the lighthouse was much less important than the public toilets located at its foot (Bishop and Foulsham 1973). Again in Harrisburg, Texas, prominent features were omitted from sketch maps, while dog houses or house numbers were included (Maurer and Baxter 1972). Details of the "floor" surface (Lukashok and Lynch 1956), roadside features, and play areas reflect the child's particular engagement with the environment. With young children, built structures are subordinate to elements of the social and natural environment (Spencer and Lloyd, 1974).

These studies bring attention to features of the environment that are important to children and suggest some of the features that can contribute to the richness of the environment for them.

A number of studies have focused on the relationship between the socioeconomic status of people and the contents of the maps they draw of the environment (for example, Ladd 1970, Porteous 1971, Orleans 1973, Stea 1974, Goodchild 1974). Socioeconomic status is a composite variable, but most studies focus on single variables such as occupation, primary mode of transportation used (although this is not necessarily an indicator of social status), years of formal education, and income. It is possible, nevertheless, to make some broad generalizations about the correlations between socioeconomic status and cognitive maps.

In the United States wealthier people have larger cognitive maps than those formed by poorer people. Appleyard (1970) found the opposite to be true in Guyana City, Venezuela. In the United States, people who own automobiles have more accurate maps than those who rely on public transportation, and middle-class people tend to conceptualize the environment better than working-class people do. This reflects not only differences in the usage of the environment, but also differences in concern for it (Michelson 1970, Goodchild 1974). This is what would be predicted by Maslow's model of human needs: the higher the motivations of people in his hierarchy, the broader the range of concerns. In the Venezuelan study, poorer people had a wider range of concerns, due to the locational distribution of residences and job opportunities.

Culture is an important predictor of the orienting schemata people use. Lynch (1960), Lowenthal (1961), Tuan (1974), and Porteous (1977) are among those who have reviewed the richness of world views and how these relate to the cognitive images people have of the environment. The people of some cultures describe total impressions, others focus on details; some pay attention to open spaces, others to boundaries and edges. It is important to recognize these differences because they reflect and are reflected in patterns of the built environment—the material artifacts of a culture (Latham 1966, Rapoport 1969).

The schemata that people develop for exploring the environment reflect what has been important to them historically. As cultures change over time so do orienting schemata and also the symbolic imagery of places and landscape structures. Paths, vistas, and linearity are reflected in European and North American design; the Japanese have emphasized spatial structure and urban patterns of named spaces. Despite all these differences, the Gestalt laws of visual organization describe the process of differentiation of patterns that all people go through in isolating the elements of the environment that form the basis of their imagery.

Above all, the structure of the built and natural environment itself is the best predictor of the cognitive images people will have of it (Porteous 1977). This is why Lynch's original work retains its importance. Those cities and buildings that are clearly organized in terms of paths or corridors, edges or perimeters, districts or use areas, landmarks or distinctive features, and nodes or visually clear gathering points are easy to read and easily imageable.

IMAGES AND SPATIAL BEHAVIOR

There is a strong correlation between activity systems and the cognitive images people have of the physical environment. Distortions in imagery do reflect and/or affect the perceptions people have of such things as the location of shops, parks and other facilities (Brennan 1948, Lee 1962, Porteous 1977). The perception of the distance of facilities is also affected by such things as the geometry of paths. A path that is circuitous or full of junctions is perceived to be longer than one of the same length that is straight. This may be a partial explanation of why people are prepared to walk longer distances in airport and regional shopping center parking lots where the destination is in sight than when it is not (Pocock and Hudson 1978). Desirable elements such as parks are often perceived to be closer to a station point than undesirable ones such as major highways that are the same distance away (Lowery 1973). Such observations may depend on personality and mood factors. For instance, an optimist may see the park closer while a pessimist may see undesirable elements closer. Such hypotheses are highly conjectural, however. It is not even clear if cognitive distances are a function of the structure of the environment or of the behavior by which the structure is learned (Briggs 1973).

Since image-development is a two-way process between person and environment, it is possible to strengthen the image of a particular place either by enhancing the competence of a person or by making the structure of a place more discernible. The former can be achieved by educating the perceiver to look at the environment with more discrimination and the latter by improving the signage of routes and places or by reshaping the physical layout of a city, neighborhood, or building. Sometimes the latter is done at the scale of building interiors, but usually people are helped in finding their way by signs. Signage is easier to implement and it works, provided care is taken with the design of the signs and the person is not overloaded with information. This is a particularly important when people are moving at high speeds (see Passini 1984).

Symbolic devices such as maps, building layout illustrations, and place signs are major ways of enhancing people's ability to orient themselves. One of the best-known such devices is the abstract map of London Transport's underground system, although the attempt to use its principles for portraying New York's subway system was not successful. Stephen Carr (1967) called for "information boards at strategic points programmed to light up the quickest or the most scenic route to any destination." These have been installed in a number of cities. Earlier Kevin Lynch (1960) cautioned:

> While such devices are extremely useful for providing condensed data on interconnections, they are also precarious since orientation fails if the device is lost, and the device must be constantly referred to and fitted to reality. . . . Moreover, the complete experience of interconnection, the full depth of the vivid image is lost.

Simultaneous with these explorations in how to make the structure of the environment more discernible, programs have been developed to educate people to look at the environment with more discernment. Environmental awareness programs take many forms. Most consist of exercises that make people think about their surroundings by asking them questions about the nature of the buildings, neighborhoods, and cities they inhabit. Some programs are aimed at children (such as Group for Environmental Education 1971) while others are aimed at adults (Eriksen 1975).

Clear environmental imagery enhances the perception of the affordances of the world around people. Stephen Carr (1967) believes that increasing the exposure of people to a greater variety of behavior settings and potential interactions will enhance their exploration of and attachment to places and will counteract the rootlessness that many people feel and the stress levels to which they are subject. (Porteous 1977).

CONCLUSION

The work on cognitive mapping provides environmental designers with an understanding of how to create legible and imageable buildings, building complexes, neighborhoods, and cities. This work is particularly important in enhancing the experience of people in places where they are not frequent visitors, such as many public buildings, hospitals, airports, and parks. The degree to which way-finding should be made easy depends on the situation. Labyrinths are designed to make it difficult. People who enter a labyrinth are challenging their way-finding ability—they are self-testing. This also occurs when people are exploring new places or driving recreationally. In cases where more instrumental purposes are being served, clarity is more important. It is also particularly important when dealing with low-competence patients such as those in some psychiatric hospitals, where even though they may be long-term residents their ability to orient themselves is reduced.

How legible should the environment be? The answer is a value-laden one. Does one design for comfort or for development? Does one design for the tourist or for the habitué? At what level does a highly legible environment become boring? Some of these issues are addressed in the research on formal aesthetics, but much rests on the subjective opinions of the architect, interior designer, landscape architect, or urban designer and on the culture of the working environment of which they are a part.

ADDITIONAL READINGS

Burnette, Charles. "The Mental Image and Design." In Jon Lang et al., eds., *Designing for Human Behavior: Architecture and the Behavioral Sciences.* Stroudsburg, Pa.: Dowden, Hutchinson and Ross, 1974, pp. 169–182.

Downs, Roger M., and David Stea. "Cognitive Maps and Spatial Behavior: Process and Products." In Roger M. Downs and David Stea, eds., *Image and Environment: Cognitive Maps and Spatial Behavior.* Chicago: Aldine, 1973, pp. 8–26.

Lynch, Kevin. *The Image of the City.* Cambridge, Mass.: MIT Press, 1960.

Moore, Gary T. "The Development of Environmental Knowing; An Overview of an Interactional-Constructivist Theory and Some Data on Within-Individual Developmental Variations." In David Canter and Terence Lee, eds., *Psychology and the Built Environment.* London: Architectural Press, 1976, pp. 184–194.

———."Knowing about Environmental Knowing: The Current State of Research on Environmental Cognition." *Environment and Behavior* 11, no. 1 (1979): 33–70.

Passini, Romedi. *Wayfinding in Architecture.* New York: Van Nostrand Reinhold, 1984.

Pocock, Douglas, and Ray Hudson. *Images of the Urban Environment.* New York: Columbia University Press, 1978.

Porteous, J. Douglas. "Macrospace Behavior: Home Range." In *Environment and Behavior: Planning and Everyday Life.* Reading, Mass.: Addison-Wesley, 1977, pp. 91–130.

Stea, David. "Architecture in the Head: Cognitive Mapping." In Jon Lang et al., eds., *Designing for Human Behavior: Architecture and the Behavioral Sciences.* Stroudsburg, Pa.: Dowden, Hutchinson and Ross, 1974, pp. 157–168.

14

PRIVACY, TERRITORIALITY, AND PERSONAL SPACE—PROXEMIC THEORY

A piece of furniture, a work station, a room, a building, or a landscape may be very well designed from an anthropometric viewpoint but still be deemed "uncomfortable" by its users (Hall 1963). The purpose of this chapter is to bring attention to the subtler factors of privacy, personal space, and territorial behavior that affect the perceptions of environmental comfort and quality. The need for privacy, personal space, and territory is universal and contributes to the meeting of other human needs such as security, affiliation, and esteem (Hall 1959, Goffman 1963, Lyman and Scott 1967, Skaburskis 1974, Sommer 1969, Altman 1975). The form in which the need is expressed and the mechanisms used for its attainment are manifested very differently in different societies, however (Hall 1966, Altman and Chemers 1980).

Some of the buildings most admired by architects have not been very good at meeting privacy and territorial needs. The reason is simple. Most aspects of these behaviors occur subconsciously. If we are unaware of a behavior is it impossible to consider it explicitly in design. One of the major contributions of behavioral scientists has been to bring the attention of designers to these behaviors and the extent to which they need to be considered in design. One of the objectives of environmental design theory is to describe and explain how the layout of the environment affords these mechanisms and the importance of designing environments that do afford them.

PRIVACY

The concepts of privacy, territorial behavior, and personal space are closely linked. Irwin Altman (1975) proposes a conceptual organizing model in which he considers personal space and territoriality to be major mechanisms for attaining privacy. Figure 14-1 shows the dynamic nature of privacy. People strive to get the appropriate level of privacy for the activity in which they are engaged. The question then arises: What is meant by privacy?

Definitions of privacy have one thing in common. They stress that it has to do with the ability of individuals or groups to control their visual, auditory, and olfactory interactions with others. For example, Amos Rapoport (1977) defines it as "the ability to control interactions, to have options, and to achieve desired interactions." Privacy should not be seen simply as the physical withdrawal of a person from others in a quest for seclusion (Schwartz 1968).

There are several kinds of privacy, each of which serves a different purpose. Westin (1970) identifies four types: *solitude,* the state of being free from the observation of others; *intimacy,* the state of being with another person but free from the outside world; *anonymity,* the state of being unknown even in a crowd; and *reserve,* the state in which a person employs psychological barriers to control unwanted intrusion. Westin also identifies four purposes served by privacy: it provides for *personal autonomy,* it allows for the *release of emotions,* it helps *self-evaluation,* and it limits and protects *communication.* Thus, privacy is important in terms of the relationship between an individual or a group and the rest of society.

The type and degree of privacy desired depends on the standing pattern of behavior, on the cultural context, and on the personality and aspirations of the individual involved. The use of walls, screens, symbolic and real territorial demarcators, and distance are all mechanisms for attaining privacy which the environmental designer can control to some extent. The qualities of surfaces (translucent, transparent, sound-absorbing) cut off the flow of information from one area to another to a lesser

or greater degree. One of the major causes of complaint about the built environment is its failure to provide desired levels of privacy.

Leo Kuper's analysis (1953) of an English housing development demonstrates some of the difficulties in attaining privacy requirements. While visual privacy was attained within the semidetached houses shown in figure 14-2, auditory privacy was not. The party wall was inadequate for this purpose and the window and door locations made it difficult to locate the beds in any position other than the one shown. People complained that they heard too much of what went on in their neighbor's house, and presumably that their neighbor's presence inhibited their own behavior.

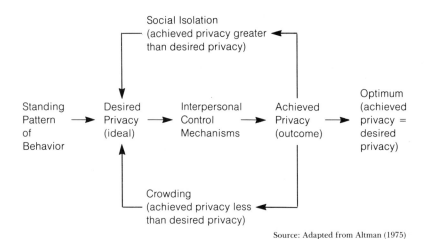

Source: Adapted from Altman (1975)

14-1. A Dynamic Model of Privacy.

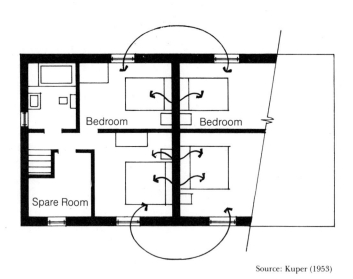

Source: Kuper (1953)

14-2. The Infringement of Privacy Requirements.

Crowding

Too much privacy leads to feelings of social isolation, and too little privacy leads to subjective feelings of crowding (Altman 1975). Crowding is stressful because it limits personal autonomy and expression and breaks down desired communication patterns. It must be distinguished from population *density*, which usually is measured in terms of the number of people per unit area (people/hectare, for example). Crowding is associated with a feeling of lack of control over the environment. It is affected by the individual's perception of the degree of control others have over the intrusions they are making (Rapoport 1977). Thus, the noise from a radio or lawn mower is perceived to be more intrusive than higher levels of traffic noise because a radio can be turned down and a lawn can be mowed at a different time.

Crowded conditions lead to negative behaviors because they are related causally to "social overload." Russell Murray (1976) suggests that such behaviors as highly punitive actions by parents toward children are related to crowded conditions. Density, on the other hand, does not seem to be *causally* linked to such behaviors. The important factors are that behavior settings should not be overmanned—that is, the number of people should be appropriate to the standing pattern of behavior—and that people should have sufficient personal space and territorial control over what is important to them (Bechtel 1977).

PERSONAL SPACE

Providing for *personal space* needs is a basic mechanism for the attainment of privacy. Personal space should not be confused with *personalized space*, although in everyday language the terms are used interchangeably. The former refers to the distance that animals of the same noncontact species maintain among themselves except for the most intimate interactions (Hall 1966, Horowitz, Duff, and Stratton 1970, Becker and Mayo 1971). The latter refers to an area of the natural or built environment that has been marked as a territory (Becker 1978).

The concept of personal space came to the attention of environmental designers with the publication of Robert Sommer's book, *Personal Space: The Behavioral Basis of Design* (1969). In it, Sommer defined personal space as follows:

Personal space refers to an area with an invisible boundary surrounding the person's body into which intruders may not come. Like the porcupine in Schopenhauer's fable, people like to be close enough to obtain warmth and comradeship but far enough away to avoid pricking one another. Personal space is not necessarily spherical in shape, nor does it extend equally in all directions . . . it has been likened to a snail shell, a soap bubble, an aura and breathing room.

If another enters this space, an individual feels encroached upon and shows displeasure (Goffman 1963). Even when outward signs of displeasure are hidden, intrusions lead to physiological responses such as heightened skin conductance levels. In work situations, this encroachment can lead to task impairment (Evans and Howard 1973). When a person is absorbed in a task or when close cooperation is required, however, this is not the case. People also seek intimacy with others and can be invited to infringe personal space boundaries.

While it is interesting as a behavioral variable, personal space does not contribute as much to the understanding of the built environment as Sommer originally thought (see Sommer 1974a). An understanding of personal space is, nevertheless, important in the design of fixed-feature environments where seating is built in. Examples of these are airport and bus terminal waiting areas and theater and park seating (Hall 1963). In other situations, people generally can array themselves comfortably or move the furniture around. Movable seats are one characteristic of many well-liked public places (Whyte 1980).

There are situations where the unwanted infringement of personal space is tolerated (Hall 1966). This occurs in behavior settings such as elevators, theater foyers, subways, and counters at fast-food restaurants. The costs to the individual are acceptable (Helmreich 1974). There are, however, behavioral mechanisms that are invoked to maintain privacy. Eye contact and conversation are avoided —people employ reserve. Many people, nevertheless, feel uncomfortable in such situations.

PERSONALIZATION AND PERSONALIZED SPACE

Personalization refers to the marking of places, or the accretion of objects within them, and thereby the staking of claim to them (see Becker 1978). The process may be a conscious one, but it is often unconscious. The behavior is a manifestation of a desire for territorial control and an expression of aesthetic tastes as well as the result of an effort to make the environment fit activity patterns better.

Some environments can be personalized without damage to them or without difficult surgery; others, called "hard architecture" by Sommer

(1974b), are more difficult to personalize. The degree to which a place is personalized depends on the affordances of the materials of its structure, the intensity of the inhabitants' need to change it, how large a stake they have in the place, and the social norms and administrative rules of the context (Rapoport 1967, Goetze 1968). In areas of homogeneous populations, streets and neighborhoods are personalized in such a way that the whole area becomes a cultural artifact of the group.

The built environment is full of examples of adaptations and personalizations. Philippe Boudon (1972) reports on the extensive changes made to Le Corbusier's Quartiers Modernes Frugès at Pessac near Bordeaux. The project consisted of seventy homogeneous "cubist" structures which have proved to be highly personalizable. The walls have been painted a wide variety of colors, many terraces and the spaces below the stilt-supported slabs have been enclosed. The original "pure" form has been lost, but what appeared to be hard architecture has turned out to be "soft."

Similar changes were made with a very different housing type in Levittown, New Jersey. Herbert Gans (1967) notes:

> Aesthetic diversity is preferred, however, and people talked about moving into a custom-built house in the future when they could afford it. Meanwhile, they made internal and external alterations in the Levit house to reduce the sameness and to place a personal stamp on the property.

The personalization of places thus serves many purposes: psychological security and symbolic aesthetic as well the adaptation of the environment to meet the needs of specific activity patterns. Above all, however, personalization marks territory.

TERRITORIALITY

Ethologists (such as Howard 1920, Nice 1941) were the first to record the territorial behavior of animals. The application of territoriality to human behavior is more recent. Leon Pastalan (1970) gives the following definition of a human territory:

> A territory is a delimited space that a person or a group uses and defends as an exclusive preserve. It involves psychological identification with a place, symbolized by attitudes of possessiveness and arrangements of objects in the area.

Irwin Altman's identification (1975) of territory as one mechanism for attaining privacy comes through in his definition of territorial behavior:

> Territorial behavior is a self-other boundary regulation mechanism that involves personalization of or marking a place or object and communication that it is owned by a person or group.

These definitions suggest some basic characteristics of territories: (1) the ownership of or rights to a place, (2) the personalization or marking of an area, (3) the right to defend against intrusion, and (4) the serving of several functions ranging from the meeting of basic physiological needs to the satisfaction of cognitive and aesthetic needs.

Humans and animals exhibit territorial behavior in different ways (Altman 1975). In animals it is biologically based. It is a localized possessiveness of place; marking is by urination and other physiological means, and defense is by fighting (often symbolic). In humans, even if territorial behavior is biologically based (Dubos 1965, Ardrey 1966), it is culturally biased. Human territories vary considerably in size and locale; not only are they of place but of artifacts and ideas as well, and they are marked by a wide array of physical barriers and symbolic markers. Humans simply have a much larger number of territories and ways of dealing with them.

The Functions of Territories

The ability of the layout of the environment to afford privacy through territorial control is important because it allows the fulfillment of some basic human needs: the need for *identity*, the need for *stimulation*, and the need for *security*. To these, Hussein El-Sharkawy (1979) adds a fourth: the need for a *frame of reference*. Although these are recurring themes in the architectural literature, the territorial function of the built environment fell outside the scope of the modern architectural concept of functionalism.

Identity—which is associated with the needs for belonging, self-esteem, and self-actualization identified by Maslow—is the need to know who one is and what role one plays in society. Stimulation needs are those concerned with self-fulfillment and self-actualization. Security needs take many forms: to be free from censure, to be free from outside attack, and to possess self-confidence. Frame-of-reference needs are those involving the maintenance of one's relationship with others and the surrounding environment. Ethologists explain these needs in terms of our biological pasts; behaviorists, in terms of reinforcement patterns within a culture; Jungian psychologists, in terms of the search for the "psychic truth."

A number of theoretical statements (for instance Sommer 1969, Altman, Nelson, and Lett

1

2

3

14-3. Symbolic Territorial Demarcators.
The ways people demarcate territories vary considerably. The demarcations may consist of real barriers such as doors and walls or they may be symbolic markers such as a sign (1), or a structure associated with an ethnic group (2), or a change in the materials of floors, or lines painted on a street (3). These markers all differentiate between one area and another and identify them with the people who control them—individuals or groups. Markers that are unrecognized do not form part of the effective environment of people.

1972, Edney 1976) explain the need for territory in terms of self-other boundary-regulating mechanisms that parallel Jungian concepts of the *self*. Altman (1975) describes territories not only as a means of attaining privacy but also as a means of stabilizing social relationships. Each of the behavior settings we inhabit has a territorial component associated with it, whether it is a residential accommodation or a work space (Becker 1981, 1982). Territorial considerations are more important in some instances than in others, however. Our lives are spent within a system of territorial definitions.

Systems of Human Territories

Recent efforts to identify types of human territories are of interest to environmental designers because they deal with people's desire to control and personalize space and behavior. J. Douglas Porteous (1977) identifies three spatial levels nested within each other: *personal space* as described above; *home base*, those spaces that are defended actively, whether they are work or residential or simply neighborhood areas; and *home range*, the behavior settings that form part of a person's life (Anderson and Tindall 1972). Some writers (such as Roos 1968, Rapoport 1977) introduce the concept of *jurisdiction* to denote the temporary ownership and control of a setting, in contrast to settings that are held more permanently by an individual or group. Jurisdictions generally are not personalized.

Hussein El-Sharkawy (1979) identifies four types of territory in his effort to build a model that deals specifically with the concerns of environmental design. These are: *attached, central, supporting,* and *peripheral.* An attached territory is one's personal "space bubble." Central territories, such as one's home, a student's room, or a work station, are those that are likely to be highly personalized unless there is strong administrative opposition to it. They are also highly defended. Oscar Newman (1972, 1979) refers to these as *private space.* Supporting territories are either *semiprivate* or *semipublic.* The former consist of places such as residents' lounges in dormitories, swimming pools in residential complexes, or areas of privately owned space, like the front lawns of houses, that are under the surveillance of others; the latter include such places as corner stores, local taverns, and sidewalks in front of houses. Semiprivate spaces tend to be owned in association, while semipublic are not owned by the users, who, nevertheless, still feel they have some possession over them. Peripheral territories are *public space.* They are areas that may be used by individuals or a group but are not possessed or personalized or claimed by them. The way the environment is laid out directly affects people's perceptions of what kind of space they are in. These perceptions are highly culture-specific.

Territorial Behavior and the Built Environment

There are many ways in which physical elements are used to demarcate territories. As an example of a central territory, the single-family detached home is "its own statement of a territorial claim" (Newman 1975). It represents the image of privacy, uniqueness, and protection held by many people in the United States, Canada, England, and Australia (Cooper 1974)—if not universally. Its continued popularity is due in part to the clarity with which territorial claims can be marked. Fences and hedges (particularly in backyards) and other symbols of boundary are easy to add.

The single-family detached home is also one that provides supporting territories without much difficulty. Supporting territories come in many forms: a frontyard, a porch, or even a flight of steps that separates the public domain from the private one by means of a semiprivate area. Clare Cooper (1974) suggests that the house is divided into two components: an intimate interior and a public exterior—"the self as viewed from within" and "the self we choose to display to others." In some instances this break occurs at the front door, in others it is at the point where semiprivate interior spaces are separated from truly private spaces.

The pattern of single-family homes almost inevitably provides a clear hierarchy of territories—from public to private, or, in El-Sharkawy's terms, from central to peripheral. Oscar Newman (1972, 1979) believes that such hierarchies of territory, or gradients in privacy, are essential to a feeling of well-being and help provide people with a sense of security (see fig. 14-4). This seems to be true of people within the mainstream of North American culture.

The typical double-loaded-corridor apartment building (such as the Van Dyke Houses, New York City) affords very poor territorial demarcators (Newman 1972). The private space, or central territory, consists of the apartment unit and stops at the door. Unlike the single-family house, there is no transition space between the public space (the corridor) and the private space (the unit). This type of layout is not an inevitable characteristic of high-rise residential buildings, however.

Newman (1972) provides a number of examples of high-rise buildings that do have a clear hierarchy of territories as part of their basic structure. Stapleton Houses on Staten Island and Riverbend Houses in Manhattan are two of them. In Stapleton Houses, entrance doors of corridors are recessed, affording tiny transition buffers between semipublic and private territories. The Riverbend example is more complex. It consists of two-story duplex apartments on single-loaded corridors. Each apartment opens onto a patio, which serves as a transitional space. A wall 4 feet high on the inside separates the patio from a public walkway. There are a couple of steps from the apartment door down to the walkway, so the patio wall is 6 feet high on the walkway side. The steps serve as a symbolic gateway, and the difference in elevation between patio and walkway affords privacy on the patio side as well as visual control over the walkway.

The campus dormitory is another example of a residential building type in which territorial-control factors make a major difference in residents' satisfaction levels. Where two students share a room, it is often difficult to create separate territories because the furniture is built in such a way that access to areas of the room cannot be controlled because they do not belong clearly to one or the other of the roommates (Sommer 1974b). This kind of arrangement is not inevitable either.

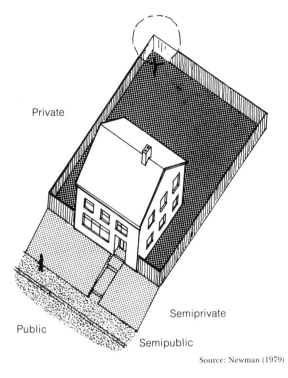

Private

Semiprivate

Public

Semipublic

1   Source: Newman (1979)

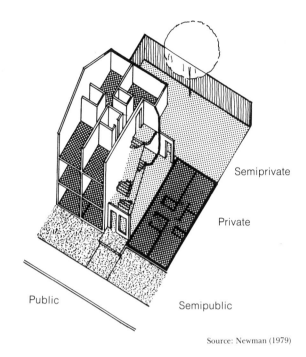

Semiprivate

Private

Public

Semipublic

2   Source: Newman (1979)

Light Traffic

Moderate
Traffic

Heavy Traffic

3   Source: Adapted from Appleyard and Lintell (1972)

The suites of rooms in International House in
Philadelphia have common living and toilet facilities
(see fig. 14-5). The rooms are thus private spaces
while the living areas are semiprivate because they
are only accessible to the residents of the residential
units. The members of the suite have free access to
it but others have to be invited in (El-Sharkawy
1979). Sim van der Ryn and Murray Silverstein
(1967) suggest similar configuration for dormitory
buildings in their study of student housing at Berke-

14-4. Territorial Hierarchies.

It is relatively easy to achieve a clear territorial hierarchy
in a single-family house as indicated in (1). In multifamily
housing a clear gradation of territories is more difficult to
achieve (2). In both cases, whether or not a semipublic
space would be perceived as such depends not only on the
house-street relationship but also on the amount of traffic
on the street (3). If there is heavy traffic, the *claim* over
the exterior space is substantially reduced (Appleyard and
Lintell 1972, Newman 1979).

ley. In the multicultural context of International
House there are some residents who find the sharing of bathrooms very difficult, but even for them
the territorial hierarchy works well.

These hierarchies of territories seem particularly important in societies where there is a great
need for security. In many areas of the United
States, for instance, social mechanisms for deterring
crime are not very effective. Oscar Newman has a
number of hypotheses about how these mechanisms
might be restored through enhancing the territorial
control that individuals and groups have over their
environments. These control mechanisms are bun-
dled together into the concept of *defensible space.*

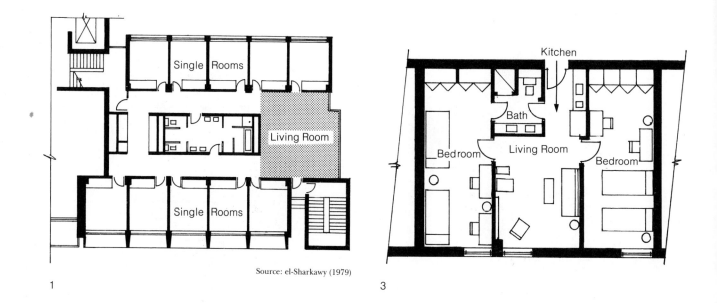

Source: el-Sharkawy (1979)

1   3

GROUND-FLOOR PLAN

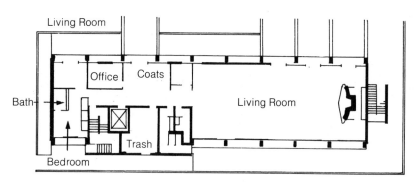

TYPICAL FLOOR PLAN

Source: Van der Ryn and Silverstein (1967)

2

14-5. Territoriality in Buildings.

The layout of some buildings affords territorial behavior much more easily than others. Thus the layout of International House, Philadelphia suites (1) clearly demarcates private, semiprivate, and semipublic territories, whereas a more typical dormitory floor plan (2) does not. Student apartment layouts such as that shown in (3) are difficult to territorialize because of the placement of built-in furniture, doors, and windows. In a study of dorms at Berkeley (Van der Ryn and Silverstein 1967), 94% of the population sample expressed a desire for rooms easier to territorialize.

DEFENSIBLE SPACE

Newman (1972) defines defensible space as follows :

> Defensible space is a surrogate term for the range of mechanisms—real and symbolic barriers, strongly defined areas of influence, and improved opportunities for surveillance—that combine to bring an environment under the control of its residents. A *defensible space* is a living residential environment which can be employed by its inhabitants for the enhancement of their lives while providing security for their families, neighbors and friends.

A defensible space is thus one whose users perceive it as affording easy recognition and control of the activities that take place within it. The assumption is that there is a predisposition, within the culture of the United States, at least, for people to exert such a control over the environment. The layout of the built environment will not cause such a predisposition to exist but it may arouse latent predispositions that will come into play once the opportunity exists (see also Gardiner 1978).

Newman provides considerable statistical evidence to support the observation that some environmental structures express a social fabric better than others. These data were obtained from interviews with the inhabitants of housing areas and project managers, from the records of crime types kept by the New York City Housing Authority, and from observations of different patterns of housing layouts. From the study of the relationships between design characteristics and crime statistics, it was possible to conclude that some building patterns afford criminal activity more readily than others.

Newman identifies four characteristics of the layout of the environment that on their own or in conjunction with each other create defensible space (see fig. 14-6). They are:

1. a clear hierarchical definition of territories, from public to semipublic, semiprivate to private;
2. the positioning of doors and windows to provide natural surveillance opportunities over entrances and open areas;
3. the use of building forms and materials that are not associated peculiarly with vulnerable populations; and
4. the location of residential developments in "functionally sympathetic" areas where residents are not threatened.

The first of these can be established through the use of symbolic barriers such as surface textures, steps, lamp posts, and bollards, or of real barriers such as walls. It works because it subdivides a development into zones over which people establish proprietary interests. The second occurs when people can see the public and semipublic areas of their environments as part of their day-to-day activities (Jacobs 1961, Angel 1968, Newman 1972); this reduces the possibility of unseen antisocial behavior. The third occurs when the massing, site planning, and materials have positive associations for people as predicted by balance-theory models (F. Heider 1946). The fourth reduces sources of antisocial behavior. It must be remembered that the layout of the environment does not cause or stop criminal activity. The roots of criminal activity lie in the social and cultural structure and environment of a society.

Recent research (Brower 1980, Brower, Dockett, and Taylor 1983), suggests that symbolic barriers are not very effective in areas of high perceived threat unless there is also a clear physical presence of residents. Under high levels of threat more redundant markers are needed to establish boundaries and claims. Apparently such elements as plantings are stronger markers of claim than artifacts such as wall decorations. The hypothesis is that plantings display a higher degree of concern because they display a greater degree of involvement with the environment; litter, weeds, and trash are marks of a lack of care. Fences are the best markers.

Newman's findings are important because, as Maslow suggests, security is a fundamental human need. For many low-income groups who live in what amounts to a hostile environment, security is a very pressing need (Rainwater 1966). Newman suggests that the ramifications of his work are even more important than they might appear. If one is insecure in one's environment then a negative attitude toward oneself, one's environment, and one's capabilities manifests itself in negative attitudes toward such things as job-seeking.

INDIVIDUAL DIFFERENCES IN PRIVACY DEMANDS

There are differences in privacy needs and in the mechanisms used to fulfill them from person to person and from group to group. Some of these differences have been researched systematically and documented but others remain as untested hypotheses based on anecdotal evidence.

Those individuals with organismic frailties are especially vulnerable to antisocial behavior. Their behavior is very much affected by their perceptions of opportunities for others to subject them to such

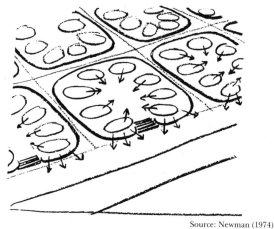

1   Source: Newman (1974)

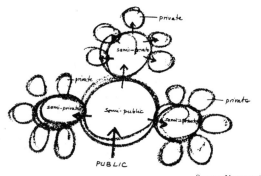

2   Source: Newman (1974)

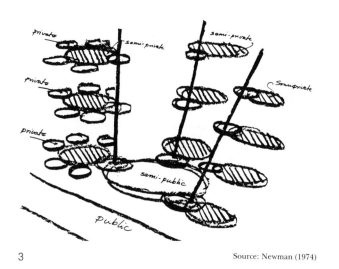

3   Source: Newman (1974)

14-6. Defensible Space.

Oscar Newman (1972) uses three diagrams to illustrate his basic hypotheses. In (1) the combination of territorial definition and natural surveillance opportunities is displayed conceptually. The hierarchy of territories from public to private that Newman found necessary to enable people to establish control over their environment is shown in (2), while the use of the hierarchy in high-rise residential buildings is shown in (3).

behavior (Lawton 1975). Their defensible-space needs are high. Similarly, their social-space distances are likely to be reduced if a perceptual system is impaired, because the amount of information picked up at a given distance will be less than it is for other people. Privacy needs may be greater for people with physical deformities, although this may be the prejudiced view of the healthy who want to be protected from seeing the infirm.

One might suspect that personality differences will be reflected in different needs for privacy (Marshall 1970). The research is confusing. There is general agreement that personal-space zones are larger for violent people (Kinzel 1970), but this has few, if

any, environmental design implications. Other research findings are contradictory.

Contrary to what one might expect, some research shows that the need for privacy is greater for extroverts than for introverts (Mikellides 1980). Daniel Cappon (1970) suggests that extroverts like contact with the environment, introverts prefer courtyard houses, misanthropes prefer buildings with complex internal relationships and clear territorial patterns, and mixers like strong central-plan houses. Other research (such as Evans and Howard 1973) does not corroborate this. A partial explanation for the variability of the research results on privacy and proxemic behavior may be differences in the moods of the individuals—their ego states—at the time the study was done. When people are under stress, for instance, they show a greater need for privacy than when they are not (Klopfer 1969).

There is another way in which house-form preferences and adaptations reflect personality differences. In a study of child-rearing attitudes, it was found that mothers who are restrictive and coercive exercise greater control over their children's privacy than mothers who are not (Parke and Sawin 1979). Such children are accorded less privacy and territorial control in their sleeping accommodations. It is difficult to make generalizations about the environment and design from such studies.

Differences in the need for privacy are partially attributable to *social group* attitudes—the roles people play in society and their socioeconomic status. The development of a person's attitude toward privacy is part of the socialization process; it is a learned value. As children grow older they need more privacy and use more privacy markers (Guardo 1969, Meisels and Guardo 1969). These developments correlate with the child's growth in physical maturity (Parke and Sawin 1979). Throughout their development, however, children in conversations keep less physical distance from their peers than from older children (Willis 1969).

In any particular housing type, space is an indicator of status and becomes a symbol of it. It must be recognized, however, that the norms of privacy for any group represent adaptations to what they can afford within the socioeconomic system of which they are a part. In low-income groups, for instance, crowded living conditions force a lack of privacy so privacy norms are much less severe than for high-income groups. Some high-income populations have major privacy demands. Alexander Kira (1966) notes:

> There are situations where all the facets of daily living are treated as an art and where only the most carefully contrived and controlled images are permitted to obtain, i.e., what is sometimes regarded as the ultimate in good breeding and civilized behavior. Here, role and format are everything, leading to separate bedrooms, bathrooms, and sitting rooms, where people come together only when fully prepared and "on stage." In these situations, privacy demands may also be regarded as being based on a sense of aesthetics.

Privacy needs are very much a part of a culture (Watson 1970, Altman and Chemers 1980). The layout of districts, buildings, and rooms depends on how people relate to each other in space, and thus it varies considerably by culture. Amos Rapoport (1969, 1977) finds that there are major cultural dif-

ferences in the privacy gradients sought by people. This is reflected in both the internal and external organization of houses. The internal organization of houses in which people feel comfortable very much reflects their culturally based attitudes toward privacy (Rapoport 1969, Zeisel 1974, Brolin 1976, Porteous 1977). While some people accept almost any relationship between the living, cooking, eating, and sleeping areas of a house, others have privacy needs that may affect not only the location of rooms but also, as in Saudi Arabia, the location of doors (Baleela 1975). In this case, the privacy needs of women are particularly high.

Rapoport stresses the importance of the threshold in establishing and reflecting privacy norms and territorial behaviors. The point at which the occupant of a house is aroused by the approach of a stranger varies from culture to culture. In the traditional Islamic dwelling it occurs at the entrance from the street. In this case there is no semipublic or semiprivate territory. The transition is from public to private. The open planning of the traditional American suburb stands in strong contrast to this.

Clare Cooper (1967), Amos Rapoport (1969, 1977), and Saim Nalkaya (1980) stress the differences in the nature of privacy expected and the nature of the personalization that takes place in frontyards and backyards in North America. Frontyards are for display—few activities take place there—while the backyard is for private activities. Not all subcultures in the United States use their frontyards in this way, and there are also socioeconomic differences in attitudes as to what a frontyard should be. These differences often lead to conflicts about how frontyards should be used and kept. Such conflicts are not unique to the United States. They are particularly acute in countries like Israel where people of very different cultural backgrounds live side by side (Nesher 1981).

Rapoport (1977) summarizes much of the research on privacy attitudes and house form as follows:

> There is a scale from self-display to extreme privacy with corresponding treatment, decorations and barriers admitting people, depending on their relationship and status, to various parts of the system—i.e., with penetration gradients. This is also related to rules about whether the street, for example, is seen as front or back region. . . . It is related to the social organization and the definition of groups so that if a whole quarter is composed of kin, it may be seen as a backstage region with a small front region for the reception of strangers, whereas in the case of an area with many nuclear families there are many front and back regions (one per house) and the treatment of the fronts defines the group front region.

Transportation technology has changed the relationship between street alley and house in many older American and European cities. Mews were once the backs of houses; visually they may still be so, but behaviorally many have become houses themselves.

Interpersonal affective behavior is influenced by ambient temperatures (Griffitt 1970, Griffitt and Veitch 1971). It is also likely that there is a trade-off between privacy and territoriality needs in housing to meet the needs for comfort, or vice versa, in different geographic settings. This results particularly from the migrations of people from one climatic zone to another. They bring their behavioral patterns developed in one place to another. Amos Rapoport (1969) shows that people often give up considerable physiological comfort to maintain cultural requirements. This is particularly evident in colonial cities.

CONCLUSION

Associated with any standing pattern of behavior is a desired level of privacy. The structure of the built environment screens activities and provides affordances for personal space and territorial needs if properly configured. The configurations and materials of the built environment also affect the ease with which it can be personalized. There is a correlation between our ability to call an area our own and our psychological comfort with it and our willingness to look after it.

The way in which buildings and the spaces between them are designed affects people's perceptions of who should be in control of them. There is a hierarchy of strengths of territorial claims. Each level in the hierarchy involves different degrees of personalization, ownership, and control. The perceived quality of the built environment is partially dependent on our ability to achieve desired levels of privacy.

Until recently these behaviors were poorly understood and difficult to consider explicitly because they are largely subconscious. Some architects have intuitively, or accidentally, incorporated features that afford these behaviors into the buildings they have designed. The research of Edward T. Hall (1959, 1966), Robert Sommer (1969, 1974a,

1974b), Irwin Altman (1975), and Oscar Newman (1972, 1979), in particular, has elucidated these processes in such a way that interior designers are better able to understand the relationship between room geography and human behavior, and architects, urban designers, and landscape architects are better able to meet privacy needs through the provision of real and symbolic barriers to demarcate territories in the internal organization of buildings and the design of open spaces.

While the desire for privacy through personal space and territorial controls may be universal, its manifestations vary considerably from culture to culture. Some cultures have more complex privacy demands and gradients than others. The work of Amos Rapoport (1969, 1977) and of Irwin Altman and Martin Chemers (1980) provides the framework for asking questions about the significance of privacy for the design of buildings and open spaces within different cultural and geographic settings.

ADDITIONAL READINGS

Altman, Irwin, and Martin Chemers. *Culture and Environment.* Monterey, Ca.: Brooks/Cole, 1980

Becker, Franklin D. "Personalization." In *Housing Messages.* Stroudsburg, Pa.: Dowden, Hutchinson and Ross, 1977, pp. 51–69.

Gardiner, Richard A. *Design for Safe Neighborhoods.* Washington, D.C.: U.S. Government Printing Office, 1978.

Hall, Edward T. *The Hidden Dimension.* New York: Doubleday, 1966.

———. "Meeting Man's Basic Spatial Needs in Artificial Environments." In Jon Lang et al., eds., *Designing for Human Behavior: Architecture and the Behavioral Sciences.* Stroudsburg, Pa.: Dowden, Hutchinson and Ross, 1974, pp. 210–220.

Mehrabian, Albert. *Public Places and Private Spaces: The Psychology of Work, Play and Living Environments.* New York: Basic Books, 1976.

Newman, Oscar. *Community of Interest.* New York: Anchor, 1979.

Saarinen, Thomas E. "Personal Space and Room Geography." In *Environmental Planning: Perception and Behavior.* Boston: Houghton Mifflin, 1976, pp. 19–43

Sommer, Robert. "Looking Back at Personal Space." In Jon Lang et al., eds., op. cit., pp. 202–309.

Skaburskis, Jacqueline. "Territoriality and its Relevance to Neighborhood Design: A Review." *Architectural Research and Teaching* 3, no. 1, (1974):39–44.

15

SOCIAL INTERACTION AND THE BUILT ENVIRONMENT

Normative theories of environmental design contain many assertions about how designs should be organized to affect the interactions between people. This has long been a concern of urban designers but it is also an issue in almost all large building design. Architects frequently make statements such as, "We have designed an open galleria three stories high so that executives and employees will be visible to each other," or that interiors will "break down hierarchies so that people will be better able to socialize." The hypothesis implicit in such claims is that the location of movement patterns and common facilities affects the degree of interaction that takes place between people. Issues of privacy and territoriality associated with behavior settings already have been introduced; the objective in this chapter is to deal more specifically with social interaction patterns and the affordances of the built environment. The topic is important because social interaction and people's attachment to social and/or built environments are interrelated (see Skaburskis 1974).

CHARACTISTICS OF THE BUILT ENVIRONMENT THAT AFFORD INTERACTION

Functional distance between units (buildings in urban and suburban areas, rooms in buildings) and the *functional centrality* of commonly used facilities (en-

tranceways in buildings, corridors and lounges in business offices) are major predictors of the interaction patterns of people who inhabit residential areas or who work in business organizations and institutions. Functional distance refers to the degree of difficulty encountered in moving from one point to another. Paths and corridors that lead straight from one place to another reduce this distance; long distances, major traffic flows across paths, and intervening opportunities for other activities increase the functional distance between two points. Functional centrality refers to the ease of access to common facilities for a group of people, the frequency with which people use them, and the amount of time they spend in them—in effect, the importance of such behavior settings in the lives of the people concerned and the ease of access to them. Much of the consideration of access has focused only on pedestrian movements, but often it is vehicular movement that should be considered. The argument is that opportunities to see and meet others are a prerequisite for promoting interactions that are informal and have no overt instrumental purpose for occurring (that is, interactions that are not premeditated for the transaction of business or the promotion of common ends). These observations have been adapted to deal with specific behavior settings and/or building types.

Jerry Finrow (1970) states that there are three bases for interactions in offices: the need for carrying out common tasks and exchanging information, accidental encounters because of the functional proximity of offices, and casual meetings in corridors. He provides empirical evidence for the importance of centralized collection points ("nodes" in Lynch's terms), the centralization of entrance points, and elevator lobbies and a greater number of units passed as enhancers of the interactions between the workers in a business organization. Others stress the importance of the spatial qualities of the built environment for affording interactions. In offices, courthouses, hospitals, nursing homes, and other institutional buildings, corridors are places that can afford casual meetings (Moleski 1974) as well as important business transactions (Perin 1970). Corridors that afford this the most easily are those that are wide enough or have alcoves, particularly at the doors of individual offices. Moleski argues for the latter because they also afford the temporary territorial control of spaces. This lends a degree of privacy and thus intimacy to the interaction. Powell Lawton (1975) notes the importance of corridors, elevator lobbies, and dining areas in congregate housing for the elderly as places where informal interactions take place (see also Zeisel 1981). If such areas are provided with seats, people's perception of them as places to gather is enhanced. This is difficult to achieve in corridors because their use as places to sit and watch what is going on may be at variance with the fire-safety regulations for institutional buildings.

One of the important variables in establishing the functional centrality of places is whether or not they are on paths of everyday activity patterns. Whether such places are desirable or not depends on whether they have seating arrangements that afford rest and comfort and allow observation of other people. In addition, such places should be group, or semipublic, territories with symbolic barriers that demarcate them. These observations apply at a variety of scales. Sproul Plaza at the University of California at Berkeley is a functionally central facility that acts as the heart of the campus: it has the common facilities that students need and is located on the main paths of movement of many people leaving and entering the campus, yet it is still clearly part of the campus (Montgomery 1971). At a smaller scale, the entrance lobbies in congregate housing for the elderly are places where residents like to gather because they can watch the passing scene. The lobbies become heavily used when comfortable seating is provided and common facilities such as a doctor's office or a store are located nearby (Lawton 1975). Whether one regards such usage as good or bad depends on one's values. Both types of places have been deemed undesirable by some critics: Sproul Plaza because it affords large

gatherings and was the scene of riots, and lobbies in housing for the elderly because the presence of people "hanging around," with little verbal interaction taking place, is perceived as aesthetically unappealing.

While these observations about the way the built environment can be designed to encourage or, if applied in reverse, to discourage interactions, may seem axiomatic, they have not always led to correct predictions about the outcome of building designs. This is because a large number of personality, social, and cultural variables intervene. Studies that support the above claims and others that do not and the reasons for these contradictory findings must be understood if designers are to apply research findings with any rationality.

The Westgate Study

The study by Leon Festinger and his colleagues of the Westgate housing of the Massachusetts Institute of Technology shortly after the end of World War II clearly showed the influence of the layout of the environment on contacts between people (Festinger, Schacter, and Back 1950, Michelson 1976). In the Westgate study the functional distance between housing units was short. Doors of units were close to each other so casual encounters were almost inevitable. In the two-story buildings the residents on the upper floor had their mailboxes located together at one place on the lower floor and had common entrances to the floor. They interacted more than the residents of the lower floor, each of whose rooms had its own entrance from the outside and its own mailbox. The population was, however, highly homogeneous on a number of dimensions: being students (or students' spouses), being veterans, and having similar financial status. They also had a need for mutual support.

Since this study, a considerable body of research has been conducted that allows the intuitions of designers to be examined and a number of conclusions to be drawn. These can be summarized in a series of observations about the major variables of concern at different scales.

SOCIAL SPACE AND ROOM GEOGRAPHY

Edward T. Hall (1966, 1974) has developed a four-level classification of basic social distances that helps interior designers and architects understand how different layouts of furniture and rooms—room geography (Saarinen 1976)—afford different degrees of formality of interpersonal interaction, from intimate conversations to formal presenta-

1

2

3

15-1. Room Geography and Social Interaction.
The way furniture is located in rooms specifies the expected interactions between people. The distance two people are apart in an office very much affects the formality of the interaction between them (1): the greater the distance, the more formal the interaction. The same holds for the design of living room furnishings. The seating layout in the lobby of a hotel (2) suggests that a fairly formal interaction pattern, if any, is expected. Public figures in formal interactions are accorded considerable deference and space (3).

tions. As the distance between people increases so the visual, olfactory, thermal, and kinesthetic information they pick up about each other decreases and the voice level rises in order to maintain contact. As distance increases so the privacy of the person increases and the privacy of the interaction decreases.

Hall differentiates among intimate, personal, social-consultive, and public interactions and the distances people maintain from each other during them. *Intimate distance* (9 to 18 inches for Hall's sample population) is the one of close physical contact; *personal distance* (1.5 to 4 feet) is the minimum dis-

tance for interaction between nonintimates; *social-consultive distance* (4 to 12 feet) is the spacing of people at casual gatherings and in working situations; people stay farthest apart when conducting formal business. Desks in offices tend to keep people at a formal distance. This is abetted by the symbolic aesthetics of the interior design (Duffy 1969, Joiner 1971). Once one goes beyond 12 feet, the interaction becomes *public*. As the distance between people increases so does the potential publicness of the interaction.

There has been considerable discussion over

the usefulness of these observations for architectural design (Broadbent 1973, Saarinen 1976, Porteous 1977). Hall was concerned originally with the "anthropology of manners," and his work does bring the designer to an awareness of how people relate to each other in space and how the layout of rooms relates to perceptions of status: people of higher status are given more space. Geoffrey Broadbent (1973) is sceptical of the utility of this research for designers: "unless it happens to be some wildly eccentric shape," a room 10 feet square can accommodate most types of interaction. The placement of windows, doors, closets, and lighting outlets, however, often severely reduces the possible furniture arrangements in a room (Sommer 1974b). In addition, much seating is built in—fixed-feature space in Hall's terms—often without consideration for what it affords for either personal interaction or observation or how it affects the potential arrangement of movable furniture.

Sociopetal and Sociofugal Space

The use of the terms *sociopetal* and *sociofugal* to describe spaces that "bring" people together and "force" them apart was introduced by Humphrey Osmond (1966) when he was Superintendent of Saskatchewan Hospital in Canada. Sociopetal layouts are those in which face-to-face contact, particularly eye contact, is easy to maintain and seating arrangements are separated at a socioconsultive distance (Argyle and Dean 1965). Sociofugal layouts are those in which it is easy to avoid interactions. Back-to-back benches are an example of a sociofugal layout and the old-fashioned drugstore booth is an example of a sociopetal layout (Hall 1974). Each is appropriate in certain contexts. One of the interesting things about the twisting pattern of seating in Güell Park in Barcelona by Antonio Gaudí is that it affords both.

The terms have been applied also to site-plan layouts. Those plans in which there are public or quasi-public places where people easily meet are referred to as sociopetal ones and those in which there are no gathering places as sociofugal. Osmond used the term in a more restricted sense to refer to smaller-scale layouts.

It is important not to assume that because face-to-face interactions are easy in sociopetal settings people will automatically seek out such settings. There must be a predisposition for such behavior, and the settings must be where people want to be. Powell Lawton (1975) found that residents at the Philadelphia Geriatric Center liked to cluster at places where there was much activity to watch in preference to places that readily afforded face-to-face interactions.

Territorial Control and Interactions

Social interactions occur more easily when people's social needs are balanced by the sense of individual autonomy that comes with privacy. Ambiguous spaces, those that are neither public nor private, tend to mitigate against interactions, since the individual is less able to control the interaction on his or her own terms. Physical privacy is a prerequisite of much socially interactive behavior because it provides a setting that allows a wider range of personal choices.

One way of obtaining privacy is through reserve—through avoiding contact. Another way is through territorial control. There is considerable evidence that when there are clear territorial boundaries for each occupant of a shared room the interaction level between them is higher than when they have to obtain privacy through reserve. This is clearly shown in a carefully controlled study conducted by Charles Holohan and Susan Saegert (1973) of interaction patterns in a psychiatric ward. The installation of 6-foot-high partitions between beds in the ward to create clear territories for each patient correlated highly with a substantial increase in the social interaction between patients and staff and between patients and visitors and with a decrease in the patients' passive behaviors such as sleeping too long. It has been accepted widely that the same occurs within residential areas.

"Private open space promotes neighboring, and neighborhood interaction provides a suitable socializing situation for children" (Porteous 1977). Anthony F.C. Wallace (1952), an anthropologist, hypothesized that the lack of privately controlled yards in housing areas tends to inhibit both family territorial control and community formation. He took this a step farther by suggesting that this is one reason for the greater degree of interaction between neighbors in areas of single-family housing than in apartment buildings. Single-family homes have clear territorial hierarchies and afford casual surveillance opportunities, provided the houses are not too far apart, in which case functional propinquity is lost.

Oscar Newman (1972) and designers such as Rijk Rietveld have shown that apartment buildings can be designed to afford these opportunities, so the important variable does not appear to be that of apartment-living versus single-family homes. Rather, the best predictors of interaction patterns appear to be the details of design and above all the residents' lifestyles, degree of affluence, and degree

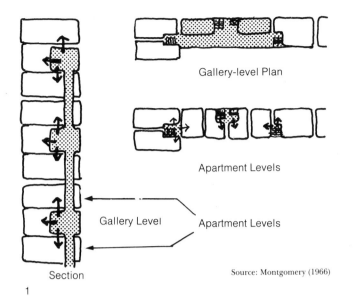

Gallery-level Plan

Apartment Levels

Gallery Level — Apartment Levels

Section

Source: Montgomery (1966)

1

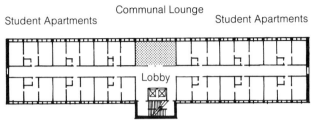

Communal Lounge

Student Apartments   Student Apartments

Lobby

2

3

15-2. Building Design for Social Interaction.
The designs illustrated above are based on the premise that the provision of facilities for people coming together will lead to the social interaction of members of the populations of concern. The conceptual basis for the Pruitt-Igoe Housing scheme is illustrated in (1) and the floor of a university dormitory building in (2). In the former case, more anti-social than social behavior became associated with the communal gallery spaces (Montgomery 1966), while in the latter case students do use the communal area but it serves a purpose different from the one intended. It has become an area for quiet study rather than interaction. The square in (3) affords a variety of interaction patterns and is heavily used and liked because it fulfills a variety of needs. It makes its larger environment a pleasant place in which to be. Architects need to be careful about imputing greater social benefits than this to a physical setting.

of need for mutual aid. This was borne out in a study of Marina Towers in Chicago, where the perception of territorial encroachment (via the believed transmission of sound from one apartment to the next) inhibited friendly interaction between neighbors (Flaschbart 1969). Certainly, Oscar Newman (1972) has shown that when territorial boundaries are clear people exert control over what goes on within them and are watchful against intrusions. Issues of privacy and interaction clearly go hand in hand, as Serge Chermayeff and Christopher Alexander (1963) recognized.

FUNCTIONAL PROPINQUITY AND INTERACTION PATTERNS IN RESIDENTIAL AREAS

The Westgate study clearly showed that functional propinquity was linked to interaction patterns between residents. This was shown also by the work of Leo Kuper (1953) in Britain. Powell Lawton (1977) states that propinquity is a major factor in the interaction patterns of elderly people because as competence levels decrease the need for mutual help increases. In face-block neighborhoods—

where the houses face each other across streets with their front doors lining the sides of the streets—there tends to be considerable interaction (Kuper 1953, Keller 1968). The road is a seam and becomes semipublic space. Although everybody has the right of admission to it, it is controlled by the residents. When accompanied by natural surveillance opportunities (windows overlooking the street) and affordances for activities (parking opportunities on the street in front of the houses, short blocks where pedestrians circulate more readily and meet at corners, and when there is a predisposition for interaction among the residents on the block, a lively living environment will ensue (see Jane Jacobs 1961). There is also supporting evidence that people who live on a cul-de-sac interact more and know each other better than people who live on through streets, but this is not necessarily something that the residents seek (Kuper 1953, Michelson 1976). Street type does not seem to be the crucial variable either. The number of houses, the width and length of the street, the amount of traffic flowing down it, and the way the houses face the street all seem to be important. As traffic increases so interaction patterns, particularly cross-street interactions, decrease (Appleyard and Lintell 1972, Appleyard et al. 1981).

When populations are not homogeneous in character, propinquity can lead to negative contacts between people, especially if they do not have enough privacy (Kuper 1953). When a working-class family locates in a middle-class area it can find itself socially isolated rather than integrated (Michelson 1976).

Much residential-area design, as well as some apartment-building and even office-building design, is based on the assumption that when the affordances for meeting, walking together, and using common facilities are part of everyday life the interaction levels between people will be higher. While this belief may seem to be axiomatic, it should be treated with caution because it can lead to a number of erroneous conclusions about the design and location of specific facilities.

Behavior settings in buildings and neighborhoods can be classified into two types in terms of the opportunities they provide for interactions between people: those whose manifest purpose is interaction between people, and those where interaction is a by-product of some other purpose. Architects (and their clients) often believe that behavior settings of the former type can be designed into buildings and urban designers imagine that cities are full of them. Certainly in Europe and in some ethnic neighborhoods in the United States it is common for taverns, streets, parks and even rail-

road stations (Sasuki 1976) to be regarded as places for meeting other people and/or for "parading" or "cruising" at certain times of the day or week, but the presence of these and the designer's ability to create them—even to know when to create them—are overestimated.

At the building level—such as apartment buildings, institutions, vacation resorts—communal lounges afford opportunities for people to meet but for this to occur there needs to be some catalyst. The catalyst may be an individual who brings people together (see Flaschbart 1969) or a common activity or topic of discussion. Public plazas attract people if there are activities and people to watch and even more so if there is food available and a safe and pleasant atmosphere (see Jacobs 1961, Whyte 1980). Parents may strike up conversations while watching their children at a playground; people working on cars in the common parking lot of an apartment house or in the street in front of their homes may discuss their problems, or people doing laundry may start a conversation while waiting for their wash to be done (although this does not seem to be as frequent as detergent advertisements would have us believe).

Herbert Gans (1967), in a study of Levittown, found that propinquity was only one of several factors in establishing interaction patterns between households. It was important when people first moved into the suburb and when the need for mutual support among neighbors was high. Thereafter, interaction patterns based on propinquity seemed to occur only when there was a need for mutual aid or a homegeneity in attitudes toward such things as child-rearing (see also Keller 1968). Taken in conjunction, these factors explain why Lawton found propinquity such a good predictor of friendship-formation in the subset of the elderly population he studied and why Seymour Bellin and Louis Kriesberg (1965) found that husbandless mothers in a public housing project in Syracuse, New York had three or four times as many friends inside the project than outside it (see Michelson 1976). In much luxury housing, in contrast, people pride themselves on not knowing their neighbors (Rapoport 1977). They also have more cosmopolitan lifestyles than poor people (Webber 1963) and rely less on their neighbors. They value privacy more.

The impact of functional propinquity on interaction patterns seems to hold best for children and tight-knit ethnic communities (Hester 1975, Michelson 1976). Even though the adults in a residential area may not know each other, the children may well do so. Children tend to be the true localites. They play on sidewalks and in the streets where they are part of the social life of a neighborhood (Jacobs 1961, Hester 1975). The places that attract them have elements of both danger and security. As they become teenagers, the lack of opportunities for them to get together and test themselves legally has been suggested as a possible contributor to antisocial behavior (Ladd 1978).

Functional Centrality and Interaction Patterns

The basic hypothesis is that the farther a housing area is from essential facilities, the less the effective social integration ("we" feeling) of its inhabitants. Anthony F. C. Wallace (1952) suggests that when the functional centrality of facilities is poor, tensions will be created within and between individuals and less use will be made of potentially common organizations. Certainly opportunities for meeting will be reduced, particularly in populations with automobiles. A counterhypothesis is that a lack of local facilities would "force" people to rely on each other for mutual aid and this would lead to greater interaction. Possibly both hypotheses hold under specific circumstances, but the supporting evidence is meager.

ARCHITECTURAL HOMOGENEITY (UNITY) AND INTERACTION PATTERNS

It is intuitively appealing to believe that a greater amount of social interaction takes place between people who live in settings that are homogeneous in terms of size, style, and value of housing units. The evidence for this is indirect. The assumption is that people who *choose* to live in such areas perceive themselves to be homogeneous in values and thus will interact more. Terrence Lee's research (1970) in Britain supports the self-perception aspect of this observation but provides no evidence for the increase in interaction between people. People who live in an architecturally homogeneous area—a "district" in Lynch's terms—are likely to have a clear image of it (Lynch 1960), but the secondary benefits of this are not clear.

IMPLICATIONS OF DESIGNING FOR SOCIAL INTERACTION

Why should we have concern for designing to increase opportunities for interaction in buildings and residential areas? This is, to some extent, within our power. It is possible to design for various degrees of privacy and territorial control. It is possible to locate lounges centrally in buildings. It is possible to design corridors so that they are wide enough

and have alcoves that afford the opportunity for people to stand out of the traffic flow to talk casually or purposefully. It is possible to design seating arrangements so that people are at a comfortable distance from each other for the time and place and the nature of the interaction desired. It is possible to design an environment that has nodes where paths cross and where there are centrally located facilities to answer people's day-to-day needs. It is possible to design parks in conjunction with their surroundings so that they can be lively places (although this is not the sole reason for having a park or plaza).

The research of Hall (1966), Sommer (1969, 1974b), and Newman (1972, 1979) informs the architect on how to achieve territorial demarcations; the work of Willis (1963) informs the architect on the mechanisms whereby the built environment affords or does not afford privacy to its inhabitants; the analyses of Whyte (1980) and of Lennard and Lennard (1984) provide the basis for generating a number of design principles for public spaces that afford interaction patterns and the circumstances under which they are likely to occur within Western cities; existing cities and new towns are full of examples of patterns where paths cross and services are centrally located. Whether these affordances are used or not depends on the predispositions of the people who inhabit and use the settings.

If people need to interact, they will find the means to do so in almost any built environment. It is easier in some environments than in others. Several reasons have been suggested to explain why interaction is a desirable end. The most basic reason is that interactions are necessary for sustaining the human relationships that are the bases for meeting human needs for affiliation and belonging. Any opportunity for achieving this end is perceived to be good. Another reason is that these activities—interacting with others and seeing them come and go—promote individual growth because they suggest new possibilities for behavior—they serve a socializing purpose. Christopher Alexander (1972, 1977) argues that people must see each other very often under informal conditions in order for intimate, primary relationships to develop. It is suggested also that interactions between people of diverse backgrounds and natures lead to positive changes in the attitudes the groups have toward each other, whether these are attitudes of employees toward management or of one ethnic group toward another. There is some supportive evidence for this (for instance, Festinger and Kelley 1951), but one study of an economically integrated housing scheme in Boston showed that over time the populations, the facilities available and their patronage, and even circulation patterns became increasingly segregated as the environment became adapted to the lifestyles of the population. Where different lifestyles are involved, propinquity leads to coolness between neighbors at best, hostility at the worst (Darke and Darke 1974).

It also has been argued that where there is considerable interaction between people at the local level crime levels are low because social obligations and the concern people have for each other is high and alienation is low. While the observations of Jane Jacobs (1961) and Oscar Newman (1972) support this hypothesis, it should be treated with some caution. There are areas where there is considerable interaction between people but crime levels are high. This may be due partially to the lack of clear territorial patterns (Newman 1972) but certainly it has more to do with the social and cultural environment than with the physical environment of which the people are a part.

It has also been suggested that residential areas where there is much neighborly interaction are well liked by their inhabitants. When people are displaced from such environments the displacement is accompanied by much grief (Fried 1963). At the same time, some people seek to be displaced because they aspire to other lifestyles which lower-density suburban environments most easily afford them (Gans 1967). It is also clear that individual differences in personality and cultural backgrounds and expectations are correlated with preferences for different levels of interaction with others.

INDIVIDUAL AND GROUP DIFFERENCES IN INTERACTION PATTERNS IN THE PHYSICAL ENVIRONMENT

It has already been shown that some generalizations can be made about the lifestyles of people (see chapter 11). It is clear that different people seek different levels of interaction. The definition of a good level can be ascertained subjectively in terms of what people themselves specify or objectively in terms of some normative position on what a good life is. Both definitions are highly value-laden, and in that sense they are social and political in character.

A strong argument has been presented for a correlation between a person's *organismic* character and his or her *personality*. On one dimension of measurement, extroverts are people who seek interactions with others while introverts do not—although they may wish to see what is going on from areas where interactions are not demanded of them (see also Cooper 1974). It has been hypothesized that

people who are physically handicapped tend to be introverted because of the stigma associated with handicaps, but this is a popular stereotype. Many people, such as the advocates for barrier-free environments, argue for mainstreaming people who have physical handicaps and building the environment so that functional distances are reduced for them. It has been argued (Lawton 1975) that people of low physical competence need the support of others and so need more immediate access to others and more opportunities for interaction than are needed by the highly competent. Personality differences also explain why some people seek interactions and others do not, people who do not need to be in control interacting more than those who do (Lofland 1973).

Social and *cultural* differences also affect the room geography and interaction patterns of people. Hall's own work notes this. People of higher status maintain larger personal spaces, greater levels of privacy, and more extensive territorial claims than are found among lower-status people. Seating arrangements in conferences and meetings reflect the status of those participating (De Long 1970). The design of table and seating arrangements is often highly symbolic. The arguments over the room layout and particularly the table and seating arrangements for the Paris peace talks during the Vietnam War attest to this (Heyman 1978).

The way in which people relate to each other in space depends considerably on their cultural background. Hall notes that Anglo-Americans, Britons, and Swedes stand farther apart in conversations than do southern Europeans, Latins, and Arabs for the same degree of formality. Latin Americans prefer to sit side by side to converse informally while Anglo-Americans prefer face-to-face conversations (Hall 1966, Sommer 1969, Watson 1970).

There are also major differences in where and how people interact with each other at a larger scale. One difference, discussed earlier, is that between people who are *localites* or *cosmopolitans* in terms of their lifestyles. Localites use local facilities and high-density environments rich in behavior settings. For them the functional centrality of facilities is important. For some this lifestyle is a personal preference; others are constricted by economic necessity and/or the lack of mobility. For large segments of the population this was the prevalent lifestyle in American cities, but changes in income levels and heavy reliance on the automobile for transportation have reduced people's need for local contacts.

Institutions and business organizations have different styles. Those whose style is paternalistic provide common facilities such as recreation rooms, cafeterias, and lounges. These are intended to instill a sense of belonging and pride in the organization, but the strategy often pulls against the users' need for autonomy. Cultural expectations also play a part. In Japan, for example, workers expect much more from their employers in the way of communal services than is expected by their American counterparts. In return, the Japanese workers feel they have a greater obligation to their employers than is felt by their American counterparts.

CONCLUSION

Architects and landscape and urban designers can design environments rich in opportunities for personal interactions of various types. When the social or administrative system supports the use of these environments, their affordances are likely to be used in the predicted manner. When support is lacking the probability of the facilities being used simply because they exist is reduced considerably. Apartment buildings and hotels can be provided with ample, well-furnished lobbies, student dormitories and offices with common lounges that afford formal and informal gatherings, but the consequences of such designs are open to debate.

There are several normative positions that one can take on this. One is that affordances for interactions will serve useful purposes if they meet people's predispositions but are a waste of money if they are not used. Another position is that they should be provided anyway because interactions are "good" and sooner or later people will learn to avail

themselves of the opportunities for interaction.

Interactions are the basis for the formation and continued existence of social organizations. Whether or not the creation of affordances for social interactions will lead to the formations of a sense of "community" in business organizations, institutions, and neighborhoods has been the subject of much debate. Recent research helps to clarify the question. This is the subject of the next chapter.

ADDITIONAL READINGS

Alexander, Christopher. "The City as a Mechanism for Sustaining Human Contact." In Robert Gutman, ed., *People and Buildings.* New York: Basic Books, pp. 406–434.

Blake, Robert, et al. "Housing, Architecture and Social Interaction." *Sociometry* 19 (1956): 133–139.

Cooper, Clare. *Easter Hill Village.* New York: Basic Books, 1975.

Gutman, Robert. "Site Planning and Social Interaction." *Journal of Social Issues* 22 (October 1966): 103–115.

Jacobs, Jane. *Death and Life of Great American Cities.* New York: Random House, 1961.

Ittelson, William, Harold M. Proshansky, Leanne Rivlin, and Gary Winkel. "The Built Environment." In *An Introduction to Environmental Psychology.* New York: Holt, Rinehart and Winston, 1974, pp. 341–396.

Wolfe, Maxine, and Harold Proshansky. "The Physical Setting as a Factor in Group Process and Function." In Jon Lang et al., eds., *Designing for Human Behavior: Architecture and the Behavioral Sciences.* Stroudsburg, Pa.: Dowden, Hutchinson and Ross, 1974, pp. 194–202.

16

SOCIAL ORGANIZATION AND THE BUILT ENVIRONMENT

There are many definitions of what constitutes an organization (Weber 1947, March, Simon, and Guetzkow 1958, W. Scott 1964). Max Weber's definition is concise: "A system of continuous purposive activity of a specific kind." Richard H. Hall (1972) provides a more detailed description:

> An organization is a collectivity with a relatively identifiable boundary, a normative order, authority ranks, communication systems, and a membership coordinating system; this collectivity exists on a relatively continuous basis in an environment and engages in activities that are usually related to a goal or set of goals.

An organization can be considered to consist of a set of behavior settings that are congruent with its existing boundaries, normative order, authority ranks, communication systems, and membership coordinating system. It consists of a set of standing patterns of behavior and milieus. The smoothness and pleasantness with which a social organization operates depends on its organizational structure and on the quality of the interpersonal relationships among its members. Neither of these is determined by the physical layout of the built environment in which the organization exists, but the affordances of the layout make a major contribution to the working of the organization at both an operational and a symbolic level.

Normative theories of architecture and urban design are replete with statements on how to achieve particular social organizations through physical design or on how to design "ideal" social organizations and the architecture to accompany them. This is true of the ideal "communities" of religious organizations such as the Shakers and Oneidas (Hayden 1976), of social reformers such as Fourier, of industrialists who were also social reformers, such as Robert Owen and Titus Salt (Mumford 1951), of architects such as Frank Lloyd Wright (1945), Le Corbusier (1925, 1934), and Percival Goodman (Goodman and Goodman 1947), and of the new town movements in a number of countries. All these people had visions of good social organizations and the architecture that was required either to achieve them or to accompany them. The same holds true, to a lesser extent, for the development of business organizations in individual buildings (Steele 1973).

Much of the thinking on architecture, urban design, and social organization has had this strong architectural deterministic overtone (Boughey 1968, Gans 1968, Lipman 1974). There are statements in the writings of architects as diverse as Paul Goodman, Romaldo Giurgola, Louis Kahn, and James Stirling about the importance of the role of architecture in organizational development (Blau 1980). This holds for both neighborhood and single-building design, particularly in those buildings that are to house institutions such as homes for the elderly, psychiatric facilities, asylums, student dormitories, and jails. Communal spaces such as lounges, for instance, often are provided in offices, apartment buildings, and student dormitories to achieve the social integration of the group. It was argued in chapter 15 that there is a relationship between the functional centrality of a communal facility and how people use it and interact socially within it. The concern in this chapter is with the patterns of the built environment that affect not only interaction patterns but also the development of social organizations. The built environment, it will be argued here, can be designed to facilitate the operation of a social organization if the design is based on an understanding of the nature of the particular social organization being considered. The claim that the built environment can bring organizations about is more problematic. One of the reasons for the lack of clarity in many architectural discussions of the built environment and social organizational behavior is a lack of clarity in our understanding of the nature of social organizations—their types and their social operational characteristics.

TYPES OF ORGANIZATIONS

There have been many efforts to classify organizations. Some writers (such as Parsons 1963) differentiate between organizations in terms of their goals; some (such as Katz and Kahn 1966) differentiate between those serving instrumental functions and those serving expressive functions, and some (such as Etzioni 1964), in terms of their source of legitimacy. The categorization that best helps environmental designers to understand the role of planning and design in organizational development is that of Shimon Gottschalk (1975), who distinguishes between *formal* and *communal* organizations.

The fundamental characteristics of the two types of organization are shown in the accompanying table. Organizations may include subsystems of both types. A planned unit development, for instance, may consist of a neighborhood maintenance organization to which all households must belong by deed. This is a formal organization but it may have subsets of communal organizations based on networks of friendships. The important point to remember is that formal organizations can be designed from the outside; communal organizations cannot be—they grow from within. A designer may well be able to design the affordances whereby neighboring and other communal behaviors take

Similarities and Differences between Formal and Communal Organizations

Some Similarities between Formal and Communal Organizations

1. Both are solidary interactional systems.
2. Both are relatively highly institutionalized in that they possess a developed normative structure, a high level of value consensus, and patterned reciprocal expectations.
3. Both may include subsystems of their own as well as of the opposite type.
4. Sentimental collectivity orientations (loyalty, commitment) are a variable.

Differences Between Formal and Communal Organizations

(Each of the dimensions may be considered as representing a continuum.)

Formal Organizations	Communal Organizations
1. Oriented toward a specific defining goal	Not oriented toward a specific defining goal
2. Functional collectivity orientation	No functional collectivity orientation
3. Linked by contract, i.e., by specified and limited cooperation	Linked by generalized cooperation (active and passive)
4. Mechanistic interaction	Structured free-wheeling
5. A variety of roles and a formal hierarchy	A variety of roles but no formal hierarchy
6. Normative, utilitarian, and coercive forms of power are legitimate	Only normative power is legitimate
7. Created externally or by its elements	Generated by its elements
8. The inclusive system defines the roles of the subsystems	The inclusive system is defined by the subsystems

place easily, but if there are no predispositions for the ends served by this type of behavior, it will not develop and the affordances will be unused for the purpose they were expected to fulfill.

FORMAL ORGANIZATIONS AND THE BUILT ENVIRONMENT

The degree of formality of social organizations varies considerably. The total institution is the most formal. This is exemplified by a typical jail. Here the bounds of the institution are clear, there is a clear distinction between caretakers and prisoners, the chain of command is highly structured, the normative behavior patterns associated with each role are clear, and there is a high degree of surveillance of the behavior of prisoners and guards. This is clearly reflected in the architecture.

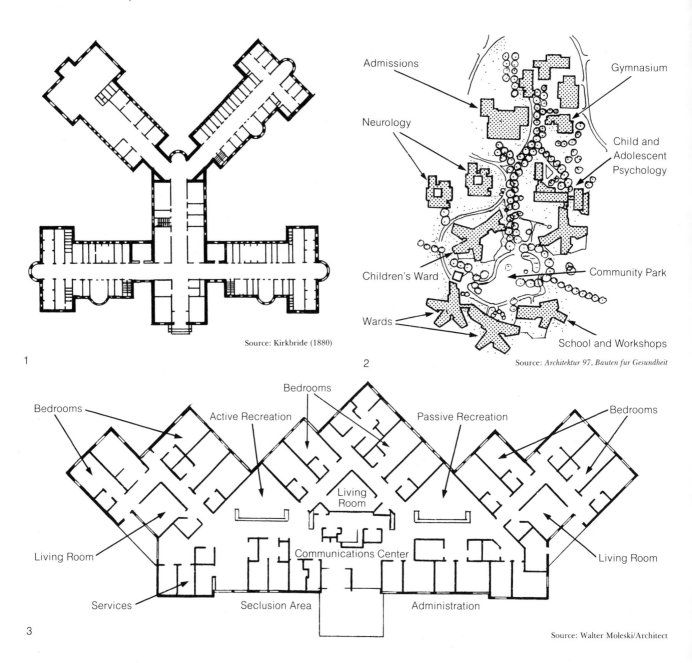

Source: Kirkbride (1880)

1

Admissions

Gymnasium

Neurology

Child and
Adolescent
Psychology

Children's Ward

Community Park

Wards

School and Workshops

2

Source: *Architektur 97, Bauten fur Gesundheit*

Bedrooms

Bedrooms

Bedrooms

Active Recreation

Passive Recreation

Bedrooms

Living
Room

Living Room

Living Room

Communications Center

Services

Seclusion Area

Administration

3

Source: Walter Moleski/Architect

16-1. Formal Organizations and Built Form.

The architecture of an institution reflects its social organization and the image of itself it wants to present to the world. The Kirkbride mental hospital in (1) was a major social and architectural innovation reflecting the belief that mental illness was curable through treatment. The individual was regarded as important, as can be seen in the individual rooms and subdivisions of the plan. Once the medical model of treatment took over, institutions grew in size and often were located in rural settings (2). Since the mid-1960s mental illness has been regarded as an issue involving the whole family and community. This has been accompanied by the emergence of smaller psychiatric hospitals with clusters of rooms (3).

The operation of a formal organization depends on the linking of subsettings with each other in terms of the flows and interactions of individuals and goods. Not all organizations are place-oriented —their settings may be linked by flows of information rather than people—but many are. Another example of a predominantly formal organization is a hospital. Its organizational structure consists of three levels of caretakers and one of patients. The

three levels of caretakers are the technical, managerial, and institutional (Souder et al. 1970). The technical level consists of the nursing, medical, and paramedical groups; the managerial level, of administrative and executive officers; and the institutional level, of directors and trustees. Each level has complete control over some activities while other activities form part of the chain of command.

Not all the organizational levels of an institution are reflected equally in the built environment (Steele 1973). Very few behavior settings, for instance, may exist at the institutional level, thus the overall impact of this level in terms of activity systems and design may be small. It may, however, be important in both the internal and external symbolic aesthetics of the building(s) and landscape of the institution.

Each level of a formal organization, be it public or private, consists of a number of behavior settings that specify its basic spatial needs given the standing patterns of behavior needed to maintain it. Design considerations go beyond this, however. The quality of a secretary's office or a nursing station goes beyond its spatial requirements since it also has to meet certain aesthetic needs. Thus the institution reflects the values that each level of its organization has about itself and about the other levels. Robert Sommer (1974b) notes that many institutions consist of "hard architecture." The built environment responds more to the needs of managerial ease than to the needs of its other users. This is apparent in the materials chosen, the general layout specifications, and the fulfillment of the needs of the equipment used rather than the needs of the technical organization or, in the case of hospitals, of the patients (Lindheim 1970).

Recently there has been much empirical research on the organizational patterns of buildings and social groups. Trites' study, "Influence of Nursing-Unit Design on the Activities and Subjective Feelings of Nursing Personnel" (1970), exemplifies the research on subsystems of organizations. In the study, three different layouts—the "radial," the "single-corridor," and the "double-corridor"—were examined. Each has its strong and weak points on various dimensions of performance, but with the radial layout much less time was spent negotiating the linkages between subsettings so more time was spent with patients. In addition, there was less absenteeism, greater morale, and higher self-esteem on the part of the personnel of the radial layouts. The hospital in which this study was conducted may be unique; it contained four units of each type.

Problems of Effectiveness in Formal Organizations

The internal layout of a building affects the effectiveness of a formal organization through the way in which it affects the flow of activities, intergroup processes, and communication patterns (see also Moleski and Lang 1982). According to Moleski (1974), an analysis of a formal organization, say, a business organization, begins with an analysis of be-

havior settings in which specific organizational activities take place. These can be classified according to their standing patterns of behavior and the milieu required to afford these well in terms of ergonomic, privacy, and symbolic aesthetic requirements. The standing patterns of behavior can be analyzed in terms of the levels of activity, thinking, routineness, attention, and the orientation of the performers themselves. These task-related behavior settings are tied together by a network of processes of communication and information flow, functional roles, collaboration, intergroup processes, and authority systems. The character and strength of these linkages are reflected in their geographic distribution in space. It is not simply the nature of task-oriented activities and linkages that determines the locations of specific activities. These often are linked for symbolic and thus for status needs. It is not simply the formal relationships that hold an organization together but also the informal. The former is defined by the policies of the organization; the latter develops outside that policy. The former is relatively easy to analyze; the latter, considerably more difficult.

The organization is the social structure uniting the components. This unification takes place through the value system of its leaders, the behavioral norms specifying the behavior expected of its members, the outcomes of the activities of the group, the types of rewards provided for appropriate behavior and the nature of the system of authority or control. It is, however, the social considerations of the activity system that tie individual members together. These depend on the organization's social structure and formalized role system, the characteristics of the task-related interactions, the level of supervision, and the social focus of the performers.

Organizations change over time. Sometimes there is a slow evolution of their purposes, structure, and size, and sometimes it occurs with dramatic suddenness. The changes may be in the task activities, but they may also be in the images that the organizations have of themselves and that they wish to communicate to others. It is possible to study growth predictions and needs for adaptation and revitalization, but external factors often result in changes very different from those forecast. A change in the self-image of an organization may or may not be accompanied by major task changes. It will, however, almost certainly result in changes in the physical design because this is how the images are manifested (Lasswell 1979). This may simply involve a change in the company's logo across the building or it may be more substantial, involving broader changes in office layout, office-planning concepts, and environmental design style.

COMMUNITIES, COMMUNAL ORGANIZATIONS, AND THE BUILT ENVIRONMENT

Residential communities, institutions such as university dormitories, and urban and suburban neighborhoods are types of communal organizations (Gottschalk 1975). They are comprised of a number of subsystems some of which are formal and some of which are communal. Gottschalk identifies three levels of social organizations in such residential settings:

Level I — External Linkages Level
Level II — Institution or Residential Area Level
Level III — Residential Unit or Family Level.

At each level the social organization may be formal or communal as specified in the table above, particularly in terms of goal orientation. The eight possible combinations of formal and communal organizations, with examples of each, are listed in the accompanying table.

The *crescive community*, exemplified by the folk village, consists of communal organizations at all levels; it is a type that can be used as the basis for understanding the others. *Administered communities* such as Pullman, Moosehaven, and Lowell, *intentional communities* such as the Bruderhof, Oneida, and Amana, and *designed communities* such as Park Forest, Columbia, Radburn, and the Levittowns deviate from the crescive. It is important to recognize this, because the folk village is often the "ideal" model for planners. In reality, the types of communities that involve or can involve any sort of conscious design from the outside have "contracts" between two levels of social organization. The built environment reflects this.

Designed communities tend to be socioeconomically homogeneous with what are considered to be high-status social architectural and landscape symbols. Intentional communities, in contrast, tend to deviate from the norms of society in both their organizations and their symbols (Hayden 1976). Administered communities reflect the values of their administering organization. Thus Pullman, Illinois reflects the position taken by the directors of the Pullman company on what constitutes a good social organization, good behavior, and good taste. Anticommunities, where individuals have to rely totally on themselves, do not seem to exist anywhere in their pure form except in novels.

In considering the relationship between social organizations and physical form, it must be remembered that some communities are local and some are

A Classification of Community Types

Residential Community Type	Examples	Organizational Level		
		I	II	III
A. Communities				
Crescive	Folk Village	C	C	C
Intentional	Oneida, Shakers	C	F +	F
Designed	Levittown, Reston	F +	C	F
Administered	Company Towns	F +	F	C
B. Anticommunities				
Orwell's 1984		F	C	C
Solipsistic		C	C	F
Total	Brave New World	C	F	C
Totalitarian		F	F	F

C: Communal organization—low goal orientation
F: Formal organization—high goal orientation
+: Partnership between levels

not. Marcia Pelly Effrat (1974) identifies four types of communities: the *compleat* [sic] *territorial community*, the *community of limited liability* (see also Suttles 1972), *community as society*, and the *personal community*. In the "compleat" territorial community many, if not most, of the behavior settings that constitute the social organization occur within a territorial boundary. The folk village was close to being a "compleat" territorial community and the pol, mohalla, or parra of northern Indian cities still remains such an example (Doshi 1974). In Gottschalk's terms, the first of these is a crescive community and the second is a designed community—designed by its inhabitants and their leaders and not by outsiders. Most designed communities are communities of limited liability; obligations, institutions, and behavior settings occur at the local level but these are few in number in comparison to the total number of behavior settings occupied by the inhabitants. The personal community does not require local territorial grounding. It consists of the network of interpersonal relationships of an individual and is based on common needs and interests. Some components of this personal community may be formal organizations but others will be communal. Society as a whole consists of many behavior settings which require no local territorial grounding.

The concepts developed by Gottschalk and by Effrat put into perspective the efforts by social planners and environmental designers to create a sense of place and community in the world—to meet people's needs for affiliation and belonging. In the proposals of environmental designers, the concept of community as something close to the "compleat" territorial community has been the design goal. At Chandigarh, "the sector may roughly be described as the home of day to day life" (Drew 1961). There is much that can be done through the design of the physical environment to achieve these ends, but there are also major limitations to what can be achieved by planning and design in democratic societies. The issue is important because it addresses what many consider to be a major problem in present-day Western societies. Seymour Sarason (1972) of the Yale Psycho-Educational Clinic states his position on this very strongly: "My belief is that the dilution or absence of a psychological sense of community is the most destructive dynamic in the lives of people in our society." This does not mean, however, that "compleat" territorial communities are needed.

CONCEPTS OF COMMUNITY AND NEIGHBORHOOD IN URBAN DESIGN

The terms *neighborhood* and *community* often are used interchangeably. Here "community" has been used to refer to the web of interpersonal relationships of a person or a group, while "neighborhood" refers to a geographic area. The two sometimes coincide, as in the pol (Doshi 1974). The goal of many planners has been to strive for the two to be conterminous.

The prototypical concepts of neighborhood formulated by the architects of the Modern Movement, such as Henry Wright, Joseph Sert, and the M.A.R.S. group of London, were based on a perceived need to fulfill certain economic, social, and aesthetic goals. Localizing facilities, they believed, was one way to achieve efficient circulation in residential areas. Along with this was the social goal of developing a sense of community through the development of a network of friends and acquaintances on the local common territorial area level. Le Corbusier advocated this in the design of high-rise buildings and Clarence Perry and Frank Lloyd Wright in the configuration and facilities of areas of single-family homes. The idea in both cases was to reduce the functional distance between households through the central placement of facilities and increasing the number of intersections of corridors, paths and routes, and to increase safety for pedestrians in societies where the automobile is much in use (see fig. 16-2).

Le Corbusier's ideas are exemplified by the design of the *Unité d'habitation* in Marseilles, France (see fig. 16-2). It is a carefully worked-out schema with shopping facilities on a central floor of the building and areas for nursery schools and other communal facilities on the roof. It is a community of limited liability. The facilities are used, although the area provided for shops has proved to be too generous for economic viability. The inhabitants are happy to be living there, although there is only a partial sense of community—which apparently is the level that is desired (Avin 1973).

Radburn, New Jersey is an early prototypical neighborhood in which the goal was to create a community conterminous with its physical boundaries (see Stein 1951). Although never completed for financial reasons, enough was built to demonstrate both the potentials and limitations of efforts to achieve social ends through physical design; from Radburn, too, were derived clearer concepts about relationships between human behavior and the built environment, as described earlier (see fig. 16-2).

Radburn consists of a superblock with segregated vehicular and pedestrian traffic, a hierarchy of roads, houses with living rooms and bedrooms facing gardens and parks, service rooms facing access roads, and a park system—the backbone of the neighborhood—containing pedestrian routes to various destinations.

Radburn has attracted much study (for instance, Lansing, Marans, and Zehner 1970). It has been found to be, above all, a safe environment for children. The behavior settings of playgrounds, playing spaces in the central green areas, and the centrally located swimming pool are well used and well liked. The decline in the percentage of families with children may lead to a decline in support for these facilities but this has not happened yet. One unanticipated play setting has been the cul-de-sac. The reason is simple: the cul-de-sacs afford the use of wheeled toys and play with balls, and they are observable by parents from the kitchens of the houses. In addition, the segregation of automobile traffic from pedestrian traffic by means of underpasses affords safe crossing of streets and saves parents much worry. It also affords self-reliant and independent behavior by the children. It cannot and does not stop destructive behavior by them on occasion, however.

The layout of Radburn affords easy access to local shops. This affordance is well used: 47 percent of Radburn's population shops for groceries on foot, in comparison to 8 percent in a matched residential area. Similarly, easy access to local recreational facilities results in fewer weekend trips by residents than are usual in the matched area. The overall social goal of Radburn has been met only partially. It is, as noted above, a community of limited liability. Its residents identify with Radburn and have community pride. There is a formal residents' association, but beyond this life centers on the cul-de-sacs and on communal facilities, though there is little sense of an overall social organization. This is something Radburn's residents do not seek

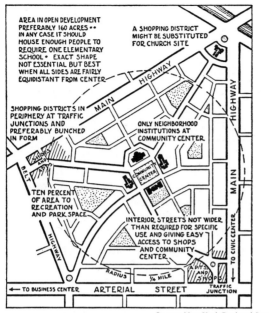

AREA IN OPEN DEVELOPMENT
PREFERABLY 160 ACRES **
IN ANY CASE IT SHOULD
HOUSE ENOUGH PEOPLE TO
REQUIRE ONE ELEMENTARY
SCHOOL • EXACT SHAPE
NOT ESSENTIAL BUT BEST
WHEN ALL SIDES ARE FAIRLY
EQUIDISTANT FROM CENTER

SHOPPING DISTRICTS IN
PERIPHERY AT TRAFFIC
JUNCTIONS AND
PREFERABLY BUNCHED
IN FORM

A SHOPPING DISTRICT
MIGHT BE SUBSTITUTED
FOR CHURCH SITE

ONLY NEIGHBORHOOD
INSTITUTIONS AT
COMMUNITY CENTER

TEN PERCENT
OF AREA TO
RECREATION
AND PARK SPACE

INTERIOR STREETS NOT WIDER
THAN REQUIRED FOR SPECIFIC
USE AND GIVING EASY
ACCESS TO SHOPS
AND COMMUNITY
CENTER

← TO BUSINESS CENTER   ARTERIAL   STREET   TRAFFIC JUNCTION

Source: New York Regional Survey

1

1. Internal Thoroughfare
2. Gymnasium
3. Cafe and Sun Terrace
4. Cafeteria
5. Children's Playground
6. Health center
7. Crèche
8. Nursery
9. Club
10. Youth Clubs and Workshops
11. Communal Laundry and Drying rooms
12. Entrance and Porter's Lodge
13. Garages
14. Standard Two-floor Flat

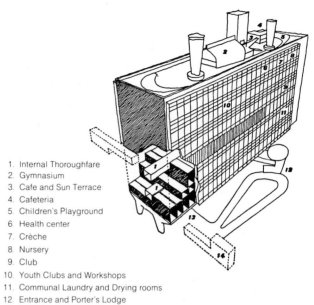

Source: Richards (1962)

2

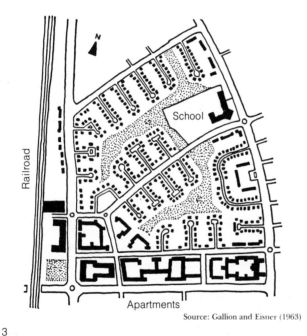

Source: Gallion and Eisner (1963)

3

16-2. Neighborhood Plans.

Two concepts of neighborhood that developed before World War II have had a profound effect on the thinking of architects and urban designers. The first is the "neighborhood unit" proposed by Clarence Perry as part of the New York Regional Plan of 1927 (1); the second is the vertical neighborhood proposed by Le Corbusier in his *Unité d'habitation* (2). The first is regressive in that it looked back to the past for a model, while the second is based on assumptions about human behavior in the future. The neighborhood unit, in particular, has been widely used across the world, often in cultures where it is inappropriate, but in Radburn (3)—although the town is not a complete social success in terms of the expectations of its proponents—it fulfills residents' perceptions of their needs extremely well (see Lansing, Marans, and Zehner 1970).

and the design cannot cause it. This is also borne out in a study of Columbia, Maryland (Brooks 1974).

The adoption of the neighborhood-unit principle by James Rouse, the developer of Columbia, was an act of faith, an intuitive belief in the inherent obviousness of an idea. He stated:

> Personally, I hold some very unscientific conclusions to the effect that people grow best in small communities. . . . I believe that a broader range of friendships and relationships occurs in a village or a small town than in a city; there is a greater sense of responsibility for one's neighbor and also a greater sense of support by one's fellow man in a small town rather than in a city; that self-reliance is promoted; that a relationship to nature—to the outdoors—to freer forms of recreation and human activity is encouraged in a smaller community.
>
> But am I right? (Brooks 1974)

Columbia is divided into villages separated by park-land; the villages are divided into neighborhoods, each with its center comprising meeting rooms and convenience stores. The meeting rooms do provide spaces for formal organizations to meet at the local level, and a by-product of using the convenience stores could be the development of primary-group relationships, but this has not occurred to any great extent.

People choose Columbia because it is a good place to live. It has what they perceive to be good homes and good recreational facilities. The convenience of the facilities is enjoyed by its residents. It is only for a few people and for certain facilities that propinquity makes much difference to useage.

In contrast to its neighborhoods, Columbia's village centers are organized around a supermarket to which people drive by car. They tend to bypass the neighborhood centers, so these are not as profitable as was predicted and hoped. Drug stores, butchers, cleaners, and banks do well at village centers but stores of the type that lend vitality to such centers have been difficult to attract. People use the facilities outside their own villages to a great extent. Some of this was planned, since some villages have a facility not common to all centers (such as an ice-skating rink), but much was unanticipated. People use the stores they prefer rather than the ones that are most convenient. Preference wins out over convenience. The teen centers, for instance, attract people across their expected service areas. At one stage they became racially segregated by choice.

Perry's concept of focusing the neighborhood on an elementary school works well in Columbia—most children do go to the local school, although fluctuating birth rates have caused some problems in maintaining desired school populations. The location of middle and high schools based on convenient distances and in conjunction with village centers so that facilities could be shared, while intuitively appealing, is less successful. One goal, that of having a library that is shared by school and village so that the liveliness of the centers might be enhanced, has not been met. The schools wanted their own libraries. Not everyone shares Rouse's zeal for communal values.

Based on all these observations, Brooks (1974) concludes that there is a variety of forces acting on the neighborhoods and villages:

> The plan to establish village centers, which was hoped would contribute to the "creation of community," appears to be yielding to a web of complicated institutional strains within the community.

The amount of cooperation between individuals and between institutions has been less than expected and the desire for an individual identity has been much higher. This reflects the broader values of American society (see also David Popenoe's description of Levittown, Pennsylvania in contrast to Valingby, Sweden, 1977). Formal organizations do exist to take care of common property, but an extended network of neighborhood friendships does not exist. The populations are heterogeneous on a local level. People do recognize the obligations they have to neighbors, but the villages and neighborhoods are not closed systems and there is little evidence that they have contributed much to the enhancement of communal values. This has also been the experience with the British new towns.

British new-town design in the post–World War II era has been based largely on the garden city principle, but the design policies regarding the overall subdivision of towns into units have been influenced by the findings of sociological research. The first generation of British new towns designed immediately after the war (such as Crawley, Stevenage) were based on the neighborhood-unit principle. It was found that people do identify with clear districts (in Lynch's terms) and with strongly promoted names. The residents know many of the people who live on their own streets, but the use of the area beyond this is less local than planners had expected—although neighborhood shops, schools, and facilities are used by local people, especially those of the traditional working class (Wilmott 1967).

In the second generation of British new towns (such as Cumbernauld), where the layout of the city is based on the concept of a strong core with little attention to concepts of neighborhood in the distribution of facilities, people describe themselves as coming from named subareas. The latest generation of British new towns (such as Milton Keynes) stresses the mobility of people in its design. This follows the writings of Melvin Webber (1963) who suggested that propinquity was not as important a factor in friendship-formation as it was once was. People belong to communities of interest—personal communities—and the members of these are likely to be located in different areas of the city. This observation, however, clearly does not take into account subsets of the population who have limited mobility.

All the studies on new towns and designed neighborhoods have led to greater clarity in discussing types of neighborhoods and their patterns. Terrence Lee (1970) differentiates between (1) the social-acquaintance neighborhood, (2) the homogeneous neighborhood, and (3) the unit neighborhood. The boundaries of the first type are set by

HARLOW

Commercial

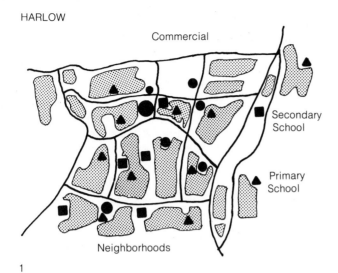

Secondary
School

Primary
School

Neighborhoods

1

CUMBERNAULD

Industry

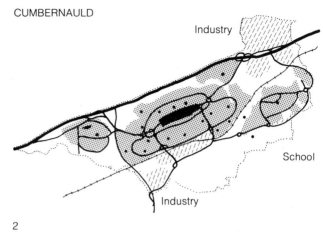

School

Industry

2

MILTON KEYNES

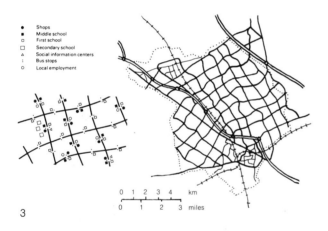

- Shops
- Middle school
- First school
- Secondary school
- Social information centers
- Bus stops
- Local employment

0 1 2 3 4   km
0 1 2 3   miles

3

16-3. Concepts of Neighborhood in the British New Towns.

The plan of Harlow (1) exemplifies the thinking behind the first generation of British new towns after World War II. It is based on the neighborhood unit concept. The plan of Cumbernauld in Scotland (2) represents a reaction to this thinking that took place when it was found that the neighborhood did not function as predicted in cities such as Harlow. In Milton Keynes (3), the latest new town, the emphasis in its design has been placed on mobility rather than local community.

human interaction patterns; their populations are probably homogeneous but this is not the defining factor as it is for the second type. The homogeneous neighborhood is characterized by a population "who live in houses like ours." The third type of neighborhood is that of a common service area for a number of residential units. Lee believes that the neighborhood is still an important factor in urban life. In existing cities there is some concordance in residents' perceptions of the boundaries of the neighborhoods in which they live. This would probably be higher if the boundaries were visually strong edges (Lynch 1960).

Suzanne Keller (1968) identifies four prevailing definitions of neighborhood: (1) the neighborhood as an area "having an ecological position in a larger area," (2) the neighborhood as a social symbol, (3) the neighborhood as an area having a special functional role, and (4) the neighborhood as an area with a "special atmosphere." All of these are sociospatial schemata. The physical components and the formal organizations of these can be designed from the outside but the communal organization has to come from within. The nature of the physical boundaries, the location and nature of streets, the way houses and other buildings enter onto them, the location of facilities and their types are all elements that can be designed to afford lively, well-liked areas that meet the needs of their populations in a multidimensional manner. Local communal organizations have to evolve, however.

A CONCEPT OF HUMAN SCALE IN DESIGNING THE BUILT ENVIRONMENT FOR SOCIAL ORGANIZATIONS

James Rouse's hypothesis about the size of an organization and participation in its life has received some empirical support. Roger Barker (1968) claimed:

> . . . there is an association between the number of people in a behavior setting and the frequency, intensity, origin and termination of forces that impinge upon these people.

Roger Bechtel (1977) outlines the development of Barker's *theory of undermanning,* which grew out of his observations in small towns in Kansas and England (see also Barker and Schoggen 1973). "He noticed profound differences in behavior that could be related to the size of behavior settings" (Bechtel 1977).

Bechtel suggests that a theory of *human scale* has been developed. This is a very different view of human scale from that characteristic of traditional architecture theory, in which it is considered to be either a purely visual phenomenon (Schubert 1965, Prak 1968) or a visual phenomenon based on the anthropometric characteristics of humans (Le Corbusier 1951). Barker's concept of human scale relates population numbers to the number of behavior settings that are available for that population's participation. This is an important concept because many expressed feelings of alienation are attributed to the built environment *per se* (it is said to be "inhumane," for instance) when they are more appropriately attributable to the overpopulation of the available and desired behavior settings. Bechtel (1977) comments:

> . . . human organizations need to be of a certain scale in order to derive positive benefits from the environment. Once the scale is exceeded not only do the benefits decrease but pressures begin to build from the environment that are detrimental to the function of any organization.

Environment in this context refers to the social situation. Bechtel believes that

> the design of a building that will enclose any organi-

zation needs to take advantage of these beneficial environmental forces and to attempt to control the detrimental effects.

This is a normative stance on his part based on his observation that social organizational policies and outcomes are related to the affordances of the physical configuration of the environment.

The basic premise of manning theory is that when there are fewer people in a behavior setting than are required optimally for its functioning they are coerced into greater participation in order to keep it going. When a church (Wicker 1969), school (Barker and Gump 1964), mental health organization (Srivastava 1975), or town (Bechtel 1970, Barker and Schoggen 1973) has relatively fewer people per behavior setting than are needed for maintaining the functioning of the unit, people participate more. Smaller schools, churches, and towns tend to have *proportionately* (to the total population) fewer people per behavior setting so those people participate more. This is not inevitable but it occurs because any institution requires a basic number of settings to survive. Large institutions, on the other hand, have specialized behavior settings, which smaller institutions cannot support. In decision-making one has to decide between participation and specialization if there are limited resources. It is possible to create large institutions with proportionately the same number of behavior settings per capita as in small institutions, but this takes considerable effort to initiate and maintain.

In an undermanned setting, the number of forces acting on an individual is greater than in a fully manned setting. In such circumstances the individual is likely to play a greater number of roles, to be challenged more, and to have more responsibility. The individual simply is more involved and less alienated (Bechtel 1977). Maybe this is why so many environmental design firms, including architectural offices, are small. It also follows that the quality of performance on specialized tasks may be low; relationships are established with outside organizations to compensate for this.

INDIVIDUAL DIFFERENCES, SOCIAL ORGANIZATIONS, AND DESIGN IMPLICATIONS

Social organizations differ in many ways. Even those with the same task orientations may differ in *personality*, and their own perceptions differ from others' of their *social status* and *culture*. Organizations differ in terms of the attitudes that members of higher and lower status roles within the organi-

PROPOSED LAW OFFICE BUILDING
Sixth-floor Plan

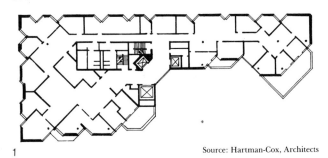

1   Source: Hartman-Cox, Architects

PROPOSED INTERIOR LAYOUT, OIL COMPANY
Typical Floor Plan

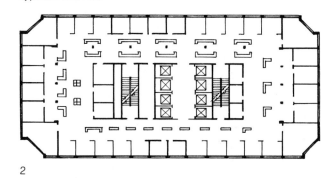

2

Scholars' Studies   Lounge

Conf.

Lounge

Dining

Conf.

Administration

Lobby

Kitchen

Services   Conf.

NATIONAL CENTER FOR THE HUMANITIES
Ground-Floor Plan

3   Source: Hartman-Cox Architects

16-4. Social Organization and Building Design.
The built environment reflects the nature of the social organizations that it houses. The floor plan for a major law firm (1) reflects the lack of emphasis on a hierarchical type of administration. This stands in strong contrast to the formality of the hierarchy and interaction patterns of a major oil company (2). The layout in (3) is that of a new building for a community of scholars. The plan reflects the simultaneous needs for opportunities for privacy and for gatherings.

zation hold toward each other. These often reflect differences in the broader society of which they are a part in terms of expectations about status roles, gender roles, and concepts of privacy accorded to different levels in the social hierarchy of the firm. In the United Kingdom, for instance, there is a much greater formality and social distance in relationships between levels in organizational hierarchy than in the United States. Even within the same broad cultural framework there are also considerable differences.

Each organization has its own personality. This will develop out of the personalities of its individual members, influenced especially by the attitudes of managers toward other staff (see Argyris 1954). Many problems arise when there is a conflict between workers who do not fit neatly into the corporate personality construct and those who do. This is resolved either by the departure of the workers whose personalities do not fit or by developing a procedure whereby the worker is permitted greater freedom of choice in meeting task goals.

The character of the organization depends on the status differences and relationships among individuals. Many organizations have a clear hierarchy of status and operate autocratically but others operate democratically (see fig. 16-4). In some societies communal values are stressed more than other values. This is reflected in the physical environment.

CONCLUSION

The built environment at every scale is a cultural cipher (A. Briggs 1966); it reflects the social organizations that created it and to which it caters. As perceptions of how society functions and should function change, so do the forms of the built world. At any given time, the built environment reflects past and present concepts of normative patterns of behavior. We thus have a circular relationship in which social organization patterns lead to patterns of built form and then social organizations, as they change, have to adapt to the affordances of the built environment and in their efforts to adapt they change the built world. They are often hampered in this process of self-conscious change by a lack of knowledge about themselves and the relationship between their behavior patterns and the built environment.

ADDITIONAL READINGS

Argyris, Chris. *Organization of a Bank.* New Haven: Labor and Management Center, Yale University, 1954.

Bennis, Warren G. *Organization Development: Its Nature, Origins and Prosepcts.* Reading, Mass.: Addison-Wesley, 1969.

Goffman, Erving. *Asylums.* Garden City, N.Y.: Anchor, 1961.

Gottschalk, Shimon S. *Communities and Alternatives: An Exploration into the Limits of Planning.* Cambridge, Mass.: Schenkman, 1975.

Hall, Richard H. *Organizations, Structure and Process.* Englewood Cliffs, N.J.: Prentice-Hall, 1972.

Moleski, Walter. "'Behavioral Analysis and Environmental Programming for Offices." In Jon Lang et al., eds., *Designing for Human Behavior: Architecture and the Behavioral Sciences.* Stroudsburg, Pa.: Dowden, Hutchinson and Ross, 1974, pp. 302–315.

——— and Jon Lang. "Organizational and Human Values in Office Planning." *Environment and Behavior* 14, no. 3 (May 1982): 319–332.

Popenoe, David. *The Suburban Environment: A Sociological Approach.* Reading, Mass.: Addison-Wesley 1976, (2nd edition).

Steele, Fred I. *Physical Settings and Organizational Development.* Reading, Mass.: Addison-Wesley, 1973.

AESTHETIC VALUES AND THE BUILT ENVIRONMENT

The term *aesthetics* was coined by Alexander Blaumgarten in 1750 to denote the study of taste in the fine arts. While, etymologically, the word means anything to do with perception, Blaumgarten was concerned principally with the perception of beauty in poetry, painting, and sculpture. Today the term is used very broadly in the discussion of both substantive and procedural matters—buildings and designing, furniture and housework, motorcycles and motorcycling.

The subject of aesthetics has been the center of much debate among speculative philosophers, artists, and architects for centuries. There has also been a search for a positive science of aesthetics (Pickford 1972). During the last hundred years the field of *empirical aesthetics* has grown substantially. Thus, one finds writings on aesthetics by philosophers, psychologists, and artists as well as by professionals associated with the environmental design professions. The goal of all these people has been to understand what gives people pleasure and why. The search for this understanding has followed different routes.

The goal of attaining a full understanding has been elusive, but we do have a basic understanding of some of the factors that contribute to the perception of environments as pleasing—beyond those factors that contribute to meeting "commodity," or "instrumental ends." The major contributions of speculative philosophers and empirical aestheticians are reviewed in chapter 17. It will be claimed that the distinction that George Santayana (1896) made among *sensory, formal,* and *symbolic* aesthetics is still a useful one.

We know very little about sensory aesthetics. What speculations there are on the topic (for instance, Rasmussen 1959, Heschong 1979) are based largely on highly subjective and fascinating introspective analyses. It remains for this field of research to attract the sustained attention of either environmental designers or behavioral scientists. For this reason, and because environmental design traditionally has been concerned with formal and symbolic issues, these issues are the chief concern of this book. This does not mean that sensory aesthetics is unimportant, only that very little is known about this field.

Chapter 18, "Formal Aesthetics," covers a topic that has long been of central concern to environmental designers and a central preoccupation at various times in the history of architecture, landscape architecture, and urban design. Formal aesthetics deals with the appreciation of shapes and structures of the environment for their own sake. This is a perceptual luxury. In discussions of formal aesthetics the question often arises as to whether or not the pleasure we feel in response to certain patterns—proportions and shapes—is biologically based. If it is not biologically based, but is based rather on a self-conscious intellectual reasoning in the examination of the patterns of the environment

per se, then Maslow is probably correct in placing aesthetic needs at the most advanced level of his hierarchical model.

Formal aesthetics has had a clear positive base during the course of this century, although this has not always been clearly articulated. It has been based on the Gestalt theory of perception. More recent theories of perception both challenge and enrich the Gestalt model.

Symbolic aesthetics is concerned with the associational meanings of the patterns of the environment that give people pleasure. It has become of research interest to behavioral scientists only recently. This research is marred by a confusion of theories of significance, meaning, and feeling. It is possible, nevertheless, to identify some major lines of investigation and their contributions to environmental design theory.

Several writers (such as Rapoport 1977, 1982) believe that, while design professionals place their emphasis on formal aesthetic issues, most people appreciate the environment mainly in terms of its symbols and its affordances for activities. Some aestheticians wonder if there even *is* such a thing as formal aesthetics. Maybe we designers simply have developed arbitrary languages which only other designers and select groups of individuals can understand. Be that as it may, symbolic aesthetics is concerned with the pleasure generated by the associations people have or make with specific configurations and characteristics of the built environment. The contribution of the behavioral sciences to our understanding of symbolic aesthetics is reviewed in chapter 19. This is an important contribution, since the symbolic aesthetics of the environment is important for the fulfillment of people's identity needs. ■

17

AESTHETIC THEORY

Interior designers, architects, landscape architects, and urban designers have long been concerned with creating aesthetic experiences for others. One of the normative issues in design today is concerned with the positions to be taken on who these "others" should be. One of the observations frequently made by both professionals (such as Montgomery 1966) and nonprofessionals (such as Wales 1984) is that we design in order to receive accolades from our peers. It suffices to say here that one of the concerns of design is with the creation of the beautiful or the delightful. The search for an understanding of what is beautiful in the built and natural environments has been an exasperating one but not one deserving of Ruskin's (1885) caricature of the endeavor:

> It is the province of aesthetics to tell you (if you did not know already) that the taste and colour of a peach are pleasant; and to ascertain (if it is ascertainable, and you have the curiosity to know) why they are so.

This does remain a good definition of the purpose of aesthetic theory, however. Aesthetics is worth pursuing because we know that taste preferences are not absolute. The taste and the color of peaches are not to everybody's liking. There are different tastes concerning peaches as well as buildings.

The science of aesthetics is concerned with (1) identifying and understanding the factors that con-

tribute to the perception of an object or a process as a beautiful or, at least, a pleasurable experience, and (2) understanding the nature of the human ability to create and to enjoy creating displays that are aesthetically pleasing. There are two broad approaches to the study of aesthetics. The first involves the study of the processes of perception, cognition, and attitude-formation, while the second involves the study of aesthetic philosophies and the creative processes. The first is psychological in character, and the second is largely metaphysical and psychoanalytical (see, for instance, Ehrenzweig 1967). The first is concerned with positive theory and the second with the normative theories of designers as artists. The concern here is with the former.

In studying aesthetics, many people, particularly in Western society since the Renaissance, differentiate between those elements in the environment that are considered works of art and those that are not—between architecture and buildings. This is an artificial distinction, and although it is not made here, it does have to be recognized. The study of aesthetic objects deals with the individual as an observer and contemplator, while the study of the experiencing of the environment as a whole considers the individual as a participant in life, of which the built environment is a part. People do indeed stand and stare and analyze the structure of buildings, landscapes, and paintings. This is not a characteristic behavior in all societies, nor was it in earlier times in Western civilization, nor is it characteristic of all people in Western cultures today. These other societies did produce what we call art but their attitudes seem to have been very different from ours today in that they did not consider such artifacts works of art (Berlyne 1974). The concern in this chapter is with the contribution of the behavioral sciences to the understanding of the aesthetic experiencing of the built world around us as part of our everyday lives.

While the psychological study of aesthetic experience can be said to have started with Gustav Fechner in 1876, there has been a prevailing feeling, as Ruskin suggested, that aesthetic values cannot be subjected to scientific study. This attitude may have been valid in the past because of the narrowness of many investigations of aesthetics. The richness of research during the past century, while by no means providing a complete understanding of the nature of environmental aesthetics, does provide a broad basis for the development of environmental design theory.

The goal of the psychological study of aesthetics has been to proceed from observation to generalization, instead of working downward from deductions. Nevertheless, the branch of philosophy and psychology known as speculative aesthetics is still very much alive for it provides a broad basis for asking what it is about the built environment that should be studied.

SPECULATIVE AESTHETICS

Speculative aesthetics, like early psychological research, relies heavily on introspective analysis by an individual of his or her own beliefs about what is beautiful and/or pleasurable. There have been several approaches to doing this (see Morawski 1977). The hermeneutic, phenomenological, existential, and political approaches are all philosophical. These can be contrasted to the scientific or quasi-scientific approaches—the psychoanalytical and the psychological. Hermeneutics relies on the interpretation of the environment as a text. While phenomenology can mean many things, in the study of aesthetics, it focuses on the gleaning of intuitive insights into the cognitive relationship between person and environment. The existential approach has focused primarily on the creative act and the created artifact. The political approach, mainly Marxist, considers art as a product and representation of the class struggle. The psychoanalytical approach has focused also on the artistic endeavor, explaining

it largely in terms of a cathartic act. All these approaches shed some light on art and the environment, but they do not tell us much about how people experience the environment. Of particular interest in creating environmental design theory is the work of a group of people who have drawn on psychological theories as well as introspective analysis in order to construct models of the nature of the aesthetic experience. These models not only provide a useful framework for architectural criticism, but they also are open to testing.

Stephen C. Pepper (1949) identified four schools of such endeavor: the *mechanistic*, the *contextualist*, the *organismicist* (also known as the school of "objective idealism"), and the *formist*. The work of George Santayana (1896), John Dewey (1934), Bernard Bosanquet (1931), and Rudolf Arnheim (1949, 1965, 1977) can be regarded as exemplars of each school, respectively (Cole 1960). The first three drew their ideas from empiricist schools of perception theory, while Arnheim is a Gestalt psychologist. More recent concepts of aesthetics draw heavily on the work of this group.

In the *mechanistic* approach to aesthetic theory, the artifact is considered to stimulate people with sensations or images coming from it or associated with it. Santayana, like many psychologists since his time, was concerned with the pleasurableness of some sensations. To Santayana, a beautiful environment is one that gives pleasure to its beholder. It is "value positive." This value is said to be intrinsic to the object or event—it is part of its structure. Many of Santayana's ideas reflect the state of psychological theory at the turn of the century. Of particular interest to us today, more than the details of Santayana's philosophy, is the overall distinction he made between sensory value, formal values, and expression or associative value (what will be called here "symbolic value"). This distinction is largely in accord with the ecological approach to perception (see Gibson 1979).

Sensory values are those generated by pleasurable sensations. They are obtained from the touches, smells, tastes, sounds, and sights of the world. Santayana stated that sensory pleasure may be an element of beauty at the same time as the ideas associated with it become elements of objects—an empiricist position. The sensory experience of the lower senses (touch, smell, and taste), however, does not serve the purpose of intelligence in human beings as well as the experience of the higher senses (sight and hearing), thus they are not as important in the aesthetic appreciation of the environment.

Formal values arise from the order of sensory material. This again is in accordance with the empiricist position on perception. Formal values deal with the pleasurableness of the structure, or patterns, of the artifact or process being considered (Santayana was also very interested in the experiencing of music). Of concern is the perception of the system of relationships that exist in the patterns. Some of these have to do with the patterns *per se*— their proportions and ordering principles. One has to do with what Santayana calls "determinate organization." In this case the form is based on its instrumental function. Santayana notes:

> The organization . . . is served by practical demands. Use requires buildings to assume certain forms, the mechanical perception of our materials; exigency of shelter, light accessibility, economy and convenience can dictate the arrangement of our buildings.

Determinate organization is the same concept as that embodied in the slogan "form follows function" of Santayana's contemporary, Louis Sullivan.

Expression or *associational values* are those that Santayana believed arose from the images evoked by sensory values. Santayana saw the associative process as an "immediate activity." This is something that both psychologists and design critics still have difficulty explaining. It is said that the association enters consciousness directly and "produces as simple a sensation as any process in any organ." He suggested that there are three types of expressive or associational value: *aesthetic, practical*, and *negative*. Aesthetic value is the perception that something is beautiful because of its associations for the observer. Practical values arise from the expression of utility of an object—not only does it have to work but it has to look as if it works. Negative values arise from the pleasure of being shocked, from the grotesque, from frightening or other supposedly unpleasant experiences.

Implicitly or explicitly, most speculations on the nature of the aesthetic experience suggest that it consists of sensory, formal, and associational values. Different writers stress different aspects. Some writers dealing with the aesthetics of the built environment (such as Prak 1968) focus on the formal and symbolic aspects of it. Some writers focus on works of art; others focus on the everyday world.

John Dewey (1934) objected to the consideration of the aesthetic experience as something apart from everyday life. The aesthetic experience, he suggested, arises from the everyday lives of people, although it may be related to specific things and activities. For Dewey, in contrast to Santayana, sensory value is not fundamental, but it provides the input for the appreciation of the forms of the environment. Unity, he believed, is the highest formal

value and can be obtained in many ways, for example, through rhythm—the ordered variation of change—or through symmetry. Dewey also stressed the intrinsic meaning of shapes and forms. In this his thinking paralleled that of the Gestalt psychologists (Köhler 1929, Koffka 1935, Wertheimer 1938) who were his contemporaries. Dewey was particularly concerned with the space-time relationship of the environment so he paid special attention to the sequential character of perception. In this way he anticipated the psychological research of James J. Gibson (1950) and the writings on environmental aesthetics by Martienssen (1956), Thiel (1961), Cullen (1962), and Halprin (1965), all of whom stress the role of *movement* in environmental perception and appreciation. Dewey introduced ideas such as the culmination, anticipation, and fulfillment of expectations in explaining what it is about sequential experiences that gives pleasure.

The organismicist philosophers offer less in the way of a structured approach to environmental analysis. Bosanquet (1931) notes that "the point of aesthetic attitude lies in the fusion of a body and soul, where the soul is a feeling and the body its expression without residue on either side." His is a poetic rather than a behavioral science approach to the study of aesthetics. Yet his philosophy echoes Dewey's.

The formist approach to aesthetics, as exemplified by Arnheim (1949, 1965, 1966, 1977) but historically associated with Albers (1963), Kandinsky (1926), and Klee (1925), stresses the role of the expressive value of patterns of form in aesthetic experience. The linkage between Gestalt theory and aesthetic philosophy is clear and often explicit (for instance, Kepes 1944, Arnheim 1977). The perception of form is explained in terms of the Gestalt principles of field forces and the process of isomorphism. Expression is a function of line and plane and form. The sensory object and the form in which it is presented are said to have direct physiognomic properties which stimulate the brain center of vision, setting up corresponding forces that form the basis of expression. In the Modern Movement in architecture, expression was regarded as the *raison d'être* of art.

All these views of aesthetics have been shaped by contemporary understandings of the perceptual processes and attitude-formation. All are weak in explaining individual differences in attitudes toward the environment. The historical development of empirical aesthetics has consisted of a more serious attempt to deal with these. It has focused more on individual experiences in order to establish what might be universal.

EMPIRICAL AESTHETICS

The behavioral sciences have relied on scientific or quasi-scientific techniques in the analysis of the aesthetic experience. Most studies have relied on correlational analysis, in which the relationship between two or more factors that vary, either naturally or because one is deliberately manipulated, is measured. Most of the current psychological research has focused on the formal, or structural, aspects of objects as the independent variable and people's subjective feelings about them as the dependent variable. Characteristics of the object are correlated with characteristics of the response which are correlated with characteristics (personality, socioeconomic status, cultural background) of the people concerned.

There have been four important theoretical orientations to these studies: *information-theory* approaches (not to be confused with the Gibson's information-based theory of perception), *semantic* approaches, *semiotic* approaches, and *psychobiological approaches* (Berlyne 1974). Research within each of these orientations is being conducted at present.

The Information-Theory Approach

Information theory deals with the environment as a set of messages that act as stimuli. There are two approaches to the use of information theory in developing aesthetic theory. The first bases its approach on empiricist theories of form, while the second uses information theory as a framework of analysis. Abraham Moles (1966) works within the first approach, while Rudolf Arnheim's work *Entropy and Art* (1971) is representative of the second.

Moles (and others such as Frank 1959 and Bense 1969) considers a building or a landscape to be a composition of elements each of which transmits messages. The pleasurableness of the message is related to its degree of structure. The greater the orderliness of the message, Moles believes, the more intelligible and pleasant it is.

The basic propositions of information-based models of aesthetics can be mapped onto Santayana's framework of *sensory value, formal value,* and *associational value.* Sensory values constitute one of the components of the aesthetic experience. The individual receives messages from the environment through the visual, oral and other sensory systems. The research has focused mainly on vision and hearing because they provide most individuals with most information. It has attempted to identify the amounts of information that a person can process optimally. Formal values arise from the structuring of the message. The structure of the built environ-

ment is said to vary principally in complexity. Moles differentiates between two types of complexity: structural and formal. The first deals with a status description ("the built environment is composed of . . .") and the second with a process description ("the built environment is made to . . ."). The degree of structure in both is the major indicator of aesthetic preferences. Structure *per se* is not, however, the only contributor to the pleasurableness of messages; the content is important, too. Messages are said to have semantic, cultural, expressive, and syntactic information, but the analyses of these has not formed a major part of the research agenda of Moles and others working within the framework of information theory.

Arnheim (1971) also deals with formal values. He does not take issue with Moles's observations on the orderliness of messages. He notes:

> The information given literally means to give form and form means structure. The rehabilitation of order as a universal principle, however, suggested at the same time that orderliness by itself is not sufficient to account for the nature of organized systems in general and for those created by man in particular. Mere orderliness leads to increased impoverishment and finally to the lowest level of structure no longer clearly distinguishable from chaos which is the absence of order.

The simplest level of order, according to Arnheim, results from the homogeneity of elements. He believes that more complex orders afford greater pleasure. Thus he concludes:

> A structure can be more or less orderly at any level of complexity. The level of ordered complexity is the level of order. The aesthetic is derived from the relation between order and complexity.

Thus, in this view of aesthetics, the perception of environmental quality is associated closely with well-ordered, complex messages. It is also associated with ambiguity in the sense that the structure of the environment contains different ordering principles perceivable by the same person or by different people (see also Rapoport and Kantor 1967). The observation is that the greater the multiplicity of meaning the greater the pleasurableness of the environment, provided a sense of order is maintained.

The Semantic Approach

The semantic approach focuses on the meaning of elements of the environment and not on the patterns of the structure *per se.* The meaning is a learned association between the object and an idea.

The approach draws heavily on some basic ideas from linguistics.

> [In a written language] the word results from the combination of a particular form with a particular meaning . . . the form of the word signifies "things" by virtue of the "concept" associated with the form . . . in the minds of the speakers of the language. (Lyons 1968)

Meanings of the built environment are considered in a similar fashion in many interpretive studies of buildings. This line of thinking is characteristic of many of the recent writings on the subject (such as Norberg-Schulz 1965).

The Semiotic Approach

Like the semantic approach, the semiotic approach to environmental aesthetics is derived from linguistics and can be seen as either an extension of the semantic approach or as a contradiction to it (Gandelsonas 1974). If one believes it to be concerned with both learning and the transfer of meaning, then it is an extension of the semantic approach. If one asserts that learning is different from the formation of associations in context, then it is a contradiction (Berlyne 1974). The approach is based on the writings of the philosopher Ferdinand de Saussure (1915). De Saussure considered the associational relationship between pattern and meaning to be internal to the sign, but he stressed that the context is important because the same element may mean different things in different places (see also Morris 1935). Thus, the semiotic approach to environmental aesthetics is concerned with the cultural system of meanings of the natural and built environments. The semantic and semiotic approaches to environmental aesthetics have had a profound influence on recent thinking about architecture (see Broadbent et al. 1980) and provide the theoretical basis for much of the ideology of Post-Modernism in architecture (Jencks 1969, 1977).

The Psychobiological Approach

The psychobiological approach has antecedents in Gestalt psychology. It explains aesthetic responses to patterns of the built environment in terms of the neurophysiological processes of the brain. Recent research within this approach is characterized by the work of D. E. Berlyne (1974). Berlyne suggests that the arousal level of an individual is correlated with his or her perception of the interestingness of the environment. The arousal level is dependent on the structure of the environment and on the personality and motivational or needs level of the individual. The environmental characteristics may be: (1) of a psychophysical nature (such as color, intensity); (2) of an ecological nature "involving a correlation with events that promote or threaten biological adaptation"; or (3) of a structural or a collative nature (variables such as simplicity or complexity, expectedness or surprisingness, clarity or ambiguity). The basic conclusion is that pleasure arises when adverse conditions are removed or moderate levels of arousal are achieved. Moderate levels of arousal occur when there are moderate levels of deviation from the norm, or the adaptation level (Helson 1948, 1964).

Empirical Aesthetics and Environmental Design Theory

The research agenda of empirical aesthetics has been concerned primarily with "the experimental investigation of judgments of preference for simple stimuli." The goal has been " to build up from below those stimuli and combinations which would be used in complete works of art" (Pickford 1972). This is the goal that Fechner set himself. The assumption is that as stimulation varies so does the perception of the aesthetic quality of the source, be it a painting, a building, or a landscape. Thus, if one could measure the stimulation afforded by different patterns of the physical environment, say, and understand the hedonic responses of different people to these, then one would have an empirical theory of environmental aesthetics. This is not possible, however. At least, it is not yet possible!

There has been much experimental research. There have been many studies of the expressiveness of lines, masses, and volumes, of what makes a form simple or complex, of perceptions of order, of color preferences, and so on. Subjects have included adults, children, and people of different socioeconomic groups and cultural backgrounds. These studies show that there are some agreements and some disagreements. Several correlations have been established and these show that "beauty is largely in the eye of the beholder." Certainly the early goal of showing that some patterns and symbols are perceived universally as beautiful has not been achieved.

No unified theory or generally accepted model of environmental aesthetics has emerged from all this research. The problem simply may be that the theories of perception implicit and explicit in the questions posed by psychologists in the course of empirical research on aesthetics are ill-founded. They are all sensation-based theories. Many are highly empiricist in nature. Yet the correlations between environmental characteristics and subjective feelings about them do exist and cannot simply be dismissed. A reinterpretation of the approaches of speculative aesthetics and empirical aesthetics allows a synthetic model to be offered. This model seems to promise much in understanding environmental aesthetics.

A TENTATIVE APPROACH TO ENVIRONMENTAL AESTHETICS

The environment, is has been argued earlier, can be considered to consist of a nested set of behavior settings. The basic hypothesis here is that people's responses to a place are to its structure as a behavior setting. Their attitude toward the behavior setting can be explained in terms of their attitudes toward the standing pattern of behavior occurring there and the people involved as well as the milieu. In terms of environmental design theory, however, the concern is largely with the milieu. This narrower concern does introduce a distorting factor in analyzing people's everyday experience.

A broad definition of aesthetic experience would encompass all the goals of design because "pleasure" is derived from the fulfillment of each of them. Thus, people get pleasure from an environment whose structure well affords standing patterns of behavior in a physiologically comfortable way. To achieve this, the structure of the environment has to be related uniquely to the needs and purposes of the people involved in terms of their organismic, personality, social group, and cultural characteristics within a specific geographic context.

Given an environment that well affords a standing pattern of behavior, it is aesthetically pleasing if it provides pleasurable sensory experiences, if it has a pleasing perceptual structure, and if it has pleasurable symbolic associations. This means that the variables of stimulus energy—the intensity of light, color, sound, odor, and touch attended to by a user or observer—are pleasurable. It means that the formal attributes—the patterning of the environment through the structuring of surfaces, textures, illumination, and colors—are pleasurable. It means that the associations evoked by the patterns are pleasurable. As Santayana suggested, these seem to be the three major dimensions of the aesthetic experiencing of the environment.

There are some major assumptions about the nature of the perceptual processes behind this statement. It assumes that aesthetics is concerned with the experiencing of beauty or pleasurableness. It assumes that inputs to the nervous system can be differentiated from perceptions of the world. There is much evidence that people do seek certain types of sensations (Gibson 1966) and that we do seek to enjoy the patterns of the environment for their own sake. It assumes that certain patterns of the environment may resonate more pleasantly than others because of the neural structure of the human perceptual system. It assumes that the associational meanings—the symbolism—of the environment is important, consciously or subconsciously, to people.

Little has been said about *sensory aesthetics* in recent years. What has been written is based largely on introspection (such as Rasmussen 1959, Heschong 1979) rather than on experimentation, although historically this was the major subject of experimental concern (see Boring 1942). The reason is that people do not pay much attention to sensations—the self-awareness of the arousal of the sensory systems—that we obtain from the environment. We can do so. We can pay attention to the environment as patches of color, or to the sensation of the wind deforming our skin, or to the tensions in our muscles as we walks across a floor, but we seldom do. We become aware of sensations when they deviate from the norm, when they become pleasant or unpleasant. There are situations when the sensations one receives are very pleasantly arousing. Walking through patches of light and shade, standing on a beach when the wind is blowing in one's face and the air one breathes is rich in ozone, being hot and feeling a cooling breeze that has blown across water—these are all situations in which one becomes aware of the sensory aspect of perception. Sensory aesthetics is an important component of a person's response to the environment. The paucity of research on the subject at a level of concern to environmental designers makes it a topic that is impossible to pursue in this book. It remains an area of potential contribution by the behavioral sciences to environmental design theory.

Formal aesthetics has been of central concern to designers since the inception of a self-conscious concern about design. The focus of this concern has been on the visual structure of the environment. It is so also in this book. This does not deny the role of sonic, tactile, and olfactory experience in a person's appreciation of the environment. The focus of research has been on the visual, except for the study of the acoustic qualities of different patterns of buildings and rooms. This research has been more the subject of physical science research rather than of behavioral science. Thus, the contribution of the behavioral sciences to environmental design theory is largely in the area of visual qualities of the environment. The concern is with its syntactic or geometric qualities. There is some concern as to whether formal aesthetics is something separate from symbolic aesthetics. Perhaps it is just another symbol system that designers have created to communicate with themselves and a few other of the cognoscenti. The concept of expression, in particular, has been the subject of much controversy. It depends on whether one accepts the Gestalt theory of perception as to whether one considers expression to be a topic of formal or symbolic aesthetics. It will be considered in both places here to illustrate the basic issue.

Symbolic aesthetics is concerned with the associational meanings of the environment that give people pleasure. The environment is inevitably a symbol system giving "concrete expression to concepts of values, meanings and the like" (Rapoport 1977). The symbolism of the environment is thus central to one's liking or disliking of it.

CONCLUSION—WORKS OF ART

An object or environment can be regarded as a work of art if it communicates a message from one person or group to another. Some objects are purposefully designed to serve this purpose; others acquire this role over time. In the latter case the work may not have been perceived originally as a work of art but it acquires this meaning. Works of art are thus artificial displays. The display may be a formal one—of patterns *per se*—or a symbolic one dealing with associational values. This definition covers works such as paintings, musical compositions, buildings, and landscapes that were created purposefully as works of art as well as objects that were perceived as serving purely utilitarian purposes but came to be regarded as works of art. Thus, a West African sculpture which was perceived to be simply a means to ward off evil spirits may come to be regarded as a work of art even though its creator never thought of it as such.

If one accepts this definition, then a number of observations can be made about buildings, landscapes, and urban designs:

1. Not all their message are regarded as those that can qualify them as works of art. Artificial criteria (norms) have been established to define what is and what is not a work of art. These norms differ for different populations and vary over time. They are established by "tastemakers" (Lynes 1954). Thus, a mill on the fall line of New England may not have been regarded as a work of art at the time of its construction but it may be now because (a) perceptions of the messages the building communicates have changed, and/or (b) the values regarding its formal patterns or its associated meanings have changed.

2. It is open to debate as to whether:

a) any of the criteria is biologically based or whether they are all culturally determined;

b) the distinction between formal and symbolic aesthetics has a basis in human psychology; it is possible that formal displays are simply a subcategory of symbolic ones;

c) there is a difference between expressive and symbolic messages communicated through built form.

The answers to the second and third of these depends on the answer to the first. There are competing theories of perception, and accepting one over another leads to different answers to the above questions.

3. The built environment can be configured to be a work of art on any dimension of human experience.

ADDITIONAL READINGS

Dewey, John. *Art as Experience.* New York: Putnam, 1958 (original edition, 1934).

Gandelsonas, Mario. "Linguistic and Semiotic Models in Architecture." In William R. Spillers, ed., *Basic Questions of Design Theory.* New York: American Elsevier, 1974, pp. 39–54.

Heschong, Lisa. *Thermal Delight in Architecture.* Cambridge, Mass.: MIT Press, 1979.

Morawski, Stefan. "Contemporary Approaches to Aesthetic Inquiry: Absolute Demands and Limited Possibilities." *Critical Inquiry* 4 (Autumn 1977): 55–83.

Mukarovsky, Jean. *Structure, Sign and Function.* New Haven: Yale University Press, 1981.

Rasmussen, Steen Eiler. *Experiencing Architecture.* Cambridge, Mass: MIT Press, 1950.

Pepper, Stephen C. *The Basis for Criticism in the Arts.* Cambridge, Mass.: Harvard University Press, 1949.

Santayana, George. *The Sense of Beauty.* New York: Dover, 1955 (original edition 1896).

18

FORMAL AESTHETICS

Sooner or later a designer has to make decisions regarding the geometrical structure of the environment. Sometimes the geometric quality of the environment is the sole issue of concern. The shapes, proportions, rhythms, scale, degree of complexity, color, illumination, and shadowing effects of the built and natural worlds are the subject matter of formal aesthetics. The concern is with the pleasure afforded people by different patterns of the world for their own sake rather than for any instrumental purpose they serve or associational meaning they provide.

The objective of this chapter is to describe different approaches to the topic: the Gestaltist approach and its limitations, and the recent theoretical and empirical research that promises much in enhancing environmental design theory.

FORMAL AESTHETICS: THE GESTALTIST APPROACH

With the rise of Post-Modern architecture there has been a major concern with environmental symbolism among design theorists. This has deempha-

sized a concern with issues of formal aesthetics. The way formal aesthetics is considered in design education is still essentially that of the Bauhaus masters of the 1930s and is thus heavily dependent on the Gestalt theory of perception for its theoretical justification. While current statements on the formal aesthetics of the built environment vary in content and scope, it is possible to represent them with a generalized model. It starts by considering the basic elements of the geometry of the environment and then considers the organization of these into compositions.

The Elements of Design

In most formulations of the Basic Design course—the central introductory course dealing with formal aesthetic issues in schools of environmental design—the basic element of design is said to be a *dot*. Dots can be accumulated together to form textures or *lines*. Lines can be grouped together to form *planes*, and planes can be structured into *volumes* (see, for example, de Sausmarez 1964, Itten 1965). The environment can be decomposed into these elements and when a designer represents the visual appearance of a building on the drawing board, these are indeed the elements that are used. The external validity of thinking about the three-dimensional world in this way is low, however.

A number of the concepts included here were presented first in Lang (1977) and published in Lang (1983). Others were presented in Lang (1984). This material is reprinted here by permission of the Environmental Design Research Association and *Visual Arts Research.*

The Principles of Composition

The Gestalt laws of visual organization form the basis for the analysis of combinations of elements into units that are perceived as either simple or complex. Governing all these laws of organization is the *law of pragnanz*, which states that the "psychological organization" of a visual composition is as "good" as the prevailing conditions allow. "Good" in this sense is not an evaluative statement. "Good figures" have the following characteristics: symmetry, inclusiveness, unity, harmony, regularity, conciseness, and "maximal simplicity." Maximal simplicity occurs when a form possesses the fewest articulated parts required to maintain its structure. Thus, parts have a degree of essentialness to the whole composition. Some are necessary to maintain the form while others may simply enhance it.

There is considerable experimental evidence to support the hypothesis that simple regular forms with repetitious elements are the easiest to see. It is easy to create simple architectural forms using the Gestalt laws of visual organization. There is nothing in Gestalt theory, however, that equates "good" form with good environments. This has been, and often is, however, the normative stance of many designers.

Many compositional principles that designers use are not directly related to Gestalt theory but have developed independently over a long period of time. The study of proportion as a means to relate larger and smaller units of a composition (particularly two-dimensional or façadal ones) has been a subject of considerable interest to designers (Banham 1960) and to many psychologists from Fechner (1876) onward. There are many ways in which façades of buildings have been subdivided into smaller units in an ordered manner. Most of these are based on some mathematical series, but some are based on musical analogies.

Order and Disorder

Questions of order and disorder, simplicity and complexity have attracted architectural theorists (such as Venturi 1966) and behavioral scientists (such as Arnheim 1966, 1977) alike for a long time. Order often is taken to be a synonym for simplicity, but it can occur at any level of visual complexity. Based on Gestalt thought, an ordered environment is one in which the parts form the whole in such a way that redundancy, self-contradiction, and conflict are avoided. The difficulty in creating design theory is that these terms have poorly articulated operational definitions.

According to Arnheim (1977), order occurs when some fundamental principle dictates the arrangement of the components of a composition. The ordering principle may not be obvious to all. A disordered environment is one where the relationship of components to each other is purely haphazard and not governed by some overall principle.

A complex structure is one that has a large number of structural components and/or a large number of ordering principles involved. The composition is ordered (if one accepts these definitions) when the priniciples of composition support each other, and it is disordered when they do not. "Disordered" is not always defined in this way. Robert Venturi (1966), for instance, takes the position that contradiction and disorder are synonyms and that they are valid goals of design in order to get visually richer environments than those achieved by following the maxims of the Modern Movement.

Perceptual Order and Proportional Schemata

The concept of proportion is related to the concept of order through the concept of rhythm in architecture. A proportional rhythm may be a simple a.b.a.b.a. relationship of adjacencies or it may be more complex. The nature of human responses to patterns of the environment, their sizes, proportions, and rhythms has long been of concern to designers. The use of "simple ratios" such as 3:2, 4:5, or 5:8 is said to produce "static" compositions, whereas ratios such as 2:3:5:8:13 are said to be "dynamic" and more interesting (de Sausmarez 1964, Isaac 1971). Interestingness is correlated with pleasingness (Berlyne 1974).

A ratio known as the "Golden Section" was an established canon of nineteenth-century academics. It is still regarded as pleasing, a conclusion that has long had some empirical support in Western societies, at least from Gustav Fechner (1876) on. Its character is such that the "ratio between bigger and smaller measurable quantities is equal to the ratio between the sum of the two and the bigger one" (de Sausmarez 1964). Several theoretical statements on why this should be so have been developed.

Anne Tyng (1975) hypothesizes, as would Gestalt theorists, that there are synchronistic processes in the brain which lead to the captivation of people by the Golden Section. Her observation is that the ratio is a recurrent one in nature, whether one is looking at a DNA molecule or at a galaxy, and thus there is a high probability that the human brain resonates in a particular way when such proportions are perceived. There are other proportional schemata, some based on mathematics and others, such as Le Corbusier's modulor schema (1951), on the human body. The goal of research is to understand

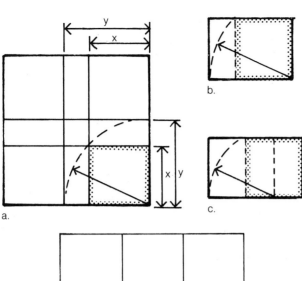

a.

b.

c.

Proportional systems are usually based on the division of an overall unit into fractions. (a), (b), and (c) illustrate how a number of shapes are derived from a few basic dimensions. In (a), for example, nine dimensions are obtained from a square and two dimensions, x and y.

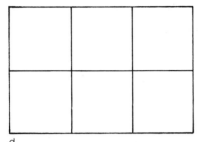

d.

Proportions that use simple numbers, such as 3:2 in (d), are said to produce static rectangles. Irrational numbers are said to produce more dynamic rectangles (e).

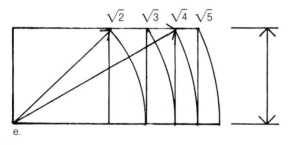

$\sqrt{2}$ $\sqrt{3}$ $\sqrt{4}$ $\sqrt{5}$

e.

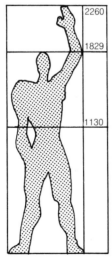

2260

1829

1130

f.

Diagram (f) illustrates Le Corbusier's use of the human body as the basis for a proportional system. This is related to the division of a 1.829-m man into key dimensions based on the Golden Section ratio.

1	2	4	8
3	6	12	24
9	18	36	72
27	54	etc	

g.

The harmonic scale in diagram (g) provides the designer with a method of relating large and small dimensions to each other in a systematic yet arbitrary way.

18-1. Proportional Scales.

Source: Adapted from de Suasmarez (1964) and Isaac (1971)

what constitutes a well-ordered environment in "human scale."

There are many positive and normative statements in the environmental design literature, particularly writings on architecture, on what human scale is, and on what should be done to achieve human scale in the built environment. For example:

> A vaulted structure over a relatively small bay will probably appear unsatisfactory because the spectator from his vast knowledge . . . will expect a certain vastness and large scale. On the other hand, a spectator without this knowledge may not experience this lack of satisfaction. (Isaac 1971)

Such statements are based on personal observation rather than on empirical research. They also suggest (1) that some mediating intellectual process, conscious or unconscious, is involved in the process, and (2) that habituation levels and familiarity are important factors in understanding an individual's or a group's attitudes toward the formal properties of the built environment. In this case we are dealing with issues of symbolic rather than formal aesthetics.

The Gestalt Theory of Expression

Gestalt psychologists, it was noted earlier in this book, hypothesized that there is a direct and immediate experience of expressive qualities in the perception of lines, planes, and volumes or masses. They postulated that these experiences were a product not of an intellectual association but of a resonance between neurological processes and environmental patterns. Thus buildings are said to appear to be lively, serene, or heavy not because of some association between the present pattern and some referent but because of a biologically based process—the Gestalt concept of isomorphism. There is considerable intuitive appeal to this assertion and some corroborative experimental support (such as Heider and Simmel 1944, Michotte 1968). David Levi (1974) summarizes this work as follows:

> In both these experiments, subjects report their experience of simple geometric shapes which have been animated. Shapes having particular movements were consistently described in terms indicative of expressive qualities. Little triangles can be perceived to be angry or afraid, depending on the form of the perceived movement.

A number of people have attempted to describe the emotional qualities that are communicated by specific patterns of the environment. One such list has been compiled by Alan Isaac (1971):

Tension:
Tension may be created by: a lack of stability; unbalanced composition; the use of large scale and extreme contrasts; unfamiliar elements in unfamiliar surroundings, intense discordant colour without relief; hard angular forms and lines; intense uneven light; discordant deafening noise; unsuitable temperatures; lack of, or limited, movement; peculiar smells.

Relaxation:
A feeling of relaxation can be achieved by placing familiar and likable elements in familiar surroundings; expected order; simplicity; the use of small scale; pleasing and soft sounds; acceptable temperatures; soft flowing forms, lines and spaces; little contrast; soft (indirect) light; analogous colour (white-blue-green); easy movement and pleasant smells.

The list recognizes (1) the multimodality of perception, (2) the symbolic quality of the environment as a major factor in its appreciation, and (3) the interrelationship between formal and symbolic aesthetics. The list assumes that empiricist and Gestalt models of perception can coexist, and it also assumes a stimulus-response model of the environment-emotional response relationship that is close to the behaviorist model of human behavior.

The most sustained analysis of the expressive content of architecture based on the Gestalt theory of perception is that conducted by Rudolf Arnheim (1949, 1965, 1977) of the formist school of aesthetics. Arnheim uses both empirical research and interpretive analysis as well as considerable deductive logic to draw conclusions about the aesthetic experience. Most of Arnheim's work has been concerned with the perception and appreciation of two-dimensional patterns. It is only with the publication of *The Dynamics of Architectural Form* in 1977 that he turned his full attention to the built environment.

Arnheim's position is clear:

> Shapes can be analyzed in detail by describing their forms in terms of geometry, size, quantity and location, also there are visual forces which expand and contract, push and pull, rise and fall, advance and recede—which determine meaning and expression in art.

The theoretical question that still remains to be resolved is whether these associations are an innate property of human thinking or are learned. Whatever theoretical explanation is provided, the basic assumption is that if one understands the expressiveness and/or associational values of lines and shapes then one can use these qualities in communicating messages through architectural design (Levi 1974). Gyorgy Kepes (1944) asserts:

1

2

3

18-2. The Gestalt Theory of Expression in Architecture.
The Gestalt psychology interpretation of the processes of visual perception suggests that the line and form of buildings communicate meanings directly through line and plane. The "soaring" quality of the Chrysler Building (1), the static quality of the building shown in (2), and the "billowing" quality of the roofs of the Sydney Opera House (3) are expressive qualities of specific configurations. An alternative interpretation to Gestalt theory is that these expressions result from learned associations.

Just as letters of an alphabet can be put together in innumerable ways to form words which can convey meaning so the optical measures and qualities can be brought together in innumerable ways.

This type of reading is exemplified by Arnheim's description of the chapel of Notre-Dame-du-Haut at Ronchamp by Le Corbusier (see fig. 18-3).

The basic theme of the design plays on the structural ambiguity of a rectangle that acquires a kind of additional symmetry around one of its diagonals. . . .

The interior . . . is more nearly rectangular, for although the room expands towards the altar wall at the east, this divergence is counteracted by perspective convergence when one views the interior from the west wall. . . . It seems to me that the teasing ambiguity between the relatively stable rectangularity of the interior and the bold dynamics of the external wedge creates a perfectly integrated, though not easily perceived unity of inside and outside. (Arnheim 1977)

Interesting and thought-provoking though this analysis may be, there are a number of questions

1

2

3

18-3. The Chapel of Notre Dame-du-Haut, Ronchamp, France.
According to the Gestalt theory of perception, the expressive meanings of this building would be biologically based and universally perceived. According to the ecological theory of perception, the meanings themselves would depend on the associations learned by the individual. Attitudes toward these meanings also are learned.

that one can raise. How generalizable to other people is Arnheim's experience? Is this how other people would automatically respond unconsciously to the building? What is the basis for such interpretations?

The influence of the force and line of gravity within the Gestaltist view of expression is a major one. While the three directions of geometric space are equally important, the pull of gravity "distinguishes the vertical as the standard direction psychologically." The horizontal plane acts as the basis for the vertical axis about which a symmetrical composition can be organized. Any other composition is seen as balanced, unbalanced, or in apparent motion around some vertical axis. This thought is a recurrent one in aesthetic philosophy (see, for example, Bachelard 1969).

Horizontal and vertical lines, when used together, are said to express a supporting surface and gravitational force, respectively (Kepes 1944). De Sausmarez (1964) believes that a balanced opposite of tensions—when a vertical line meets a horizontal —provides a deeply satisfying experience because it symbolizes "the human experience of the absolute

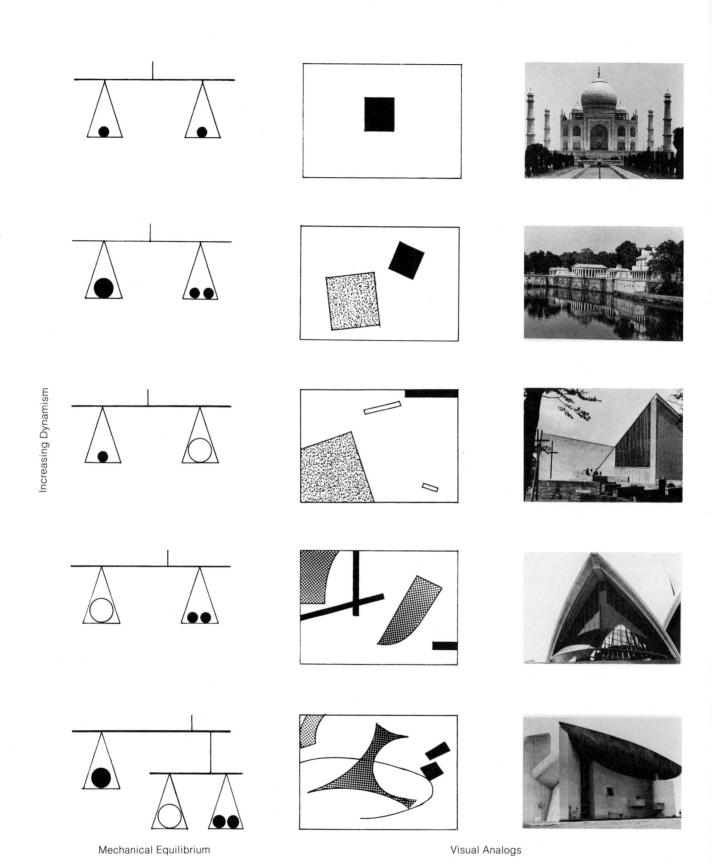

Increasing Dynamism

Mechanical Equilibrium

Visual Analogs

Two-dimensional Field

Three-dimensional Field

18-4. Concepts of Static and Dynamic Equilibrium.

balance of standing on the ground." Once diagonals are introduced, a "dynamism which is the outcome of unresolved tendencies toward the vertical and horizontal which are held in balanced suspension" is noted. The analogy with Newtonian physics is clear (see Koffka 1935).

Kepes (1944) and Arnheim (1949, 1977), among others, pay particular attention to the Gestalt concept of field forces in the hope of deducing a theory of liveliness and expressiveness of form from it. Kepes observed:

If the forces and their induced field are of equal quality and spatial strength, a balance will be reached but it will be without tension, static and lifeless.

In contrast, a lively organization is one in which

. . . movements are different in terms of their optical measures and qualities—that is, opposite in direction, weight and intensity—but if they are equal in strength in terms of their spatial fields a dynamic equilibrium is reached.

Gravitational forces are said to affect also the perceived weight of a building. Kepes (1944), like Koffka (1935), uses a Newtonian analogy to explain how this occurs. Arnheim provides three possible explanations: (1) an object loses apparent weight with distance from the center of attention—the visual center of gravity of a composition; (2) the visual weight is affected by the distribution of elements on the façade of the building being observed; and (3) elements elevated from the ground or higher up on the façade of a building add "to the object's potential energy—the same black spot looks heavier in the top of the picture than below." If one accepts this view then the expressive effects of the visual environment can be analyzed in terms of the way such features as the contours, edges, and façade elements of a building relate to the horizontal and the vertical.

While Gestalt psychologists conducted considerable experimental research on the attributes of form and expression, there has been very little systematic research on environmental preferences. Implicit, if not explicit, in the views of the modern masters who drew so heavily on Gestalt theory is the belief that "good figures" are desirable, that "unity" is good, and that "simplicity" is good. This seems to have been more of a reaction to the eclectic ideas of nineteenth-century architects than to anything else —a difference in form empathy, perhaps.

PROBLEMS WITH THE GESTALT-THEORY-BASED MODEL OF FORMAL AESTHETICS

While the Gestalt theory of perception was based on much experimental research, the extrapolation of Gestalt principles of perception to aesthetic theory has been highly personal. Thus, it is difficult to distinguish between positive and normative theory. Those statements that are clearly positive remain static representations of Gestalt thought of the 1930s. In particular, they pay little attention to the specific characteristics of the three-dimensional world and the role of movement as the basis for its perception, or to the research of the last fifty years that questions the whole concept of isomorphism as developed by Gestalt theorists and thus the Gestalt theory of expression.

There has been considerable research on perception and on aesthetics during the past four decades; new theories have been established and new hypotheses generated. The Gestalt model of formal aesthetics is an important basis for asking questions about the experiencing of the geometric qualities of the environment *per se*. It needs to be adapted, amended, and extended, however, if it is to provide a positive theoretical basis for design (see also Jones 1969).

RECENT EMPIRICAL RESEARCH

Gestalt theory has been extended and, at least partially, replaced by the ecological and transactionalist theories of perception. There has also been much empirical research that needs to be considered in stating our present understanding of the formal aesthetics of the built environment. This research has covered a wide variety of topics, but the emphasis has been on studying the relationship between environmental complexity/simplicity and hedonic values. Amos Rapoport (1977) summarizes this research as follows:

(1) Recent psychological and ethological research shows that animals and humans (including infants) prefer complex patterns in the visual field.
(2) There is an optimum preference range of perceptual input, with both simple and chaotically complex visual fields disliked.
(3) There are two ways of achieving complexity; through ambiguity (in the sense of multiplicity of meanings rather than uncertainty of meanings) and hence using allusive and open-ended design, or through the use of varied and rich environments and environments not visible from one view, i.e., which unfold and reveal themselves and thus have an element of mystery.

(4) Much modern design has aimed at simplicity and total control which is unsatisfactory.

Complexity has been measured in a number of ways: the number of elements in a system, their novelty and surprisingness, their texture patterns, and their levels of order. Much of this research has focused on the perception of two-dimensional line drawings but some has looked specifically at building façades (Sanoff 1974, Krampen et al. 1978). Structural order correlates with perceptions of geometric regularity. Complexity thus has a variety of meanings in this research. The basic goal in this research is to understand how the relational aspects of a visual system are perceived as simple or complex (Valentine 1962). It is clear that learning and experience make a difference in perceptions of levels of complexity.

The visual complexity of environments is related positively to how interesting they are—measured subjectively or objectively (in terms of the length of time that people pay attention to a pattern) (Smets 1971, Wohlwill 1981). The relationships between interestingness and complexity, and between complexity and pleasantness are portrayed in figure 18-5. Pleasantness also tends to increase the longer one examines a complex pattern. This is done, possibly, for the reward of ascertaining the ordering principles (Nasser 1985). There have been several attempts to ascertain optimal levels of stimulation (Fiske and Maddi 1961), but the number of factors that influence perceptions of the physical environment is so high that no clear statement can yet be made. According to information-theory approaches to aesthetics, however, and also according to Arnheim (1977), if there is perceived order to high levels of complexity the pattern is evaluated to be more pleasant than if there is not that order.

Attempts to segregate formal values from symbolic ones are difficult in the analysis of real built environments. In a study of façades, for instance, Martin Krampen and his colleagues (1978) found that the newness of façades was an intervening variable in the judged attractiveness of façades of various degrees of complexity. Most studies do, however, indicate a positive correlation between façades subjectively evaluated to be "stimulating," "sensuous," "dynamic," and pleasing (for instance, Sanoff 1974).

The theoretical explanations of these empirical findings have not paralleled the research, but there are several potential explanations for them. D. E. Berlyne (1974) has developed the thesis that hedonic values are related to the degree of arousal that visual patterns initiate, provided the degree is not too high. It seems that arousal is related also to

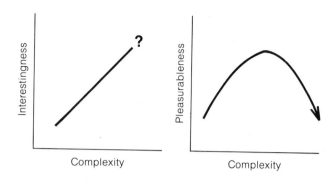

18-5. The Relationship of Complexity, Interestingness, and Pleasure.

deviations from the level of complexity in the environment to which people are accustomed. The magnitude and threshold of change in the environment required to arouse people depends on their habituation level and on the mood of the perceiver. Anne Tyng (1975) presents the hypothesis that people's preferences for complexity and simplicity go in cycles, that we are now going through a period demanding greater complexity and that this is tied to the state of individuation of a person or the society of which he or she is a part—a Jungian model of individual psychological growth. The psychobiological approach to the study of aesthetics (such as Berlyne 1974) explains the relationship between complexity and pleasure in terms of supposed degrees of activation in the brain, with one tending to drive arousal upward and the other tending to keep it within bounds.

Recent empirical research provides some insights into people's preferences for geometric patterns of various characteristics. One of the problems with the research from the point of view of someone interested in how people experience the environment in order to build environmental design theory is that little of it seems to be tied into an image of the design task or a broad picture of aesthetic theory. This may be an explanation of why aesthetic concepts derived from Gestalt theory still hold sway. They were closely linked to an artistic endeavor.

UPDATING FORMAL AESTHETIC THEORY

Formal aesthetics is concerned with the pleasures that arise from the visual, sonic, olfactory, and haptic scanning of the environment in order to discriminate, perceive, and enjoy its structure. The visual sense is the most important for environmental design theory, thus we will consider it first.

Delight with the geometric structure of the visual environment seems to arise in four ways: (1) the recognition that the structure is in accordance with some canon, or normative principle, of importance to the viewer; (2) the perception that the structure affords its purpose well; (3) the congruence of the level of its visual complexity and order with the viewer's habituation level or the level to which he or she can adapt; or (4) the maintenance of the viewer's attention.

When the characteristics of the environment are related to some normative canon which the observer enjoys or holds in high esteem, then his or her attitude toward the environment will be a positive one, according to balance-theory concepts. For instance, those architects who believe and value the concept of "dynamic balance" will get pleasure from the perception of a pattern of walls, ground, and other elements of the environment which when seen from a particular viewpoint are in "dynamic balance." If a person does not know about the concept, his or her appreciation of the environment will depend on other qualities. People who do not know the canons of taste frequently are referred to as "aesthetically illiterate."

Understanding the logic of the layout of the environment is self-rewarding. Attaining this understanding involves a process of learning. Perceptual learning is a process of developing one's ability to pay attention to finer details and broader classes of characteristics of the environment.

If one accepts this view, which owes much to the ecological model of perception (Gibson 1966, 1979), the distinction between formal aesthetics and symbolic aesthetics is blurred. The question then arises as to whether there are some characteristics of the environment that are universally appealing. The need for clarity—the reduction of uncertainty—seems to fall into this category. Clarity is valued. A perceptual system hunts until it finds clarity. The process occurs at many levels: first, the pickup of information reinforces exploratory adjustments (Gibson 1966); second, the registering of information reinforces the neural activity in the brain that brings it about. Not much is known about this process. While the basic process may be universal, the degree of clarity, complexity, or orderliness that is pleasing depends on the circumstances, perceptions, and attitudes of the people involved. People also can be fooled. Apparent clarity may be based on illusions—of depth, of line, and of form. Illusions have been used by architects for centuries to attain specific aesthetic ends (Lukiesch 1922, Gibson 1966).

Clarity can be achieved by using the Gestalt principles of visual organization in terms not of lines and planes but of texture, color, inclination of surfaces, and effects of illumination and shadowing inherent in the structure of the environment. In urban design, Kevin Lynch's identification of the form-giving elements of cities and neighborhoods, as described in chapter 13, provides a set of principles for achieving both richness and clarity in urban design and architecture.

Of particular importance in environmental perception is the role of movement. As Rapoport noted in the quotation above, environments hold our attention when they present sequences of vistas as we move through them; they are perceived as being more interesting than environments where such vistas are lacking. If, however, the connections between one vista and the next occur too frequently, the resulting profusion of transformations in the optic array will be confusing and insufficiently clear. The sequential experiencing of the environment as a factor in aesthetics has been well documented (Thiel 1961, Cullen 1962, Hassan 1965, Martienssen 1956, Halprin 1965). It must be remembered that the speed with which one moves through the environment varies from that of a pedestrian to that of a high-speed train. One of the problems in environmental design is to reconcile the needs of the pedestrian with those of people moving through it at higher speeds (see Appleyard, Lynch, and Myer 1964).

Environments in which there are many well-ordered juxtapositions of surfaces and/or colors and/or illumination levels and/or textures are also interesting ones. More intricate patterns require more scanning. At high levels of complexity and low levels of order, and particularly when the environment is partially obscured by very high levels or low levels of illumination, the clarity gets lost and the environment is perceived as being unpleasant. The difficulty is to define this point of balance between interestingness and confusion objectively, whether one is dealing with surfaces, colors (Birren 1965, 1969, Porter and Mikellides 1976), or light and shade (Heschong 1979). This also applies to the layout of neighborhoods and cities. Lynch (1960) claimed that environments that are rich in paths, nodes, edges, landmarks, and districts are pleasurable ones. Each of us can identify subjectively an environment that is rich and one that is confusing, but there is at present no measurement for this point nor any way of explaining our individual preferences.

Other environments that attract attention and maintain interest are those in which there are moving objects, people, automobiles—in other words, *busy* environments. The portions of the environment in motion draw, at least initially, the foveae of the eyes toward them rather than toward their backgrounds. At high levels of intricacy and when there is too much motion, the environment becomes chaotic and people stop paying attention to it and

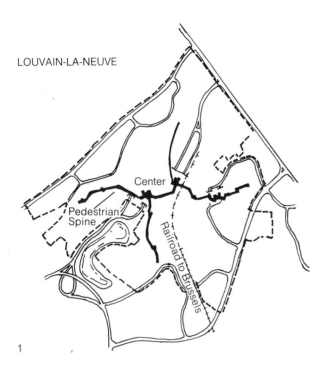

LOUVAIN-LA-NEUVE

Center

Pedestrian Spine

Railroad to Brussels

1

2

3

18-6. Sequential Experience.
Much modern architecture and urban design has failed to make use of the way vistas open up as one moves through the environment. Here, however, is an example of a recent urban design that illustrates how changes in view (2, 3) occur as one moves along the pedestrian spine street (1) of Louvain-la-Neuve in Belgium.

withdraw, or else their attentions become highly selective.

People's apprehension over time seems to be a matter of detecting progressively larger patterns that are composed of smaller ones. The pattern in any view and the temporal relationship in a sequence of views allow the viewer to take in progressively larger spatial or temporal units or "chunks." As one scans the environment, one can take in a complex composition—a panel of instruments or a façade of a building or the geography of a city. The process of apprehension is aided when the layout of the environment follows ordering principles.

Order is, as Gestalt psychologists recognized, a fundamental requirement for the aesthetic appreciation of the environment. This applies both to static views from a single station point and to dynamic views from a sequence of station points. There needs to be some level of continuity in the view for order to be maintained. In the case of the sequential experiencing of the environment, this can be achieved by some constancy in the sequence of transitions between overlapping connected episodes. Not only does this provide some order, but it also makes orientation and way-finding easier.

Perception is multimodal. Thus, one would expect the patterning of sounds, odors, and haptic experiences to be other dimensions of formal aesthetics. There appears to be no systematic research and little speculation on these. The little that has been done has focused on associational meanings. Steen Eiler Rasmussen (1959) brings the designer's attention to the sonic qualities of the environment, and Michael Southworth (1969) shows that the sonic quality of the environment affects our perceptions of its overall quality—meaning that formal and symbolic visual qualities are not alone in determining aesthetic quality. Study is needed of the systematic structuring of sounds, odors, and other sensory input in order to achieve aesthetic effects.

There have been one or two examples of the coordination of the visual, sonic, and haptic patterns of the environment in the work of individual artists such as Remo Saraceni. One of his works consisted of an illuminated tunnel in which the footsteps of the person passing through it triggered musical sounds and caused its illumination level and color to change—the pattern depending in the sequence of the steps. The systematic examination of the interrelationships between patterns discerned by the different perceptual systems is minimal, however.

INDIVIDUAL DIFFERENCES IN ATTITUDES TOWARD THE FORMAL QUALITIES OF THE BUILT ENVIRONMENT

Different people pay attention to different elements and patterns in the environment. If there are some fundamental shapes or patterns that appeal to all people, the research does not show it. Much of what has been written about individual differences in responses to patterns of the environment is highly speculative, but there have also been several experimental studies in which hedonic responses to patterns and variables of pattern have been correlated with characteristics of individuals.

There is little research on how a person's *organismic* characteristics affect that individual's responses to environmental patterns. Heinreich Wölfflin (1888) did suggest that people are habituated to seeing other people of the same ethnic type and so prefer patterns in the environment that have the same proportions as the facial proportions of that ethnic type. While there may seem to be some logic to this hypothesis, it has not received any empirical validation.

The proportional schema that can be perceived visually are not of importance to a blind person. One can speculate that the sound reverberations are affected by the proportional attributes of a space and that these might be more or less pleasing depending on the proportions of the space. Whether a blind person, on walking through a space, gets a feeling for its shape via the sense of sound or touch in conjunction with other experiences is also open to speculation.

There is some evidence that the preference for different visual forms is related to *personality* differences. A generalized model of the relationship between the levels of stimulation and the preferences of introverts and extroverts is shown in figure 18-7. The hypothesis is that introverts, in contrast to extroverts, prefer lower levels of stimulation from the environment (Eysenck 1973). This is really a tautology because it is a definition of one dimension of introversion: receptivity to environmental information.

Individual experimental studies show a variety of linkages between personality and visual pattern preferences. First-born children have a lower tolerance for ambiguity than their younger siblings (Eisenmann 1966). Creative people like complex line drawings (Barron 1965). The hypothesis is that they have come to terms with their individual unconscious—a Jungian interpretation (see Jung 1968). Amos Rapoport argues that rich, vivid, and complex forms are liked by people in general, although there may be groups who are undergoing cultural change for whom low levels of complexity are desired (Rapoport 1977).

Anne Tyng's hypothesis (1975) is more complex. Her model of form empathy, already mentioned, suggests that people like more and more complex forms as the process of individuation proceeds. When a person goes through psychological rebirth, the preference reverts from very complex to simple forms and the process begins again. She suggests that this process occurs more rapidly for things like clothing fashions than for architecture and that the process applies to the personality of societies as well as that of individuals.

There is some speculation on the shapes of artifacts that people of different personalities like. People who are content and dependable are said to prefer round shapes; ovals are said to be liked by creative and organized people; squares by those who are clearheaded. Whether or not these observations are accurate and universal and applicable to buildings and landscapes is open to conjecture. Most of these speculations on pattern preferences, like most of current research on aesthetics, assume a sensation-based model of perception. This is a be-

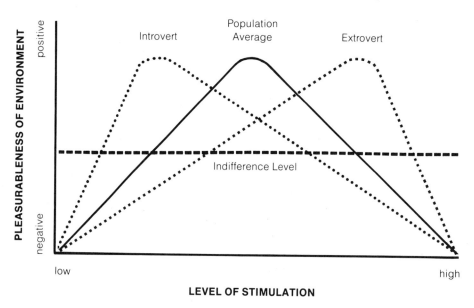

18-7. The Relationship of Personality, Levels of Environmental Stimulation, and Pleasingness.

ginning but it is a limited approach.

Relatively few people seem to explore self-consciously the patterns of the environment for their own sake. Members of some *social groups* and *cultures* do so more than others but we do not understand these differences well. Architects and artists have been taught to appreciate certain formal aesthetic principles and are thus able to recognize patterns in the environment that others do not. Certainly, the interpretation of the work of abstract artists seems to stem more from an understanding of their "vocabulary" or the assignment of a language by the viewers than from any innate processes.

The *geographic environment* in which people live affects their attitudes toward the novelty and complexity of their environment and of new scenes. People enjoy deviations from the norm on a temporary basis provided these deviations are not too large (Wohlwill 1971). Presumably, too, people who inhabit highly complex environments seek less complex ones in order to get a sense of relief. In terms of the competence-environment press model (Lawton 1977), people sometimes seek more comfortable environments and sometimes want more stressful ones depending on their degree of competence in dealing with the situations of everyday life. The nature of these processes is also highly conjectural.

CONCLUSION

The nature of the formal aesthetics of the built environment has been the subject of much debate among adherents of different schools of positive thought. Many ideas that are currently part of environmental design theory, particularly architec-

tural theory, are derived from Gestalt psychology. The Gestalt laws of visual organization provide a theoretical basis for achieving many visual ends in design, but they do not specify what those ends should be. The research overwhelmingly, but by no means universally, indicates that people, nowadays, at least, prefer patterns more complex than those produced by the modern masters. But is this simply part of a cyclical trend?

Usually when designers (and behavioral scientists) think of issues of complexity and simplicity in the formal aesthetics of buildings, they are thinking of façadal treatments. Most of the research has focused on the perception of two-dimensional patterns. Perception of the world, however, involves the movement of the observer. Movement results in transformations in the optic array. The complexity-simplicity of these transformations needs to be better understood.

Much of our understanding of formal aesthetics relies on the introspective analyses of the speculative philosophers and on the research of a relatively small group of psychologists working with very different assumptions about the perceptual processes. Studying formal aesthetic preferences is difficult. Many of the issues that traditionally were regarded as formal aesthetic ones may more appropriately be regarded as symbolic aesthetic ones.

ADDITIONAL READINGS

Arnheim, Rudolf. *The Dynamics of Architectural Form.* Berkeley and Los Angeles: University of California Press, 1977

Cullen, Gordon. *Townscape*. London: Architectural Press, 1962.

Kepes, Gyorgy. *Language of Vision*. Chicago: Paul Theobold, 1944.

Hesselgren, Sven. *Man's Perception of the Man-Made Environment: An Architectural Theory*. Stroudsburg, Pa.: Dowden, Hutchinson and Ross, 1975, pp. 98–110.

Lang, Jon. "Theories of Perception and 'Formal Design.' " In Jon Lang et al., eds., *Designing for Human Behavior: Architecture and the Behavioral Sciences*. Stroudsburg, Pa.: Dowden, Hutchinson, and Ross, 1974, pp. 98–110.

Levi, David. "The Gestalt Psychology of Expression in Architecture." In Jon Lang et al., eds., op. cit., pp. 111–119.

Martienssen, Rex. *The Idea of Space in Greek Architecture*. Johannesburg: University of Witwatersrand Press, 1956.

Rapoport, Amos. "The Importance and Nature of Environmental Perception." In *Human Aspects of Urban Form*. New York: Pergamon, 1977, pp. 178–247.

Rasmussen, Steen Eiler. *Experiencing Architecture*. Cambridge, Mass.: MIT Press, 1959.

Venturi, Robert. *Complexity and Contradiction in Architecture*. New York: Museum of Modern Art, 1966.

19

SYMBOLIC AESTHETICS

The built environment is full of potential symbolic meanings for people. The recognition of these meanings, consciously or subconsciously, contributes to people's feelings about the environment and about themselves. While it is not the sole factor, identification with the symbolic meanings of the built environment is an important way whereby people attain a sense of belonging to a group of people or a place (Cooper 1974, Rapoport 1982, Rykwert 1982).

Designers have taken a variety of normative stances on what these meanings should be. Geoffrey Scott (1935) collected the statements of a number of architects associated with the early years of the Modern Movement on this. Architecture must be "expressive of its purpose"; architecture must be "expressive of the national life." Designers also take stances on what meanings individual schemes should communicate. An example is architect Louis Kahn's statement on the design of a United States embassy: "I wanted to have a clear statement of a way of life" (Hershberger 1970). The positive basis required to understand how such meanings are abstracted from the patterns of the built environment

is limited. This has been very much recognized during the last decade as the importance of the symbolic meanings of the environment in people's lives has been recognized and there has been a concomitant growth in desire on the part of environmental designers to enhance their understanding of the nature of symbolism and symbolic aesthetics.

The recent concern of interior designers, architects, landscape architects, and urban designers with the nature of symbolism coincides with three other developments:

1. the growth of the tertiary sector of the economy—the postindustrial society—and the search by designers for new design ideologies;
2. the recognition that much of what has been built in the United States and chosen by many people is rich in symbolism not recognized by the ideology of the Modern Movement; the Levittowns and Las Vegases were seldom studied by designers until brought to their attention by Robert Venturi and his colleagues (Venturi, Scott Brown, and Izenour 1977);
3. the demand by clients and the public that buildings be in styles with which they can identify.

Any design ideology with a humanistic basis needs

Parts of this chapter were published previously in Jon Lang, "Symbolic Aesthetics in Architecture: Towards a Research Agenda," in Polly Bart et al., eds., *Knowledge for Design: Proceedings of EDRA12*, EDRA, Inc., 1982, pp. 172–182. Reprinted by permission of the Environmental Design Research Association.

a clear positive theory of symbolic aesthetics if it is to achieve its purpose. The objective of this chapter is to review our understanding of the nature and purposes of symbols, their aesthetic dimension, and the relationship between individual differences and aesthetic interpretations of the environment.

THE NATURE OF SYMBOLIC MEANING

Different categorizations of meaning (such as Gibson 1950, Hershberger 1974) have already been introduced. They all suggest that some meanings of the environment have to do with its potential instrumental use and others have to do with the emotional qualities that an observer or user reads into it. The latter is of concern here.

There is more confusion over the nature of symbolic meaning than any other level of meaning. The terms *image, sign,* and *symbol* often are used interchangeably. An image, it will be assumed here, is an imitation or a reproduction or a similitude of something. "The image of St. Peter's is an image of St. Peter's and nothing more; if it suggests Rome or the Holy Catholic Church, the image becomes a symbol" (Gibson 1966).

A symbol is the result of a cognitive process whereby an object acquires a connotation beyond its instrumental use. An "object" in this sense may be an environment or a person as well as a material artifact. These meanings are derived from what an observer imputes to an object (Kepes 1966). This may result from a psychological association, a social convention, or even an accident (Burchard and Brown 1966). A sign, in contrast, is a convention or device that stands for something else in a literal rather than an abstract sense.

Semiology

Semiology, a young field concerned with the nature of symbols, already has influenced the thinking of a number of environmental designers, architects in particular (such as Broadbent, Bunt, and Jencks 1980). The concerns of the field are summarized in the basic semiological triangle which specifies a relationship connecting symbol, thought, and referent as shown in figure 19–1 (Barthes 1967). The built environment consists of a structure of surfaces of various materials, pigmentations, and illumination levels. The pattern of these elements is the signifier. The ideas and meanings associated with the pattern—that which is signified—may vary from individual to individual or group to group because the referent is different. It might have meaning to some architects to refer to a house as "a

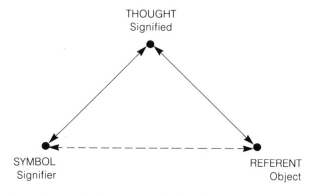

19-1. The Basic Semiological Triangle.

second canonical De Stijl house" but the referent will be obscure to most people. The important referents for a group also change over time.

During the course of the last century in the Chicago area, synagogues have been built in Moorish, Byzantine, classical, Italian Renaissance, European Modern, Gothic, and what has pejoratively been called "Supermarket Modern" styles. These choices have not been haphazard. Different referents were important at different times. For example, the classical style followed the archaeological discovery of classical synagogues from Roman times; the Moorish style was associated with Middle Eastern roots, and the Byzantine style also had archaeological associations (Hine 1978).

The symbolic meaning of a particular pattern of the built environment also depends on its context. Charles Morris (1938) suggested that there are three levels of meaning: *syntactic, semantic,* and *pragmatic.* Syntactical meaning results from, say, the location of a building in its surroundings. Semantic meanings refer to the "norms, idea or attitude that an element represents or designates" (Rainwater 1966). Thus, much public housing in the United States represents the idea of a small group of people of how the working class should live (Wolfe 1981). *Pragmatic* meaning relates the symbol to those who use it.

The processes of stimulus-and-response generalization explain why some of the confusion over the interpretations of symbols exists. It is known that the same variables (such as the façades of buildings) may have different meanings for different people. Architect Minoru Yamasaki has used essentially the same basic pattern in the façades of a synagogue, the World Trade Center in New York, and Dhahran airport in Saudi Arabia. "Yamasaki must be a very good explainer," wrote critic Thomas Hines (1978). Different forms may also communicate the same meaning.

Within a homogeneous society, there may be a general agreement on the symbolism of specific building styles or decorations. When experiences and values differ there is likely to be a diversity of meanings attributable to the same pattern. Design theory needs to recognize this because symbolic meanings serve a number of purposes for people and are important to them in a number of ways.

THE PURPOSES SERVED BY SYMBOLS

"Human beings are symbol mongers" (Langer 1953). One way in which people communicate with each other is through symbols. The symbolic meaning of furniture, building layouts, and style and landscape designs is a nonverbal mechanism that people use to communicate messages about themselves, their backgrounds, social statuses, and world views (Beinart 1975, Rapoport 1982). Other material artifacts, such as automobiles and clothing and even such things as household pets, also carry symbolic meaning.

Using material artifacts in this way is more important for some people than for others. A tentative explanation for this can be derived from an interpretation of Maslow's model of human motivations (1954). When one is struggling for survival, the symbolic aesthetics of the environment will not be the focus of one's attention. The physical environment will still communicate messages about the status of the people concerned and they may be very aware of this, but they will have less energy and, therefore, less inclination to act purposively to change the environment and thus its meanings. For people whose prime concern is with security, architectural variables—particularly those associated with symbolic barriers representing territorial demarcations—become more important, but it is in fulfilling people's affective needs and their needs for a sense of belonging and esteem that the symbolism of the built environment is particularly important.

The symbols people choose to have around them may reflect their perception of who they are or who they aspire to be, or they may be simply a rejection of the past. Socially mobile people find the symbols associated with the group they aspire to join particularly important. The perception of important symbols associated with a group might well, however, be different for those outside the group than for those who are full members of it. If we have full membership in a group—be it socioeconomic, cultural, or ethnic—the symbols of membership are less important and those chosen are more likely to reflect personality or other idiosyncrasies. This is also true for people whose needs are primarily those associated with self-actualization and cognitive and aesthetic fulfillment.

Probably the clearest statement on identity and environment is that by Clare Cooper (1974), whose concepts are based on those of Carl Jung. Cooper's research suggests that people select houses, to the extent they can, that represent themselves. A house can be divided into public and private parts. The façade represents the public image that a person wants to convey to society. The interior reveals the nature of the person's inner self; this is revealed only to special individuals. Cooper notes that the public image often extends to the interior so that what is personal is very much depleted. Sometimes the whole interior seems to have been designed for public display.

The same type of analysis can be extended from individuals to groups of people and to institutions. Business corporations, for instance, attempt to present an image of themselves to the world (Lasswell 1979). This is reflected not only on the exterior façades and massings of buildings but also in the landscape design and interior design. Thus, very little of the CBS Building in New York, for instance, takes on anything but a corporate image. The office of the then Chairman of the Board was done the way he wanted, however, and the senior administrators of the organization were allowed to select their furnishings from a menu, but the lower-echelon workers had to accept the symbolism of the corporation and little personalization was allowed. This resulted in conflicts between managers and staff over how personal possessions could be displayed (Rapoport 1967).

In using Maslow's model of human motivations in this kind of analysis, it must be remembered that human needs are largely fulfilled through social and cultural mechanisms not related to the built environment. The attributes of the built world are still important, however.

VARIABLES OF THE BUILT ENVIRONMENT THAT CARRY MEANING

A content analysis of the writings of architects, artists, and art historians and of the few studies that have dealt empirically with the symbolism of the built environment enables us to compile a tentative list of variables that carry symbolic meaning. These are also the variables over which environmental designers have some control.

Building Configuration

The shapes and patterns that comprise an architectural style carry meaning. Within certain cultures specific shapes such as a circle, or a pattern such as symmetry, have associational meanings themselves, but these have largely been lost in the Western world except in certain religious institutions where the linkage has become a social convention.

The simplicity or complexity of overall configurations is associated with specific eras. Simple clear shapes with few historical allusions have been used to represent the machine age and modernity, and an emerging complexity of shapes and patterning has been used to represent the postindustrial society. In terms of housing, the meanings of the rectangular single-family structure are mentioned frequently in both the architectural and the social science literature. The association, it is suggested, is with a lifestyle and with individualism of action. The roots of these meanings are said to lie deep in the Anglo-Saxon psyche (Handlin 1972). The meanings are also recognized, however, by almost all the people of the United States (Hinshaw and Alott 1972, Cooper 1974), including those who choose other environments to live in for themselves (Michelson 1968).

Venturi, Scott Brown, and Izenour (1977) identify two basic types of building in terms of the relationship between instrumental and symbolic functions. These are reflected in the nature of the building configuration:

1. Where the architectural system of space, structure and program is submerged and distorted by an overall symbolic form. This kind of building-becoming-sculpture we call a *duck* in honor of the duck-shaped drive-in, "The Long Island Duckling," illustrated in *God's Own Junkyard* by Peter Blake.

2. Where systems of space and structure are directly at the service of the program, and ornament is applied independently of them . . . we call it a *decorated shed.*

In these definitions "program" refers to room and circulation requirements and not to aesthetic specifications. The basic point is that the overall building configuration is the symbol in the "duck," while in the "decorated shed" the decoration is applied to the façade (see fig. 19–2). Most modern architectural works are ducks; while most "commercial vernacular architecture" consists of decorated sheds.

In decorated sheds, the associational meanings of the applied decoration are reasonably explicit. Decorated sheds look like what they are because of what they call to mind in the observer. The associational meanings of ducks arise from the architect's intentions. In decorated sheds the associational meanings rely on past history—in terms of everyday experiences; with ducks, the recognition of the as-

sociation depends on knowing the designer's philosophy. In Santayana's terms, it is an intellectual association.

Spatial Configurations

The volume, degree of enclosure, and proportions of enclosed space carry meaning. The consumption of space *per se* is an important symbol. People of higher status in most organizations, formal or informal, inhabit physical settings that are larger in size than those of people of lower rank. People have little difficulty in recognizing this. Maxwell Fry (1961) noted the following about Le Corbusier's Secretariat building in Chandigarh, India:

One can see the preferential treatment given to the higher ranks of government breaking into the regular façade by way of [the] recessed balcony and larger windows. . . .

In many capital cities, government buildings are widely spaced with sweeping vistas. This has the impact of symbolizing the importance and power of the government and/or country. While this is historically true of the United States, in many cities the opposite has been the case in recent times (Lasswell 1979).

The meanings of other spatial relationships have hardly been studied rigorously. Christian Norberg-Schulz (1971) refers to architectural space as the concretization of existential space—"a psychological concept denoting the schemata man develops interacting with the environment to get along satisfactorily." He is thus concerned with linking concepts in the mind with architectural space but the linkages are unclear. In an empirical study (Beck 1970), simple dichotomous spatial variables were identified as potential carriers of architectural meaning. These are *diffuse* versus *dense space*, *delineated* versus *open space*, *verticality* versus *horizontality*, *right* and *left* in the *horizontal plane*, *up* and *down* in the *vertical plane*. A summary of one of these sets, delineated versus open space, will give a feeling for Beck's research goal. "Delineated space refers to bounded, constricted, contained, contracted or centripetal space; open space suggests inward and outward movement, spatial penetration, liberty and freedom." His research shows that different people have different associations with architectural spaces located at different points on those scales but the patterns of these differences are not clear.

Materials

A plain wood interior may be chosen for a ski shop, marble for the Kennedy Arts Center in Wash-

1

2

3

19-2. Ducks and Decorated Sheds.
Venturi, Scott Brown, and Izenour (1977) differentiate between two types of buildings based on whether the whole structure is the symbol itself or whether the symbolism is applied. The former they call "ducks" and the latter, "decorated sheds." In (1), a duck, the symbolism communicated depends considerably on whether or not the architect's intentions are understood. Decorated sheds (2) tend to have associational meanings that are part of a broader culture, but this is not always the case (3).

ington, or metal for a museum of technology. These materials may be chosen partially for their technical attributes but also for the associations they afford. Not only does the visual character of a material have associations but also its sonic, haptic, and sometimes its olfactory nature. For example, the sound made by walking on floors of different materials varies considerably and contributes to the perceived ambiance of a setting. Certain materials have, through usage, become associated with specific building types. Glazed tiles, hard surfaces, and mercury

vapor lamps are associated with institutions. Often these now have negative connotations. The result is that there is often a clash between what is technically sensible and the symbolic aesthetic requirements in design. This is also true of the use of synthetic materials.

The artificiality or naturalness of materials has associations for people. Kyoshi Izumi (1969) believes that the use of plastics to simulate wood and other materials sets up doubts in viewers because their perceptual systems are fooled and/or because there is a lack of congruence between what a material looks like and what it feels or sounds like. This is an appealing hypothesis.

The Nature of Illumination

The effects of the directionality, source, color, and level of illumination of a behavior setting have long been regarded as fundamental variables in the experiencing of both indoor and outdoor space. There is a considerable, if scattered, body of introspective and interpretive analyses of the psychological impact of the use of light as a compositional element. For instance, Walter Gropius (1962) wrote:

Imagine the surprise and animation experienced when a sunbeam shining though the stained glass window in a cathedral wanders slowly through the twilight of a nave and suddenly hits the altar piece. What a stimulus for the spectator.

The effort to use explicitly the symbolic qualities of light in design has a long history. Abbot Suger, the patron of what is regarded as the first work of Gothic architecture, the choir for the church of Saint-Denis in the Île de France (1140–1150) had a clear, if challengeable, concept of the metaphysics of light:

The physical "brightness" of the world of art will "brighten" the minds of the beholder with a spiritual illumination . . . [thus] his insatiable passion for everything lustrously beautiful. (Panofsky 1946)

On a more mundane level, there are strong correlations between illumination level, types of light fittings, and the nature of certain behavior settings. For instance, a student study of restaurants in Philadelphia revealed a correlation between illumination type and restaurant quality. The less expensive restaurants with large numbers of patrons daily have high levels of illumination from overhead fluorescent lighting while the more exclusive tend to have much lower levels of illumination from incandescent light fittings on tables and/or walls.

While such anecdotal statements exist in abundance and there are many data on the human engineering aspects of lighting in the built environment, the theoretical underpinnings for the assertions about the symbolic uses of light are weak. We may know a fair amount about the pragmatics of light but we have little systematic knowledge about its semantic or syntactic meanings, in Morris's terms.

Color

The colors and coloring of the built environment carry meanings at a variety of scales. These are often carried by explicit social conventions. These conventions may be understood by broad segments of a population even though the antecedents of the convention may be unknown. For example, in traditional Beijing, color was a symbol of status. Bright colors were reserved for palaces, temples, and other buildings housing rituals; ordinary buildings were made artificially less colorful.

Color conventions differ from society to society. Within Western cultures red is supposed to be a fiery color; green is said to be soothing. Both are supposed to have behavioral implications. Colors often are associated with specific building types where they may have been selected originally for highly pragmatic reasons (such as railroad brown for its dirt-hiding qualities). Used in other contexts they still carry the old associational meaning. The evidence on the meanings of colors within different social and cultural contexts is highly contradictory (Hayward 1974, Porter and Mikellides 1976). Often it seems that it is not the color itself that carries meaning but the way in which it deviates from the norm, from habituation levels.

The Nonvisual Environment

The sounds that reverberate from the surfaces of the environment as one acts and talks in it carry meanings. These meanings are both instrumental and symbolic (Rasmussen 1959). This is true also of the tactile and olfactory qualities of surfaces and of textures, even though people may not be conscious of them. Some of the associations are pleasant; some are unpleasant. Very little research has been done on these types of meanings, although novels and motion pictures are full of them.

The Meaning of Nonmaterial Attributes of the Built Environment

To make matters more complex, the symbolic meanings of specific environments are not dependent simply on their physical qualities. They are dependent also on such things as place-names; as the developers of new residential areas well know (see fig. 19–3); on perceptions of who was involved in the decision process; and on the people present and the activities taking place within the setting. Buildings and urban designs reflect the way decisions were made and who made them. They act as symbols of the process which, in turn, reflects the

1   Source: Charles Spuhler, Inc.

2   Source: FPA Corporation

3   Source: Windon Property Management

19-3. The Symbolism of Residential Areas.

A variety of meanings are afforded by housing, as developers and advertisers recognize (Michelson 1976). Within Anglo-American culture, rural imagery is important, as many advertisers show (1, 2). The urban image (3) is less common. Residential areas often are chosen by people, consciously or unconsciously, because of the self-images they reinforce (Cooper 1974). The names for these residential areas are highly symbolic.

distribution of power in society and the attitudes of people toward each other. Robert Goodman (1971) is among those who now perceive the urban renewal efforts of the 1950s and 1960s in the United States as symbols of the efforts of politicians and architects to impose their values on others and of the continuing oppression of the poor. Other people see the same artifacts as symbols of concern for the poor.

Some buildings are associated with certain people or events. A particular setting may have meaning to people not because of its physical attributes but because of the events that took place there. The building becomes a symbol of the events. These events may have been recurrent or there may have been a single event. Independence Hall in Philadelphia and the Ann Frank House in Amsterdam act in this way. The forms of the building are largely irrelevant in terms of their associational meanings but the style of the building may become a symbol of the occurrence. This type of symbolism is thus beyond the control of the environmental designer; it is acquired over time or through an idiosyncratic occurrence. Issues of this type have to be addressed in urban renewal and historic preservation.

Cities and buildings are changing constantly. These changes are both symptoms and symbols of new needs and ideas, of decay and growth. Thus, although Chandigarh, India may be perceived as a poor design because of the incongruences between what the layout affords and the lifestyle of its inhabitants (Brolin 1976) and to contain culturally inappropriate symbolism (Nilsson 1973), it is also perceived by many as a symbol of progress and a new era. An Indian official commented:

> Anyhow Le Corbusier and his associates got away with it. And considering the hindrances offered by ignorance, routine behavior, official machinery and the mediocre thinking inevitable to a democratic structure, this town of the future seems like a miracle, wrung out of the heritage of indifference and bad taste left by the Victorian British minds who ruled us for two centuries. (Nilsson 1973)

It is clear from such statements that what constitutes good or bad taste is highly subjective (and often highly political). Changes in the environment shake up the old order and may be perceived by people as a loss of part of themselves or as progress or as both (Fried 1963). Whether it is liked or disliked depends on the referent and attitudes toward it.

THE AESTHETIC DIMENSION

Attitudes are composed of beliefs and values. Attitudes toward specific symbolic meanings in the environment arise from the attribution of a value to a belief about them. Whether one regards specific symbols as positive can be explained, at least partially, by Heider's balance theory. One's attitude toward a symbol depends on one's attitude toward the referent and the perceived linkage between symbol and referent.

Writing about attitudes toward the symbolism in the buildings and landscapes of suburbia, Venturi and his colleagues (1972) note:

> The content of the symbols, commercial hucksterism and middle-class social aspirations, is distasteful to many architects. . . . They recognize the symbolism but do not accept it. To them the symbolic decoration of the split-level suburban shed represents the debased, materialistic values of a consumer economy where people are brainwashed by mass marketing and have no choice but to move to tickey-tackey, with its vulgar violations of the natural materials and its visual pollution of architectural sensibilities and therefore the ecology.

People strive for a consensus of attitudes, notes psychologist Leon Festinger (1957). The symbolic value of a Levittown or a Las Vegas is found to be acceptable by many people. Figure 19–4 places the symbolic meanings, taste culture, and oneself at the corners of a triangle of relationships. A population that likes the symbolism of Levittown's housing also will have a positive attitude toward the middle-class values that generated Levittown, provided it can see the linkage between those values and the physical environment. A question of importance to environmental design theory is: How are those attitudes established? A clear answer to this question will enable designers to better understand the people with whom they are working and also themselves. At present our ability to provide such an answer is limited.

THE ACQUISITION OF SYMBOLIC MEANINGS AND AFFECTIVE VALUES

A number of coexisting theories attempt to explain why certain patterns in the built environment communicate specific meanings to specific groups of people. These theories may act simultaneously, each explaining some aspect of symbolism. No integrative model exists.

The Theory of Physiognomic Properties

This theory states that buildings have physiognomic properties that are directly perceivable by the observer. This observation is derived from the Gestalt theory of perception (Levi 1974). Rudolf Arnheim (1949, 1977) calls this approach "spontaneous symbolism through perceptual dynamics." The meanings are inherent in the forms themselves. He contrasts this with "conventional symbolism" (for example, the Lincoln Memorial has thirty-six columns because that was the number of states at the time of Lincoln's death; the Presbyterian Church designed by Harrison & Abramovitz in Stamford, Connecticut is in the shape of an important Christian symbol—a fish). Line and form are said to carry meaning because of the human neurological system. Another position is that these shapes carry meaning because of natural empathies with natural phenomena.

Spontaneous symbolic meanings are said to arise from directly perceivable analogies—that is, those that require no intellectual thought. Many of these empathies are said to develop because they are tied to aspects of the natural world, including the characteristics of the human body (Wöllflin 1885), or to the nature of natural materials (Rasmussen 1959), or to the nature of the DNA molecule (Tyng 1969). These types of empathies are different from what Arnheim has in mind. He is a pure Gestaltist.

1

Source: Venturi, Rauch and Scott Brown

2

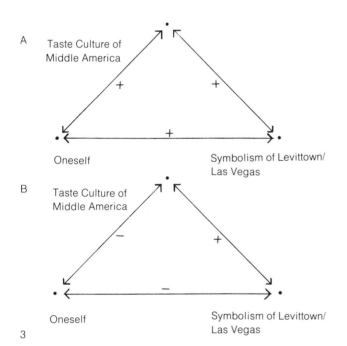

A Taste Culture of
Middle America

      +   +

              +

Oneself   Symbolism of Levittown/
                           Las Vegas

B Taste Culture of
Middle America

      −   +

              −

Oneself   Symbolism of Levittown/
                           Las Vegas

3

19-4. Learning from Levittown and Las Vegas.
Heider's balance theory helps explain attitudes toward Las Vegas (1) and toward houses such as this one (2). Diagrams (3a and b) show two consonant positions on the symbolism of these two places. The design professions consistently have remained aloof from the popular culture and found it very difficult to relate to it positively. In this way they have maintained their own identity.

There has been criticism of this approach by psychologists such as Gregory (1966) and Gibson (1966, 1979) and by architects such as Alan Colquhoun (1967), as cited by Venturi et al. (1977):

> . . . the arrangement of forms as found in a painting by Kandinsky is, in fact, very low in content, unless we attribute to them some conventional meaning not inherent in the forms themselves.

Jungian Approaches to Symbolism

Jung's concepts of collective unconscious and individuation have been used to explain why certain forms take on meaning for us. Jung postulated that people have a collective unconscious linking them to the past (Jung 1968). In this unconscious are "bundles of psychic energy"—archetypes. One of the most fundamental archetypes is the self—"the inner heart of our own being, our soul, our uniqueness." Since such archetypes are difficult to grasp, people attempt to express their personalities and aspirations through the environments they select for themselves. They might do this, as mentioned above, in the forms of the houses they build or select (Cooper 1974).

Anne Tyng (1969) links the concept of uni-

1

2

3

4

19-5. The Cycle of Form Empathy.

The process of individual or group individuation goes through a cycle, according to Carl Jung (1968). Anne Tyng (1969) suggests that each phase is associated with an empathy for a type of pattern or style in the history of architecture. The sequence starts with an empathy for bilateral, twofold, or fourfold symmetry (1); this is followed by empathies for rotational (2), helical (3), and spiral (4) forms. After this the empathy returns to that for bilateral symmetry in a new cycle of rebirth and continuance.

versal symbols—those common to all human experience—to the unconscious. She also links the Jungian concept of "individuation" (von Franz 1968) to empathies for certain forms. Individuation is the process of growth in personality in which the individual is able to integrate more and more of the unconscious in his or her conscious life. This can also be an attribute of a group of people. The ability to accommodate the unconscious increases until a "rebirth occurs." This involves a restructuring of what is unconscious. The process is accompanied by an empathy for increasingly complex forms until a rebirth occurs. Then the empathy returns to simple forms.

The Behaviorist Model

The behaviorist approach to the understanding of symbols suggests that because elements of the built world and specific meanings have been associated in situations that people find pleasing, they continue to be sought because these associations are rewarding. What may once have been a deterministic relationship between "function" and form is carried on as a symbolic association because the pattern of the form is important to people. This is one explanation for the timber construction details used in marble buildings by the Greeks. What was once important in structural terms remained important in symbolic decorative terms.

The Ecological Model of Perception and Cognition

The correspondence between a particular pattern of the built environment, according to this theory, has to be learned. Sometimes the process is clear, as shown in figure 19–6 (Gibson 1966). When it is, the social convention is learned naturally through the processes of socialization. The psychological association also is learned. The behaviorist model would claim that this is through the process of outside reinforcements—rewards and punishments. The ecological model rejects this position, maintaining that learning can occur for its own sake; this model stresses the importance of culture in understanding the meanings of the built environment.

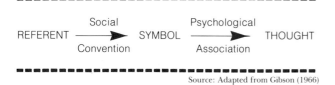

Source: Adapted from Gibson (1966)

19-6. The Ecological Model of Environmental Symbolism.

INDIVIDUAL DIFFERENCES IN SYMBOLIC AESTHETIC VALUES

The environment around us contains, as Norbert Wiener once said, "a thousand and one to-whom-it-may-concern messages." The symbolic meanings people perceive in the natural and built environments and the values that they consciously or unconsciously attribute to them depend on who they are as physiological, social, and psychological beings. There are a number of studies on, and much speculation about, who sees what messages and why.

Some of these differences have been attributed to variations in people's *organismic* character. There are as many different concepts of beauty as there are people of different physiological types. Heinreich Wöllflin (1885), as mentioned in the earlier discussion of formal aesthetics, suggests that people have an empathy for forms that reflect the facial character of the ethnic group to which they belong. This has not been clearly demonstrated, although it is intuitively appealing. Certainly, peoples of different physiological attributes differ in their concepts of human beauty, and they also are likely to look at the environment in different ways for different purposes. There is likely to be a relationship between physiological competence and attitudes toward the environment. The lack of affordances for access to facilities for a segment of the population, for instance, becomes a symbol of those people's role in society and of the attitude of others toward them.

Personality differences are likely to be a predictor of the importance of various symbolic meanings of the environment to individuals and groups. Individuals with a high need for achievement frequently have a high need to bolster their self-images. This takes on different forms depending on who one is. Carl Werthman (1968, reported in Cooper 1974) noted that:

> . . . self-made business people . . . tended to choose somewhat ostentatious, mock colonial display homes, while people in the helping professions, whose goals revolve around personal satisfaction rather than financial success, tended to opt for the inward looking architect designed styles conforming to current standards of good design.

Frank Lloyd Wright's Oak Park clients also were self-made men but of a different character from those studied by Werthman. They were inventors directly involved with the manufacturing process. Their feelings of security and satisfaction were derived from individual definitions. This is clear in the work of the architect they chose. They did not seek to emulate the dwellings of the commercial leaders of Chicago who were more concerned with their place in the social hierarchy and wanted their houses to reflect this (Eaton 1969).

The need for achievement and recognition is not the only personality variable that has attracted research attention. A number of studies (Cooper 1974) have found the introversion-extroversion dimension of personality to be a more useful predictor of people's attitudes toward the environment. People who are extrovert in terms of their actions on the environment tend to decorate their houses more than others. This applies not only to extrovert individuals but also to extrovert groups.

Environmental attitudes go hand in hand with social attitudes and *social group membership* (Rapoport 1977). In residential areas, the size of the house, the nature of the land around it, the ways the front yard is handled, the degree of difference among houses, the facilities provided—particularly those with rural connotations such as bridle paths, lakes, winding roads—even if seldom used, all contribute to the symbolic effect desired by many middle-class Americans (Eichler and Kaplan 1967). In a study of the symbolism of landscape in a prestigious suburb of New York, James S. Duncan (1973) found two contrasting attitudes toward privacy and the maintenance of outdoor areas. Residents in the higher-status group, valuing privacy highly, had less-well-kept grounds with less elaborate displays of decorative elements than those in the lower-status group.

The same variables seem to be important in areas of higher density, but they take on different values due to constraints of space, traffic patterns, and social organization. This applies to apartment buildings as well. The details of the entranceway, the types of furnishings used, and the attire of the doorman and his manners are implicit symbols of status.

The symbolic meaning of the built environment must be perceived within the broad set of values about people and the universe that constitutes a *culture*. Within the Western cultural system, for instance, there is a deeply rooted belief that the natural is superior to the man-made. This is an aspect of the Judeo-Christian ethic that has been traced back to the story of Cain and Abel in Genesis (Saarinen 1976). Traditional patterns of landholding, activities, and social organizations also affect the nature of architectural symbolism.

Perhaps the most important differences in the perception and appreciation of the symbolic meanings of buildings arise from a person's training. There are, for instance, major differences in the appreciation of Post-Modern architecture between architects and lay people. A study (Groat and Canter 1979) showed that a major concern among non-architects was that buildings look like the kinds of buildings they are. This echoes the Modernist ideology. They also seem to appreciate Post-Modern buildings when they can be related to one clear historical style. Most architects studied prefer more complex associations.

The single-family house is a symbol of a belief system that emphasizes individual and territorial rights. This is a characteristic of many countries (Raymond et al. 1966). Clare Cooper (1974) and William Michelson (1976) point out that the single-family house is a powerful image of "home" and that apartments are seldom seen as home in the same way. Such images of what is good and bad, beautiful and ugly, acceptable or not acceptable, have shaped cities and landscapes throughout the world (Jackson 1951).

The United States is an example of a country in which several philosophical systems operate simultaneously. The landscape often reflects the values of the people who first settled it (Pillsbury 1970). This is true of urban as well as rural patterns. The relationship of squares to streets is a function of those who created the city. For example, settlers of English origin in the United States created squares separate from streets; non-English settlers tended to create squares by widening streets (Saarinen 1976).

The way in which a culture overrides other conditions in the development of housing patterns has been explored by Amos Rapoport (1969, 1977, 1982). The results are very clear in cities that have been built up by people of diverse cultures, as occurs especially in colonial societies where an indigenous and a colonial city exist side by side. New Delhi, Khartoum, and Jakarta are good examples. If one simply looks at East Africa, for instance, one finds:

> . . . the Bavarian character of Dar-es-Salaam, the Belgian of Elizabethville [now Lubumbashi], the English character of the Zambian Copperbelt towns or the sidewalk cafes, inlaid sidewalks and Portuguese buildings of Lourenço Marques [now Maputo].

The national character also shows in the design of houses. Much of the housing in Israel, for example, reflects the concept of "good house" that designers brought with them from another country—in this case, Germany—or from an education that drew on Bauhaus principles. In all these cases the symbol of "home" or "good housing unit" has been the decisive factor; the nature of the geographical environment has been subordinate in decision-making.

The process of socialization takes place not only in a social and cultural setting but also in a *geographic* setting. Such settings are rich in symbols, both man-made and natural. Something that is commonplace in one setting may be rare and thus more highly valued in another (Santayana 1896). This is illustrated by a study conducted by Ross Thorne and David Canter (1970). In Scotland, the attached house is common; in Australia it is not. Architectural students in Australia prefer the row house, while those in Scotland prefer the detached one (Rapoport 1977).

The form of cities and houses is, in part, a response to climate. Roof pitches, for instance, are associated with climate zones and become symbols for them. The same is likely to hold true for materials and vegetation. When people move from one area to another they take their symbols of identity with them and use them in the new situation where the patterns may well be "functionally" inappropriate.

CONCLUSION

The symbolism of patterns of furnishings, buildings, and landscapes is central to the aesthetic appreciation of the world. The choices people make of where they will work and live often are made on symbolic grounds. Rapoport (1977) notes that by changing the appropriate symbols associated with a place, people's perceptions of its qualities can change (Manus 1972). Some cities, notably Baltimore, have created new images for themselves by selective changes in land use and building design.

Environmental designers such as architects and landscape architects often have attempted to create new symbols through the manipulation of variables of built form. Interior designers have striven to create images of individuals and corporations through the layout and furnishings of interiors. Many designers have a good intuitive feeling for this, but the record of the profession shows that we have some serious difficulties in understanding and using symbols in the design of the built environment. The architects of the postrevolutionary Soviet Union, for instance, created the architectures that we know as Constructivist and Rationalist to represent the new order, but these symbols never were widely accepted, as Stalin recognized. Predicting the outcome of such efforts is complicated by the lack of a clear positive theory of environmental symbolism. Many fundamental questions still exist. To what extent can buildings be designed to afford specific symbolic values? What are the codes that specific populations understand and enjoy? How do these change over time? What methods are available to ascertain them? Recently we have begun to ask serious questions about symbolic aesthetics and to seek answers in a systematic way using behavioral science research techniques.

ADDITIONAL READINGS

Bonta, Juan. *Architecture and its Interpretation.* New York: Rizzoli, 1979.

Broadbent, Geoffrey, Richard Bunt, and Charles Jencks. *Signs, Symbols and Architecture.* New York: John Wiley, 1980.

Cooper, Clare. "The House as Symbol of the Self." In Jon Lang et al., eds., *Designing for Human Behavior: Architecture and the Behavioral Sciences.* Stroudsburg, Pa.: Dowden, Hutchinson and Ross, 1974, pp. 130–146.

Groat, Linda, and David Canter. "A Study of Meaning: Does Post-Modernism Communicate?" *Progressive Architecture* 60, no. 12, 84–87.

Hershberger, Robert G. "Predicting the Meaning of Architecture." In Jon Lang et al., eds., op. cit., pp. 147–156.

Lasswell, Harold D., with the collaboration of Merritt B. Fox. *The Signature of Power: Buildings, Communications, Policy.* New Brunswick, N.J.: Transaction Books, 1979.

Norberg-Schulz, Christian. *Meaning in Western Architecture.* New York: Praeger, 1975.

Rapoport, Amos. *The Meaning of the Built Environment: A Non-Verbal Communications Approach.* Beverly Hills, Ca.: Sage, 1982.

Rykwert, Joseph. "Meaning and Building." In *The Necessity of Artifice.* New York: Rizzoli, 1982, pp. 9–16.

Venturi, Robert, Denise Scott Brown, and Steven Izenour. *Learning from Las Vegas.* Cambridge, Mass.: MIT Press, 1977 (revised edition).

PART III

NORMATIVE ENVIRONMENTAL DESIGN THEORY

POLEMICS AND PRACTICE

Normative theory in environmental design is concerned with both the professed and the practiced positions that architects, urban designers, landscape architects, and others take and have taken on these questions: What are good designed environments? What attitudes should designers have? What should be the nature of the design process? In this segment of the book, the focus of attention is with that area of theory for the design professions shown in the following diagram:

	Orientation of Theory	
Subject Matter of Theory	*Positive*	*Normative*
Procedural		
Substantive		

This is the traditional domain of theory for the environmental design professions, although the explicit concern has been with substantive rather than procedural issues. The behavioral sciences can make a major contribution to an understanding of the normative stances that different designers and schools of architecture, landscape architecture, and urban design have taken toward the development of a science of design ideologies. As stated at the outset of this book, this does not mean that any normative design theory can be scientific or even quasi-scientific, but that the ideas and positions taken by designers can be studied, described, and explained scientifically (to the extent that the behavioral sciences can be scientific), even though this is often very difficult. The objective of developing an explicit and rigorous body of knowledge about the normative positions that designers have taken and are taking is simply to enable us to understand ourselves, our attitudes, and our actions and so give clarity to the potential normative roles and positions we might select.

The nature of the self-consciously designed built environment depends on a variety of factors. Among them is the need of design professionals to shape values in order to attain their own ideals. Their ability to do this depends not only on their own knowledge and skills, but also on the marketplace. The processes of profit and loss, supply and demand, costs and benefits, and commercial and institutional rules are reflected in urban design and architecture. Similarly, the nature of the technology available affects built form. The availability of steel, electricity, refrigeration, and new heating systems has had a major impact on what architects have created. Some architects have quickly absorbed new technologies into their work while others have sided with handicraftsmen. Some architects have allied themselves with the pure fine arts tradition and others with architecture as one of the serving professions. In some societies, climate and topography—the natural factors of the geographic environment

—exert a predominant influence on the shape of buildings and cities, while in other societies the geographic environment is less important.

Since the Industrial Revolution the work of designers has been less constrained by the traditional factors controlling their work. Rather than making the designer's task easier, this has made it more difficult because the number of choices of how to build has increased considerably as have the activities to be housed and the range of aesthetic values of the populations who are clients of the designer's work. Any specific building, building complex, or system of open spaces represents some balance of the impact of all these factors on the designer.

The objective here is not to describe the ideologies of individual designers or schools of design thought, but rather to identify the current thinking on the values that underlie and thus distinguish the work of different designers. If one can differentiate the attitudes that distinguish the work of one designer from that of another, then one can understand the potentials and the limitations of the behavioral sciences in explicating and clarifying the various normative stances that have existed in the past and the stances that now coexist.

Each designer has a set of values. Some designers deviate more than others from the norms of their era. Some are tastemakers and pacesetters; others are followers. Within one societal and professional culture, the work of some architects and schools of thought is easier to recognize than others. Differences in style manifest differences in perceptions of what the concerns of architecture are and the pattern preferences of the designers themselves. Johnson, Wright, Kahn, Le Corbusier, Alto, Mies van der Rohe, and countless other less-well-sung

and often less self-congratulatory architects were contemporaries. They have designed buildings in the same cities for similar purposes, yet their designs are startlingly different. Analyses of these differences have long been the heart of architectural theory and have provided models for practitioners and students alike.

It has been difficult to imagine the application of empirical research and/or theories from the behavioral sciences in the analysis of the work of designers. One of the objectives of this part of the book is to show that this is occurring and that it promises much in enhancing our understanding. This discussion of normative theory is divided into two parts. Chapter 20, "Understanding the Normative Theories of Environmental Design," is concerned with describing the attitudinal differences that are reflected in a designer's work and the contribution of the behavioral sciences to further elucidating them. Some of these attitudes are those of the broader society, some are those of the design professions, and some are those of the individual designer. It is clear that designs would be different even if every designer had the same understanding of positive theory. Goals are not established scientifically or even rationally, but our knowledge of the world does affect the decisions we make. This book would have no purpose if that were not so. This is shown in chapter 21, "Current Sociophysical Issues in Environmental Design: a Normative Stance," which describes some of the subjects of debate on what the normative positions of designers should be. The two chapters thus show what seems to be a basis for describing the value positions of designers and some of the issues that have to be faced in designing new value positions. ∎

20

UNDERSTANDING NORMATIVE THEORIES OF ENVIRONMENTAL DESIGN

Many actions in the world are dictated by perceptions of how they *ought* to be done. The action is the behavioral correlate of an attitude. Social scientists have positions on how research should be carried out and what good research is. These positions are used to evaluate how research has been done and the direction it should take in the future. While there may be a generally agreed-upon ethos that guides these positions, one can identify a variety of positions taken by different social scientists. Similarly, the action-oriented professions have normative positions on the processes and end products of their work. This is reflected in what they do.

The normative statements of designers are, by definition, value-full. There are two types of normative statements made by designers: verbal statements of their ideological positions and the projects they design. Sometimes there is a high coincidence between the two and at other times not. Many environmental designers are reluctant to specify verbally what their ideological positions are; they take the position that their "designs speak for themselves."

It is not always clear what is the nature of the values underlying the statements or work of an environmental designer or why one designer follows a particular direction rather than another. The reasons are likely to be highly complex because personalities are complex and because working environments differ from one designer to another. We know less than we are wont to believe about the objectives that many designers have set for themselves and why certain themes occur in their work.

Each normative position of an architect, landscape architect, or urban designer consists, consciously or unconsciously, of a series of deontological statements which, when applied to practice, can be seen in the designs that result. A well-known example of such a set is Frank Lloyd Wright's tenets of good house design which guided (or, perhaps, explained) his designs during his prolific Oak Park period between the years 1893 and 1913:

> First—
> To reduce the number of necessary parts of the house and the separate rooms to a minimum, and make all come together as enclosed space—so divided that light, air and vista permeate the whole with a sense of unity.
>
> . . . .
>
> Ninth—
> Eliminate the decorator. He was all curves and efflorescence if not all period. (Wright 1960)

A collection of such statements by architects of the first half of the twentieth century has been ably as-

Much of this chapter was prepared for a forthcoming issue of *Environment and Behavior* on political behavior and design, edited by Andrew Seidel.

1

2

3

20-1. The Work of an Architect is the Behavioral Correlate of His or Her Normative Theory.
Buildings reflect the perceptions and values of those who designed them and those for whom they are designed. These three examples of the work of Frank Lloyd Wright during his Oak Park period reflect his stated tenets of good house design. Or do his basic tenets reflect his house design?

sembled by Ulrich Conrad (1970) who calls them "programs and manifestoes." At least implicit in the work of every architect is such a set of beliefs.

Some normative statements specify design objectives rather than design patterns. A recent example of such a statement appears in the National Endowment for the Arts Guidelines for Research Applications:

> Professionals in the field have suggested that a liveable community offers an environment that: stimulates the development of the physical, mental and spiritual potential of individuals; provides a sense of security, pride, privacy, community, vitality; is on a scale in keeping with human needs rather than the needs of machines or computer-compiled statistics;

encourages a harmonious relationship between nature and everything that is built; helps conserve energy and our natural resources . . .

Such statements are not scientific ones but normative ones based on a set of values and thus a vision of a good world.

ASCERTAINING THE NORMATIVE POSITIONS OF ENVIRONMENTAL DESIGNERS

There are, as just noted, two basic sources to use in ascertaining the normative positions of individual designers and schools of thought: their verbal statements and their buildings and/or urban designs. From Vitruvius to Venturi, many architects have stated their normative positions in writing. Changes over time in these positions can be evaluated in terms of changes in the content and nature of verbal statements as well as by changes in the character of the works they have designed.

In taking designers' writings as statements of their normative positions two problems have to be recognized. The first is that the writings are often at such a high level of generality that, although they may characterize the thinking of the designers of an era, it is difficult to differentiate between the thinking of individual designers. The second is that there is frequently a discrepancy between the professed position of a designer and his or her position in practice. In some recent writings on modern architecture, it has been suggested that there is little or no correspondence between the two (see, for example, Gadamer 1976, 1982). While this position does not seem tenable (Eslami 1985), discrepancies between what is said and what is done frequently do exist.

Discrepancies between what architects say is good architecture and what they actually design can arise for a number of reasons: (1) the professed statements and the practiced work are for different audiences; (2) the architect was unable to get his or her professed position accepted in the marketplace; (3) the professed position was developed before the attempt to implement it, and the architectural consequences of holding such a position were not foreseen; (4) the architect consciously or unconsciously treated the verbal position and actions as independent of each other; (5) the architect did not possess the intellectual or design skills to achieve what he or she was seeking; and, possibly (6) the architect was deliberately misleading in his or her written or oral statements. Perhaps a seventh reason is the most important: architects have a highly ambiguous and imprecise vocabulary for describing their intentions and work. Thus, words such as "organic," "dynamic," "function," "pure," "honest," have a number of meanings or, possibly, as George Orwell (1954) argued, no meaning.

Architects like to think of themselves as individualists, and this is certainly their popular image (see Rand 1968, Saint 1983, Prak 1984). Their values are shaped by many forces, however. While most buildings clearly do bear the hallmark of their creators, a study of architectural history also indicates that what an architect does is very much affected by the nature of the society of which he or she is a part. Major revolutions in architectural design are correlated with the emergence of new social organizations (societal and professional), new types of

clients, a revision in values and thus changes in the perception of the purposes of the built environment, and an architect or set of architects who are anxious to develop new design patterns with new materials and/or new technologies.

If one traces the changes in architecture from the Romanesque to the Gothic to the Renaissance and ultimately to the Modern Movement, one sees that the changes followed major changes in the power structure of society with the concomitant arrival of new types of patrons, new professional roles, and new world views (Eaton 1969). Each new movement is based on some model of man, some belief about the nature of the natural and social worlds and the interaction between them. While the work of all the environmental design professions is governed largely by the society of which they are a part, we recognize the work of individual designers by the configurations, or patterns, they use. Each act of design implies that a decision has been made about a problem and the means to solve it. This requires the application of a value to the prediction of the performance of a pattern or set of patterns.

It is not always clear what is the nature of the values underlying the statements of a designer, or why a designer uses one set of patterns rather than another. The reasons are likely to be highly complex, having to do with individual differences between designers in personality and culture and the working environments in which they find themselves.

APPROACHES TO STUDYING THE NORMATIVE VALUES OF ENVIRONMENTAL DESIGNERS

In the past, few analyses of the normative theories of designers went very far beyond the descriptive level. More recently some effort has been made to get beyond mere descriptions of buildings, programs, and manifestoes to explain: (1) why an architect or school of architecture focused on certain variables rather than others, (2) why some designs were considered to be important and others not, (3) what the role of the client was, and (4) the world view implicit or explicit in the results obtained. In doing so, these analyses draw on a variety of models of socialization, human personality, and motivation.

There are several approaches to the study of normative theories in the design disciplines. Some rely on the introspective analyses of designers themselves, some on the interpretive analysis of the designer's work, especially if the designer is dead and/ or has not talked or written much about it; some use psychoanalytic techniques, and some rely on interviews with and observations of the designer at work.

Most of the research on the normative theories of artists, architects, and schools of art or architecture has been conducted by architectural and art historians rather than behavioral scientists. While the *Journal of Aesthetics and Art Criticism* contains many such studies, the journals with a social science orientation have very few. There are two reasons for this: first, the subject has not attracted behavioral scientists; second, it is impossible to conduct attitudinal research using interview techniques, for instance, on architects of the past. Autobiographies have proven to be a valuable source of information on the lives and beliefs of architects but have been less valuable in the design fields where professionals have written even less. Each of the sources and approaches used to identify and explain the normative positions of designers has its strengths and weaknesses.

Historical research is biased by the material available—by what has survived. Autobiographies rely on recollections of past experiences, sometimes decades old. These are subject to errors of memory —selective retention—at best, and can be extraordinarily self-serving at the worst. Frank Lloyd Wright's portrayals of his relationships with his clients have been shown by diligent, partly empirical, research to have been much warmer than he presents them in his own writings (Eaton 1969). Le Corbusier portrayed himself as a loner who did not read very much. An analysis of his colleagues' participation in his work and the annotations he made in the books of his voluminous library show that the view he presented of himself to the world is misleading (Turner 1977). The reasons for these discrepancies are unclear but presumably they have to do with the image architects want to have of themselves and/or the image they want others to have of them (Saint 1983).

Another problem with traditional art-history approaches to the study of the development of normative theories in the design fields is that art-history approaches are theoretically weak. This is particularly true in the area of attitude-formation and in understanding the informal political nature of the act of design (see Cranz 1982). This represents not only a bias in the art-history approach to the study of normative theory but also the difficulty of doing research on past positions. Despite these difficulties, the art-history approach and the writings and public pronouncements of designers remain the basic sources of information on their normative positions.

Some designers, however, make few oral or written statements about their design goals or beliefs, and those they do make often are not recorded. Of the modern architectural masters, for instance, Alvar Aalto wrote very little, although some of his speeches have been recorded. The motives behind the making or not making of such statements need to be understood. Those who produce rationalizations of their work have diverse motives. A major one is to promote or justify one's position to one's peers and/or one's clients. Other reasons might be to promulgate a specific thesis or to achieve certain political ends.

There are also reasons for *not* making explicit statements. One is that there is no demand to clarify one's position. Another is that silence is helpful in maintaining a professional mystique. In addition, exposing one's value position to society requires considerable psychic energy and can be a very stressful experience. Such exposures open one to criticism.

Despite all these problems, it is possible to make a list of the variables that differentiate the position of one environmental designer from another.

VARIABLES DIFFERENTIATING ONE NORMATIVE POSITION FROM ANOTHER

The first step in building an explicit body of normative theory of the design professions is to understand the variables that enable the position of one designer to be differentiated from another. There is much that we do know about designers' normative theories. While the nature of normative theory *per se* has not attracted the attention of architectural or landscape architectural historians, there has been considerable speculation and some partly empirical research on the positions architects have taken. This enables us to make a generalized statement on our present understanding.

A designer's world view is the basis for his or her normative position on design. One is seldom aware of one's own world view or that of one's culture—professional or societal—until confronted by another one. Even within a single overriding culture, the visions of a good world differ considerably. Thus, in urban design, for instance, the proposals of architects based in France—Yona Friedman, Michael Ragon, and Le Corbusier are very different from one another (Rapoport 1977). To some extent, each is a product of the society of which he is a part. To some extent each is unique. Each has his own view of what a good city is. Each has his own political orientation.

Recent research and conjecture suggest the basic variables that constitute a designer's professional world view. These consist of a series of attitudes, partially reinforcing each other but sometimes conflicting and thus unstable, toward phenomena and processes. Each attitude represents a belief about how a particular phenomenon works and a value toward it. Identifying the characteristics of the attitudes of architects on each variable enables a comparison of their positions to be made with some clarity.

Attitudes Toward the Societal Culture

Each designer is a member of two cultures—a broader *societal culture* and a *professional culture*. These are not independent cultures. The way the land is laid out, the place of buildings on it, the characteristics of the buildings, and the processes of design are affected by both.

The attitude of individual designers toward their societal culture is important in shaping their work. Some environmental designers are comfortable with the culture of which they are a part; others want to change it. In the case of a society like the United States, it is difficult to understand what is meant by "American culture" and to understand what aspects of it individual designers like and dislike. Wilbur Zelinsky (1973) has identified some major aspects of American culture that distinguish it from others. These are reflected in the design of both cities and buildings. Thomas Saarinen (1976) summarizes them as follows:

- an intense, almost anarchistic individualism
- a high value placed on mobility
- a mechanistic vision of the world
- a messianic perfectionism.

Building and urban designs within the mainstream of recent American culture are characterized by a high degree of privacy, territorial control, ease of accessibility (by automobile), and individual symbolism.

These values are reflected in the Levittowns of the country (Popenoe 1977) and in the proposals of architects such as Frank Lloyd Wright. His Broadacre City (1945) reflects Wright's belief in Jeffersonian democracy and his strong antiurban bias (White and White 1964). On the other hand, many designers do not particularly care for the strong individualism of American society and have produced idealized schemes that are a reaction to it. Paul and Percival Goodman's *Communitas*, as its name suggests, reflects a belief that strong, tightly knit communal organizations are good (Goodman and Goodman 1947). Here the Goodmans, like Wright, were taking a strong political stance. Many designers, however, do not like to state openly their positions on the nature of society. In practice they often

are forced to compromise their beliefs in order to get work, and, as dissonance theory (Festinger 1957) explains, this is not something that people care to acknowledge even unconsciously.

In order to get work designers often end up supporting the status quo. Their livelihood depends largely on political stability and economic growth. They are the "soft cops" enforcing the orders of the ruling class through design (R. Goodman 1971). Thus, Mies van der Rohe gave support to National Socialism in Germany at a time when he was awarded a commission to design the Reichs Bank in 1933 (Jencks 1971). South African architects who are totally opposed to apartheid have been designing racially segregated facilities for years.

Designers whose work is unacceptable to the powers that be may overcome this by arguing that it represents something desirable and even nationalistic. In this century this argument was more successful in Nazi Germany than in the Soviet Union. When the Nazis came to power in Germany in 1933, Walter Gropius and other leading architects of the Bauhaus tried to justify modern architecture in nationalistic terms—its Germanness (Jencks 1971). Interestingly, the Gestalt theory of perception in psychology, whose development parallels the development of architectural aesthetics in Germany, also was appealing on the same patriotic grounds (Overy 1969). The Rationalist and Constructivist movements in Soviet architecture in the postrevolutionary era, however, found that their concepts were totally unacceptable to Stalin, even though they were trying to express in their work the development of a new society (Senkevitch 1974).

The structure of the built environment can be understood only within the economic system, the judicial system, and the political system of which it is a part. The power of architects and planners is also delimited by these. The commercial strip development along highways outside cities in the United States can be understood only in terms of these variables. The strip has been labeled a "visual slum" by many people, but it is the architectural correlate of an economic and social system. Some architects (such as Goodman 1971, Venturi, Scott Brown, and Izenour 1977) recognize this. One's attitude toward the strip depends on one's attitude toward the nature of society, as balance theory (Heider 1946) and dissonance theory (Festinger 1957) in psychology, as argued earlier, would suggest (see also Lang 1982). Robert Goodman (1971) is forthright on the topic:

> Venturi . . . takes the products of a sick social order (an order which he himself dislikes) and says that by aesthetically interpreting them as a new visual order

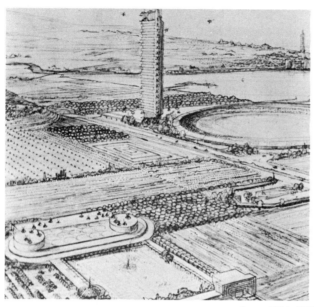

1   Source: Wright (1958)

2   Source: Hayden (1976)

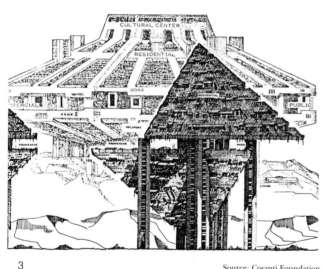

3   Source: Cosanti Foundation

20-2. World Views and Urban Design.
Broadacre City (1), designed by Frank Lloyd Wright, reflects a belief in Jeffersonian democracy as an ideal for
American society. The emphasis is on individualism, private ownership, and mobility. The Oneida complex with
its communal buildings (such as 2) reflects John Humphrey Noyes's comment on the dedication of the Mansion
House: "Communism has made itself a home." Paolo Soleri's proposal for a city (3) falls between the other two.
Much greater emphasis is placed on communality than in
Broadacre City and on much greater privacy than in the
Oneida community. All three schemes are based on clear,
but different, images of what a good society and good
human behavior are.

outside the context of how they are used we can learn
to enjoy them. What he doesn't do is go the next
logical step in the argument. By learning to perceive
this "garbage" through his new set of glasses, by giving it an aesthetic rationale, *the society is being immu-
nized against the causes which presented the banalities in
the first place.* Why bother to fight the capitalist interests that produced the blighted landscape when an
architecture which assails your visual sense at every
turn can be seen as an "architecture of bold communication rather than a subtle persuasion."

Whether one accepts or rejects the strip because it
is not well ordered in traditional architectural or
Gestalt psychological terms depends on one's world
view. There often has been a tension between the

architect's view of an ideal society and the view implicit, if not explicit, in that society's behavior.

In addition to the societal culture, most designers participate in a professional culture. The concept of "architect" or "landscape architect" or
"urban designer" is important because it gives the
designer a self-image. There is, for example, a
broad image of what an architect should be like that
is often in conflict with the reality of the work situation. The admired image is that of the architect as
an artist fighting for his ideals (for example, see
Rand 1968). The reality is often more mundane
(Saint 1983, Blau 1984).

The concept of architect and the concept of an
architectural profession, as we know them today,

are mainly nineteenth-century phenomena coinciding with the development of the Industrial Revolution and the increasing specialization of occupations. Professional organizations developed during the latter part of the century in response to the desire to control a market for their members who had some specific expertise (Larson 1979). This is true of architecture. The history of the architectural profession is also a history of its struggle for legitimacy and of its efforts to define its area of expertise and control entry into the profession (S. Dostoglu 1982). The other design fields have had a similar experience.

In some countries almost all the buildings are architect-designed; in others, almost none are. This has to do with the state of technological development in the country and its overall social organization. The appearance of the environment has much to do with whether or not it was and is professionally designed. Through their formal education, professional designers are taught that certain designs are good and others bad. Often these positions have differed from those held by the broader society (Michelson 1968). This partially accounts for the cultural insensitivity that designers have displayed during the course of this century (see Brolin 1976, Wolfe 1981).

The standards set by schools of environmental design reflect and shape the values of the professions. The professions, in turn, through the presentation of awards and the conducting of competitions, shape and are shaped by their members. There is considerable pressure to conform to the professional norms of a period in terms of style and content of design (Montgomery 1966). Some architects break away from this and manage to set new trends, often after a period of considerable criticism from their peers; others may establish a reputation for idiosyncratic designs but establish no trends (Prak 1984). The former can be seen in the recent work of architects such as Robert Venturi and Michael Graves. In contrast, the work of Bruce Goff, while often much lauded by architects, set no new direction. One of the factors that distinguishes the work of one designer from the work of others is the degree to which the designer is prepared to deviate from standard professional ideology in dealing with clients, addressing problems, and developing patterns to solve them.

Attitudes Toward People

The concepts of people—the "models of man" —that are used as a basis for design very much affect the image of what a good world is in the mind of the designer and thus they affect the character of the built environment that ensues. The views designers hold of the nature of their clients and their attitudes toward them depend very much on the way the society to which they belong views those people and the obligations it has toward them. In the Introduction to this book it was noted that much of the ideology of the Modern Movement in housing design was based on what Isreal and Tajfel (1972) call an *organismic* model of man (Stringer 1980). In this model the physiological character of the human organism is stressed. The whole range of human needs is reduced to a few universal, constant, physiological requirements. This image has been contrasted to a *role* model emphasizing human activities in a social system, and to a *relational* model emphasizing social relationships, and to a *self-actualizing* model that stresses the need for people to achieve what they are capable of achieving (Maslow 1954). While lip service frequently is paid to social and cultural needs as a basis for design (that is, it is part of an architect's manifesto), the organismic model is often the basis for design. This was true of much of the ideology of the Bauhaus (see Meyer 1928) but less true of the urban design, landscape architecture, and architecture of people such as Henry Wright and Clarence Stein (see Stein 1957).

Issues of territoriality, privacy, social interaction, and symbolic aesthetics, for example, simply are not considered when an organismic model of man is used as a basis for housing design. The same is true in the design of other types of buildings and urban areas (see Parr 1967a, Rapoport 1967, Perin 1970, Lang et al. 1974, Blake 1974, Brolin 1976, Fitch 1979, Wolfe 1981). It is also noteworthy that the model of man implicit in the manifestoes of the early congresses of CIAM (Congrès Internationaux d'Architecture Moderne) in the 1930s was an organismic and role model. There was consensus in drafting these manifestoes, but as the model of man implicit in the discussion about design goals in the post–World War II era shifted to a relational and self-actualizing emphasis, controversies arose. Team 10 broke away from CIAM and CIAM soon dissolved (see Smithson 1968). With the rise of Post-Modernism has come an increased concern with the symbolic nature of the built environment—the model of man as a relational one—but there is very little evidence of any systematic concern with a broader model of man and a broader concern with human issues.

Attitudes Toward Nature

In the Western world, the way land is used and buildings are designed relates closely to the Judeo-Christian tradition. This is particularly true in the attitude displayed toward the natural world. The prevailing attitude has been that man has dominance over nature. Some Eastern philosophies, in contrast, see man as part of nature. There are many examples in both the East and West, however, where the correspondence between philosophical stances and actions cannot be discerned.

The traditional Japanese garden was designed to provide the occupant of the house with a view. The view is something to contemplate. In Western society the garden often is regarded as a setting for activities and/or as a demarcator of territory or as a ground against which to view the house. In the Japanese garden, trees are used to give an illusion of depth so the larger ones are placed near the house and the smaller ones farther away; in the West, trees are used as a backdrop for the house or as a means of creating a sense of enclosure (Eliovson 1971). Such generalizations describe different philosophies, but within Eastern and Western settings there is considerable variability in what is practiced.

Countries as diverse as the United States, the Soviet Union, India, and South Africa contain many subcultures each with its own attitudes toward the natural environment and elements of that environment, such as trees. These attitudes are reflected in the normative positions of designers. In the United States some subgroups prefer the environment to look "natural" in the manner of the English landscape garden. Others prefer it to appear manicured in the French Baroque style. The people of some subcultures like trees; others regard them as a nuisance. Environmental designers also display a wide variety of attitudes toward the natural environment and how it should be integrated into the city—or, as Le Corbusier argued, how the city should be integrated into the natural environment.

While the Judeo-Christian attitude toward nature has been largely exploitive, there are differences in the manner of exploitation within this ethic. The English landscape reflects a concern for appearance and amenity, while the American landscape has been exploited in a more directly instrumental way for profit (Lowenthal and Prince 1965, Lowenthal 1968). There has been a strong response to this attitude by many designers (such as Ian McHarg's ecological view of nature in *Design with Nature* [1969] and Randolph Hester's environmental or conservation aesthetics [1975]).

Public policies toward the environment change over time to reflect people's attitudes toward it—their perceptions of how it works and how it should be used, and their values toward these (Parker 1969, Tuan 1974, Saarinen 1976). In the Soviet Union, for example, there have been significant changes in policy concerning the natural environment since the October Revolution of 1917. These reflect the attitudes of those in power at the time. Lenin's view of Marxist doctrine led to public policies concerned with local ecology after the revolution. Under Stalin, however, with the strong push toward central government and its promotion through development, the focus of effort was to get things done—get new towns built and large engineering schemes such as dams constructed. The resulting public policies very much exploited the natural environment. Architects, engineers, and landscape architects had to work within this policy framework. This parallels the movement from Rationalism and Constructivism to Social Realism in Soviet architecture (see Senkevitch 1974).

The attitude of the design professions toward the natural elements of the world and their attitudes toward people are interwoven. Galen Cranz (1982) has shown how attitudes toward people and nature are reflected in the successive eras of park design in the United States: the Pleasure Ground, the Reform Park, the Recreation Facility, and the Open-Space System.

Many writers (such as Jackson 1951) have stated that exposure to the natural elements of the landscape is important for man's well-being and happiness. These statements are highly polemical and are based as much on a normative view of human life as on scientific evidence. With very little systematic research on such topics it is difficult to assess the effect of such exposure on people's psychological well-being. It is thus difficult to assess the claims made for positions such as that of Jackson.

Attitudes Toward the Built Environment

Designers' attitudes toward the built environment are allied closely to their attitudes toward people. There are two aspects to this: (1) beliefs about how the built environment works and affects people, and (2) values about the concerns of the design professions.

The built environment serves many purposes. In this book Maslow's model of human motivations and needs has been used in considering the range of needs which the built environment can, at least partially, supply. At the outset, other ways of considering the built environment were discussed (Vitruvius, Norberg-Schulz, Steele). Similarly, an approach to the relationship between environment and behavior based on environmental perception and cognition has been accepted here as the one with greatest external validity in comparison to other views. There are many overlaps among all these views, but there are also different beliefs about how patterns of the built environment afford different human behaviors and aesthetic experiences.

There are several theories about how people perceive, think about, like, and behave in the built environment and in the natural environment. For instance, the Bauhaus theory of aesthetics, it has been argued here, is closely allied to Gestalt theories of perception. Whether a designer consciously or unconsciously accepts or rejects this view biases his or her view of how buildings and open spaces work and thus his or her view of the nature of the aesthetic experience (see Lang 1982, 1983). Similarly, there are different explanations of how people use space and the degree to which the built environment is coercive in dictating behavior (Lipman 1974).

The focus of concern of an environmental designer also will be evident in his or her work. All buildings, provided they do not collapse, perform to some extent on all the basic dimensions of architectural concern, but different architects emphasize different aspects. There have been various statements on what the primary concerns of architecture should be. There are many slogans: "form follows function," a building "should be true to materials," it "should be honest," it "should contribute to architecture itself." These reflect what architects believe to be the essence of architecture, although often the statements are open to many interpretations. Sometimes the aspects of architectural concern that an architect regards as central to his or her work are idiosyncratic, but they usually reflect the concerns of an era or a school of architectural thought. Nevertheless, one can differentiate the work of the Modernists and the work of individual Modernists on the basis of the patterns—spatial, structural, and façadal and the interactions among them—that they use consistently in response to the problems they define as worth solving. Robert Venturi (1966) quotes Paul Rudolf to reinforce this point:

> . . . architects are highly selective in determining which problems they want to solve. Mies, for instance, makes wonderful buildings only because he ignores many aspects of a building. If he solved more problems, his buildings would be far less potent.

Attempts to understand architects' normative positions have to deal with the apparent contradictions between the architects' statements about what they admire and what they actually design and build. While Venturi agrees with Rudolf that Mies's buildings are wonderful, he also says that he himself is opposed to the attitude they represent:

> [An architect] can exclude important considerations only at risk of separating architecture from life and the needs of society. If some problems prove insoluble he can express this; in an inconclusive rather than an exclusive architecture there is room for the fragment, for contradiction, for improvisation, and for the tensions these produce.

It must be recognized that Mies believed he was addressing central issues in building design and meeting the needs of society.

Different designers emphasize different things (Prak 1984). Some stress the interrelatedness of the concerns of architecture; some deal with them as independent issues. James Marston Fitch (1979) sees the latter as the trend in the work of many architects today. The environmental designers held in the highest esteem by the profession are those who have presented convincing arguments for the set of problems they consider to be the most important and for the patterns they use in addressing them. The variables chosen by many architects do seem, as Venturi fears, to separate architecture from life. Douglas Porteous (1971) notes this in quoting the words that Graham Greene puts into the mouth of his character, the architect Querry, in *A Burnt-Out Case* (1963): "I wasn't concerned with the people who occupied my space—only with the space." Querry's concern with his own values and attitudes toward formal aesthetics reflects one public image of the architect—that of a sculptor concerned primarily with his own views of the aesthetics of shape. This position is reflected in some of the "clientless" abstract conceptual architecture currently being practiced, as exemplified by Peter Eisenman's numbered houses (Eisenman 1977).

Recently, with the development of the Post-Modern school of architecture has come a self-conscious concern with the symbolic aesthetics of the built environment. Here the work of different architects can be recognized by the referents that they believe are important; some (such as Graves) rely heavily on classical Italian referents, others on French. Paralleling this concern with the creation of more lively appearances for buildings has been a concern with the creation of livable and lively places (see Whyte 1980). Both of these concerns are responses to the tenets of the Modern Movement and to the criticism of observers such as Jane Jacobs (1961) who feared that economic forces combined with the design principles of the Modernists were turning cities into boring places.

The attitude that designers have toward different aspects of architecture is closely related to their attitudes toward people. Whether individuals are seen as such or as parts of the mass is reflected in design. These attitudes are reflected also in designers' attitudes toward the design process.

1

2

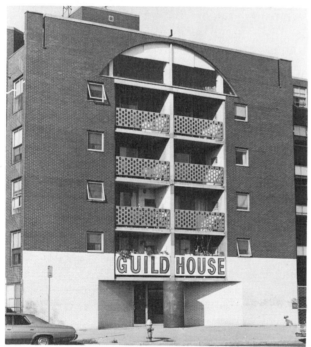

3

20-3. The Aesthetics of Post-Modernism.

Post-Modern buildings are distinguishable by the referents used by their architects in composing them. The AT&T Building (1) has referents to Serlio's work at the base and to "Chippendale" at the top. The building of the University of Louvain-la-Neuve in Brussels (2) has allusions to a hill town but also reflects its architect's belief about the changeability of the elements of a building as its inhabitants change. The residential building for the elderly in (3) reflects its architect's position that historical precedents adapted to new conditions are important referents in buildings. The attitudes of an observer toward these buildings depend on the referents perceived by that person and the attitude that he or she has toward the relationship between the referent and the building.

Attitudes Toward the Design Process

Almost all designers recognize the importance of intuition in the design process; almost all designers recognize that the process consists of a number of discrete activities. The arguments arise over the degree to which the process can be and should be operated in a systematic fashion and the degree to which its should be based on a program or on a paradigm (Rowe 1983). Since much current practice is carried out in an unselfconscious manner, designers find it difficult to articulate what they feel the process should be. The basic differences in the normative positions of designers seem to arise over (1) how the process is and/or should be structured, (2) what the relationship between client and professional should be, and (3) what specific methods, or techniques, of analysis, synthesis, and evaluation should be used. These are interrelated issues.

The Overall Structure of the Design Process

Some architects believe that the design process should be operated as far as possible in a linear fashion with a thorough programming process prior to the major design effort. Others believe that programming should be done cursorily because the act of designing brings problems to light. Some believe that explicit systematic procedures should be used throughout the process to display it to all concerned; others believe that this is a waste of time and that common sense is all that is needed (Bazjanac 1974).

Many prominent architects have claimed that it is pointless to focus heavily on analytical activities. There is considerable anecdotal if not scientific evidence that some of those who profess this most loudly have been very thorough analysts of problem situations. People who are perceived as form-givers and/or pattern-makers might better be seen as problem-redefiners. Shifts in normative positions from one era to another reflect shifts in perceptions about the problems of design as much as a shift in forms used. Other arguments arise over the usefulness of generating more than one potential design solution at a time; that is, should the evaluating activity be separated from the activities of design? Still other arguments arise over the nature of the evaluation of schemes—for example, should the traditional intuitive and argumentative process of evaluation by architectural juries be replaced by systematic approaches such as cost-benefit studies? The basic issue is that there are different opinions as to how systematic and open the design process can be and should be made. The conflict is reflected in the distinction, noted earlier, that Horst Rittel (1972) made between first- and second-generation models of the design process.

First-generation models of the process reflect the position that design can and should be carried out in a logical and rational fashion by experts (architects and other design professionals), while in the second-generation models designing is regarded as an argumentative or learning process (Bazjanac 1974). Implicit in all this are different positions on the roles of the designer and the client.

The Professional-Client Relationship

The work of environmental designers is almost invariably carried out for a client other than themselves. Frequently there is a multiplicity of clients. These include the ultimate users of a building, landscape design, or urban design, its sponsors (Zeisel 1974), and the public, whose interests are represented in the rules and regulations imposed by society on the building form and structure. Sometimes the sponsor and the user are the same person, but often the sponsor is a committee or a public agency which is organizing the design and construction of a facility on behalf of some other people. The "public interest," as perceived by the designer or his other clients, may also be a hidden client. The peer group of both designers and clients may act in a similar fashion as a potent force that is considered, consciously or unconsciously, as a "client" whose values have to be met. Each building reflects, to a greater or lesser extent, the values of the different client groups. The more powerful clients—often those controlling the financial resources—are the ones whose values are most clearly reflected or the ones who say whose values should be reflected. Designers' power comes from their expertise, their reputation, and their ability to argue effectively.

Alan Lipman (1974) points out that when an architect is sponsoring his own work "a relationship between artist as a professional specialist and a client is a *sine qua non* of the process." Beyond this situation there have been a number of positions taken on what the professional-client relationship should be (see, for instance, Pawley 1971, Goodman 1971, Mitchell 1974). There have also been a number of historical studies of how the present relationship emerged (Kaye 1960, Jenkins 1961, Ackerman 1969).

Until World War I, the design professional, an architect for instance, typically enjoyed the patronage of a wealthy client. With the Industrial Revolution and the rise of both capitalism and socialism and the development of professional organizations, the situation changed. Architects today seldom design for a patron of the arts. More frequently, particularly in socialist societies, they are designing for the "masses" with some sponsor being in control of the designing and building process. When patronage prevailed, architects and clients had similar social backgrounds, although there may have been a difference of status. Architects were in a position to understand the character of the activities and aesthetic values of their clients; often these were shared.

James Ackerman (1969) suggests that there are two polar opposite ways in which architects can and do relate to their clients. Some architects are egotists and others are pragmatists. A pragmatist takes the view that the architect should "give-'em-what-they-say-they-want," while the egotist takes the view that he or she should "give-'em-what-I-want" or "give-'em-what-I-think-is-good-for-'em." Clients in the former group tend to be interested mainly in the short run economic viability of a building. The result is an architecture of "fashionable modernism" or something highly eclectic. Ackerman describes the egotistical architect as someone who

> . . . gets the less hard-headed clients . . . some discriminating, some just soft. He is the form giver our architectural schools are trying to produce (and he usually teaches them on the side)—the inheritor of the mantle of Frank Lloyd Wright, Mies van der Rohe and Le Corbusier. He and his client silently agree that a building is an isolated work of art, an inhabited sculpture . . .

The pragmatist simply listens to his client's demands, while the egotist relies on his or her own intuitions. Although there are no hard data available on which to base conclusions, most architects are probably partly pragmatists and partly egotists, depending on what dimension of architectural concern is being considered. They tend to be pragmatists when dealing with the nature of activities to be housed and egotists in dealing with aesthetic issues. There have been a number of pleas for a more collaborative relationship between client and professional (for example, Mitchell 1974, Zeisel 1981).

A collaborative relationship between a designer, a sponsor, and a set of users has a number of characteristics: programming involves the mutual setting of goals; information is shared by all those involved; the designer is explicit about his or her intentions and the positive theoretical and ideological basis for them; the designer brings the attention of the other participants to the implications of decisions regarding the objectives of the design itself and vice versa; and decisions are made on a basis of agreement. This is the usual process in the design of custom-designed houses. In carrying out such a process the designer gives up some ego gratification. Some designers are prepared for this and favor it and others are not and do not.

The positions that designers and their clients take on the nature of their roles and their relationship depend, first, on their respective self-images and their views of the social and cultural world and, second, on the environment in which professional work is carried out. George Howe put his view of clients and their impact on design quite bluntly: "Architects and dogs are as good as their masters" (Stern 1975).

Methods and Techniques

Every designer has a set of methods that he or she uses during the various phases of the designing process. These methods depend on the designer's attitudes toward the clients, the landscape, and the built environment. Schools of design can be recog-

nized as much by their modes of analysis, synthesis, and evaluation as by the products they generate. Designers of the Tendenza (or Neo-Rationalist) movement of Italy, for instance, use typologies as a basic analytical tool. The types that Aldo Rossi and Carlo Aymonino study, for instance, are those concerned with the city—the building-street relationship, the boulevard, the piazza. They use different design methods, however. Aymonino relies heavily on the application of patterns associated with the Modern Movement; Rossi relies more on the use of analogy.

Attitudes toward Technology

The attitudes that designers have toward technology and technological changes affect the nature of the buildings they design. Some architects embrace the latest technological developments, while others remain attached to technologies of the past. There seem to be four different attitudes that one can identify. Some architects regard technology as a means to an end; the architect specifies the surfaces of the desired layout and somebody else, usually an engineer, is expected to make the whole system stand up. Some architects use what appear to be advanced technologies in a symbolic way; superficially their buildings may appear to be very advanced in their use of the latest technological breakthroughs in construction and materials, but these items are largely decorative. Another position holds that technological efficiency—efficiency in terms of structural systems and materials for their purposes—is the basis for the aesthetics of building design; this is the position generally associated with the Modern Movement in design. Yet another position is that the structure of a building should be expressed and used as part of its aesthetic character; with this approach different architects display a greater or lesser degree of understanding of the nature of the structural aspects of design.

EXPLAINING THE NORMATIVE STANCES OF ENVIRONMENTAL DESIGNERS: THEIR ESSENTIALLY POLITICAL NATURE

The normative theory of any environmental designer can be described in terms of his or her stance on the variables outlined above. In conducting such an analysis, it must be remembered that the act of designing is a creative, value-laden act in which specific ends representing the values of specific people or interest groups are advocated. All designing involves some advocacy—for a set of patterns, a set of objectives, and/or a set of human needs. The evaluation of buildings, landscapes, and urban designs, however objectively it is done, is based on some value system. The design professions can exist only by providing a service to other people. It is almost inevitable that the work of individual designers is directly or indirectly in the service of those who hold power in society, either because they have the economic resources necessary to build or the political power to muster those resources. The decision to build, the objectives set, and the means chosen are based on a combination of attitudes as described above. It must not be thought, however, that designers are simply at the beck and call of those who have this power.

Designers as a body can be thought of as a special-interest group advocating special ends. This can be seen most clearly in the development of the architectural profession in the late nineteenth century in the effort to control professional services (Larson 1979, S. Dostoglu 1982) but it holds true throughout history. Each movement in architecture is essentially political in nature as it fights to get its attitudes —its beliefs and values—accepted in the marketplace and/or in the formal political arena. Sometimes this is a highly overt act that receives formal political support. An example of this was the 1932 decree that Soviet architecture should be in the style of Socialist Realism (see Senkovitch 1974), but more often it is simply the bold advocacy of ends over a period of time in order to capture the attention of other designers, educational institutions, and the economically and politically powerful people in society (see Watkin 1977). This is as true of the movement from Modernism to Post-Modernism as of the movement from the Victorian era to Modernism and of the shifts that took place before that. It is not surprising that shifts from one era of architectural design to another have almost inevitably paralleled a shift in the power structure of society. We do not fully understand these shifts or the full nature of the change in attitudes of the profession that accompanied them. Until we do, our self-images are likely to go on being distorted.

THE POTENTIAL CONTRIBUTION OF THE BEHAVIORAL SCIENCES

This chapter is a highly descriptive one. In it, a number of dimensions of environmental design philosophy and practice that distinguish, particularly, the work of one architect or school of architectural thought from another have been identified. It has been based on an interpretive analysis of the papers cited. The chapter is theoretically weak. This reflects the weaknesses of the present literature in explanations of the normative positions of designers. There is little explanation within the design disciplines of why different professionals take different positions on the goals, procedures, and means of design, apart from saying that they perceive problems differently as a result of being educated in a particular way or, if one accepts the behaviorist view of human development, because they have received different patterns of reinforcement. One of the major contributions of the behavioral sciences is in providing methods and concepts for documenting and enhancing our understanding of how normative positions are developed. This involves coming to an understanding of the value orientation of the profession as a whole and that of individual architects toward their work, toward the people who inhabit it, and toward the social and cultural system to which they belong. This requires an understanding of the economic system and of the way the power to make decisions is distributed. It must be remembered that each new movement in the fields of design regards itself as more moral than its predecessors (Watkin 1977). Each believes it is serving the ends of society better. One of the major contributions the behavioral sciences can make to the development of design theory is in clarifying the normative positions taken by designers and explaining the reasons for those positions being taken.

There are two ways of doing this. One is by applying theoretical constructs to the analysis of normative positions; the other is by using the research methods of the behavioral sciences, particularly with reference to attitudinal development and value conflicts, in analyzing these positions (see Mayo 1984 on planners). The former approach can be applied to written statements and to the analysis of autobiographies and biographies of past designers. Interviews can be carried out only with living designers, although one important study found out about two architect's views by interviewing people who knew the architects directly or indirectly (see Eaton 1974). Personality studies of architects have been carried out to ascertain the characteristics associated with people regarded by the profession as the most creative, but these have not been done recently (for example, Barron 1965). Twenty years ago MacKinnon (1962a, 1962b) found architects, in general, to be highly cooperative in doing such studies. Whether the situation still prevails is unknown.

We have only partial knowledge of how attitudes toward nature, toward people, toward the act of intervention into the environment develop. We know little about the relationship between creativity and attitudes toward the world, even though we do know something about the attitudes required for creative problem-solving (Barron 1965). Until more systematic research is done on the normative positions architects take, either implicitly or explicitly, we will have to rely on the partial and anecdotal insights of critics such as Wolfe (1981) and Jencks (1971) and the interpretation of the statements of architects themselves (such as Le Corbusier 1923, Wright 1958). There is, however, no substitute for the information yielded by systematic empirical research (such as Eaton 1969, Turner 1977). It is also important to apply the understanding yielded by psychological research on attitude-formation to the interpretation of the positions taken by schools of thought within the design professions. It must not be thought that this will yield a value-free analysis of these positions, but it will enhance our understanding considerably.

ADDITIONAL READINGS

Conrad, Ulrich, ed. *Programs and Manifestoes on Twentieth Century Architecture.* Cambridge, Mass.: MIT Press, 1970.

Cranz, Galen. *The Politics of Park Design—A History of Urban Parks in America.* Cambridge, Mass.: MIT Press, 1982.

Eaton, Leonard K. *Two Chicago Architects and their Clients: Frank Lloyd Wright and Norman Van Doren Shaw.* Cambridge, Mass.: MIT Press, 1969.

Larson, Magali. *The Rise of Professionalism.* Berkeley and Los Angeles: University of California Press, 1979.

Mayo, James. "Conflicts in Roles and Values for Urban Planners." *Journal of Architectural and Planning Research* 1, no. 1 (June 1984): 67–78.

Mitchell, Howard. "Professional and Client: An Emerging Collaborative Relationship." In Jon Lang, et al., eds., *Designing for Human Behavior: Architecture and the Behavioral Sciences.* Stroudsburg, Pa.: Dowden, Hutchinson and Ross, 1974, pp. 15–22.

Montgomery, Roger. "Comment on 'House-as-Haven in the Lower Class.'" *Journal of the American Institute of Planners* 32, no. 1 (1966): 31–36.

Prak, Niels Luning. *Architects: The Noted and the Ignored.* New York: Van Nostrand Reinhold, 1984.

Rowe, Colin. "Program versus Paradigm." *The Cornell Journal of Architecture,* no. 2 (1982): 8–19.

Watkin, David. *Morality and Architecture.* Oxford: Clarendon Press, 1977.

Zeisel, John. "Fundamental Values in Planning with the Nonpaying Client." In Jon Lang et. al., eds., *Designing for Human Behavior: Architecture and the Behavioral Sciences.* Stroudsburg, Pa.: Dowden, Hutchinson and Ross, 1974, pp. 293–301.

Zelinsky, Wilbur. *The Cultural Geography of the United States.* Englewood Cliffs, N.J.: Prentice-Hall, 1973.

21

CURRENT SOCIOPHYSICAL ISSUES IN ENVIRONMENTAL DESIGN— A NORMATIVE STANCE

As discussed throughout this book, environmental design problems are "wicked" ones. The result is that design praxis is an argumentative process during which opposing sides can be identified on almost every question that a designer has to address. This is because decision-making is a value-laden activity, and while much unity on value positions does exist there are also many differences. The objective of this chapter is to identify current issues of concern to both designers and environmental psychologists. They are of concern to designers because the stances taken in dealing with them contribute to a designer's normative position. They should be of central interest to those environmental psychologists whose research commitment is based largely on improving the knowledge base for design rather than on enhancing the quality of psychological theory for its own sake. An enhanced knowledge base clarifies but does not resolve the issues. The resolution is political in nature.

The key question is: What should be the perimeter of concern of the design professions as a whole and of an individual designer? This is an all-embracing question. It focuses on the world view of the profession and its members. All other questions about the positions designers should take on current issues are subsidiary to this.

DESIGNERS' RESPONSIBILITIES

What are the responsibilities of the design professions? Are designers simply technicians delivering what their sponsors say they want? Are they simply fine artists whose medium is the physical and architectural form of the environment? Should they be involved in designing behavioral systems and in shaping the aesthetic values of society? If so, toward what end? There are different views on what a good behavioral system is—what a good life is. Which one should be used as the basis for design? A design based on one will not necessarily afford another. Do these issues fall within the perimeter of concern of environmental designers? Whether they like it or not, designers do take implicit stances on all these questions in their work.

There are three basic issues here. The first has to do with the degree to which environmental design professionals should become involved in establishing the behavioral program, which is the basis for establishing a building program. The second has to do with the degree to which they should become involved in establishing the objectives a design has to meet. The third has to do with the question of how far designs should be taken—the degree of control the designer has over the designed object.

There is no consensus on any of these subjects.

Different designers take different stances on these topics, and the same designer may take different stances when faced with different problem situations. The stance taken here—and the whole book is based on it—is that all designers have the social responsibility to know as much as they can about the relationship between human behavior, in all its dimensions, and the built environment so that they can participate in discussions about the behavioral program and the advantages and limitations of design options to afford it.

It must be recognized that all designers have value positions. It is advocated here that designers should understand their own value position as well as that of the design professions as a whole. It is advocated here that designers should participate in the debates regarding the design of the behavioral programs upon which building programs are designed. In doing this they must recognize the limits of their knowledge about the system under investigation.

SOCIAL CONCERNS: THE BEHAVIORAL PROGRAM

In a democratic society every designer has the right to speak out on the issues that confront that society. Most of these are social issues but many also have implications for design, and their resolution is reflected in the designed environment. Members of the environmental design professions have aligned themselves with political parties of almost every conceivable dimension from the extreme right to the extreme left. They have supported the status quo in almost every society and they have fought for social change. The important thing to remember is the limitation of the designed environment as a force in shaping society. It is also important to recognize that every act of design is a political act; some are trivial but some are major.

There are a number of social concerns which have had a direct impact on design and on which designers have taken stances. This is particularly so in architects' idealized designs of cities and neighborhoods. While ideal designs seem to have been generated from the earliest historical times, major social concerns are most readily apparent in the innumerable designs, some of which were built, generated by architects since the beginning of the Industrial Revolution. In these designs social issues have been understood to fall well within the architect's concerns.

Homogeneity and Heterogeneity of Populations, Land, and Building Uses

What is a good society? Is it one in which populations are segregated by income, stage in life cycle, ethnicity, or sex? Is it one in which there is integration on some dimensions and segregation on others? Is it one with a rich variety of behavior settings on the local level? Is it one in which market forces are allowed to dictate? Since discussion of these issues is controversial, designers usually let the market dictate. Some ideal communities have been based on a philosophy of egalitarianism; others have accepted the existing social structure of society (see Benevolo 1967, Hayden 1976).

It has been pointed out that environmental designers have limited roles as professionals in dealing with broad societal issues. In an open society people choose where they want to work and live within the limits of the resources they have available to them. Individuals and organizations hire the architects who they feel can provide buildings within the bounds of their own philosophies. Different designs do, however, afford different opportunities for integration and segregation of people and activities, even though they cannot by themselves cause it. Retirement communities, for instance, have many facilities that are attractive to a broad spectrum of people, but they have a set that is particularly attractive to the elderly. Thus, it is a decision on both what to build and how to administer it that affects the results. A broader question is whether it is good for society as a whole for such segregation, albeit self-chosen, of the middle- and upper-income elderly, to exist. In the United States it is regarded as acceptable. The position taken here is that the designer should be an advocate for the richness of experience in terms of importance to the population of concern. The designer should bring to that population's attention opportunities to create such an environment, whether it be at an urban or a building level. This advocacy tends to lead toward an integrationist stance.

Many countries have been through a period in their history when land uses were highly integrated. This was regarded as bad for health and aesthetic reasons, and policies were designed to combat it. These policies led to segregated land use—industrial, commercial, residential, and so on. The results have been liked by large segments of the population, although critics often regard such environments as dull. Advocates for mixed land use are arguing, implicitly or explicitly, for mixed populations and the liveliness of environments (for instance, Jacobs 1961). They also are advocating a change from an economic system that leads to a larger and larger scale of activities. Criticism of the built environment often is a criticism of the broader societal structure.

Individual Roles and Activity Patterns

Many changes in the roles people play in society are taking place. Gender roles are changing; occupational roles are changing; the patterns of interactions between people are changing. The structure of the family is changing. At one stage nearly all members of society were members of a traditional three-generation family or a nuclear family. Now only 35 percent of the United States population lives in such families (Moore and Hofferth, 1979). The family with a working husband and a supporting wife who stays at home to rear the children still exists but it is atypical (Smith 1979). Residential environments designed for such families no longer work as well when the nature of the family and family roles within it change. Similar observations can be made about business organizations, institutions, and communications media.

What assumptions about these changing patterns should designers make? What are good social organizations? What is a good environment for a child, a good working environment for an office worker? How much should designers get involved in such debates? Those architects, for instance, who regard architecture as a pure art say not at all. Those who do not hold this view are asking questions such as: What are the issues that are involved?

It is possible to identify a number of basic points in the debate over (1) the design of behavioral systems that should form the basis for design, and (2) the patterns that are used to fulfill the requirements of whatever behavioral system is chosen as the basis for design. It is also possible to take a stance on how to deal with these.

Behavioral Systems

Questions arise about how to predict the stability of the behavioral systems used as a basis for design; about whether one should accept a given system simply because it is stable; about who has the right to say whether it is good or bad; about who designs new systems and the degree to which the designer should be a follower or a leader.

Design Patterns

Questions arise about the stability of the mechanisms that have made patterns work in the past; about the degree to which the designer should seek novel solutions to problems that have been resolved in particular ways in the past; about how adaptable or flexible the environment should be; about where the designer should contribute his or her own ideas.

While there is no "right" answer to these questions, we know a lot about how to deal with them as a result of research and theoretical developments in the behavioral sciences. Many patterns of behavior are stable. Not all of these are regarded as socially desirable. Thus, the designer has to start off with a normative model of behavior as the basis for design. This can be generated in a number of ways. One way is simply to follow what the designer believes to be good to the extent he or she can get away with this. It is advocated here, however, that this should be done within a collaborative framework in which designers participate with other professionals, social and behavioral scientists, and clients. The issues and their architectural implications become clearer when looking at specific questions.

An Egalitarian or a Socially Hierarchical Society

This is both a social and an aesthetic issue and has been asked mainly in connection with housing design. In much of the Western world housing designs now tend to reflect the social status of their inhabitants both in terms of space and aesthetics (Chapman 1955). There is not a complete positive correlation between the two variables because social values also shape housing choice (Feldman and Tilly 1960). Thus, some people of high status may choose what are generally regarded as lower-status homes within a culture while some people of low status may spend a disproportionate amount of their incomes—given societal norms—on higher-status housing. A basic philosophical question that is being asked in a number of societies is: Should the designed environment reflect the social status of its inhabitants? This is implicitly a broader question about societal norms.

In the design of Brasília, the federal capital of Brazil, the housing type selected as policy—the slab apartment building—was chosen partially because it was thought it would be impossible to differentiate the social status of people by the external appearance of the buildings. There is a social value implicit in this position. This social value is not reflected in the designs of the Post-Modernists, who seem quite willing to accept the social structure of society as it is in the development of their design philosophies. Architecture reflects society.

The position taken here is the traditional liberal stance. An egalitarian society in which there is equal opportunity is an end for which it is worthy to strive.

This does not mean that people have to be indistinguishable. Individual tastes and emphases on what is important should be reflected in society. The symbolism of architecture should reflect both the individual and the society of which he or she is a part. This position is reflected also in stances on other societal issues that impinge on architecture.

Institutional Scale

Large institutions tend to have fewer behavior settings per capita than smaller ones because there is a basic number of behavior settings that are required to keep any institution going. Larger institutions provide their members with a greater array of behavior settings from which to choose but there is a tendency for these settings to be overmanned, and thus some people tend not to participate fully in them and to withdraw. In contrast, the behavior settings of smaller institutions tend to be undermanned, requiring that people participate in a greater number of settings in order to keep them going. Which is better? How one answers or avoids this question is obvious in the designs that ensue.

There is a tendency to regard small institutions as better both socially and architecturally (see Alexander 1975, 1977, for example). They are regarded as socially better because people are required to participate more in their life. Larger institutions, however, provide the opportunity for specialized behavior settings and often are regarded as being better in economic terms because their administration tends to be more efficient. The delight with large buildings on the part of some architects is reflected in the megastructure phase of recent architectural ideology.

Large institutions can be designed socially to have subsystems that provide the richness of smaller institutions. The reason that they have not been so designed is that the cost-savings benefit of larger institutions is then lost. Thus, there is a trade-off between tangible economic benefits and the not-immediately-tangible social benefits.

Smaller institutions result in smaller buildings. This is regarded by some as better on the grounds that such buildings are easier to adapt to change and provide greater opportunities for the establishment of an identity and a sense of belonging (Alexander 1977). The world view implicit in the stances taken on the earlier questions is that environmental designers should be advocates for smaller institutions because they enhance the participation and liveliness of life but larger ones are better than none at all. Smaller institutions should, however, be nested as identifiable units within larger ones that provide for a variety of opportunities.

Arguments over the optimum size for formal institutions such as hospitals and schools and for physical structures such as neighborhoods in which desirable communal institutions can develop have been a part of policy formulation for a long time. This is clear from an analysis of British new-town policies over the last thirty years, where the ideal city size has increased substantially. The debate focuses on the issues of opportunities available to people versus greater participation in life. It is a debate that will continue.

Accessibility to All? With Dignity?

During the past decade there has been a considerable increase in legislation to make environments barrier-free for all people. The position taken has been that people with physical handicaps, at least, should be able to gain access to all the places that are accessible to people without these handicaps. This position closely follows the ideology of the civil rights movement in the United States. Itzhak Perlman, the Israeli violinist now living in the United States, expressed his hope for 1981:

> It would be my greatest cultural wish for 1981 that all concert halls in the United States might have access with dignity for the disabled . . . so that I can perform and that the public who make the effort to come, under handicap, should have access . . . with dignity.

It is clear that the issue is not simply one of accessibility but of accessibility with dignity. Perlman's hope has not been realized.

A number of controversies arise. Should all existing places which the public uses be made barrier-free? Is it acceptable to use other than front doors to get access to buildings? Who should bear the cost of making the environment barrier-free? To what extent can the additional cost incurred in making the environment barrier-free deprive the majority of the population of opportunities for better environments? Should existing transportation facilities be adapted for the handicapped or should an independent transportation system be established for them?

The position taken here is that all people should be able to participate in the mainstream of life to the extent that they wish. If this were a universal policy, universally implemented, say, in the United States, it would not place an onerous burden on the remainder of the population. In new buildings it is easier to consider these issues; in adapting the existing environments it is not so easy. It places a disproportionate financial burden on some people.

DESIGN GOALS: DESIGNERS' ADVOCACIES

Much of the argumentative nature of the designing process arises from the incompatibility of the various ends that the built environment is supposed to serve. The usual professional response to this observation is that the designer should strive to do the best for all concerned. All designers, however, end up being advocates for certain ends that represent the needs of specific populations. Often this happens without conscious thought. The question is: Whose ends should the designer serve? The ultimate decision-maker is usually the sponsor of a scheme or a legal or quasi-legal body that has jurisdiction over the context in which the scheme is to be built. Their ends usually have to be met in order for the project to be implemented. It is advocated here, nevertheless, that designers should attempt to persuade these decision-makers to accept specific ends when the evidence suggests that this is a benefit. Where designers have hard evidence for their stances, their arguments are more likely to be accepted, but there is no guarantee of this.

The fundamental stance taken here is that designs should be based on the users' needs while recognizing that the basic requirements of the sponsors should be met. Where there is a clash between these, the designer is obligated to represent the user. This becomes confusing because in almost all designs there is a multiplicity of users. Almost inevitably there will be some clash between the needs of the different sets of users. The position taken here is that the most basic needs, in terms of Maslow's hierarchy, should be met first by order of importance, according to the problems being addressed, of each of the user groups. Then, step by step up the scale, the needs of each group should be met, with those of the most important users, in terms of the project, being given precedence. The designer should represent the needs of those who do not represent themselves well in this process—children, the handicapped, the less powerful socially and politically. Accepting this position leads to subsidiary positions on other questions such as: Is it more important to design for activity systems or for aesthetics?

The Centrality of Activity Systems or Aesthetics as a Design End?

Is the design of the environment concerned with aesthetic goals or with activity-system goals? Many architects take the view that the primary concern is with aesthetics and that meeting people's spatial needs well is not a prime consideration for the profession. Their argument is either that the spatial purpose of the building will change over time but the building will remain the same, or that the spatial behavior needs that the building meets are incidental to the true purpose of architecture. The advocacy position implicit in this is that the timeless needs of society, real or imagined and as defined by the architect, are more important than those of the present population.

The position advocated here is that neither activity systems nor aesthetic ends are paramount *per se*. The basic needs of the population concerned, in terms of Maslow's hierarchy, must be met first. Buildings must work at this level at least. Then higher needs should be addressed. Both lower- and higher-order needs have an activity component and an aesthetic component. In striving to meet these needs the designer has to address the question of how specifically the designed environment should meet them.

Designing for Comfort or Development?

A question arises in those situations where one of the objectives of a design is to cater to the needs of a standing pattern of behavior: Does one design for comfort or for development? More broadly, another question must be addressed first in the intelligence phase of design: How close to the ideal should the set of behavior settings be to that needed by individuals or groups to make it easier for them to attain their goals? These are not simply physical-design issues, they are also social-design issues.

In the everyday environment of cities and neighborhoods this is often a moot point. The demands of the physical environment are so many and often so conflicting that the environment cannot be made easy and comfortable to use for everybody. Thus, striving for a comfortable environment seems to be a legitimate end. The question is more meaningful in the design of specific institutional settings or for specific populations—the everyday environment for children in schools, special learning settings for the mentally impaired, geriatric hospitals for the senile elderly. Powell Lawton (1977) suggests that an ecological approach for design should be to create situations that are modestly demanding on an individual. This is the position advocated here.

Arguments arise over the meaning of "modestly demanding." How much of a challenge should it be for children to get to school in the morning? Is the segregated traffic pattern of a Radburn too easy? Does it help children to develop better—that is, develop greater competence in dealing with the world—if their daily experiences are in an urban, a suburban, or a rural environment? What constitutes an environment that is too difficult or too easy for different groups?

These questions apply across all the substantive issues discussed in this book. How complex should designers make the layout of the environment? Labyrinths are fun in their place, but should the designer strive to create challenges to orientation in buildings, cities, and neighborhoods? Similar questions can be asked of aesthetics. How complex should the aesthetic interpretation of the environment be for the everyday user? Should the challenge be akin to that presented by a crossword puzzle, the solving of which is rewarding?

These questions are seldom addressed by designers. Where they are, they are answered subjectively. One of the problems is that they cut across many dimensions of human experience and the answers have to be specific to the situation. An examination of one basic issue clarifies the problem facing the designer.

Life-Safety Qualities versus Livability Qualities

Among the major determinants of building form, both internally and externally, are the building codes designed to reduce the affordances for loss of life due, in particular, to fire. The stringent application of fire codes has resulted from the tremendous loss of life associated with some major disasters. (On Saturday, November 18, 1942, 492 people lost their lives in a fire at the Coconut Grove nightclub in Boston. More recently, in 1971, 196 died in a fire at the Beverly Hills Supper Club in Southgate, Kentucky.) The fire codes, legally mandated, often clash with the layout requirements for enhancing the livability of buildings, especially institutional buildings.

Some of the features of high-rise housing that Oscar Newman (1972) criticizes as reducing the territorial control of its inhabitants and increasing the opportunities for egress for criminals are those designed for fire safety (such as scissors staircases). Often code requirements dictate that corridors must be free of furniture, making it impossible to use a corridor as, say, a gathering place for institutionalized psychiatric patients, who are very much wont to use corridors in this way. Similarly, much dormitory design ends up being hard architecture (Sommer 1974b). The location of exits and windows and the materials chosen for construction are based on requirements for reducing the potential for loss of life due to fire.

A similar issue is raised by Romedi Passini (1984) with reference to way-finding in buildings.

He suggests that the basic instrumental purpose of way-finding—finding a destination, getting out of a building on fire—has priority but that the aesthetic aspect is also important. The position taken here is essentially his. In many instances, such as strolling or driving for pleasure or when visiting exhibitions, complexity is important because it provides an opportunity for people to test way-finding skills. In these situations, however, way-finding support systems—overall clarity, directional signs, and the like —must exist and be functional for the population of concern.

Such clashes between safety needs and other human needs are common. There is no clear way of analyzing the trade-offs involved. We are reluctant to place a value on human life, although this is implicit in the design of housing and transportation systems. We do not go on indefinitely attempting to design places so that the loss of life through accidents is impossible. The fields of anthropometrics and ergonomics developed partially in response to the need for information that could be used to reduce the high fatality rate from household accidents. What should be the balance between demands for building layouts that are ultrasafe and the demands for livability? Can we achieve both?

The position taken here is that life safety needs come first but that they cannot be the sole focus of attention. Designers should be advocates for making the built environment more livable. Many present codes remain as a legacy of responses to past problems and they need to be changed. In the meantime, designers will be successful advocates for the ends they seek only if their arguments are sound. This depends on both the internal logic and the external validity of the arguments.

The "Desire" for "Space" versus the "Need" for Access

Many studies have shown that most people in countries such as the United States, Australia, and Canada, at least, prefer single-family detached homes to other housing types. They want the space. They also want easy access to facilities. These ends are not easy to reconcile. Many people have been willing to pay dearly in time and energy for access to work and recreation. High-density living, as we know it today, has been a solution of last recourse for many people. Yet as populations increase, so do pressures for high-density living. This is particularly acute in political entities such as Singapore where there are major limitations to the supply of land.

The position taken here is that designers should be advocates for the environments that best meet the needs of the population of concern. They should also be concerned with the long-run implications for society in doing so. This is difficult to do because the future is not a paying client in the present. Designers should strive to create environments that afford levels of privacy and control within people's cultural norms. It is possible to achieve this in both high-density and low-density environments. The difficulty is rather to provide individuals with the same level of identity—a symbolic aesthetic issue—in high-rise environments that they achieve with the single-family house. Not everybody seeks a clear external identity to their individual dwelling unit. Designers should strive to meet the need for identity in the ways desired by their client populations. When this situation changes, new advocacies will be necessary.

The same issues exist in the design of individual buildings. There is a trade-off between cost, size of room, pleasantness of corridors and communal spaces, and efficiencies in circulation. Within our culture, it is the public spaces that, without much thought, tend to be slighted. Then we wonder why the buildings are not pleasant places to visit.

Whose Meaning in Architecture?

Most designers are prepared to accept specifications from clients, consultants, and others for the activities that the designs they are creating are expected to afford. When it comes to aesthetic goals, however, the situation is different because this is where the designer gets his or her opportunity for self-expression. Most designers are comfortable working within one aesthetic style and with a selection of patterns that they strongly defend as the correct way of doing things. The designer's thinking may evolve over time. Designers are selected by clients on the basis of the style of their work as much as anything else. If a client wants a classical design, and knows the work of present-day architects, he or she is likely to approach Alan Greenberg or John Blatteau or one of a handful of other architects who believe strongly in the importance of classical style. If they wish to have modern adaptations of classical styles they may choose Robert Stern. If they want an architect working within the mainstream of Post-Modernism they can select a Michael Graves. The argument for such diversity is that each architect can develop a far-reaching expertise in a specific intellectual area. Few designers have been taught or have educated themselves to work within different design idioms. Their work may develop over time but this is usually an evolutionary process in which design styles evolve in sequence. Sometimes it changes more dramatically.

It is clear from the study of stimulus generalization that people have the same feelings about many patterns of built form, either because of the physical similarities among the patterns or because of a mediated generalization of associational meanings. The position taken here is that architectural education should make students aware of these underlying psychological processes because this will make them more sensitive and appreciative of the different stances taken by designers and the logic of their arguments. Designers themselves should be less arrogant in defending their work on moral grounds and need to recognize the legitimacy of alternative positions and the limitations of their own. It is also hoped that many designers will develop the expertise to be able to work systematically in different design idioms. This places a great burden on the education of architects and stresses the need for more theoretical approaches to it. The position designers take on the degree to which they should be involved in goal-setting is affected by their position on the degree to which the environment should be designed.

The symbolism of buildings is of major importance to the people who own them and live in them. It is frequently of less importance to people for whom buildings are a means to achieve financial rewards, although recently some developers have taken the position that having a big-name architect adds to a building's salability. Symbolism is also less important to people who have a low psychic investment in buildings, such as workers in an office building. It is seldom, if ever, totally irrrelevant because it has to do with people's perceptions of themselves and of others and the degree of control they desire over the spaces they inhabit. Aesthetic issues become particularly important in the environments that people choose for themselves.

Architects focused on the formal aspects of design for much of this century and allowed the symbolic qualities to be a by-product of other decisions. This still represents one value orientation that designers can take. At the same time, there is now a more explicit consideration of architectural symbolism in building design. The question is: Whose meanings should be considered? What are designers' aesthetic obligations to society, to their sponsors, to the users of the environments being designed, to themselves?

Many architects and landscape architects and some urban designers take the position that their contribution to society is their aesthetic philosophy as exhibited in their work. The position taken here is that the meanings of buildings and urban designs have to be more pluralistic—they have to communicate meanings at a variety of levels so that a broader segment of society can relate to them. The limitations of our present positive theory of symbolic aesthetics make this a difficult position to implement with any confidence, as other advocates of this position have found. Taken to its logical extension, this position suggests that architects must be capable of designing buildings within a variety of stylistic media, and that they understand the workings of symbolism within the framework of semiotic and balance theory. Traditionally, architects who work outside the conventions of the mainstream of architectural values have been shunned by critics. Provided the architects are serving somebody's purposes without being detrimental to society as a whole, the shunning should not occur. Arguments will still arise, however, because such words as "detrimental" are value-laden and raise a host of broader social issues.

DESIGN SCOPE

The concept of "total design," where the designer is responsible for the design of everything from large-scale urban design to the design of ashtrays and floral decorations, has been a popular architectural philosophy. Designers, such as Arne Jacobson, who addressed design problems at all scales have been much admired. This philosophy leads to a unity in design products, but it also leads to a reduction in opportunities for people to adapt the environment as their needs change and to personalize it as an expression of their own personalities and aspirations without destroying the original aesthetic intention. This becomes an issue when the original intention is deemed to be of historical importance as a representation of an era or the work of an individual.

The need for the built environment, especially housing, to be adaptable and personalizable, it has been argued in this book, is a fundamental need for many people. Thus, the logical extension of this position is that designers should not strive for total design except in those instances where the paying client is the same as the user client and such a design is what is sought.

One of the characteristics of recent built form is that it is constructed of materials that are not very flexible. Some architects have looked at societies where technological levels are not those of Western societies and have perceived a close fit between behavioral needs and built form. This relationship must be perceived within its cultural context:

As in other societies, the buildings reflect the composition of the dwelling group. But the fit is much closer in a society where the houses are built of mud than when they are made of more permanent materials such as stone. On account of heavy rains, repair work is an annual affair. And if a room is not required because of the death or departure of an occupant, it will soon fall into ruins. The plan of the homestead acts therefore as a fairly exact map of the social relations of the members of the dwelling group. (Goody, 1962)

Can this occur in modern societies? It certainly cannot without much difficulty in a situation of total design. All designs, unless there is a complete administrative prohibition on change, will take on the patina of their inhabitants' use and attitudes over time. This is happening in Brasília, where ostensibly the same building patterns are now differentiable by the socioeconomic statuses of their inhabitants. This does not, however, answer the broad philosophical question of what the designer should specify and what should be left to the inhabitants of a building.

There are two basic views of the degree of fit that architects should be designing into the environment. One states that an architect is responsible only for the overall framework and the inhabitants should be responsible for the infill. The other states that the architect should be responsible for the details as well. Those espousing the former position, especially in housing design (such as Habraken 1971), believe that architects cannot be and should not try to be certain about what the interior layouts are that people desire or need. Lucien Kroll (1972) extends this argument to the exterior of buildings. If one accepts this position, the structure and range of possible adaptations to units should be the focus of concern in the design of large-scale housing developments. Presumably the same arguments can be made for the design of the public environment, although here questions about who controls what become paramount.

The position advocated here is based on the observation that there are much greater regularities in design than are suggested by people such as John Habraken (1971). It is possible to ascertain the range of activity patterns and aesthetic values of the potential users of the environment and these are likely to be stable for a generation. It is possible to design specifically for this range. This implies greater flexibility in design than that advocated by much of the Modern Movement, but it also recognizes that designs are not changed by users as rapidly or as frequently as many designers like to believe. The student dormitories for the medical school of the new Catholic University of Louvain in Brussels by Lucien Kroll attest this as do countless office interiors. The "failure" of much modern housing is attributable to the failure of policymakers and architects to understand the activity systems and aesthetic values of people in whose culture they themselves were not saturated. The position taken here is that any environment one designs should be tailor-made as far as possible to meet the needs of those concerned and should allow for easy personalization. "Hard" architecture should be avoided.

CONCLUSION

While positive theory may clarify many of the issues facing the designer, it cannot specify the ends of design. They depend on what an individual designer believes and the degree to which society as a whole and individual clients are willing to accept those beliefs. In this chapter a number of issues confronting almost all designers have been identified. It is possible to identify a number of value stances that designers have taken and might take on how to deal with these issues. A value stance has been taken on what designers should do. This is my stance. It has shaped the topics I have chosen to cover in this book. The same topics could be covered by somebody with a value stance different from mine. They would differ only to the extent we differ in our knowledge of these processes. The decision as to what to do with this information could, however, be radically different.

ADDITIONAL READINGS

Conway, Don, ed., *Social Sciences and Design: A Process Model for Architect and Social Scientist Collaboration.* Washington, D.C.: AIA Research Department, 1974.

Deasey, C.M. *Design for Human Affairs.* New York: McGraw-Hill, 1977.

Heimseth, Clovis. *Behavioral Architecture.* New York: John Wiley, 1974.

Lang, Jon, Charles Burnette, Walter Moleski, and David Vachon, eds., *Designing for Human Behavior: Architecture and the Behavioral Sciences.* Stroudsburg, Pa.: Dowden, Hutchinson and Ross, 1974.

Sommer, Robert. *Social Design: Creating Buildings with People in Mind.* Englewood Cliffs, N.J.: Prentice-Hall, 1983.

Zeisel, John. *Inquiry by Design.* Monterey, Ca.: Brooks/Cole, 1981.

PART IV

CONCLUSIONS

22

THE PRESENT AND POTENTIAL CONTRIBUTION OF THE BEHAVIORIAL SCIENCES TO ENVIRONMENTAL DESIGN THEORY—A SUMMATION

In this book an attempt has been made to provide a framework for discussing the development of environmental design theory and, in particular, the contribution of the behavioral sciences to it. During the past twenty years a number of anthropologists, sociologists, and psychologists have shown an interest in studying the design professions, designers, and the nature of designers' concerns. In addition, an increasing number of people with training and professional experience in interior design, architecture, landscape architecture, and urban design are doing systematic research using behavioral science techniques. Both groups of people have felt that the behavioral sciences should be able to provide designers with substantive theories, models, and concepts that will lead to a clearer understanding of both design praxis and the nature of the person-environment relationship. Both groups believe that research will enhance theory. The goal is to enhance designers' abilities to design "better" interiors, buildings, building complexes, and landscapes. This is the ultimate test of the basic hypothesis of this book—that the behvioral sciences afford the design professions much through the building of theory. It is not an easy hypothesis to test.

The assumption made in this book is that the goal of design is to meet human needs in a manner that is not detrimental to the lives of other organisms. Sometimes designers are advocates for other organisms partly for their own sake but also because they can enrich human experience (Leedy, Maestro, and Franklin 1978, Spirn 1984). It has been assumed here that the goal of design is to solve problems and to enhance human experience.

It was noted at the outset of this book that, while the Modern Movement in design has made a vast contribution to human life, there have been some serious limitations in its perceptions of the problems of the world and in the design principles that were created to solve them. While many of the modern masters of design were very socially concerned people, their knowledge of human life was limited by their own experience. Systematic research enables us to go beyond this; many psychological constructs enable us to place our own experiences in context and to go beyond them. There are, however, many behavioral scientists and many architects who do not see this.

Some behavioral scientists believe that the role of the built environment in human life is minor and not worthy of their attention; some designers believe that the behavioral sciences have nothing more to offer than some complex terms for the simple ones they have used traditionally and some pseudoscientific jargon that cannot replicate the quality of ideas developed through common sense. Other designers fear that the complexity that they believe they handle very well intuitively will be reduced through the application of a reductionist philosophy. It will be seen that these fears are misplaced if one understands the nature of the contribution of the behavioral sciences to the development of environmental design theory.

It has been suggested here that in order to clarify the nature of the contribution of the behavioral sciences to environmental design it is useful to distinguish between two types of theory: *positive* and *normative*. This has been done at a time when the distinction often is challenged in the traditional academic disciplines (see Bernstein 1978). In an applied field this distinction makes sense because it enables an individual to distinguish between what the field purports its knowledge base to be and its positions on what to do with this base in action. At the same time, the role of values in theory-building both now and in the future must be recognized.

Building a body of theory for the environmental design disciplines is perceived by some to be a search for objective facts. Traditionally this has been the view of theory-building in the behavioral sciences. It was believed that the values of observers could be removed from the observations they made and that the world is "capable of being investigated in a wholly neutral way" (Skinner 1938). Thomas Kuhn, in his book *The Structure of Scientific Revolutions* (1965) warned that not even the natural scientist can hope to observe facts neutrally. What we accept as scientific is based on a set of assumptions which act as a schema to guide explorations, perceptions, and analyses (Neisser 1977). The role of creative thought and values in building positive theory is now acknowledged even though neutrality is still the goal—but that, in itself, is a value.

The goal of creating an explicit positive theory base for environmental design is to have a set of descriptions and explanations of patterns of: (1) the decision process in environmental design praxis, (2) the built environment and how people use and respond to it, and (3) the structural nature of the materials of the built environment and what they afford people in creating an artificial world. The concern here has been with the first two. It has been argued that positive theory can be created scientifically or, at least, quasi-scientifically. Normative theories, on the other hand, are statements on what should be done to make better worlds. They involve the identification and explanation of statements of belief. They can be studied in the same way as positive theories, but they themselves cannot be scientific—although some designers claim their normative positions to be scientific. To them science consists not of methods for describing and explaining phenomena, but rather of the use of erudition and logic in design (Banham 1960).

THE CONTRIBUTION OF THE BEHAVIORAL SCIENCES

Perhaps the major contribution the behavioral sciences can make to the development of environmental design theory is a way of looking at the world. They provide a learning model in which conceptual formulations are confronted and compared to real experience; hypotheses are tested rather than just generated and believed. In this way the environmental design professions will take on more of the quality of the professions that have incorporated science/research as the basis for professional practice (Sims 1983). Many regard these professions as more successful than the environmental design professions. Their practitioners certainly seem to be more highly paid! Environmental designers, architects in particular, have stressed the role of the individual as a creative artist and they promote this self-image (Turner 1977). This is often the image that others have of us and the way we are portrayed in novels (such as Rand 1968, Greene 1963). Maybe it is time for us to see the similarities rather than the differences between the design professions and the other applied professions. This does not deny the essential creativity in the act of environmental design—or in professional action in other fields, for that matter.

Depending on the nature of the phenomena of concern, there are a number of approaches to the development of architectural theory. Hypotheses about some concerns can be subjected to rigorous experimental research. This is certainly true of many technological factors and may even be true of areas, such as aesthetics, that we have believed to be beyond the scope of systematic research. There has, however, been much greater difficulty in applying scientific research methods to the study of aesthetics and to the study of the normative positions architects hold than in studying a topic such as spatial behavior. It is easier to design and conduct studies of spatial behavior than studies of the design process or studies of an individual architect's beliefs or studies of aesthetics. The reason is simple: spatial behavior is observable. Nevertheless, in areas such as aesthetics, diligent research has uncovered more than we are often wont to acknowledge. It has yielded knowledge of some of the regularities of the world and has suggested explanations that can be scrutinized from different theoretical positions. In creating positive theory for environmental design, one must acknowledge that different world views affect what is deemed to be worthy of investigation and the reasons given for the states observed. It was for this reason that the major views of the processes of perception, cognition and affect, and spatial behavior have been presented in this book. This may make the presentation more complex, but it does represent the state of our knowledge.

VALUES, RESEARCH, AND THEORY-BUILDING

The way in which environmental design theory has been presented in this book is biased by the model of theory presented in it. This model shapes the whole book. It is also clear that there has been an uneven development of knowledge and conceptual models in the different areas of concern to designers. The quality of knowledge is not always commensurate with the energy spent on research. While both architects and psychologists have spent much effort in coming to an understanding of formal aesthetic issues during the last hundred years, our understanding is still limited. We seem to understand issues of privacy and territoriality much better, although the sustained effort to do research on these topics with reference to the built environment is much more recent. This unevenness in our understanding reflects the ease of doing research and our willingness to do it in different areas. It also reflects the funding available for that research. There is little money available today to do systematic research on symbolic or formal aesthetics in comparison to, say, crime and the environment. Such differences are to some extent a reflection of what society deems to be important and to some extent a reflection of what individual researchers want to study. All these factors bias the contents of this book.

The goal here has been to update the humanistic orientation that the architectural profession generally has professed. In doing this, an attempt has been made to avoid a reductionist philosophy. Perhaps, by doing this, it has been implied that designers need to take more variables into consideration than they do now. Howard Mitchell (1974) noted a student's observation about this:

> Architecture is difficult enough having to learn about form, structure, perspective, and how to deal with ignorant clients, and now you bring in all these other behavioral factors.

This book is biased by the belief that any creative work of design that is truly helpful to society can only grow out of empathy for people and out of a rich understanding of the environment and what it affords people—a cultivated knowledge that recognizes cultural differences. The information in this book is, however, neutral: it can be used for creating environments that are inhospitable to people as well as environments that are humane. The goal of this book has not been to present guidelines for designing within a particular ideological framework, but rather to bring to the reader an organized awareness of the present state of the contribution of the behavioral sciences to environmental design theory. The goal has been to further the sharing of ideas.

This book represents one of a number of attempts to synthesize the scattered theories and research findings of the behavioral sciences that can tell designers something about their activities. It is different in scope and focus from books dealing with environmental psychology (such as Saarinen 1976, Rapoport 1977, Levy-Le Boyer 1982, Holohan 1982) and from those dealing with design methods *per se* (such as Moore 1970, Koberg and Bagnall 1974), even though it overlaps them in content and owes much to them. It is written by an architect and urban designer who teaches architects and architectural students. Its bias is reflected in the following statement which appears at the conclusion of *Designing for Human Behavior* (Lang et al., eds. 1974):

> It has been suggested that if the profession would recognize the habits, needs and desires of building users as primary determinants of form, it will need to know more about the relationship between the designed environment and human behavior than it does at present. Moreover, if the profession is to use this information creatively, it must be organized in such a way which lends itself to that use. The design process is presently largely mimetic; typological solutions are adjusted to new situations and approaches to designing imitated. The emphasis in teaching, as in practice, has been the formal generation of the product with little attention to the understanding of the problem involved.

Such a belief is held by a large number, but not necessarily a majority, of designers. It has been the impetus for much of the recent research. Some environmental design research is done simply to assuage the curiosity of the researcher. Even in this case it is motivated by the values of that person.

THE FUTURE

Where do we go from here? The quality of research in the future will depend not only on the quality of research design—subject selection, sampling procedures, measurement techniques, and so forth—but also on the quality of the hypotheses being tested. How does one select useful hypotheses for testing? One way is to look at gaps in the existing theories. Another is to identify conflicting explanations and to design studies to settle the matter. This is no easy task. Useful hypotheses also can be derived from the casual examination of the work we do in practice. One can, for instance, look at what we do well and what we do badly in the process of design. One can analyze where we have been successful in our prediction of the outcomes of design in terms of the use and enjoyment the designs have brought to people. These outcomes can be correlated not only with the methods of analysis and design but also with the personal characteristics and aspirations of the people concerned.

In practice there has been a growing collaboration between researcher and practitioner in the programming and design-review phase of architectural praxis. Many architectural firms now offer systematic programming services as part of their professional work. There has, however, been little collaboration in an area of research that is essential to theory-building—postconstruction evaluation. Indeed there has been little postconstruction evaluation. Where there has been, it has focused more on the individual problems of a specific building or building type than on theory-building. There has been very little evaluation of the process of design in praxis. All this has been highly detrimental to the development of environmental design theory and thus to the intellectual growth and practice of the design professions.

The following statement was made over ten years ago:

> There must be a change in attitude within the profession toward questions of architectural criticism and evaluation. A system which brooks no criticism by peers and makes no effort to scientifically evaluate its products in human terms is intolerable. Improvements depend on the critical and constructive assessment of experience and learning from one another's mistakes [and successes]. (Lang et al., eds. 1974)

A number of people (such as Bechtel 1977) have pointed out that this statement is unfair, that it expects too much of the practitioner. This may be so. Professions are not good at monitoring themselves or the quality of their work. Expecting practitioners to broadcast weaknesses in their design solutions and in the theoretical assumptions on which those solutions are based may be asking too much. The working environment of designers is too competitive. This means that the academic community must get much more involved in basic theoretical research.

It is less important to know the successes and failings of specific buildings than it is to identify specific patterns and what they do and do not afford. This is what Oscar Newman (1972) did in developing his concept of "defensible space" and what William H. Whyte (1980) did in identifying the characteristics of urban spaces that possess the affordances necessary for the development of social life within our culture. It behooves those in the academic environment to initiate programs of systematic research to foster the development of positive theory.

There has been an increase in the amount of systematic research being done in schools of environmental design. Much of this research has to do with the natural sciences—architectural structures, acid rains, and soils, for example. Much of it involves the topics addressed in this book, however, as the references in the Bibliography will attest. Much of this research is very situation-specific and more useful as a programming exercise than as an aid in theory-creation, in the making of generalizations.

It is not the purpose here to establish a research agenda for environmental design. There are, however, some major gaps in our knowledge that must be recognized and addressed in the future. One of the criticisms of the arguments presented in this book might be that they are highly ethnocentric; another is that they are ahistorical. Much of the research that has been done *is* ethnocentric despite the contributions of people like Amos Rapoport (1969, 1977) and Irwin Altman and Martin Chemers (1980). Perhaps this is due to the paucity of anthropologists who have found research on environmental design issues to be of interest. Much of the research that has been done *is* ahistorical. We have little understanding of the changes in patterns of territorial behavior of groups over time, although we do have some anecdotal information. We have little understanding of how taste cultures have been structured and how they have changed over time. Even our information on lifestyle and housing change is incomplete. The ahistorical nature of environmental design research makes it difficult to make predictions of change with accuracy. Good historical data and models will not enable us to predict changes with total accuracy but certainly will enhance our ability. Traditional research in architectural history is not very helpful. It has focused on monuments rather than on the everyday environments of people within different cultures. As a basis for making predictions about the future, we need to be able to look at past trends and to understand the reasons for change. This is happening and so, in the future, books like this one should be more explicit and contain more powerful models that can be used as the basis for asking questions about the environment and about people, change, and the processes of design that respond to change.

Much about what the present built environment affords people is unclear, as any designer having to make decisions will tell. It is intuitively appealing, for instance, to use the Maslow model of human needs and motivations as an organizing model for considering the concerns of environmental design. But is it a model that really liberates us from past thinking, or not? Our knowledge of aesthetics is limited, although books and articles by designers are full of untested hypotheses about what makes specific patterns of the built and natural environments appealing to people. The very organization of aesthetics into sensory, formal, and symbolic categories, as has been done here, is open to question. We have only limited knowledge about behavioral opportunities, the interaction of value systems, and the choices people make, and so our ability to discuss these issues is restricted.

In the area of design methodology there are many issues that need to be addressed. Much of what has been presented in this book is as much the product of introspective analysis as it is of systematic research. Introspective analysis is fine for generating hypotheses but these need to be checked against what really happens: What processes lead to what outcomes? Sometimes the research is there but we designers prefer to rely on our own beliefs. The subject of creativity is a good example. We have far more knowledge about the processes of creative thinking than we like to admit, but our willingness to apply it in asking serious questions about environmental design is limited. As a result, we know considerably less about creativity in environmental design than one would expect from the amount of research done in other applied areas. This is also true of normative theory, which, after all, has long been the central concern of courses on architectural theory in schools of design.

There is much confusion about the normative positions that environmental designers have taken and why they have taken these positions. We should be in a position to understand these better in the future. The relationship of professionals to their professional cultures is now being explored by a number of people (such as Gutman 1977, Larson 1979, S. Dostoglu 1982, Blau 1984). A useful next step in enhancing our understanding of ourselves, our predecessors, and our colleagues would be for this research to focus on the attitudes of specific schools of designers toward the environment, to-

ward their clients and society, toward the use of environmental knowledge, and toward the design process. At the moment, we tend to classify designers in terms of the aesthetic style of the products they create. To some extent this does represent their value positions but it tends to be a unidimensional categorization.

With advances in computer technology, the information overload that designers often labor under may well be reduced if not eliminated. Storing in a computer a series of design principles in which specific goals are linked with the specific patterns that afford their attainment (and which have a history of working within specific cultures for specific problems) is conceivable now and may become a reality in the future. If and when it does, it will be essential that designers have a strong theoretical understanding of how the built and natural environments work so that such easily recallable design principles can be evaluated. Otherwise we designers will lose our role in society and become technicians. Good technicians are scarce, but this should not be the sole role of design professionals. One of their roles surely is to consider what might enhance human experience that has not been done before. This requires creative thought.

Future research must address the questions of importance to people and to environmental designers. We need to better understand the concept of *fit* (or congruence or synomorphy) between persons, values, and environment. We need to understand the consequences of ill-fitting environments and to understand when a degree of "ill-fittingness" may not be bad. Some of these issues will always be debatable. Explicit, externally valid positive theory will enable the discussion to take place with some clarity. It will also enable the designer to deduce what should be done in a particular circumstance.

The achievement of these goals is important. Learning based on first-hand tutorial or practical experience must be augmented by the development of generalized models and theory drawn from systematic research. The education and work of designers will be advanced significantly if this is done. This book, it is hoped, continues the work of many people who perceive that environmental design can have a much clearer and more theoretical basis than it now enjoys. Furthering the achievement of this goal demands greater research efforts to enhance the accuracy of observations and the understanding of causal relationships between phenomena. It also demands the criticism, refinement, and elaboration of the ideas presented here.

ADDITIONAL READINGS

Churchman, Arza, and Yona Ginsberg. "The Use of Behavioral Science Research in Physical Planning." *Journal of Architectural Research and Teaching* 1, no. 1 (1984): 57–66.

Kantrowitz, Min. "Has Environment and Behavior Research Made a Difference?" *Environment and Behavior* 17, no. 1 (January 1985): 25–46.

BIBLIOGRAPHY

Ackerman, James S. (1969), "Listening to Architecture," *Harvard Educational Review* 39, no. 4: 4–11.

Adams, Bert N. (1968), *Kinship in an Urban Setting*, Chicago: Markam.

Adams, James L. (1974), *Conceptual Blockbusting*, San Francisco: Freeman.

Albers, Josef (1963), *Interaction of Color*, New Haven: Yale University Press.

Alberti, Leone Battista (1485), *De re aedificatoria*. English translation by James Leoni (1726), *Ten Books on Architecture*, London: Alec Tiranti, 1955.

Alexander, Christopher (1964), *Notes on the Synthesis of Form*, Cambridge, Mass.: Harvard University Press.

—— (1965), "The Theory and Invention of Form," *Architectural Record* 137, no. 4: 177–186.

—— (1969), "Major Changes in Environmental Form Required by Social and Psychological Demands," *Ekistics* 28: 78–85.

—— (1972), "The City as a Mechanism for Sustaining Human Contact," in Robert Gutman, ed., *People and Buildings*, New York: Basic Books, pp. 406–434.

—— (1984), *The Search for a New Paradigm in Architecture*, Boston: Oriel.

——, Sara Ishikawa, and Murray Silverstein (1967), "A Pattern Language which Generates Multi-Service Centers," Berkeley: Center for Environmental Structure.

——, et al. (1969), "Houses Generated by Patterns," Berkeley: Center for Environmental Structure.

——, and Barry Poyner (1970), "Atoms of Environmental Structure," in Gary Moore, ed., *Emerging Methods in Environmental Design and Planning*, Cambridge, Mass.: MIT Press, pp. 308–321.

——, et al. (1975), *The Oregon Experiment*, New York: Oxford University Press.

——, et al. (1977), *A Pattern Language*, New York: Oxford University Press.

——, et al. (1979), *The Timeless Way of Building*, New York: Oxford University Press.

Alger, John R. M., and Carl V. Hays (1964), *Creative Synthesis in Design*, Englewood Cliffs, N.J.: Prentice-Hall.

Allen, Marjorie (1968), *Planning for Play*, Cambridge, Mass.: MIT Press.

Allsop, Bruce (1974), *Towards a Humane Architecture*, London: Frederick Muller.

Altman, Irwin (1975), *Environment and Social Behavior*, Monterey, Ca.: Brooks/Cole.

——, P. A. Nelson, and E. E. Lett (1972), "The Ecology of Home Environments," Washington D.C.: U.S. Dept. of Housing, Education and Welfare, Office of Education.

——, and Martin Chemers (1980), *Culture and Environment*, Monterey, Ca.: Brooks/ Cole.

Ames, Adelbert (1960), *Morning Notes of Adelbert Ames*, edited by Hadley Cantril, New Brusnwick, N.J.: Rutgers University Press.

Anastasi, Anne (1958), *Differential Psychology*, New York: Macmillan.

—— (1965), *Individual Differences*, New York: John Wiley.

Anderson, Jeremy, and Margaret Tindall (1972), "The Concept of Home Range: New Data for the Study of Territorial Behavior," in William J. Mitchell, ed., *Environmental Design: Research and Practice, Proceedings of the EDRA3/AR8 Conference*, Los Angeles, pp. 1.1.1.–1.1.7.

Angel, Shlomo (1968), "Discouraging Crime through City Planning," Berkeley: University of California, Center for Planning and Development Research.

Appleyard, Donald (1969), "Why Buildings are Known," *Environment and Behavior* 1, no. 3: 131–156.

—— (1970), "Styles and Methods of Structuring a City," *Environment and Behavior* 2, no. 3: 100–107.

—— (1973), "Notes on Urban Perception and Knowledge," in Roger M. Downs and David Stea, eds., *Image and Environment*, Chicago: Aldine, pp. 109–114.

——, Kevin Lynch, and John Myer (1964), *The View from the Road*, Cambridge, Mass.: MIT Press.

——, with M. S. Gerson and M. Lintell (1981), *Livable Streets*, Berkeley: University of California Press.

——, and M. Lintell (1972), "The Environmental Quality of Streets," *Journal of the American Institute of Planners* 38 (March): 84–101.

ARC (1975), *Places and Settings*, Columbus, Ohio: Architectural Research Construction.

Archer, L. Bruce (1970), "An Overview of the Structure of the Design Process," in Gary T. Moore, ed., *Emerging Methods in Environmental Design and Planning*, Cambridge, Mass.: MIT Press, pp. 285–307.

Architectural Education Study Vol. II (1981), Consortium of Eastern Schools of Architecture.

Architektur Weltbewerbe (1979), *Bauten für die Gesundheit*, Stuttgart: Karl Krämer Verlag.

Ardrey, Robert (1966), *The Territorial Imperative*, New York: Atheneum.

Argüelles, Jose (1972), *Charles Henry and the Formation of a Psychophysical Aesthetic*, Chicago: University of Chicago Press.

Argyle, M., and J. Dean (1965), "Eye Contact, Distance and Affiliation," *Sociometry* 28: 289–304.

Argyris, Chris (1954), *Organization of a Bank*, New Haven: Labor and Management Center, Yale University.

Arnheim, Rudolf (1949), "The Gestalt Theory of Expression," *Psychological Review* 56: 156–171.

——— (1965), *Art and Visual Perception*, Berkeley and Los Angeles: University of California Press.

——— (1966), *Towards a Psychology of Art*, Berkeley and Los Angeles: University of California Press.

——— (1968), "Gestalt Psychology and Artistic Form," in Lancelot Law Whyte, ed., *Aspects of Artistic Form*, London: Lund Humphries.

——— (1971), *Entropy and Art: An Essay on Disorder and Order*, Berkeley and Los Angeles: University of California Press.

——— (1977), *The Dynamics of Architectural Form*, Berkeley and Los Angeles, University of California Press.

Arnold, Henry F. (1980), *Trees in Urban Design*, New York: Van Nostrand Reinhold.

Ås, Dagfin (1975), "Observing Environmental Behavior: The Behavior Setting," in William Michelson, ed., *Behavioral Research Methods in Environmental Design*, Stroudsburg, Pa.: Dowden, Hutchinson and Ross, pp. 280–300.

Auden, W. H. (1965), "Prologue: The Birth of Architecture," in *About the House*, New York: Random House.

Avin, Uri (1973), "Le Corbusier's Unité d'habitation: Slab for all Seasons," unpublished master's thesis, University of Cape Town.

Ayer, A. J. (1936), *Languages, Truth, Logic*, republished in New York: Dover.

Bachelard, Gaston (1969), *The Poetics of Space*, Boston: Beacon Press.

Bacon, Edmund (1974), *The Design of Cities*, New York: Viking (revised edition).

Bagley, Christopher (1965), "Delinquency in Exeter: an Ecological and Comparative Study," *Urban Studies* 2: 33–50.

Bailey, Joe (1975), *Social Theory for Planning*, London and Boston: Routledge and Kegan Paul.

Baleela, Mustafa (1975), "Design for Liveability: The Housing for Middle Income Families in Saudi Arabia," unpublished doctoral dissertation, University of Pennsylvania.

Banham, Reyner (1960), *Theory and Design in the First Machine Age*, New York: Praeger.

Barker, Roger (1960), "Ecology and Environment," in Stephen Friedman and Joseph B. Juhasz, eds., *Environments: Notes and Selections on Objects, Spaces and Behavior*, Monterey, Ca.: Brooks/Cole, 1974, pp. 50–69.

——— (1968), *Ecological Psychology: Concepts and Methods for Studying Human Behavior*, Stanford, Ca.: Stanford University Press.

——— and Herb Wright (1951), *One Boy's Day*, New York: Harper & Row.

——— and Paul Gump (1964), *Big School, Small School*, Stanford: Stanford University Press.

——— and Phil Schoggen (1973), *Qualities of Community Life*, San Francisco: Jossey-Bass.

Barron, Frank (1965), "The Psychology of Creativity," in *New Directions in Psychology II*, New York: Holt, Rinehart and Winston, pp. 1–134.

Barthes, Roland (1967), *Elements of Semiology*, translated by Annette Lavers and Colin Smith, London: Cape.

Bartley, William W. (1965), "How Is the House of Science Built?" *Architectural Association Journal* 80, no. 889 (February): 213–218.

Bates, F. L. (1956), "Position, Role and Status: A Reformulation of Concepts," *Social Forces* 34: 313–321.

Bayes, Kenneth (1967), *The Therapeutic Effect of the Environment on Emotionally Disturbed and Mentally Sub-Normal Children*, London: Unwin Brothers.

———, and Sandra Franklin (1971), *Designing for the Handicapped*, London: George Godwin.

Bazjanac, Vladimir (1974), "Architectural Design Theory: Models of the Design Process," in W. R. Spillers, ed., *Basic Questions of Design Theory*, New York: American Elsevier, pp. 3–20.

Bechtel, Robert (1970), "A Behavioral Comparison of Urban and Small Town Environments," in John Archea and Charles Eastman, eds., *EDRA2: Proceedings of the Second Annual Environmental Design Research Association Conference*, Pittsburgh, pp. 347–353.

——— (1974), "Experimental Methods in Environmental Design Research," in Jon Lang et al., eds., *Designing for Human Behavior: Architecture and the Behavioral Sciences*, Stroudsburg, Pa.: Dowden, Hutchinson and Ross, pp. 286–293.

——— (1977), *Enclosing Behavior*, Stroudsburg, Pa.: Dowden, Hutchinson and Ross.

Beck, Robert (1970), "Spatial Meaning and Properties of the Environment," in Harold Proshansky et al., eds., *Environmental Psychology: Man and His Physical Setting*, New York: Holt, Rinehart and Winston, pp. 134–153.

Becker, Franklin D. (1978), *Housing Messages*, Stroudsburg, Pa.: Dowden, Hutchinson and Ross.

——— (1981), *Workspace: Creating Environments in Organizations*, New York: Praeger.

——— (1982), *The Successful Office: How to Create Workspace That's Right for You*, Reading, Mass.: Addison-Wesley.

———, and C. Mayo (1971), "Delineating Personal Distance and Territoriality," *Environment and Behavior* 3: 375–381.

Bednar, James (1977), *Barrier-Free Environments*, Stroudsburg, Pa.: Dowden, Hutchinson and Ross, 1977.

Beinart, Julian (1975), "Patterns of Change in an African Housing Environment," in Paul Oliver, ed., *Shelter, Sign and Symbol*, London: Barrie and Jenkins, pp. 160–182.

Bellin, Seymour, and Louis Kriesberg (1965), "Informal

Social Relations of Fatherless Families: A Study of Public Housing and Social Mobility," paper delivered to the 1965 Annual Meeting of the American Sociological Society.

Benevolo, Leonardo (1967), *The Origins of Modern Town Planning*, Cambridge, Mass.: MIT Press.

Bennett, Corwin (1977), *Spaces for People*, Englewood Cliffs, N.J.: Prentice-Hall.

Bennis, Warren (1969), *Organization Development: Strategies and Models*, Reading, Mass.: Addison-Wesley.

Bense, M. (1969), *Einführung in die informationstheoretische Aesthetik*, Reinbek: Rohwolt.

Beranek, Leo L. (1962), *Music, Acoustics and Architecture*, New York: John Wiley.

Berlyne, D. E. (1960), *Conflict, Arousal and Curiosity*, New York: McGraw-Hill.

——— (1974), *Studies in the New Experimental Aesthetics*, Washington, D.C.: Hemisphere Publishing Corp.

———, and K. B. Madsen, eds. (1973), *Pleasure, Reward, Preference*, New York: Academic Press.

Bernstein, Richard J. (1978), *The Restructuring of Social and Political Theory*, Philadelphia: University of Pennsylvania Press.

Birren, Faber (1965), *Color Psychology and Color Theory: A Factual Study of the Influence of Color on Human Life*, New Hyde Park, N.Y.: University Books.

——— (1969), *Light, Color and Environment*, New York: Van Nostrand Reinhold.

Bishop, J., and J. Foulsham (1973), "Children's Images of Harwich," Working Paper No. 3, Architectural Psychology Research Unit, Kingston Polytechnic.

Black, Max (1961), *Models and Metaphors*, Ithaca, N.Y.: Cornell University Press.

Blake, Peter (1964), *God's Own Junkyard: The Planned Deterioration of America's Landscape*, New York: Holt, Rinehart and Winston.

——— (1973), *Architecture for the New World: The Work of Harry Seidler*, New York: Wittenborn.

——— (1974), *Form Follows Fiasco*, Boston: Atlantic-Little, Brown.

——— (1984), "What Is Happening to our Buildings?" *Pennsylvania Gazette* 82, no. 4 (February): 32–38.

Blake, Robert, et al., "Housing, Architecture and Social Interaction," *Sociometry* 19 (1956): 133–139.

Blau, Judith (1980), "A Framework of Meaning in Architecture," in Geoffrey Broadbent et al., eds., *Signs, Symbols and Architecture*, New York: John Wiley, pp. 333–368.

Blau, Judith (1984), *Architects and Firms: A Sociological Perspective on Architectural Practice*, Cambridge, Mass.: MIT Press.

Blaut, J., and David Stea (1971), "Studies of Geographical Learning," *Annals of the Association of American Geographers* 61: 387–393.

Bloomer, Kent, and Charles W. Moore (1977), *Body, Memory and Architecture*, New Haven: Yale University Press.

Bonta, Juan P. (1979), *Architecture and Its Interpretation*, New York: Rizzoli.

Boring, Edwin G. (1942), *Sensation and Perception in the History of Experimental Psychology*, New York: Appleton-Century.

Bosanquet, Bernard (1931), *Three Lectures on Aesthetics*, London: Macmillan.

Boudon, Philippe (1972), *Lived-In Architecture: Le Corbusier's Pessac Revisited*, translated by G. Orm, Cambridge, Mass.: MIT Press.

Boughey, Howard N. J. (1968), "Blueprints for Behavior: The Intentions of Architects to Influence Social Action through Design," unpublished doctoral dissertation, Princeton University.

Boulding, Kenneth (1956), *The Image*, Ann Arbor: University of Michigan Press.

Brebner, John (1982), *Environmental Psychology and Building Design*, London: Applied Science Publishers.

Brehm, J. W., and A. R. Cohen (1962), *Explorations in Cognitive Dissonance*, New York: John Wiley.

Brennan, T. (1948), *Midland City*, London: Dobson.

Briggs, Ronald (1973), "Urban Cognitive Distance," in Roger M. Downs and David Stea, eds., *Image and Environment*, Chicago: Aldine, pp. 361–388.

Brill, Michael (1974), "Evaluating Builings on a Performance Basis," in Jon Lang et al., eds., *Designing for Human Behavior: Architecture and the Behavioral Sciences*, Stroudsburg, Pa.: Dowden, Hutchinson and Ross, 1974, pp. 316–319.

Broadbent Geoffrey (1966), "Creativity," in S. A. Gregory, ed., *The Design Method*, New York: Plenum Press.

——— (1973), *Design in Architecture: Architecture and the Human Sciences*, New York: John Wiley.

——— (1975), "Function and Symbolism in Architecture," in Basil Honikman, ed., *Responding to Social Change*, Stroudsburg, Pa.: Dowden, Hutchinson and Ross, pp. 73–95.

——— (1983), "Architects and their Symbols," in John S. Pipkin, Mark E. Le Gory, and Judith E. Blau, eds., *Remaking the City: Social Science Perspectives on Urban Design*, Albany, N.Y.: SUNY Press, pp. 77–100.

———, Richard Bunt, and Charles Jencks (1980), *Signs, Symbols and Architecture*, New York: John Wiley.

———, Richard Bunt, and Thomas Llorens, eds. (1980), *Meaning and Behavior in the Built Environment*, New York: John Wiley.

Broady, Maurice (1966), "Social Theory in Architectural Design," *Arena* 81, no. 898: 149–154.

Brodey, Warren (1969), "The Other than Visual World of the Blind," *Ekistics* 28: 100–103.

Brolin, Brent (1976), *The Failure of Modern Architecture*, New York: Van Nostrand Reinhold.

———, and John Zeisel (1970), "Social Research and Design: Applications to Mass Housing," in Gary Moore, ed., *Emerging Methods in Environmental Design and Planning*, Cambridge, Mass.: MIT Press, pp. 239–246.

Brooks, Richard O. (1974), *New Towns and Communal Values: A Case Study of Columbia, Maryland*, New York: Praeger.

Bross, Irwin D. J. (1953), *Design for Decision*, New York: Macmillan.

Brower, Sidney N. (1980), "Territory in Urban Settings," in Irwin Altman et al., eds., *Human Behavior and Environment*, 4, New York: Plenum.

————, Kathleen Dockett, and Ralph B. Taylor (1983), "Residents' Perceptions of Territorial Features and Perceived Local Threat," *Environment and Behavior* 15, no. 4 (July): 419–437.

Brown, R. (1965), *Social Psychology*, New York: Free Press.

Brunner, Jerome S. (1966), "On Cognitive Growth," in Brunner et al., *Studies in Cognitive Growth*, New York: John Wiley, pp. 1–67.

————. (1970), "Constructive Cognition," *Contemporary Psychology* 15, no. 2: 81–83.

Burchard, John Ely, and Albert Bush Brown (1966), *The Architecture of America, A Social and Cultural History*, Boston: Little, Brown.

Burnette, Charles (1974), "The Mental Image and Design," in Jon Lang et al. eds., *Designing for Human Behavior: Architecture and the Behavioral Sciences*, Stroudsburg, Pa.: Dowden, Hutchinson and Ross, pp. 169–182.

————, Jon Lang, and David Vachon, eds. (1971), *Architecture for Human Behavior*, Philadelphia: American Institute of Architects/Philadelphia Chapter.

Burton, I., C. D. Fowle, and R. S. McCullough (1982), *Living with Risk: Environmental Risk Management in Canada*, Toronto: University of Toronto, Institute for Environmental Studies.

Byerts, Thomas O., Sandra Howell, and Leon Pastalan, eds. (1979), *Environmental Context of Aging: Life-Styles, Environmental Quality and Living Arrangements*, New York: Garland STPM Press.

Callender, John Hancock, ed. (1974), *Time-Saver Standards for Architectural Design Data*, New York, McGraw-Hill.

Campbell, Joan M. (1983), "Ambient Stressors," *Environment and Behavior* 15: 355–380.

Cantril, Hadley, and William Ittelson (1954), *Perception: A Transactionalist Approach*, Garden City, N.Y.: Doubleday.

Caplow, T., and R. Forman (1955), "Neighborhood Interaction in a Homogeneous Community," *American Sociological Review* 15: 357–366.

Cappon, Daniel (1970), "You Are Living in the Wrong House," *Financial Post Magazine* 64: 2–10.

Carmichael, L., H. P. Hogan, and A. A. Walter (1932), "An Experimental Study of the Effect of Language on the Reproduction of Visually Perceived Forms," *Journal of Experimental Psychology* 15: 73–86.

Carr, H. A. (1935), *An Introduction to Space Perception*, New York: Longmans, Green.

Carr, Stephen (1967), "The City of the Mind," in H. Ewald, ed., *Environmeent for Man*, Bloomington, Ind.: Indiana University Press, pp. 197–231.

————, and D. Schissler (1969), "The City Is a Trip: Perceptual Selection and Memory in the View from the Road," *Environment and Behavior* 1: 7–35.

Cassirer, Ernst (1953), *The Philosophy of Symbolic Form*, translated by Ralph Manheim, New Haven: Yale University Press.

Chadwick, George (1978), *A Systems View of Planning*, New York: Pergamon.

Chapin, F. Stuart (1951), "Psychology of Housing," *Social Forces* 30: 11–15.

Chapin, F. Stuart, Jr., (1965), *Urban Land Use Planning*, Urbana, Ill.: University of Illinois Press.

————, and R. K. Brail (1969), "Human Activity Systems in the Metropolitan United States," *Environment and Behavior* 1: 107–130.

Chapman, Denis (1955), *The Home and Social Status*, London: Routledge and Keagan Paul.

Chermayeff, Serge, and Christopher Alexander (1963), *Community and Privacy*, New York: Doubleday.

Chomsky, Noam (1957), *Syntactic Structure*, The Hague: Mouton.

Churchman, Arza, and Yona Ginsburg (1984), "The Uses of Behavioral Science Research in Physical Planning: Some Inherent Limitations," *Journal of Architectural Research and Planning* 1, no. 1: 57–66.

Churchman, C. West, Russell L. Ackoff, and E. Leonard (1967), *Introduction to Operations Research*, New York: John Wiley.

Clay, Grady (1973), *Close Up, How to Read the American City*, New York: Praeger.

Cole, Margaret Van B. (1960), "A Comparison of Aesthetic Systems: Background for the Identification of Values in City Design," University of California at Berkeley (mimeographed).

Collins, Peter (1965), *Changing Ideals of Modern Architecture 1750–1950*, London: Faber and Faber.

Colquhoun, Alan (1967), "Typology and Design Method," *Arena: Journal of the Architectural Association* 83, no. 913 (June): 11–14.

Conant, James B. (1953), *Modern Science and Modern Man*, Garden City, N.Y.: Doubleday.

Conrad, Ulrich, ed. (1970), *Programs and Manifestoes on Twentieth-Century Architecture*, Cambridge Mass.: MIT Press.

Conway, Donald, ed. (1974), *Social Science and Design: A Process Model for Architect and Social Scientist Collaboration*, Washington, D.C.: AIA Research Department.

Cooley, Charles H. (1909), *Social Organization: A Study of the Larger Mind*, New York: Scribner's.

Cooper, Clare (1967), "Fenced Back Yard—Unfenced Front Yard—Enclosed Porch," *Journal of Housing* 24 (June): 268–274.

———— (1974), "The House as Symbol of Self," in Jon Lang et al., eds., *Designing for Human Behavior: Architecture and the Behavioral Sciences*, Stroudsburg, Pa.: Dowden, Hutchinson and Ross, pp. 130–146.

————, (1975), *Easter Hill Village*, New York: Basic Books.

———— and Phylis Hackett (1968), "Analyses of the Design Process at Two Moderate Income Housing Developments," Berkeley: Center for Planning and Development Research, University of California.

Corbett, Michael N. (1981), *A Better Place to Live: New Designs for Tomorrow's Communities*, Emmaus, Pa.: Rodale Press.

Cowan, Peter (1962–63), "Studies in the Growth, Change and Aging of Buildings," *Transactions of the Bartlett Society* 1: 53–84.

Craik, Kenneth H. (1970), "Environmental Psychology," in *New Directions in Psychology 4*, New York: Holt.

Cranz, Galen (1974), "Using Parsonian Structural-Functionalism for Environmental Design," in William R.

Spillers, ed., *Basic Questions in Design Theory*, New York: American Elsevier, pp., 475–484.

——— (1982), *The Politics of Park Design—A History of Urban Parks in America*, Cambridge, Mass.: MIT Press.

Croney, John (1971), *Anthropometrics for Designers*, New York: Van Nostrand.

Crutchfield, R. S., and M. V. Covington (1965), "Programmed Instruction and Creativity," *Programmed Instruction* 4 (January): 1–2, 8.

Cullen, Gordon (1962), *Townscape*, London: Architectural Press.

Cutler, Laurence Stephan, and Sherrie Stephens Cutler (1982), *Recycling Cities for People: The Urban Design Process* (2nd edition), Boston, Mass.: CBNI Publishing.

Cutting, James E. (1982), "Two Ecological Perspectives: Gibson vs. Shaw and Turvey," *American Journal of Psychology* 95, no. 2: 199–222.

Darke, J., and R. Darke (1974), "Planned Paradise," *Habitat* 17: 36–40.

Davidoff, Paul (1965), "Advocacy and Pluralism in Planning," *Journal of the American Institute of Planners* 31, no. 4 (November): 331–338.

Davis, Gerald, and Virginia Ayers (1975), "Photographic Recording of Environmental Behavior," in William Michelson, ed., *Behavioral Research Methods in Environmental Design*, Stroudsburg, Pa.: Dowden, Hutchinson and Ross, pp. 235–279.

Deasey, C. M. (1974), *Design for Human Affairs*, New York: John Wiley.

De Chiara, Joseph, and Lee Koppelman (1975), *Urban Planning and Design Criteria*, New York: Van Nostrand Reinhold.

De Jonge, Derk (1962), "Images of Urban Areas: Their Structure and Psychological Determinants," *Journal of the American Institute of Planners* 28: 266–276.

De Long, Alton (1970), "Coding Behavior and Levels of Cultural Integration: Synchronic and Diachronic Adaptive Mechanisms in Human Organization," in John Archea and Charles Eastman, eds., *EDRA Two: Proceedings of the 2nd Annual Environmental Design Research Association Conference, October 1970*, Pittsburgh, pp. 354–365.

de Montmollin, Maurice (1967), *Les Systèmes Hommes–Machine*, Paris: Presses Universitaires de France.

de Sausmarez, Maurice (1964), *Basic Design: The Dynamics of Visual Form*, New York: Reinhold.

de Saussure, Ferdinand (1915), *Course in General Linguistics*. Translated by Wade Barker, New York: McGraw-Hill, 1959.

Descartes, René (1637), *Discourse on Method*, translated by A. Wollaston, Harmondsworth: Penguin, 1960.

Deutsch, Morton, and Robert M. Krauss (1965), *Theories in Social Psychology*, New York: Basic Books.

Dewey, John (1920), *How We Think*, London: Heath.

——— (1934), *Art as Experience*, New York: Putnam, 1958.

———, and A. Bentley (1949), "Interaction and Transaction," in *Knowing and the Known*, Boston: Beacon Press, pp. 103–108.

Dickerson, Steven L., and Joseph E. Robertshaw (1975),

Planning and Design, Lexington, Mass.: Lexington Books.

Diffrient, Niels, Alvin R. Tilley, and Joan Bardagjy (1974), *Humanscale 1/2/3*, Cambridge, Mass.: MIT Press.

Doshi, Harish (1974), *Traditional Neighbourhoods in a Modern City*, New Delhi: Abhinov.

Dostoglu, Neslihan (1986), "Architectural Deterministic Thinking in the Development of Urban Utopias, 1882–1933," unpublished doctoral dissertation, University of Pennsylvania.

Dostoglu, Sibel B. (1982), "Towards Professional Legitimacy and Power: An Inquiry into the Struggle, Achievements, and Dilemmas of the Architectural Profession through an Analysis of Chicago 1871–1909," unpublished doctoral dissertation, University of Pennsylvania.

Downs, Roger, and David Stea, eds. (1973), *Image and Environment*, Chicago: Aldine Press.

Dreyfuss, Henry (1968), *The Measure of Man: Human Factors in Design*, New York: Whitney Library of Design.

Drew, Jane B. (1959), "Sector 22," *Urban and Regional Planning Thought*, 2, no. 4 (December): 124–130.

Dubos, René (1965), *Man Adapting*, New Haven: Yale University Press.

Duffy, Francis (1969), "Role and Status in the Office," *Architectural Association Quarterly* 1: 4–13.

Duncan, H. D. (1972), *Symbols in Society*, New York: Oxford University Press.

Duncan, James S., Jr. (1973), "Landscape Taste as a Symbol of Group Identity," *Geographic Review* 63: 334–355.

———, (1982), *Housing and Identity: Cross Cultural Perspectives*, New York: Holmes and Meier.

Eastman, Charles (1970), "On the Analysis of the Intuitive Design Process," in Gary T. Moore, ed., *Emerging Methods in Environmental Design and Planning*, Cambridge, Mass.: MIT Press, pp. 21–37.

Eaton, Leonard K. (1969), *Two Chicago Architects and Their Clients: Frank Lloyd Wright and Norman Van Doren Shaw*, Cambridge, Mass.: MIT Press.

Edney, J. J. (1976), "Human Territories: Comment on Functional Properties," *Environment and Behavior* 8, no. 1: 31–47.

Effrat, Marcia Pelly (1974), "Approaches to Community: Conflicts and Complementarities," in Effrat, ed., *The Community: Approaches and Applications*, New York: Free Press, pp. 1–32.

Ehrenzweig, Anton (1967), *The Hidden Order of Art, A Study in the Psychology of Artistic Imagination*, Berkeley: University of California Press.

Eichler, Edward P., and Marshall Kaplan (1967), *The Community Builders*, Berkeley and Los Angeles: University of California Press.

Eisenman, Peter (1977), "House VI," *Progressive Architecture* 58, no. 6 (June): 57–67

——— (1982), "Introduction," in Aldo Rossi, *The Architecture of the City*, Cambridge, Mass.: MIT Press.

Eisenmann, Russell (1966), "Pleasingness and Interesting Visual Complexity: Support for Berlyne," *Perceptual and Motor Skills* 23: 1167–1170.

Eliovson, Sima (1971), *Gardening the Japanese Way*, London: George C. Harup.

Ellis, Willis D., ed. (1939), *A Source Book of Gestalt Psychology*, New York: Harcourt Brace.

El-Sharkawy, Hussein (1979), "Territoriality: A Model for Design," unpublished doctoral dissertation, University of Pennsylvania.

Eriksen, Aase (1975), *Learning about the Built Environment*, New York: Educational Facilities Laboratory.

Erikson, Eric H. (1950), *Childhood and Society*, New York: Norton.

Eslami, Manoucher (1985), "Architecture as Discourse: The Idea of Method in Modern Architecture," unpublished doctoral dissertation, University of Pennsylvania.

Etzioni, Amitai (1964), *Modern Organization*, Englewood Cliffs, N.J.: Prentice-Hall.

Evans, C. R., P. A. Purcell, and J. Wood (1971), "An Investigation of Design Activities Using Analytical Time-Lapse Photography," National Physical Laboratory, Division of Computer Science.

Evans, Gary W., ed. (1982), *Environmental Stress*, New York: Cambridge University Press.

———, and R. B. Howard (1973), "Personal Space," *Psychological Bulletin*, 80: 334–344.

Evans, Robin (1982), *The Fabrication of Virtue—English Prison Architecture, 1750–1840*, New York: Cambridge University Press.

Everitt, J., and M. Cadwallader (1972), "The Home Range Concept in Urban Analysis," in William J. Mitchell, ed., *Environmental Design: Research and Practice: Proceedings of the EDRA3/AR8 Conference*, Los Angeles, pp. 1.2.1–1.2.10.

Eysenck, Hans J. (1973), "Personality and the Law of Effect," in D. E. Berlyne and K. B. Madsen, eds., *Pleasure, Reward, Preference*, New York: Academic Press.

Fechner, Gustav T. (1876), *Vorschule der Aesthetik*, Leipzig: Gebr. Mann.

Feldman, Arnold, and Charles Tilly (1960), "The Interaction of Social and Physical Space," *American Sociological Review* 25, no. 6: 877–884.

Fellman, Gordon, and Barbara Brandt (1970), "A Neighborhood a Highway Would Destroy," *Environment and Behavior*, 2: 281–301.

Ferguson, G. A. (1966), *Statistical Analysis in Psychology and Education*, New York: McGraw-Hill.

Festinger, Leon (1957), *A Theory of Cognitive Dissonance*, Evanston, Ill.: Row, Peterson.

———, S. Schacter, and Kurt Back (1950), *Social Pressures in Informal Groups*, Stanford, Ca.: Stanford University Press.

———, and Harold H. Kelley (1951), "Changing Attitudes Through Social Contact: An Experimental Study of a Housing Project," Ann Arbor, Mich.: Research Center for Group Dynamics, Institute for Social Research, University of Michigan.

Finrow, Jerry (1970), "Urban Human Contact: 1. A Limited Theoretical Overview; 2. Two Cases," *Man-Environment Systems* (July): S33.

Fiske, D. W., and S. R. Maddi (1961), *Functions of Varied Experience*, Homewood, Ill.: Dorsey Press.

Fitch, James Marston (1965), "Experiential Bases for Aesthetic Decision," *Annals of the New York Academy of Science:* 706–714.

——— (1972), *American Building 2: The Environmental Forces That Shape It*, New York: Schocken Books.

——— (1979), "A Funny Thing Happened . . ." *AIA Journal*, 68: 82.

Flaschbart, Peter G. (1969), "Urban Territorial Behavior," *Journal of the American Institute of Planners* 25, no. 6: 412–416.

Fodor, J. A. (1981, "The Mind–Body Problem," *Scientific American* 224, no. 1 (January): 114–123.

Foott, Sydney (1977), *Handicapped at Home*, London: Design Centre.

Frampton, Kenneth (1980), *Modern Architecture: a Critical History*, New York: Oxford University Press.

Franck, Karen (1984), "Exorcising the Ghost of Physical Determinism," *Environment and Behavior* 10, no. 4 (July): 411–430.

Frank, H. (1959), *Grundlagenprobleme der Informationsästhetik und erste Anwending auf die mime pure*, Quickborn: Verlag Schnelle.

Freedman, Jonathan L., David O. Sears, and J. Merrill Carlsmith (1981), *Social Psychology*, Englewood Cliffs, N.J.: Prentice-Hall.

Fried, Marc (1963), "Grieving for a Lost Home," in J. Duhl, ed., *The Urban Condition*, New York: Simon & Schuster, pp. 151–171.

Friedman, Stephen, and Joseph B. Juhasz (1974), *Environments: Notes and Selections on Objects, Spaces and Behavior*, Monterey, Ca.: Brooks/Cole.

Fromm, Eric (1950), *The Sane Society*, New York: Reinhart.

Frump, Bob (1978), "Why Projects Fail," *Philadelphia Inquirer*, April 16, p. 1–L.

Fry, Maxwell (1961), "Problems of Chandigarh Architecture," *MARG* 25, no. 1 (December): 20–21, 25.

Gadamer, Hans Georg (1976), *Philosophical Hermeneutics*, translated by David E. Linge, Berkeley: University of California.

——— (1975), *Truth and Method*, translated by Garrett Barden and John Cumming, New York: Seabury.

Galitz, Wilbert O. (1980), *Human Factors in Office Management*, Life Office Management Association.

Gallion, Arthur B., and Simon Eisner (1963), *The Urban Pattern*, New York: Van Nostrand (2nd edition).

Gandelsonas, Mario (1974), "Linguistic and Semiotic Models in Architecture," in W. R. Spillers, ed., *Basic Questions of Design Theory*, New York: American Elsevier, pp. 39–54.

Gans, Herbert J. (1961), "Planning and Social Life," *Journal of the American Institute of Planners* 27: 134–140.

——— (1962), *The Urban Villagers*, New York: Free Press.

——— (1967), *The Levittowners*, New York: Pantheon.

——— (1968), *People and Plans*, New York: Basic Books.

——— (1972), "Integrating New Towns," *Design and Environment* 3, no. 1: 28–29, 50–51.

——— (1975), "Foreword," in Clare Cooper, *Easter Hill*

Village, New York: Free Press, pp. ix–xxi.

Garcia, Raul (1982), "Towards a Comprehensive Design Methodology" (mimeographed).

Gardiner, Richard A. (1978), *Design of Safe Neighborhoods,* Washington, D.C.: U.S. Government Printing Office.

Gastal, Alfredo (1982), "Towards a Model of Cultural Analysis for the Designing Process," unpublished doctoral dissertation, University of Pennsylvania.

Gerard, Robert M. (1958), "The Differential Effects of Colored Lights on Psychophysical Functions," unpublished doctoral dissertation, University of California at Los Angeles.

Gertkus, K. (1969), *Die Temperaturverhaltnisse in Raumer bei Sonneneinstrahlung durch Fenster,* Deutsche Bauzeitting, Sonderduik, Stuttgart: Deutsche Verlags-Anstalt.

Gibson, Eleanor J. (1969), *Principles of Perceptual Learning and Development,* New York: Appleton-Century-Crofts.

———, and R. D. Walk (1960), "The 'Visual Cliff,'" *Scientific American* 202 no. 4 (April): 64–71.

Gibson, James J. (1950), *The Perception of the Visual World,* Boston: Houghton Mifflin.

——— (1961), "Ecological Optics," *Vision Research* 1: 253–262.

——— (1966), *The Senses Considered as Perceptual Systems,* Boston: Houghton Mifflin.

——— (1971), "The Legacies of Koffka's Principles," *Journal of the History of the Behavioral Sciences* 7, no. 1: 3–9.

——— (1975), "Pickford and the Failure of Experimental Aesthetics," *Leonardo* 8: 319–321.

——— (1979), *An Ecological Approach to Visual Perception,* Boston: Houghton Mifflin.

———, and Eleanor J. Gibson (1955), "Perceptual Learning: Differentiation or Enrichment?" *Psychological Review* 62: 32–41.

Gideon, Siegfried (1941), *Space, Time and Architecture, The Growth of a New Tradition,* London: Oxford University Press, 1971.

Gillfillan, S. G. (1970), *The Sociology of Invention,* Cambridge, Mass.: MIT Press.

Glassie, Henry (1975), *Folk Housing in Middle Virginia: A Structural Analysis of Historical Artifacts,* Knoxville: University of Tennessee Press.

——— (1982), *Passing the Time in Ballymenone,* Philadelphia: University of Pennsylvania Press.

Goetze, R. (1968), "Recreating Responsive Environments," *Architectural Design* 38: 365–366.

Goffman, Erving (1961), *Asylums,* Garden City, N.Y.: Anchor.

——— (1963), *Behavior in Public Places,* New York: Free Press.

——— (1972), *Relations in Public: Microstudies of Public Order,* London: Penguin.

Goldberg, Theodore (1969), "The Automobile: A Social Institution for Adolescents," *Environment and Behavior* 1, no. 2: 157–185.

Goldfinger, Erno (1942), "The Elements of Enclosed Space," *The Architectural Review* 91, no. 541: 5–8.

Goldsmith, Selwyn (1976), *Designing for the Disabled,* London: Royal Institute of British Architects.

Gombrich, E. H. (1960), *Art as Illusion: A Study of the Psychology of Pictorial Representation,* London: Pantheon.

——— (1963), *Meditations on a Hobby Horse and Other Essays on Art,* London: Pantheon Press.

——— (1975), *Art History and the Social Sciences,* Oxford: Oxford University Press.

Goodchild, B. (1974), "Class Differences in Environmental Perception," *Urban Studies* 11: 157–169.

Goodman, Paul, and Percival Goodman (1947), *Communitas,* Chicago: University of Illinois Press.

Goodman, Robert (1971), *After the Planners,* New York: Touchstone.

Goodrich, Ronald (1974), "Surveys, Questionnaires and Interviews," in Jon Lang et al., eds., *Designing for Human Behavior: Architecture and the Behavioral Sciences,* Stroudsburg, Pa.: Dowden, Hutchinson and Ross, pp. 234–243.

Goody, James, ed. (1962), *The Development Cycle in Domestic Groups,* Cambridge: Cambridge University Press.

Gordon, William J. J. (1961), *Synectics: The Development of Creative Capacity,* New York: Harper Bros.

——— (1978), *The Metaphorical Way,* Washington, D.C.: Porpoise.

Gottschalk, Shimon S. (1975), *Communities and Alternatives: An Exploration of the Limits of Planning,* Cambridge, Mass.: Schenkman.

Grandjean, Etienne (1973), *Ergonomics of the Home,* New York: Halsted.

———, ed. (1984), *Ergonomics and Health in Modern Offices,* Philadelphia: Taylor and Francis.

Grant, Donald P. (1975), "Aims and Potentials of Design Methodology," in Basil Honikman, ed., *Responding to Social Change,* Stroudsburg, Pa.: Dowden, Hutchinson and Ross, pp. 96–108.

——— (1982), *Design by Objectives: Multiple Objective Design Analysis and Evaluation in Architectural, Environmental and Product Design,* San Luis Obispo, Ca.: Design Methods Group.

Gray, Christopher (1953), *Cubist Aesthetic Theories,* Baltimore: Johns Hopkins University Press.

Green, Ronald, *The Architect's Guide to Running a Job,* London: Architectural Press.

Greenbie, Barrie (1976), *Design for Diversity,* Amsterdam: Elsevier.

Greene, Graham (1963), *A Burnt-Out Case,* London: Penguin.

Greene, Herb (1976), *Mind and Image,* Lexington, Ky.: University of Kentucky Press.

Gregory, Richard L. (1966), *Eye and Brain, The Psychology of Seeing,* New York: McGraw-Hill.

Griffen, C. W. (1972), *Development Building: The Team Approach,* Washington, D.C.: American Institute of Architects.

Griffitt, William (1970), "Environmental Effects on Interpersonal Affective Behavior: Ambient Effective Temperature and Attraction," *Journal of Personality and Social Psychology* 15: 240–244.

———, and Russell Veitch (1971), "Hot and Crowded:

Influence of Population Density and Temperature on Interpersonal Affective Behavior," *Journal of Personality and Social Psychology* 17: 92–98.

Groat, Linda, and David Canter (1979), "A Study of Meaning: Does Post-Modernism Communicate?" *Progressive Architecture* 60, no. 12: 84–87.

Gropius, Walter (1947), "Design Topics," *Magazine of Art* 40: 229–244.

—— (1962), *The Scope of Total Architecture*, New York: Collier.

Group for Environmental Education (1971), *Our Man-Made Environment*, Philadelphia: GEE.

Guardo, C. J. (1969), "Personal Space in Children," *Child Development* 40: 143–151.

Guilford, J. P. (1959), "Three Faces of Intellect," *American Psychologist* 14: 469–479.

—— (1967), *The Nature of Human Intelligence*, New York: McGraw-Hill.

Gump, Paul (1971), "Milieu, Environment and Behavior," *Design and Environment* 2: 48–50, 60.

—— (1979), *An Introduction to Ecological Psychology*, Monterey, Ca.: Brooks/Cole.

Gutman, Robert 1966), "Site Planning and Social Behavior," *Journal of Social Issues* 22: 103–115.

—— (1972), "The Questions Architects Ask," in R. Gutman, ed., *People and Buildings*, New York: Basic Books, pp. 337–369.

—— (1977), "Cast of Characters; Architecture, the Entrepreneurial Profession," *Progressive Architecture* 58 (May): 55–58.

—— and Barbara Westergaard (1974), "Building Evaluation, User Satisfaction and Design," in Jon Lang et al., eds., *Designing for Human Behavior: Architecture and the Behavioral Sciences*, Stroudsburg, Pa.: Dowden, Hutchinson and Ross.

Habraken, N. John (1971), *Supports: An Alternative to Mass Housing*, New York: Praeger.

Hack, Gary (1979), "Environmental Programming," unpublished doctoral dissertation, Massachusetts Institute of Technology.

Hall, Calvin S., and Gardner Lindzey (1957), *Theories of Personality*, New York: John Wiley.

Hall, Edward T. (1959), *The Silent Language*, New York: Doubleday.

—— (1963), "What Is Quality?" *AIA Journal* 40, no. 1: 44–48.

—— (1966), *The Hidden Dimension*, New York: Doubleday.

—— (1974), "Meeting Man's Spatial Needs in Artificial Environments," in Jon Lang et al., eds., *Designing for Human Behavior: Architecture and the Behavioral Sciences*, Stroudsburg, Pa.: Dowden, Hutchinson and Ross, pp. 210–220.

Hall, Richard H. (1972), *Organization: Structure and Processes*, Englewood Cliffs, N.J.: Prentice-Hall.

Halprin, Lawrence (1965), "Motation," *Progressive Architecture* 46, no. 7: 126–133.

Handlin, David P. (1972), "The Detached House in the Age of the Object and Beyond," in William Mitchell, ed., *Environment and Design, Research and Practice: Pro-ceedings of the EDRA3/AR8 Conference*, Los Angeles, pp. 7.2.1–7.2.8.

Harris, Britton (1967), "The Limitations of Science and Humanism in Planning," *Journal of the American Institute of Planners* 35, no. 5: 324–325.

Hart, Roger, and Gary T. Moore (1973), "The Development of Spatial Cognition," in R. M. Downs and David Stea, eds., *Image and Environment: Cognitive Mapping and Spatial Behavior*, Chicago: Aldine, pp. 246–288.

Hartman, Chester (1963), "Social Values and Housing Orientations," *Journal of Social Issues* 19: 113–131.

Hassan, Y. (1965), "The Movement System as an Organizer of Visual Form," unpublished doctoral dissertation, Massachusetts Institute of Technology.

Hassid, Sami (1961), "Systems of Judgment in Architectural Design," *New Building Research*, Washington, D.C.: National Academy of Science and the Building Research Council.

Haviland, David (1967), "The Activity/Space: A Least Common Denominator for Architectural Programming," paper presented to the American Institute of Architects Conference (dittoed).

Hawley, Amos (1950), *Human Ecology: A Theory of Community Structure*, New York: Ronald Press.

Hayden, Delores (1976), *Seven American Utopias: The Architecture of Communitarian Socialism*, Cambridge, Mass.: MIT Press.

Hayward, D. Geoffrey (1974), "Psychological Factors in the Use of Light and Lighting in Buildings," in Jon Lang et al., eds., *Designing for Human Behavior: Architecture and the Behavioral Sciences*, Stroudsburg, Pa.: Dowden, Hutchinson and Ross, pp. 120–129.

Heath, Tom (1984), *Method in Architecture*, New York: Van Nostrand Reinhold.

Heider, F. (1946), "Attitudes and Cognitive Organization," *Journal of Psychology* 21: 107–112.

Heider, R., and M. Simmel (1944), "An Experimental Study of Apparent Behavior," *American Journal of Psychology* 57: 43–59.

Heimseth, Clovis (1977), *Behavioral Architecture*, New York: McGraw-Hill.

Helmholtz, Herman L. F. von (1925), *Physiological Optics*, edited by J.P.C. Southall, Washington D.C.: Optical Society of America.

Helmreich, Robert (1974), "The Evaluation of Environments: Behavioral Research in an Undersea Habitat," in Jon Lang et al., eds., *Designing for Human Behavior: Architecture and the Behavioral Sciences*, Stroudsburg, Pa.: Dowden, Hutchinson and Ross, pp. 274–285.

Helson, Harry (1948), "Adaptation Level as a Basis for a Quantitative Theory of Frames of Reference," *Psychological Review* 55: 297–313.

—— (1964), *Adaptation-Level Theory*, New York: Harper & Row.

Herdeg, Klaus (1983), *The Decorated Diagram, Harvard Architecture and the Failure of the Bauhaus Legacy*, Cambridge, Mass.: MIT Press.

Hershberger, Robert G. (1970), "Architecture and Meaning," *Journal of Aesthetic Education* 4, no. 4: 37–55.

—— (1974), "Predicting the Meaning of Architecture," in Jon Lang et al., eds., *Designing for Human Behavior: Architecture and the Behavioral Sciences*, Stroudsburg, Pa.: Dowden, Hutchinson and Ross, pp. 147–156.

Heschong, Lisa (1979), *Thermal Delight in Architecture*, Cambridge, Mass.: MIT Press.

Hesselgren, Sven (1975), *Man's Perception of the Man-Made Environment: an Architectural Theory*, Stroudsburg, Pa.: Dowden, Hutchinson and Ross.

Hester, Randolph (1975), *Neighborhood Space*, Stroudsburg, Pa.: Dowden, Hutchinson and Ross.

Heyman, Mark (1978), *Places and Spaces: Environmental Psychology in Education*, Bloomington, Ind.: Phi Kappa Delta Educational Foundation.

Hill, Morris (1972), "A Goal Achievement Matrix for Evaluating Alternative Plans," in Ira M. Robinson, ed., *Decision-Making in Urban Planning*, Beverly Hills, Ca.: Sage, pp. 185–207.

Hine, Thomas (1978), "Stalking the Style of the Synagogue," *Philadelphia Inquirer*, Sunday, June 26.

Hinshaw, M., and K. Alott (1972), "Environmental Preferences of Future Housing Consumers," *Journal of the American Institute of Planners* 38: 102–107.

Hipple, Walter (1957), *The Beautiful, the Sublime and the Picturesque in Eighteenth-Century British Aesthetic Theory*, Carbondale, Ill.: Southern Illinois University Press.

Hochberg, Julian (1964), *Perception*, Englewood Cliffs, N.J.: Prentice-Hall.

Holohan, Charles (1982), *Environmental Psychology*, New York: Random House.

——, and Susan Saegert (1973), "Behavioral and Attitudinal Effects of Large-Scale Variations in the Physical Environments of Psychiatric Wards," *Journal of Abnormal Psychology* 82: 454–462.

Hood, A. (1963), "A Study of the Relationship between Physique and Personality Variables Measured by the MMPI," *Journal of Personality* 31: 97–107.

Horowitz, M. J., D. F. Duff, and L. C. Stratton (1970), "Personal Space and the Body Buffer Zone," in Harold Proshansky et. al., eds., *Environmental Psychology: Man and His Physical Settings*, New York: Holt, Rinehart and Winston, pp. 214–220.

Howard, E. (1920), *Territory in Bird Life*, New York: Dutton.

Howard, Ebenezer (1902), *Garden Cities of Tomorrow*, London: Sonnenschein.

Howell, Sandra (1980), *Designing for Aging: Patterns of Use*, Cambridge, Mass.: MIT Press.

Hunt, E. (1983) "On the Nature of Intelligence," *Science* 219, no. 4581 (January 14): 141–146.

Isaac, A.R.G. (1971), *Approach to Architectural Design*, Toronto: University of Toronto.

Israel, J., and H. Tajfel (1972), *The Context of Social Psychology*, London: Academic Press.

Ittelson, William H. (1960), *Visual Space Perception*, New York: Springer.

—— (1973), "Environmental Perception and Contemporary Perceptual Theory," in Ittelson, ed., *Environment and Cognition*, New York: Seminar Press, pp. 1–19.

——, and Hadley Cantril (1954), *Perception: A Transactionalist Approach*, Garden City, N.Y.: Doubleday.

——, Leanne Rivlin, and Harold Proshansky (1970), "The Uses of Behavioral Maps in Environmental Psychology," in H. Proshansky et al., eds., *Environmental Psychology: Man and his Physical Setting*, New York: Holt, Rinehart and Winston, pp. 658–668.

——, Karen Franck, and Timothy O'Hanlon (1976), "The Nature of Environmental Experience," in Seymour Wapner, Saul D. Cohen, and Leonard Kaplan, eds., *Experiencing the Environment*, New York: Plenum, pp. 187–206.

——, Harold M. Proshansky, Leanne Rivlin, and Gary Winkel (1974), *An Introduction to Environmental Psychology*, New York: Holt, Rinehart and Winston.

Itten, Johannes (1965), "The Foundation Course at the Bauhaus," in Gyorgy Kepes, ed., *The Education of Vision*, New York: George Braziller, pp. 104–121.

Izumi, Kiyo (1965), "Some Architectural Considerations in the Design of Facilities for the Care and Treatment of the Mentally Ill," paper prepared for the American Schizophrenia Foundation (mimeographed).

—— (1967), "LSD and Architecture," Human Ecology Program, University of Saskatchewan (mimeographed).

—— (1968), "Some Psycho-Social Considerations of Environmental Design" (mimeographed).

Jackson, Barry (1967), *Zodiac 17*, pp. 210–211.

Jackson, J. B. (1951), "Ghosts at the Door," *Landscape* 1: 3–9.

—— (1956–57), "Other-directed Houses," *Landscape* 6, no. 2: 29–35.

—— (1972), *American Space: The Centennial Years 1865–1876*, New York: Norton.

Jacobs, Jane (1961), *The Death and Life of Great American Cities*, New York: Random House.

—— (1969), *The Economy of Cities*, New York: Random House.

Jain, R. K., et al., eds. (1977), *Environmental Impact Analysis*, New York: Van Nostrand Reinhold.

James, William (1890), *The Principles of Psychology*, New York: Holt.

Jencks, Charles (1969), "Semiology and Architecture," in Charles Jencks and George Baird, eds., *Meaning in Architecture*, New York: George Braziller, pp. 11–26.

—— (1971), *Architecture 2000: Predictions and Methods*, New York: Praeger.

—— (1977), *The Language of Post-Modern Architecture*, London: Academy.

—— and George Baird, eds. (1969), *Meaning in Architecture*, New York: George Braziller.

Jenkins, Frank (1961), *Architect and Patron*, New York: Oxford University Press.

Joiner, Duncan (1971), "Social Ritual and Architectural Space," *Architectural Research and Teaching* 1, no. 3: 11–22.

Jones, Barclay G. (1958), "Prologomena to the Study of the Aesthetic Effects of Cities," *The Journal of Aesthetics and Art Criticism* 18, no. 4: 419–429.

—— (1962), "Design from Knowledge not Belief," *AIA*

Journal 38, no. 6: 104–105.

———, and David E. Sparrow (1980), "Major Themes in the Evolution of Planning Thought" (mimeographed).

Jones, J. Christopher (1970), *Design Methods: Seeds of Human Futures,* New York: John Wiley.

Jones, Michael A., and John H. Catlin (1978), "Design for Access," *Progressive Architecture* 59, no. 4: 65–71.

Jones, Peter Lloyd (1969), "The Failure of Basic Design," *Leonardo* 2: 155–160.

Jung, Carl G. (1968), "Approaches to the Unconscious," in Jung, ed., *Man and His Symbols,* New York: Dell, pp. 1–94.

Kandinsky, Wassily (1926), *Punkt und Linie zu Flache,* Munich: Langen; published in English as *Point and Line to Plane* (c. 1947), New York: Guggenheim Museum.

Kantowitz, Barry H., and Robert D. Sorkin, eds. (1983), *Human Factors: Understanding People–System Relationships,* New York: John Wiley.

Kantrowitz, Min (1985), "Has Environment and Behavior Research Made a Difference?" *Environment and Behavior* 17, no. 1 (January): 25–46.

Kaplan, Abraham (1964), *The Conduct of Inquiry,* Scranton: Chandler.

Kaplan, Stephen (1973), "Cognitive Maps in Perception and Thought," in Roger M. Downs and David Stea, eds., *Image and Environment,* Chicago: Aldine, pp. 63–78.

——— (1982), *Cognition and Environment: Functioning in an Uncertain World,* New York: Praeger.

——— (1983), "Person–Environment Compatibility," *Environment and Behavior* 15, no. 3 (May): 311–322.

———, and Rachel Kaplan (1978), *Humanscape: Environments for People,* North Scituate, Mass.: Duxbury.

Katz, Daniel, and Robert L. Kahn (1966), *The Social Psychology of Organizations,* New York: John Wiley.

Katz, David (1950), *Gestalt Psychology,* translated by Robert Tyson, New York: Ronald Press.

Kavolis, Vytautas (1968), *Artistic Expression—a Sociological Analysis,* Ithaca, N.Y.: Cornell University Press.

Kaye, B. (1960), *The Development of the Architectural Profession in Britain,* London: Allen and Unwin.

Keller, Suzanne (1968), *The Urban Neighborhood,* New York: Random House.

Kenny, Anthony (1973), *Wittgenstein,* London: Allen Lane.

Kepes, Gyorgy (1944), *Language of Vision,* Chicago: Paul Theobold.

———, ed. (1966), *Sign, Image, Symbol,* New York: George Braziller.

Keyerserlingk, Edward W. (1979), *Sanctity of Life or Quality of Life in the Context of Ethics, Medicine and Law,* Ottawa: Law Reform Commission of Canada.

Khan-Mahomedov, S. O. (1971), "N. A. Ladovsky 1881–1941," in O. A. Shvidovsky, ed., *Building in the U.S.S.R., 1917–1932,* New York: Praeger, pp. 72–76.

Khazanova, V. (1971), "Vkhutemas, Vkutein," in O. A. Shvidovsky, ed., *Building in the U.S.S.R., 1917–1932,* New York: Praeger, pp. 31–34.

Kinzel, Augustus F. (1970), "Body-Buffer Zone in Violent Prisoners," *The American Journal of Psychiatry* 127: 59–64.

Kira, Alexander (1966), *The Bathroom: Criteria for Design,* Ithaca, N.Y.: Center for Housing and Environmental Studies, Cornell University.

Kirk, W. (1963), "Problems of Geography," *Geography* 37: 357–371.

Kirkbride, Thomas (1888), *Hospitals for the Insane,* Philadelphia: J. B. Lippencott.

Klausner, Samuel Z. (1968), *Why Man Takes Chances: Studies in Stress-Seeking,* Garden City, N.Y.: Anchor.

Klee, G. D., et al. (1967), "An Ecological Analysis of Diagnosed Mental Illness in Baltimore," in R. R. Moore et al., eds., *Psychiatric Epidemiology and Mental Health Planning,* Washington, D.C.: American Psychiatric Association.

Klee, Paul (1925), *Pädagogisches Skizzenbuch,* Munich: Langen; translated by S. Moholy-Nagy as *Pedagogical Sketchbook,* New York: Praeger, 1953.

Klopfer, P. H. (1969), *Habitats and Territories: A Study of the Use of Space by Animals,* New York: Basic Books.

Koberg, Don, and Jim Bagnall (1974), *The Universal Traveler,* Los Altos, Ca.: William Kaufman (2nd edition, 1977).

Koestler, Arthur (1964), *The Act of Creation,* New York: Macmillan.

Koffka, Kurt (1935), *Principles of Gestalt Psychology,* New York: Harcourt Brace.

Köhler, Wolfgang (1929), *Gestalt Psychology,* New York: Liveright.

Krampen, Martin (1976), "A Possible Analogy between (Psycho-)Linguistic and Architectural Measurement," in David Canter and Terrence Lee, eds., *Psychology and the Built Environment,* London: Architectural Press, pp. 87–95.

———, Kutzal Ozturk, and Hasan Saltik (1978), "Some Impressions and Objective 'Old' and 'New' Façades," *Architectural Bulletin,* no. 3, Karadeniz Technical University, Trabzon.

Krech, D., and R. S. Crutchfield (1948), *Theory and Problems of Social Psychology,* New York: McGraw-Hill.

Kretschner, Ernst (1925), *Physique and Character,* New York: Harcourt, Brace and World.

Kriedberg, Marshall, Herman Field, et al. (1965), "Problems of Pediatric Hospital Design," Final Report, Research Project HM00235, U.S. Public Health Service.

Krier, Rob (1979), *Urban Space,* New York: Rizzoli.

Krippendorf, Klaus (1980), *Content Analysis,* Beverly Hills, Ca.: Sage.

——— (1981), interview with author.

Kroll, Lucien (1972), "La Zone Molle: The Soft-Zone" (photocopied).

Kuhn, Alfred (1974), *The Logic of Social Systems,* San Francisco: Jossey-Bass.

Kuhn, Thomas (1965), *The Structure of Scientific Revolutions,* Chicago: University of Chicago Press.

Kuller, Rikard (1981), *Non-Visual Effects of Light and Colour,* Stockholm: Swedish Council for Building Research.

Kunzel, H., and Ch. Snatzke (1969), "Zur Wirkung von Sonnenschutzglasern auf die Sommerlichen Temperature in Raumen," *Gesunheits-Ing.* 90: 2–10.

Kuper, Leo, et al. (1953), *Living in Towns*, London: Cresset Press.

Ladd, Florence C. (1970), "Black Youths View Their Environment: Neighborhood Maps," *Environment and Behavior* 2: 74–99.

——— (1978), "City Kids in the Absence of Legitimate Adventure," in Stephen Kaplan and Rachel Kaplan, eds., *Humanscape*, North Scituate, Mass.: Duxbury, pp. 443–447.

Lalo, C. (1908), *L'Esthétique Expérimentate Contemporaine*, Paris; republished 1977.

Lang, Jon (1971), "Architecture for Human Behavior—The Nature of the Problem," in Charles Burnette et al., eds., *Architecture for Human Behavior*, AIA/Phildelphia Chapter, pp. 5–14.

——— (1977), "Applying the Behavioral Sciences to Theory-Building for the Design Professions: A Case Study of Basic Design," unpublished doctoral dissertation, Cornell University.

——— (1980a), "The Built Environment and Social Behavior: Architectural Determinism Reexamined," *VIA IV*, Cambridge, Mass.: MIT Press, pp. 146–153.

——— (1980b), "The Nature of Theory for Architecture and Urban Design," *Urban Design International* 1, no. 2: 41.

——— (1982), "Symbolic Aesthetics in Architecture: Towards a Research Agenda," in Polly Bart et al., eds., *Knowledge for Design*, Washington, D.C.: EDRA Inc., pp. 172–182.

——— (1983), "Perception Theory, Formal Aesthetics and the Basic Design Course," in Doug Amedo et al., eds., *Proceedings of the Fifteenth International Conference of the Environmental Design Research Association*, pp. 48–55.

——— (1984), "Formal Aesthetics and Visual Perception: Questions Architects Ask," *Visual Arts Research* 10, no. 1: 66–73.

———, and Charles Burnette (1974), "A Model of the Design Process," in Lang et al., eds., *Designing for Human Behavior: Architecture and the Behavioral Sciences*, Stroudsburg, Pa.: Dowden, Hutchinson and Ross, pp. 43–51.

———, Charles Burnette, Walter Moleski, and David Vachon, eds. (1974), *Designing for Human Behavior: Architecture and the Behavioral Sciences*, Stroudsburg, Pa.: Dowden, Hutchinson and Ross.

———, Sengul Gur, et al. (1982), "Uzamsal Imgeler, Bilis (Stilleri) ve Estik Yeğlemelerin Dogasi: Trabzon'da 5 pilot Calisma," *Mimarlik Bülteni* 7: 71–94.

Langdon, F. J. (1966), "The Social and Physical Environment: A Social Scientist's View," *Journal of the Royal Institute of British Architects* 73: 460–464.

Langer, Susanne K. (1953), *Feeling and Form*, New York: Scribner's.

Lansing, John B., and Robert W. Marans (1969), "Evaluation of Neighborhood Quality," *Journal of the American Institute of Planners* 35: 195–199.

———, ———, and Robert B. Zehner (1970), *Planned Residential Environments*, Ann Arbor, Mich.: Institute for Social Research, University of Michigan.

Larson, Magali (1979), *The Rise of Professionalism*, Berkeley and Los Angeles: University of California Press.

Lashley, K. S., K. L. Chow, and J. Semmes (1951), "An Examination of the Electric Field Theory of Cerebral Integration," *Psychological Review* 58: 123–136.

Lasswell, Harold (1979), *The Signature of Power: Buildings, Communication and Policy*, New Brunswick, N.J.: Transaction Books.

Latham, Richard S. (1966), "The Artifact as Cultural Cipher," in Laurence B. Holland, ed., *Who Designs America?* Garden City, N.Y.: Doubleday, pp. 257–280.

Laugier, Marc-Antoine (1753), *Essai sur l'architecture;* republished 1966, Farnborough: Gregg Press.

Lauman, Edward, and James House (1972), "Living Room Styles and Social Attitudes: Patterning Artifacts in an Urban Community," in Lauman et al., eds., *The Logic of Social Hierarchies*, Chicago: Markham, pp. 189–193.

Lawton, M. Powell (1975), *Planning and Managing Housing for the Elderly*, New York: Wiley Interscience.

——— (1977), "An Ecological Theory of Aging Applied to Elderly Housing," *Journal of Architectural Education* 31, no. 1: 6–10.

Leary, Michael (1968), "Individual Stress in the Urban Environment," unpublished master's thesis, Graduate School, Cornell University.

LeCompte, William (1972), "Behavior Settings: The Structure of the Treatment Environment," in William J. Mitchell, ed., *Environmental Design: Research and Practice, Proceedings of the EDRA3/AR8 Conference*, Los Angeles, pp. 4.2.1–4.2.2.

——— (1974), "Behavior Settings as Data-Generating Units for the Environmental Planner and Architect," in Jon Lang et al., eds., *Designing for Human Behavior: Architecture and the Behavioral Sciences*, Stroudsburg, Pa.: Dowden, Hutchinson and Ross, pp. 183–193.

———, and Edwin Willems (1970), "Ecological Analysis of a Hospital," in John Archea and Charles Eastman, eds., *EDRA2: Proceedings of the Second Annual Environmental Design Research Association Conference*, Pittsburgh, pp. 226–245.

Le Corbusier (1923), *Vers une architecture*, English translation by F. Etchells, *Towards a New Architecture*, New York: Praeger, 1970.

——— (1925), *Urbanisme*, English translation by F. Etchells, *The City of Tomorrow and its Planning*, London: Architectural Press, 1947.

——— (1934), *La ville radieuse*, English translation by Pamela Knight and Eleanor Levieux, *The Radiant City*, New York: Orion Press, 1967.

——— (1951), *Le Modulor*, English translation by Peter de Francia and Anna Bostock, *The Modulor*, Cambridge, Mass.: MIT Press, 1968.

——— (1960), *Creation Is a Patient Search*, translated from the French by James Palmer, New York: Praeger.

——— (1973), *The Athens Charter*, translated from the French by Anthony Bardley, New York: Grossman.

Lee, Terrence (1962), "Brennan's Law of Shopping Behavior," *Psychological Reports* 11: 662.

——— (1970), "Urban Neighborhood as a Socio-Spatial

Schema," in Harold M. Proshansky et al., eds., *Environmental Psychology: Man and His Physical Setting*, New York: Holt, Rinehart and Winston, pp. 349–370.

—— (1971), "Psychology and Architectural Determinism," *The Architects' Journal* (August 4): 260–261.

Leedy, Daniel L., Robert M. Maestro, and Thomas M. Franklin (1978), *Planning for Wildlife in Cities and Suburbs*, Chicago: American Planning Association.

Leighton, Alexander H. (1959), *My Name Is Legion: Foundations for a Theory of Man in Relation to Culture*, New York: Basic Books.

Leighton, John (1881), *Suggestions in Design*, New York: Appleton.

Lennard, Suzanne, H. Crowhurst, and Henry L. Lennard (1984), *Public Life in Urban Places: Social and Architectural Characteristics Conducive to Public Life in European Cities*, Southampton, NY.: Gondlier.

Levi, David (1974), "The Gestalt Psychology of Expression in Architecture," in Jon Lang et al., eds., *Designing for Human Behavior: Architecture and the Behavioral Sciences*, Stroudsburg, Pa.: Dowden, Hutchinson and Ross, pp. 111–119.

Levy-LeBoyer, Claude (1982), *Psychology and Environment*, Beverly Hills, Ca.: Sage.

Lewin, Kurt (1936), *Principles of Topological Psychology*, New York: McGraw-Hill.

—— (1951), "Field Theory and Learning," in D. Cartwright, ed., *Field Theory in Social Science: Selected Theoretical Papers by Kurt Lewin*, New York: Harper & Row, pp. 60–86.

Lewis, Oscar (1965), *La Vida*, New York: Random House.

Lindblom, Charles, and David Cohen (1979), *Usable Knowledge: Social Sciences and Social Problem Solving*, New Haven: Yale University Press.

Lindheim, Roslyn (1970), "Factors Which Determine Hospital Design," in Harold M. Proshansky et al., eds., *Environmental Psychology: Man and his Physical Setting*, New York: Holt, Rinehart and Winston, pp. 579–587.

Lindzey, G., and E. F. Borgetta (1959), "Sociometric Measurement," in G. Lindzey, ed., *Handbook of Social Psychology*, Reading, Mass.: Addison-Wesley.

Linton, Ralph (1945), *The Cultural Background of Personality*, New York: Appleton-Century-Crofts.

Lipman, Alan (1974), "The Architectural Belief System and Social Behavior," in Jon Lang et al., eds., *Designing for Human Behavior: Architecture and the Behavioral Sciences*, Stroudsburg, Pa.: Dowden, Hutchinson and Ross, pp. 23–30.

Litchfield, Nathaniel (1960), "Cost-Benefit Analysis in City Planning," *Journal of the American Institute of Planners* 26, no. 4 (November): 273–279.

Little, Brian R. (1983), "Personal Projects: A Rationale and Method for Investigation," *Environment and Behavior* 15: 273–309.

Lofland, Lyn H. (1973), *A World of Strangers*, New York: Basic Books.

Lord, Peter, and Duncan Templeton (1983), *Detailing for Acoustics*, London: Architectural Press and Nichols.

Lowenthal, David (1961), "Geography, Experience and Imagination: Towards a Geographical Epistemology," *Annals of the Association of American Geographers* 51: 241–260.

—— (1968), "The American Scene," *The Geographical Review* 58, no. 1: 61–88

——, and Hugh C. Prince (1965), "English Landscape Tastes," *The Geographical Review* 55, no. 2: 188–222.

——, and Marcus Binney, eds. (1981), *Our Past before Us: Why Do We Save It?* London: Temple Smith.

Lowery, R. A. (1973), "A Method for Analyzing Distance Concepts of Urban Residents," in Roger Downs and David Stea, eds., *Image and Environment*, Chicago: Aldine, pp. 338–360.

Lukashok, A. K., and Kevin Lynch (1956), "Some Childhood Memories of the City," *Journal of the American Institute of Planners* 22: 142–152.

Lukiesch, M. (1922), *Visual Illusions: Their Causes, Characteristics and Applications*, reprinted in New York: Dover, 1965.

Lyman, Stanford M., and Marvin B. Scott (1967), "Territoriality—A Neglected Sociological Dimension," *Social Problems* 15: 236–249.

Lynch, Kevin (1960), *The Image of the City*, Cambridge, Mass.: MIT Press.

—— (1977), *Growing up in Cities: Studies of the Spatial Environment of Adolescents in Cracow, Melbourne, Mexico City, Salta, and Warszawa*, Cambridge, Mass.: MIT Press.

—— (1981), *Good City Form*, Cambridge, Mass.: MIT Press.

Lynes, Russell (1954), *The Tastemakers*, New York: Harper.

Lyons, John (1968), *Introduction to Theoretical Linguistics*, New York: McGraw-Hill.

MacKinnon, Donald W. (1962a), "The Personality Correlates of Creativity: A Study of American Architects," in G. S. Nielsen, ed., *Proceedings of the XIV International Congress of Applied Psychology*, Copenhagen: Munksgaard.

—— (1962b), "The Nature and Nurture of Creative Talent," *American Psychologist* 16: 484–495.

—— (1963), "The Characteristics of Creative Architects and Further Reflections on the Implications for Architectural Education," in Marcus Wiffen, ed., *The Teaching of Architecture*, Washington, D.C.: AIA.

—— (1967), "The Study of Creative Persons: A Method and Some Results," in Jerome Kagan, ed., *Creativity and Learning*, Boston: Houghton Mifflin.

Maier, N.R.F. (1967), "Assets and Liabilities of Group Problem-Solving: The Need for an Integrative Function," *Psychological Review* 74, no. 4: 239–249.

Maltzman, I. (1960), "On the Training of Originality," *Psychological Review* 67 no. 4: 229–242.

Mandelbaum, Seymour (1985), "The Institutional Focus of Planning Theory," *Journal of Planning, Education and Research* 5, no. 1: 3–9.

Manheim, Marvin L. (1970), "A Design Process Model: Theory and Applications to Transportation Planning," in Gary T. Moore, ed., *Emerging Methods in Environmental Design and Planning*, Cambridge, Mass.: MIT Press, pp. 331–348.

Manis, Melvin (1966), *Cognitive Processes*, Belmont, Ca.:

Wadsworth.

Manus, Willard (1972), "Hostelboro," *Ekistics* 34, no. 204: 369–376.

Marans, Robert W. (1975), "Survey Research," in William Michelson, ed., *Behavioral Research Methods in Environmental Design*, Stroudsburg, Pa.: Dowden, Hutchinson and Ross, pp. 119–179.

March, James G., and Herbert A. Simon with Harold Guetzkow (1958), *Organizations*, New York: John Wiley.

March, Lionel, and Philip Steadman (1971), *The Geometry of the Environment: An Introduction to Spatial Organization in Design*, London: Methuen.

Markus, T. A. (1969), "The Role of Building Performance, Measurement and Appraisal in Design Method," in Geoffrey Broadbent and Anthony Ward, eds., *Design Methods in Architecture*, New York: Wittenborn.

Marmot, Alexi (1982), "The Legacy of Le Corbusier and High-Rise Housing," *Built Environment* 7, no. 2: 82–95.

Marshall, Nancy (1970), "Personality Correlates of Orientation Towards Privacy," in John Archea and Charles Eastman, eds., *EDRA2: Proceedings of the Second Annual Environmental Design Research Association Conference*, Pittsburgh, pp. 316–319.

Martienssen, Rex D. (1956), *The Idea of Space in Greek Architecture*, Johannesburg: Witwatersrand University Press.

Maslow, Abraham (1943), "Theory of Human Motivation," *Psychological Review* 50: 370–396.

——— (1954), *Motivation and Personality*, New York: Harper & Row.

Maurer, R. J., and J. C. Baxter (1972), "Images of the Neighborhood and City among Black-, Anglo-, and Mexican-American Children," *Environment and Behavior* 4: 351–388.

Maver, Thomas (1975), "Three Paradigms for Design: A Tentative Philosophy," *DMG-DRS Journal* 9, no. 2 (April–June): 130–132.

May, Hayden B. (1965), "Technological and Methodological Advances in Design," unpublished master's thesis, Graduate School, Cornell University.

Mayer, Albert (1967), *The Urgent Future*, New York: McGraw-Hill.

Mayo, James (1984), "Conflicts in Roles and Values for Urban Planners," *Journal of Architectural and Planning Research* 1, no. 1 (June): 67–78.

McConnell, W. J., and M. Spiegelman (1940), "Reactions of 75 Clerks to Summer Air Conditioning," *Heating, Piping, Air Conditioning*, vol. 12, pp. 317–322.

McHarg, Ian L. (1969), *Design With Nature*, Garden City, N.Y.: Natural History Press.

Mead, George (1903), "The Definition of the Physical," in H. Peck, ed., *The Selected Writings of George Herbert Mead*, Indianapolis: Bobbs-Merrill.

Medawar, P. B. (1983), *The Limits of Science*, New York: Harper & Row.

Mehrabian, Albert (1976), *Public Places and Private Spaces: The Psychology of Work, Play and Living Environments*, New York: Basic Books.

———, and James Russell (1974), *Approach to Environmental Psychology*, Cambridge, Mass.: MIT Press.

Meisels, M., and C. J. Guardo (1969), "Development of Personal Space Schematas," *Child Development* 40: 1167–1178.

Meyer, Hannes (1928), *Hannes Meyer*, London: Schnaidt Tiranti.

Michelson, William (1968), "Most People Don't Want What Architects Want," *Transaction* 5, no. 8: 37–43.

——— (1970), "Selected Aspects of Environmental Research in Scandinavia," *Man–Environment Systems* 1 (July): 2.

———, ed. (1975), *Behavioral Research Methods in Environmental Design*, Stroudsburg, Pa.: Dowden, Hutchinson and Ross.

——— (1976), *Man and His Urban Environment: A Sociological Approach*, Reading, Mass.: Addison-Wesley (revised edition).

———, and Paul Reed (1975), "The Time Budget," in William Michelson, ed., *Behavioral Research Methods in Environmental Design*, Stroudsburg, Pa.: Dowden, Hutchinson and Ross, pp. 180–234.

Michotte, A. E. (1968), "The Emotional Significance of Movement," in M. Arnold, ed., *The Nature of Emotion*, Baltimore: Penguin Books.

Mikellides, Byron (1980), *Architecture for People*, New York: Holt, Rinehart and Winston.

Mills, C. W. (1956), *The Power Elite*, New York: Oxford University Press.

Mitchell, Howard E. (1974), "Professional and Client: An Emerging Collaborative Relationship," in Jon Lang et al., eds., *Designing for Human Behavior: Architecture and the Behavioral Sciences*, Stroudsburg, Pa.: Dowden, Hutchinson and Ross, pp. 15–22.

Mitchell, William J. (1977), *Computer-Aided Architectural Design*, New York: Petrocelli/Charter.

Mitroff, Ian I. (1983), *Stake Holders of the Organizational Mind*, San Francisco: Jossey-Bass.

Moholy-Nagy, Lazlo (1965), *Vision in Motion*, Chicago: Paul Theobold.

Moholy-Nagy, Sybil (1968), *Matrix of Man*, New York: Praeger.

Moles, Abraham (1966), *Information Theory and Esthetic Perception*, Urbana, Ill.: University of Illinois Press.

Moleski, Walter (1974), "Behavioral Analysis and Environmental Programming for Offices," in Jon Lang et al., eds., *Designing for Human Behavior: Architecture and the Behavioral Sciences*, Stroudsburg, Pa.: Dowden, Hutchinson and Ross, pp. 302–315.

——— (1978), "Programming for Human Needs," in Wolfgang Preiser, ed., *Facility Programming*, Stroudsburg, Pa.: Dowden, Hutchinson and Ross, pp. 107–126.

——— (1979), "The Usefulness of Man–Environment Knowledge in Development Housing Design," Philadelphia: Environmental Research Group.

———, and Jon Lang (1982), "Organizational Needs and Human Values in Office Planning," *Environment and Behavior* 14, no. 3: 319–332.

Moller, Clifford (1968), *Architectural Environment and Our Mental Health*, New York: Horizon.

Montgomery, Roger (1966), "Comment on 'Fear and

House-as-Haven in the Lower Class,' " *Journal of the American Institute of Planners* 32, no. 1: 31–37.

—— (1971), "Center of Action," in Walter McQuade, ed., *Cities Fit to Live In and How We Can Make Them Happen*, New York: Macmillan, pp. 69–78.

Moore, Gary T., ed. (1970), *Emerging Methods in Environmental Design and Planning*, Cambridge, Mass.: MIT Press.

—— (1972), "Elements of a Genetic-Structural Theory of the Development of Environmental Cognition," in William Mitchell, ed., *Environmental Design: Research and Practice: Proceedings of the EDRA3/AR8 Conference*, Los Angeles, pp. 30.9.1–30.9.13.

—— (1973), "Developmental Differences in Environmental Cognition," in Wolfgang F. Preiser, ed., *Environmental Design Research*, Stroudsburg, Pa.: Dowden, Hutchinson and Ross, vol. 2, pp. 232–239.

—— (1976), "The Development of Environmental Knowing: An Overview of an Interactional-Constructivist Theory and Some Data on Within-Individual Development Variations," in David Canter and Terrence Lee, eds., *Psychology and the Built Environment*, London: Architectural Press, pp. 184–194.

—— (1979), "Knowing about Environmental Knowing: The Current State of Research on Environmental Cognition," *Environment and Behavior* 11, no. 1 (1979): 33–70.

——, and Lynne Meyer Gay (1967), "Creative Problem-Solving in Architecture—a Pilot Study," Department of Architecture, University of California at Berkeley.

——, and Reginald G. Golledge, eds. (1976), *Environmental Knowing: Theories, Research and Methods*, Stroudsburg, Pa.: Dowden, Hutchinson and Ross.

Moore, Kristin, and Sandra Hofferth (1979), "Women and Their Children," in Ralph E. Smith, ed., *The Subtle Revolution*, Washington, D.C.: Urban Institute.

Morawski, Stefan (1977), "Contemporary Approaches to Aesthetic Inquiry: Absolute Demands and Limited Possibilities," *Critical Inquiry* 4 (Autumn): 55–83.

Morris, Charles (1938), *Foundations of a Theory of Signs*, Chicago: University of Chicago Press.

Mukarovsky, Jean (1981), *Structure, Sign and Function*, New Haven: Yale University Press.

Mumford, Lewis (1951), *The City in History*, London: Secker and Warburg.

—— (1952), *Art and Technics*, New York: Columbia University Press.

Murray, Henry A. (1938), *Explorations in Personality*, New York: Oxford University Press.

Murray, Russell (1976), "The Influence of Crowding on Children's Behavior," in David Canter and Terrence Lee, eds., *Psychology and the Built Environment*, London: Architectural Press, pp. 112–117.

Murrell, K.F.H. (1965), *Ergonomics: Man in His Working Environment*, London: Chapman and Hall.

Nadler, Gerald (1970), "Engineering Research and Design in Socioeconomic Systems," in Gary Moore, ed., *Emerging Methods in Environmental Design and Planning*, Cambridge, Mass.: MIT Press, pp. 322–331.

Nalkaya, Saim (1980), "The Personalization of a Housing Environment: A Study of Levittown, Pennsylvania," unpublished doctoral dissertation, University of Pennsylvania.

Na Nangara, Yongyudh (forthcoming), "A Psychological Study of Design Behavior: The Correlations between Preconceptions and Outcomes in Architectural Designing," unpublished doctoral dissertation, University of Pennsylvania.

NASA (1978), *Anthropometric Sources Books. Vol. I: Anthropometry for Designers; Vol, II: Handbook of Anthropometric Data; Vol. III: Annotated Bibliography of Anthropometry*, Webb Associates for NASA.

Nasser, Jack (1985), "IXth International Colloquium on Emperical Aesthetics, U.C. Santa Cruz, August 19–22, 1985," *American Society for Aesthetics Newsletter 6*, no. 1: 3.

Neisser, Ulrich (1977), *Cognition and Reality*, San Francisco: Freeman.

Nesher, Arie (1981), "Socio-Cultural Factors in Israeli Public Housing Design," unpublished doctoral dissertation, University of Pennsylvania.

Neuckermans, Herman (1975), "The Relevance of Systematic Methods for Architectural Design," *DMG-DRS Journal* 9: 140–144.

Neutra, Richard (1954), *Survival Through Design*, New York: Oxford University Press.

Newman, Oscar (1972), *Defensible Space: Crime Prevention Through Urban Design*, New York: Macmillan.

—— (1973), *Architectural Design for Crime Prevention*, Washington, D.C.: U.S. Government Printing Office.

—— (1975), *Design Guidelines for Creating Defensible Space*, Washington, D.C.: U.S. Government Printing Office.

—— (1979), *Community of Interest*, New York: Anchor.

Nice, M. M. (1941), "The Role of Territory in Bird Life," *American Midland Naturalist* 26: 441–487.

Nilsson, Sten (1973), *The New Capitals of India, Pakistan and Bangladesh*. London: Curzon Press.

Norberg-Schulz, Christian (1965), *Intentions in Architecture*, Cambridge, Mass.: MIT Press.

—— (1971), *Existence, Space and Architecture*, New York: Oxford University Press.

—— (1975), *Meaning in Western Architecture*, New York: Praeger.

Olgay, Victor (1963), *Design with Climate*, Princeton: Princeton University Press.

Orlenas, P. (1973), "Differential Cognition of Urban Residents: Effects of Social Scale on Meaning," in Roger Downs and David Stea, eds., *Image and Environment*, Chicago: Aldine, pp. 115–130.

——, and S. Schmidt (1972), "Mapping the City: Environmental Cognition of Urban Residents," in William J. Mitchell, ed., *Environmental Design: Research and Practice, Proceedings of the EDRA3/AR8 Conference*, Los Angeles, pp. 1.4.1–1.4.9.

Orwell, George (1954), "Politics and the English Language," in *Shooting an Elephant*, New York: Harcourt Brace, pp. 77–92.

Osborne, A. F. (1957), *Applied Imagination: Principles and Practices of Creative Thinking*, New York: Scribner's.

Osgood, C. E., and P. H. Tannenbaum (1955), "The Principles of Congruity in the Prediction of Attitude

Change," *Psychological Review* 62: 42–55.

Oskamp, Stuart (1977), *Attitudes and Opinions*, Englewood Cliffs, N.J.: Prentice-Hall.

Osmond, Humphrey (1966), "Some Psychiatric Aspects of Design," in Laurence B. Holland, ed., *Who Designs America?* New York: Doubleday, 281–318.

Overy, Paul (1969), *Kandinsky: The Language of the Eye*, New York: Praeger.

Palmer, Mickey A. (1981), *The Architect's Guide to Facility Programming*, Washington, D.C.: AIA and Architectural Record Books.

Panofsky, Erwin, ed. (1946), *Abbot Suger on the Abbey Church of St. Denis and Its Art Treasures*, Princeton, N.J.: Princeton University Press.

——— (1955), *Meaning in the Visual Arts: Papers in and on Art History*, New York: Doubleday.

Park, Robert E., Ernest Burgess, and R. D. Mackenzie, eds. (1925), *The City*, Chicago: University of Chicago Press.

Parke, Ross, and Douglas B. Sawin (1979), "Children's Privacy in the Home Development: Ecological and Child-Raising Determinants," *Environment and Behavior* 11, no. 1: 87–104.

Parker, W. H. (1969), *The Soviet Union*, Chicago: Aldine.

Parnes, S. J. (1962), "The Creative Thinking in the Problem-Solving Course and Institute at the University of Buffalo," in S. Parnes and H. Harding, eds., *A Source Book for Creativity*, New York: Scribner's.

Parr, Albert E. (1967a), "In Search of Theory," *Arts and Architecture* 82, no. 9: 14–16.

——— (1967b), "The Child and the City: Urbanity and the Urban Scene," *Landscape* 16 (Spring): 3–5.

——— (1969), "Lessons of an Urban Childhood," *American Montessori Society Bulletin* 7, no. 4.

Parsons, Talcott (1937), *The Structure of Social Action*, New York: Free Press.

——— (1959), *Structure and Process in Modern Society*, New York: Free Press.

——— (1963), "Some Ingredients of a General Theory of Formal Organization," in Joseph A. Litterer, ed., *Organizations, Systems, Control and Adaptation*, New York: John Wiley, vol. 2, pp. 214–219.

——— (1966), *Societies*, Englewood Cliffs, N.J.: Prentice-Hall.

Passini, Romedi (1984), *Wayfinding in Architecture*, New York: Van Nostrand Reinhold.

Pastalan, Leon A. (1970), "Privacy as an Expression of Human Territoriality," in Leon A. Pastalan and Daniel H. Carson, eds., *Spatial Behavior of Older People*, Institute of Gerontology, University of Michigan–Wayne State University, pp. 88–101.

Patricios, N. N. (1975), "Consumer Behavior and Attitudes in Spatial Choice Behavior and Implications for the Planning and Designing of Convenience-Goods Shopping Areas," Occasional Paper No. 1, University of the Witwatersrand.

Patterson, Arthur (1974), "Unobtrusive Measures. Their Nature and Utility for Architects," in Jon Lang et al., eds., *Designing for Human Behavior: Architecture and the Behavioral Sciences*, Stroudsburg, Pa.: Dowden, Hutchinson and Ross, pp. 261–273.

Pawley, Martin (1971), *Architecture versus Housing*, New York: Praeger.

Peña, William (1977), *Problem Seeking*, Boston, Mass.: Cahners.

Pepper, Stephen C. (1949), *The Basis of Criticism in the Arts*, Cambridge, Mass.: MIT Press.

Perez-Gomez, Alberto (1983), *Architecture and the Crisis of Modern Science*, Cambridge, Mass.: MIT Press.

Perin, Constance (1970), *With Man in Mind*, Cambridge, Mass.: MIT Press.

Perry, Clarence (1927), "The Neighborhood Unit Formula," reprinted in William L. C. Wheaton et al., eds., *Urban Housing*, New York: Free Press of Glencoe, 1966, pp. 94–109.

Pevsner, Nikolaus (1936), *Pioneers of the Modern Movement from William Morris to Walter Gropius*, London: Faber and Faber.

Piaget, Jean (1953), *The Child's Construction of Reality*, reprinted (1964), New York: Basic Books.

Pickford, Ralph W. (1972), *Psychology and Visual Aesthetics*, London: Hutchinson Educational.

Pillsbury, Richard (1970), "The Urban Street Pattern as a Cultural Indicator, Pennsylvania 1682–1815," *Annals of the Association of American Geographers* 60, no. 3 (September): 428–446.

Pipkin, John S., Mark E. La Gory, and Judith Blau (1983), *Remaking the City; Social Science Perspectives on Urban Design*, Albany, N.Y.: SUNY Press.

Pocock, Douglas, and Ray Hudson (1978), *Images of the Urban Environment*, New York: Columbia University Press.

Pollowy, Anne-Marie (1977), *The Urban Nest*, Stroudsburg, Pa.: Dowden, Hutchinson and Ross.

Polya, G. (1957), *How to Solve It*, New York: Doubleday.

Popenoe, David (1977), *The Suburban Environment*, Chicago: University of Chicago Press.

Popper, Karl (1962), *Conjecture and Refutation*, New York: Basic Books.

Porteous, J. Douglas (1971), "Design with People," *Environment and Behavior* 3, no. 2: 206–223.

——— (1977), *Environment and Behavior: Planning and Everyday Urban Life*, Reading, Mass.: Addison-Wesley.

Porter, Tom, and Byron Mikellides (1976), *Color for Architecture*, New York: Van Nostrand Reinhold.

Prak, Niels Luning (1968), *The Language of Architecture*, The Hague: Mouton.

——— (1984), *Architects: The Noted and the Ignored*, New York: John Wiley.

Pratt, Joanne H., James Pratt, Sarah B. Moore, and William T. Moore (1979), *Environmental Encounters*, Dallas: Reverchon.

Preiser, Wolfgang, ed. (1978), *Facility Programming: Methods and Applications*, Stroudsburg, Pa.: Dowden, Hutchinson and Ross.

Prince, H. C. (1971), "Real, Imagined and Abstract Worlds of the Past," in C. Board et al., eds., *Progress in Geography*, London: Arnold.

Propst, Robert (1970), "The Human Performer in the Machine-Related Office," *Environmental Planning and Design* 8: 25–31.

Proshansky, Harold (1974), "Environmental Psychology

and the Design Professions," in Jon Lang et al., eds., *Designing for Human Behavior: Architecture and the Behavioral Sciences*, Stroudsburg, Pa.: Dowden, Hutchinson and Ross, pp. 72–97.

———, William Ittelson, and Leanne G. Rivlin, eds. (1970), "The Influence of the Physical Environment on Behavior: Some Basic Assumptions," in Proshansky, Ittelson, and Rivlin, eds., *Environmental Psychology: Man and His Physical Setting*, New York: Holt, Rinehart and Winston, pp. 27–36.

Rainwater, Lee (1966), "Fear and House-as-Haven in the Lower Class," *Journal of the American Institute of Planners* 32, no. 1: 23–31.

Rand, Ayn (1968), *The Fountainhead*, Indianapolis: Bobbs-Merrill.

Rapoport, Amos (1967), "The Personal Element in Housing: An Argument for Open-Ended Design," *Interbuild-Arena* 14 (October 1967): 44–46.

——— (1969), *House Form and Culture*, Englewood Cliffs, N.J.: Prentice-Hall.

——— (1977), *Human Aspects of Urban Form*, New York: Pergamon.

——— (1982), *The Meaning of the Built Environment: A Non-Verbal Communications Approach*, Beverly Hills, Ca.: Sage.

———, and Robert E. Kantor (1967), "Complexity and Ambiguity in Environmental Design," *Journal of the American Institute of Planners* 33, no. 4: 210–221.

———, and Newton Watson (1972), "Cultural Variability in Physical Standards," in Robert Gutman, ed., *People and Buildings*, New York: Basic Books, pp. 33–53.

Rasmussen, Steen Eiler (1959), *Experiencing Architecture*, Cambridge, Mass.: MIT Press.

Raymond, H., et al. (1966), *L'Habitat Pavillonnaire*, Paris: Centre de Recherche d'Urbanisme.

Razjouyan, Mahmood (1979), "Population Density and the Liveability of Residential Environments," unpublished doctoral dissertation, University of Pennsylvania.

Relph, E. C. (1976), *Place and Placelessness*, London: Pion.

Ricouer, Paul (1977), *The Rule of Metaphor*, translated by R. Czerny, et al., Toronto: University of Toronto Press.

Rittel, Horst (1971), "Some Principles for the Design of an Educational System for Design," *Journal of Architectural Education* 26, no. 1–2 (Winter–Spring): 16–26.

——— (1972), "Son of Rittelthink," *Design Methods Group 5th Anniversary Report* (January): 5–10.

———, and Melvin M. Webber (1972), "Dilemmas in a General Theory of Planning," Working Paper no. 194, Institute of Urban and Regional Development, University of California, Berkeley.

Roberts, E. (1969), *Theory Building*, New York: Free Press.

Robinetter, Gary O., ed. (1985), *Barrier-free Exterior Design: Anyone Can Go Anywhere*, New York: Van Nostrand Reinhold.

Robins, W. J. (1968), "Minimum Standards for Circulation Spaces Between Walls, Tables and Chairs Established by Photography of Body Movements," thesis, Faculty of Technology, University of Manchester.

Roos, P. D. (1968), "Jurisdiction: An Ecological Concept," *Human Relations* 21: 75–84.

Rosenberg, M. J., and R. P. Abelson (1960), "An Analysis of Cognitive Balancing," in C. I. Hovland and I. L. Janis, eds., *Attitude Organization and Change*, New Haven: Yale University Press, pp. 112–283.

Rosmarin, Adena (1984), "Theory and Practice: From Ideally Separately to Pragmatically Joined," *The Journal of Aesthetics and Art Criticism* 43, no. 1 (Fall): 31–40.

Rosow, Irving (1961), "The Social Effects of the Physical Environment," *Journal of the American Institute of Planners* 27: 127–133.

Rossi, Aldo (1982), *The Architecture of the City*, Cambridge, Mass.: MIT Press.

Rowe, Colin (1972), "Introduction" in *Five Architects: Eisenman, Graves, Gwathmey, Hejduk, Meier*, New York: Wittenborn, pp. 3–7.

——— (1983), "Program vs. Paradigm," *The Cornell Journal of Architecture*, no. 2: 8–19.

Rubin, Arthur, and Jacqueline Elder (1980), *Building for People*, Washington, D.C.: U.S. Department of Commerce.

Ruchelman, Leonard I. (1977), *The World Trade Center*, Syracuse NY.: Syracuse University Press.

Rudofsky, Bernard (1964), *Architecture Without Architects*, New York: Museum of Modern Art.

Rusch, Charles W. (1969), "On the Relation of Form to Behavior," *DMG Newsletter* (October): 8–11.

Ruskin, John (1885), *Works*, New York: John Wiley.

Rykwert, Joseph (1982), *The Necessity of Artifice*, New York: Rizzoli, pp. 9–16.

Saarinen, Thomas F. (1968), "Image of the Chicago Loop" (mimeographed).

——— (1969), *Perception of Environment*, Washington, D.C.: Association of American Geographers.

——— (1976), *Environmental Planning: Perception and Behavior*, Boston: Houghton Mifflin.

Saint, Andrew (1983), *The Image of the Architect*, New Haven: Yale University Press.

Salvadori, Mario G. (1974), "Is Automated Design Possible?" in R. Spillers, ed., *Basic Questions of Design Theory*, New York: American Elsevier, pp. 95–102.

Sanoff, Henry (1968), "Activities Gameboard," *Techniques of Evaluation for Designers*, Raleigh, N.C.: Design Research Laboratory, School of Design, North Carolina State University.

——— (1974), "Measuring Attributes of the Visual Environment," in Jon Lang et al., eds., *Designing for Human Behavior: Architecture and the Behavioral Sciences*, Stroudsburg, Pa.: Dowden, Hutchinson and Ross, pp. 244–260.

——— (1977), *Method of Architectural Programming*, Stroudsburg, Pa.: Dowden, Hutchinson and Ross.

Santayana, George (1896), *The Sense of Beauty*, reprinted (1955) New York: Dover.

Sarason, Irwin G., and Charles D. Spielberger, eds. (1979), *Stress and Anxiety*, vol. 6, Washington, D.C.: Hemisphere.

Sarason, Seymour (1972), *The Creation of Settings and the Future Society*, San Francisco: Jossey-Bass.

Sasuki, Peter (1976), "Germans and Turks at Germany's Railroad Stations: Interethnic Tensions in the Pursuit of Walking and Loitering," *Urban Life: A Journal of Ethnographic Resesrch* 4: 387–412.

Scheflen, Albert E. (1976), *Human Territories, How We Behave in Space and Time*, Englewood Cliffs, N.J.: Prentice-Hall.

Schon, Don (1984), *The Reflective Practitioner*, New York: Basic Books.

Schubert, Otto (1965), *Optik in Arckitektur und Stadebau*, Berlin: Gebr. Mann.

Schwartz, Barry (1968), "The Social Psychology of Privacy," *American Journal of Sociology* 73, no. 6: 541–542.

Scott, Geoffrey (1935), *Architecture of Humanism: A Study in the History of Taste*, London: Constable (2nd edition).

Scott, W. Richard (1964), "Theory of Organizations," in Robert E. L. Faris, ed., *Handbook of Modern Sociology*, Chicago: Paul McNally.

Selltiz, Claire, Marie Jahoda, Martin Deutsch, and S. W. Cook, eds. (1959), *Research Methods in Social Relations*, New York: Holt.

Semple, E. C. (1911), *Influences of the Geographical Environment*, New York: Holt.

Senkevitch, Anatole (1974), "Trends in Soviet Architectural Thought 1917–1937," unpublished doctoral dissertation, Graduate School, Cornell University.

Sennett, Richard (1970), *The Uses of Disorder*, New York: Alfred Knopf.

Sheldon, William (1954), *Atlas of Man: A Guide for Somatyping the Adult Male Population*, New York: Harper.

———, and S. S. Stevens (1942), *The Varieties of Temperament*, New York: Harper.

Sherwood, Roger (1978), *Modern Housing Prototypes*, Cambridge, Mass.: Harvard University Press.

——— (1960), *The New Science of Management Decision*, New York: Harper.

——— (1969), *The Sciences of the Artificial*, Cambridge, Mass.: MIT Press.

——— (1970), "Style in Design," in John Archea and Charles Eastman, eds., *EDRA Two: Proceedings of the 2nd Annual Environmental Design Research Association Conference*, October 1970, Pittsburgh, pp. 1–10.

Simon, Herbert A. (1957), *Models of Man*, New York: John Wiley.

Sims, William (1983), personal communication.

Sivadon, Paul (1970), "Space as Experienced: Therapeutic Implications," in Harold Proshansky et al., eds., *Environmental Psychology: Man and His Physical Environment*, New York: Holt, Rinehart and Winston, pp. 409–419.

Skaburskis, Jacqueline V. (1974), "Territoriality and Its Relevance to Neighborhood Design: A Review," *Architectural Research and Teaching* 3, no. 1: 39–44.

Skinner, B. F. (1938), *The Behavior of Organisms*, New York: Appleton-Century-Crofts.

——— (1953), *Science and Human Behavior*, New York: Free Press.

Smets, G. (1971), "Pleasingness vs. Interestingness of Visual Stimuli with Controlled Complexity: Their Relationship to Looking Time as a Function of Exposure Time," *Perceptual and Motor Skills* 40, no. 1: 3–10.

Smith, Ralph E., ed. (1979), *The Subtle Revolution*, Washington, D.C.: Urban Institute.

Smithson, Alison (1968), *Team 10 Primer*, Cambridge, Mass.: MIT Press.

Sobal, Geoffrey (1978), "Social and Physical Factors Involved in the Experience of Crowding," unpublished doctoral dissertation, University of Pennsylvania.

Soen, D. (1970), "Neighborly Relations and Ethnic Problems in Israel," *Ekistics* 177: 133–138.

Sommer, Robert (1969), *Personal Space: The Behavioral Basis of Design*, Englewood Cliffs, N.J.: Prentice-Hall.

——— (1971), *Design Awareness*, Corte Madera, Ca.: Rinehart.

——— (1974a), "Looking Back at Personal Space," in Jon Lang et al., eds. *Designing for Human Behavior: Architecture and the Behavioral Sciences*, Stroudsburg, Pa.: Dowden, Hutchinson and Ross, pp. 202–209.

——— (1974b), *Tight Spaces: Hard Architecture and How to Humanize It*, Englewood Cliffs, N.J.: Prentice-Hall.

——— (1983), *Social Design: Creating Buildings with People in Mind*, Englewood Cliffs, N.J.: Prentice-Hall.

———, and Franklin D. Becker (1969), "Territorial Defense and the Good Neighbor," *Journal of Personality and Social Psychology* 11, no. 2: 85–92.

Soudet, J. J. et al. (1970), "A Conceptual Framework for Hospital Planning," in Harold M. Proshansky et al., eds., *Environmental Psychology: Man and his Physical Setting*, New York: Holt, Rinehart and Winston, pp. 579–587.

Southworth, Michael (1969), "The Sonic Environment of Cities," *Environment and Behavior* 1, no. 1: 49–70.

Spencer, D., and J. Lloyd (1974), "The Small Health Schools Session: Mental Maps of Routes from Home to School," Working Paper 24, Centre for Urban and Regional Studies, University of Birmingham.

Spirn, Anne (1984), *The Granite Garden*, New York: Basic Books.

Srivastava, Rajendra K. (1971), "Environmental Psychology: An Introduction," *Journal of Education and Psychology* 29, no. 1: 29–40.

——— (1975), "Undermanning Theory in the Context of Mental Health Care Environments," in Daniel H. Carson, ed., *Man–Environment Interactions, Part II*, Stroudsburg, Pa.: Dowden, Hutchinson and Ross, pp. 245–258.

Stea, David (1965), "Space, Territoriality and Human Movements," *Landscape* 15: 13–16.

——— (1969), "The Measurement of Mental Maps: An Experimental Model for Studying Conceptual Spaces," in K. R. Cox and R. G. Golledge, eds., *Behavioral Problems in Geography*, Evanston, Ill.: Northwestern University Studies in Geography 17, pp. 228–253.

——— (1974), "Architecture in the Head: Cognitive Mapping," in Jon Lang et al., eds., *Designing for Human Behavior: Architecture and the Behavioral Sciences*, Stroudsburg, Pa.: Dowden, Hutchinson and Ross, pp. 157–168.

——, and James A. Blaut (1973), "Some Preliminary Observations on Spatial Learning in School Children," in Roger Downs and David Stea, eds., *Image and Environment*, Chicago: Aldine, pp. 27–50.

Steele, Fred (1973), *Physical Settings and Organizational Development*, Reading, Mass.: Addison-Wesley.

Stein, Clarence (1951), *Towards New Towns for America*, New York: Reinhold.

Steinitz, Carl (1968), "Meaning and Congruence of Urban Form and Activity," *Journal of the American Institute of Planners* 34: 233–248.

Stern, Robert A. M. (1975), *George Howe: Toward a Modern American Architecture*, New Haven: Yale University Press.

Sternberg, Eugene D., and Barbara Sternberg (1971), *Community Centers and Student Unions*, New York: Van Nostrand Reinhold.

Strauss, Anselm (1961), *Images of the American City*, Glencoe: Free Press.

Stringer, Peter (1980), "Models of Man in Casterbridge and Milton Keynes," in Byron Mikellides, ed., *Architecture for People*, New York: Holt, Rinehart and Winston, pp. 176–186.

Studer, Raymond (1969), "The Dynamics of Behavior-Contingent Physical Systems," in Anthony Ward and Geoffrey Broadbent, eds., *Design Methods in Architecture*, London: Lund Humphries, pp. 59–70.

Summerson, John (1949), *Heavenly Mansions*, New York: Cresett.

—— (1966), *Classical Language of Architecture*, Cambridge, Mass.: MIT Press.

Suttles, Gerald (1972), *The Social Construction of Community*, Chicago: University of Chicago Press.

Swinburne, Herbert H. (1967), "Change Is the Challenge," *AIA Journal* (May): 83–90.

Tanner, J. M. (1964), *The Physique of the Olympic Athlete*, London: G. Allen and Unwin.

Taylor, G. Brooke, Lewis Keeble, and Wyndham Thomas (1960), "New Towns and Neighborhood Planning," *Architecture and Building* 35 (April): 138–139.

Thieberg, S. (1965–70), *Anatomy for Planners, Parts I–IV*, Stockholm: Statens Institute for Byggnadsforskning.

Thiel, Philip (1961), "A Sequence-Experience Notation for Architectural and Urban Spaces," *Town Planning Review* 32: 33–52.

—— (1964), "The Tourist and the Habitué: Two Polar Modes of Environmental Experience, with Some Notes on an Experience Cube" (mimeographed).

Thorne, Ross, and David Canter (1972), "Attitudes Towards Housing: A Cross-Cultural Comparison," *Environment and Behavior* 4, no. 1: 3–32.

Titchner, Edward B. (1910), *Textbook for Psychology*, New York: Macmillan.

Tolman, E. C. (1932), *Purposive Behavior in Animals and Man*, New York: Century.

—— (1948), "Cognitive Maps in Rats and Man," *Psychological Review* 55: 189–208.

Trites, David K., et al. (1970), "Influence of Nursing-Unit Design on the Activities and Subjective Feeling of Nursing Personnel," *Environment and Behavior* 2, no. 3: 303–334.

Tuan, Yi-Fu (1974), *Topophilia: A Study of Environmental Perception, Attitudes and Values*, Englewood Cliffs, N.J.: Prentice-Hall.

Turner, John F. C. (1976), *Housing by People: Towards Autonomy in Building Environments*, New York: Pantheon.

Turner, Paul V. (1977), *The Education of Le Corbusier*, New York: Garland.

Tyng, Anne (1975), "Simultaneous Randomness and Order: The Fibonacci-Divine Proportion as a Universal Forming Principle," unpublished doctoral dissertation, University of Pennsylvania.

—— (1969), "Geometric Extensions of Consciousness," *ZODIAC 19*, Edrioni di Communita, Milan, pp. 130–162.

Ushenko, Andrew Paul (1953), *Dynamics of Art*, Bloomington, Ind.: Indiana University Press.

Valentine, C. W. (1962), *The Experimental Psychology of Beauty*, London: Methuen.

Van der Ryn, Sim, and Murray Silverstein (1967), *Dorms at Berkeley: An Environmental Analysis*, Berkeley: University of California, Center for Planning and Development Research.

Vayda, Andrew, ed., (1969), *Environment and Cultural Behavior*, Garden City, N.Y.: Natural History Press.

Venturi, Robert (1966), *Complexity and Contradiction in Architecture*, New York: Museum of Modern Art.

——, Denise Scott Brown, and Steven Izenour (1977), *Learning from Las Vegas*, Cambridge, Mass.: MIT Press (revised edition).

Vidler, Anthony, ed. (1973), "News from the Realm of No-Where," *Oppositions*, no. 1 (September): 83–92.

Vitruvius Pollio (c. 10 B.C.); translated by Morris H. Morgan, *The Ten Books on Architecture*, Cambridge, Mass.: Harvard, 1914.

von Franz, M. L. (1968), "The Process of Individuation," in Carl J. Jung, ed., *Man and His Symbols*, New York: Dell, pp. 157–254.

von Frisch, Karl (1974), *Animal Architecture*, New York: Harcourt Brace Jovanovich.

Wade, John (1977), *Architecture, Problems and Purposes*, New York: John Wiley.

Wales, Prince of (1984), quoted in the *Times of India*, May 27, p. v.

Walker, Edward L. (1970), "Complexity and Preference in Animals and Men," *Annals of the New York Academy of Science* 169: 619–653.

Wallace, Anthony F. C. (1952), "Housing and Social Structure," Philadelphia Housing Authority.

Wampler, Jan (1978), *All Their Own: People and the Places They Build*, Oxford: Oxford University Press.

——, ed. (1969), *Design Methods in Architecture Symposium*, New York: Wellentstorn.

Ward, John W. (1966), "The Politics of Design," in Laurence B. Holland, ed., *Who Designs America?* Garden City, N.Y.: Anchor, pp. 51–85.

Warfield, John, and Douglas Hill (1973), "Assault on Complexity," Battelle Monograph.

Watkin, David (1977), *Morality and Architecture*, Oxford: Clarendon.

Watson, O. Michael (1970), *Proxemic Behavior: A Cross-Cultural Study*, The Hague: Mouton.

Webber, Melvin (1963), "Order in Diversity: Community without Propinquity," in Lowden Wingo, ed., *Cities and Space*, Baltimore: Johns Hopkins University Press, pp. 23–54.

Weber, Max (1947), *The Theory of Social and Economic Organization*, translated by A. M. Henderson and Talcott Parsons, New York: Free Press.

Wertheimer, Max (1938), "Gestalt Theory," "The General Theoretical Situation," and "Laws of Organization," in William D. Ellis, ed., *A Source Book of Gestalt Psychology*, London: Routledge and Kegan Paul, pp. 1–88.

Werthman, Carl (1968), "The Social Meaning of the Physical Environment," unpublished doctoral dissertation, University of California, Berkeley.

Westin A. (1970), *Privacy and Freedom*, New York: Ballantine.

White, Edward T. (1972), *An Introduction to Architectural Programming*, Tucson, Arizona: Architectural Media.

White, Morton G., and Lucia White, eds. (1964), *The Intellectual versus the City from Thomas Jefferson to Frank Lloyd Wright*, New York: New American Library.

Whiting, J.W.M., and I. Child (1953), *Child Training and Personality*, New Haven: Yale University Press.

Whyte, William H., Jr. (1954), "The Web of Word-of-Mouth," *Fortune* 50, no. 5: 140–143, 204–212.

——— (1956), *The Organization Man*, Garden City, N.Y.: Anchor

——— (1980), *The Social Life of Small Urban Spaces*, New York: Conservation Foundation.

Wickelgren, Wayne A. (1974), *How to Solve Problems: Elements of a Theory of Problems and Problem-Solving*, San Francisco: Freeman.

Wicker, Alan (1969), "Size of Membership and Member's Support of Church Behavior Settings," *Journal of Personality and Social Psychology* 13: 278–288.

——— (1979), *An Introduction to Ecological Psychology*, Monterey, Ca.: Brooks/Cole.

Willis, Margaret (1963), "Designing for Privacy," *The Architects' Journal* 137 (29 May, 5 June, 12 June): 1137–1141, 1181–1187, 1231–1236.

——— (1969), "Sociological Aspects of Urban Structure," *Town Planning Review* 39: 296–396.

Wilmott, Peter (1967), "Social Research and New Communities," *Journal of the American Institute of Planners* 33, no. 5: 387–397.

———, and Michael Young (1960), *Family and Class in a London Suburb*, London: Routledge and Kegan Paul.

——— (1973), *The Symmetrical Family*, New York: Pantheon.

Wilson, Edward O. (1978), *On Human Nature*, Cambridge, Mass.: Harvard University Press.

Windley, Paul G., and Gerald Weisman (1977), "Social Science and Environmental Design," *Journal of Architectural Education* 31, no. 1: 16–19.

Wingler, Hans (1969), *The Bauhaus*, translated by Wolfgang Jabs and Basil Gilbert, edited by Joseph Stein, Cambridge, Mass.: MIT Press.

Wöllflin, Heinreich (1885), *Principles of Art History*, translated by M. D. Hotlinger, New York: Dover, 1948.

——— (1888), *Renaissance and Baroque;* reprinted (1964) New York: Fontana Library.

Wohlwill, Joachim F. (1966), "The Physical Environment: A Problem for the Psychology of Stimulation," *Journal of Social Issues* 22: 29–38.

——— (1971), "Behavioral Response and Adaptation to Environmental Stimulation," in A. Damen, ed., *Physiological Anthropology*, Cambridge, Mass.: Harvard University Press.

Wolfe, Maxine, and Harold Proshansky (1974), "The Physical Setting as a Factor in Group Process and Function," in Jon Lang et al., eds., *Designing for Human Behavior: Architecture and the Behavioral Sciences*, Stroudsburg, Pa.: Dowden, Hutchinson and Ross, pp. 194–202.

Wolfe, Tom (1981), *From Bauhaus to Our House*, New York: Farrar Straus Giroux.

Wotton, Sir Henry (1624), *The Elements of Architecture;* reproduced (c. 1897), Springfield, Mass.: F. A. Basette Company.

Wright, Frank Lloyd (1945), *When Democracy Builds*, Chicago: University of Chicago Press.

——— (1958), *The Living City*, New York: Horizon.

——— (1960), "Prairie Architecture," in Edgar Kaufman and Ben Raeburn, eds., *Frank Lloyd Wright; Writings and Buildings*, New York: Horizon Press.

Young, Michael, and Peter Wilmott (1957), *Family and Kinship in East London*, London: Routledge and Kegan Paul.

Young, Robert C. (1966), "Goals and Goal Setting," *Journal of the American Institute of Planners* 32, no. 2: 76–85.

Zeisel, John (1974), "Fundamental Values in Planning with the Nonpaying Client," in Jon Lang et al., eds., *Designing for Human Behavior: Architecture and the Behavioral Sciences*, Stroudsburg, Pa.: Dowden, Hutchinson and Ross, pp. 293–301.

——— (1975), *Sociology and Architectural Design*, New York: Russel Sage.

——— (1981), *Inquiry by Design: Tools for Environment–Behavior Research*, Monterey, Ca.: Brooks/Cole.

———, and Mary Griffen (1975), "Charlesview Housing," Architectural Research Office, Graduate School of Design, Harvard University.

Zelinsky, Wilbur (1973), *The Cultural Geography of the United States*, Englewood Cliffs, N.J.: Prentice-Hall.

Zevi, Bruno (1978), *The Modern Language of Architecture*, Seattle, Wash.: University of Washington Press.

Zwicky, Fritz (1948), "A Morphological Method of Analysis and Construction," *Studies and Essays* (Courant Anniversary Volume), New York: Interscience.

PERMISSIONS

Fig. 1-1(3) Reprinted by permission of Walter Moleski.

Fig. 1-2(1) Drawing by Le Corbusier. Reprinted by permission of Foundation Le Corbusier and VAGA, New York.

Fig. 1-2(2) Reprinted by permission of Van Nostrand Reinhold.

Fig. 1-3(2) Photograph reprinted by permission of Fondation Le Corbusier and VAGA, New York.

Fig. 1-5(2) Photograph reprinted by permission of FRIDAY Architects/Planners.

Fig. 2-2 Copyright © Philadelphia Museum of Art 68-165-1, Philadelphia Museum of Art: 68-165-1 Purchased.

Fig. 3-3(1) Reprinted by permission of the artist, K. A. Kolnick.

Fig. 3-3(2) *Architectural Design* Magazine, London.

Fig. 3-3(3) Copyright © Philadelphia Museum of Art 50-134-104: Philadelphia Museum of Art, Louise and Walter Annenberg Collection.

Fig. 4-1 Reprinted by permission of *Architecture*.

Fig. 4-3 Reprinted by permission of Raymond Studer and Lund Humphries.

Table 6-1 Reprinted by permission of Battelle.

Fig. 6-1 From J. P. Guilford. Copyright © 1953 by the American Psychological Association. Reprinted by permission of J. P. Guilford.

Fig. 8-1(2) Reprinted by permission of Lee Copeland.

Fig. 9-1 James J. Gibson, *The Senses Considered as Perceptual Systems*, p. 50. Copyright © 1966 by Houghton Mifflin Company. Reprinted by permission.

Fig. 9-2 Julian E. Hochberg (1978), *Perception*, 2nd ed., copyright © 1978, pp. 137–138. Adapted by permission of Prentice-Hall, Englewood Cliffs, New Jersey.

Fig. 9-3 Adapted from James J. Gibson, *An Ecological Approach to Visual Perception*, p. 71. Copyright © 1979 by Houghton Mifflin Company. Reprinted by permission.

Fig. 9-4 Adapted from James J. Gibson, *The Perception of the Visual World.* Copyright © renewed 1978 by James J. Gibson. Reprinted by permission of the publishers, Houghton Mifflin.

Fig. 9-5 Reprinted by permission of Van Nostrand Reinhold.

Fig. 10-1(1) Used by permission of Sei-Kwan Sohn.

Fig. 10-2(1) Photograph used by permission of Venturi, Rauch and Scott Brown.

Fig. 10-3 From Lawton and Nahemow (1973); Copyright (1973) by the American Psychological Association/Used by permission of Powell Lawton.

Fig. 10-4 Used by permission of Van Nostrand Reinhold.

Fig. 10-6 Used by permission of Kiyo Izumi.

Fig. 11-2 Used by permission of John Zeisel.

Fig. 11-5(1) Used by permission of CEPT Ahmedabad.

Fig. 11-5(2) Used by permission of the School of Planning and Architecture, New Delhi.

Fig. 11-5(3) Used by permission of *inside outside*, the Indian design magazine (April-May, 1984)

Fig. 12-1(1) Photograph used by permission of *The New York Times Pictures*.

Fig. 12-1(3) Used by permission of the University of Pennsylvania Press.

Fig. 12-2(1) Used by permission of Van Nostrand Reinhold.

Fig. 12-2(2) Used by permission of Van Nostrand Reinhold.

Fig. 12-3 Used by permission of Taylor and Francis, Ltd. and Architectural Publishers, Artemis, Zurich.

Fig. 12-5 Used by permission of Amos Rapoport.

Table 13-1 Used by permission of Columbia University Press.

Fig. 13-2 Used by permission of MIT Press.

Fig. 14-1 Used by permission of Irwin Altman.

Fig. 14-2 Used by permission of the Faculty of Commerce and Social Science, University of Birmingham.

Fig. 14-4(1) Used by permission of the Law Enforcement Assistance Administration, U.S. Department of Justice.

Fig. 14-4(2) Used by permission of the Law Enforcement Assistance Administration, U.S. Department of Justice.

Fig. 14-4(3) Reprinted by permission of the *Journal of the American Institute of Planners*.

Fig. 14-5(1) Reprinted by permission of Hussein El-Sharkawy.

Fig. 14-5(2) Reprinted by permission of Sim Van der Ryn.

Fig. 14-6(1,2,3) Reprinted by permission of Macmillan Publishing Company from *Defensible Space: Crime Prevention through Urban Design*. copyright © 1972 by Oscar Newman.

Fig. 15-2(1) Reprinted by permission of Roger Montgomery and *The Journal of the American Institute of Planners*.

Fig. 16-1(2) Reprinted by permission of Karl Krame Verlag GmbH + Co.

Fig. 16-1(3) Reprinted by permission of Walter Moleski, Architect.

Fig. 16-2(2) From J. M. Richards, *An Introduction to Modern Architecture* by J. M. Richards (Pelican Books, 1940, rev. ed. 1962). Copyright © by J. M. Richards, 1940, 1962. Reproduced by permission of Penguin Books Ltd.

Fig. 16-2(3) Reprinted by permission of Van Nostrand Reinhold.

Fig. 16-4(1) Reprinted by permission of Hartman-Cox, Architects.

Fig. 16-4(3) Reprinted by permission of Hartman-Cox, Architects.

Fig. 18-1 Reprinted by permission of Van Nostrand Reinhold and Alan R. G. Isaac.

Fig. 19-3(1) Reprinted by permission of the FPA Corporation.

Fig. 19-3(2) Reprinted by permission of Charles Spuhler, Inc.

Fig. 19-3(3) Reprinted by permission of Windon Property Management.

Fig. 19-4(1) Reprinted by permission of Venturi, Rauch and Scott Brown.

Fig. 19-6 Adapted from James J. Gibson, *The Senses Considered as Perceptual Systems*, p. 244. Copyright © 1966 by Houghton Mifflin Company. Reprinted by permission.

Fig. 20-2(1) Reprinted from *The Living City* by Frank Lloyd Wright. Copyright © 1978. Reprinted by permission of the publisher, Horizon Press, New York.

Fig. 20-2(2) Photograph by William Logan from Dolores Hayden, *Seven American Utopias* (MIT Press, 1976), reprinted by permission of Dolores Hayden and MIT Press.

Fig. 20-2(3) Drawing by Paolo Soleri. From *The City in the Image of Man*. Reprinted by permission of the Cosanti Foundation.

INDEX